U.S. History

Volume 2: 1840 to 1900

By OpenStax College
at Rice University

Arranged by Traci Hodgson
Chemeketa Community College

A Chemeketa Press Reprint

U.S. History, **Volume 2: 1840 to 1900**

ISBN: 978-1-943536-08-5

The contents of this book are reprinted directly from U.S. History by OpenStax College.
© May 15, 2015 by OpenStax College. Textbook content produced by OpenStax College
is licensed under a Creative Commons Attribution 4.0 license.

Chemeketa Press
Managing Editor: Steve Richardson
Production Editor: Brian Mosher
Production Designer: Kristen MacDonald
Cover Layout: Cierra Maher

Printed in the United States of America.

Volume 2: 1840 to 1900

CHAPTER 1

Industrial Transformation in the North, 1800–1850

Figure 1.1 *Five Points* (1827), by George Catlin, depicts the infamous Five Points neighborhood of New York City, so called because it was centered at the intersection of five streets. Five Points was home to a polyglot mix of recent immigrants, freed slaves, and other members of the working class.

Chapter Outline
1.1 Early Industrialization in the Northeast
1.2 A Vibrant Capitalist Republic
1.3 On the Move: The Transportation Revolution
1.4 A New Social Order: Class Divisions

Introduction

By the 1830s, the United States had developed a thriving industrial and commercial sector in the Northeast. Farmers embraced regional and distant markets as the primary destination for their products. Artisans witnessed the methodical division of the labor process in factories. Wage labor became an increasingly common experience. These industrial and market revolutions, combined with advances in transportation, transformed the economic and social landscape. Americans could now quickly produce larger amounts of goods for a nationwide, and sometimes an international, market and rely less on foreign imports than in colonial times.

As American economic life shifted rapidly and modes of production changed, new class divisions emerged and solidified, resulting in previously unknown economic and social inequalities. This image of the Five Points district in New York City captures the turbulence of the time (**Figure 1.1**). Five Points began as a settlement for freed slaves, but it soon became a crowded urban world of American day laborers and low-wage workers who lived a precarious existence that the economic benefits of the new economy largely bypassed. An influx of immigrant workers swelled and diversified an already crowded urban population. By the 1830s, the area had become a slum, home to widespread poverty, crime, and disease. Advances in industrialization and the market revolution came at a human price.

1.1 Early Industrialization in the Northeast

By the end of this section, you will be able to:
- Explain the role of the putting-out system in the rise of industrialization
- Understand industrialization's impact on the nature of production and work
- Describe the effect of industrialization on consumption
- Identify the goals of workers' organizations like the Working Men's Party

Northern industrialization expanded rapidly following the War of 1812. Industrialized manufacturing began in New England, where wealthy merchants built water-powered textile mills (and mill towns to support them) along the rivers of the Northeast. These mills introduced new modes of production centralized within the confines of the mill itself. As never before, production relied on mechanized sources with water power, and later steam, to provide the force necessary to drive machines. In addition to the mechanization and centralization of work in the mills, specialized, repetitive tasks assigned to wage laborers replaced earlier modes of handicraft production done by artisans at home. The operations of these mills irrevocably changed the nature of work by deskilling tasks, breaking down the process of production to its most basic, elemental parts. In return for their labor, the workers, who at first were young women from rural New England farming families, received wages. From its origin in New England, manufacturing soon spread to other regions of the United States.

FROM ARTISANS TO WAGE WORKERS

During the seventeenth and eighteenth centuries, **artisans**—skilled, experienced craft workers—produced goods by hand. The production of shoes provides a good example. In colonial times, people bought their shoes from master shoemakers, who achieved their status by living and working as apprentices under the rule of an older master artisan. An apprenticeship would be followed by work as a journeyman (a skilled worker without his own shop). After sufficient time as a journeyman, a shoemaker could at last set up his own shop as a master artisan. People came to the shop, usually attached to the back of the master artisan's house, and there the shoemaker measured their feet in order to cut and stitch together an individualized product for each customer.

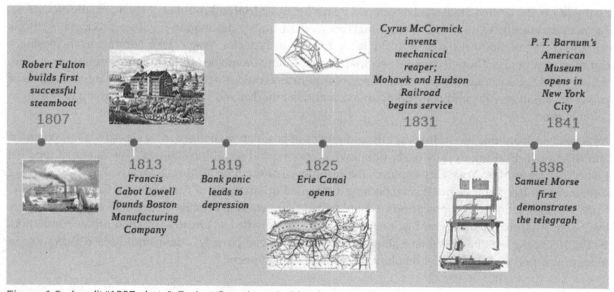

Figure 1.2 (credit "1807 photo": Project Gutenberg Archives)

In the late eighteenth and early nineteenth century, merchants in the Northeast and elsewhere turned their attention as never before to the benefits of using unskilled wage labor to make a greater profit by reducing labor costs. They used the **putting-out system**, which the British had employed at the beginning of their own Industrial Revolution, whereby they hired farming families to perform specific tasks in the production process for a set wage. In the case of shoes, for instance, American merchants hired one group of workers to cut soles into standardized sizes. A different group of families cut pieces of leather for the uppers, while still another was employed to stitch the standardized parts together.

This process proved attractive because it whittled production costs. The families who participated in the putting-out system were not skilled artisans. They had not spent years learning and perfecting their craft and did not have ambitious journeymen to pay. Therefore, they could not demand—and did not receive—high wages. Most of the year they tended fields and orchards, ate the food that they produced, and sold the surplus. Putting-out work proved a welcome source of extra income for New England farm families who saw their profits dwindle from new competition from midwestern farms with higher-yield lands.

Much of this part-time production was done under contract to merchants. Some farming families engaged in shoemaking (or shoe assemblage), as noted above. Many made brooms, plaited hats from straw or palm leaves (which merchants imported from Cuba and the West Indies), crafted furniture, made pottery, or wove baskets. Some, especially those who lived in Connecticut, made parts for clocks. The most common part-time occupation, however, was the manufacture of textiles. Farm women spun woolen thread and wove fabric. They also wove blankets, made rugs, and knit stockings. All this manufacturing took place on the farm, giving farmers and their wives control over the timing and pace of their labor. Their domestic productivity increased the quantity of goods available for sale in country towns and nearby cities.

THE RISE OF MANUFACTURING

In the late 1790s and early 1800s, Great Britain boasted the most advanced textile mills and machines in the world, and the United States continued to rely on Great Britain for finished goods. Great Britain hoped to maintain its economic advantage over its former colonies in North America. So, in an effort to prevent the knowledge of advanced manufacturing from leaving the Empire, the British banned the emigration of mechanics, skilled workers who knew how to build and repair the latest textile machines.

Some skilled British mechanics, including Samuel Slater, managed to travel to the United States in the hopes of profiting from their knowledge and experience with advanced textile manufacturing. Slater (**Figure 1.3**) understood the workings of the latest water-powered textile mills, which British industrialist Richard Arkwright had pioneered. In the 1790s in Pawtucket, Rhode Island, Slater convinced several American merchants, including the wealthy Providence industrialist Moses Brown, to finance and build a water-powered cotton mill based on the British models. Slater's knowledge of both technology and mill organization made him the founder of the first truly successful cotton mill in the United States.

(a)   (b)

Figure 1.3 Samuel Slater (a) was a British migrant who brought plans for English textile mills to the United States and built the nation's first successful water-powered mill in Pawtucket, Massachusetts (b).

The success of Slater and his partners Smith Brown and William Almy, relatives of Moses Brown, inspired others to build additional mills in Rhode Island and Massachusetts. By 1807, thirteen more mills had been established. President Jefferson's embargo on British manufactured goods from late 1807 to early 1809 (discussed in a previous chapter) spurred more New England merchants to invest in industrial enterprises. By 1812, seventy-eight new textile mills had been built in rural New England towns. More than half turned out woolen goods, while the rest produced cotton cloth.

Slater's mills and those built in imitation of his were fairly small, employing only seventy people on average. Workers were organized the way that they had been in English factories, in family units. Under the "Rhode Island system," families were hired. The father was placed in charge of the family unit, and he directed the labor of his wife and children. Instead of being paid in cash, the father was given "credit" equal to the extent of his family's labor that could be redeemed in the form of rent (of company-owned housing) or goods from the company-owned store.

The Embargo of 1807 and the War of 1812 played a pivotal role in spurring industrial development in the United States. Jefferson's embargo prevented American merchants from engaging in the Atlantic trade, severely cutting into their profits. The War of 1812 further compounded the financial woes of American merchants. The acute economic problems led some New England merchants, including Francis Cabot Lowell, to cast their gaze on manufacturing. Lowell had toured English mills during a stay in Great Britain. He returned to Massachusetts having memorized the designs for the advanced textile machines he had seen in his travels, especially the power loom, which replaced individual hand weavers. Lowell convinced other wealthy merchant families to invest in the creation of new mill towns. In 1813, Lowell and these wealthy investors, known as the Boston Associates, created the Boston Manufacturing Company. Together they raised $400,000 and, in 1814, established a textile mill in Waltham and a second one in the same town shortly thereafter (**Figure 1.4**).

Figure 1.4 The Boston Manufacturing Company, shown in this engraving made in 1813–1816, was headquartered in Waltham, Massachusetts. The company started the northeastern textile industry by building water-powered textile mills along suitable rivers and developing mill towns around them.

At Waltham, cotton was carded and drawn into coarse strands of cotton fibers called rovings. The rovings were then spun into yarn, and the yarn woven into cotton cloth. Yarn no longer had to be put out to farm families for further processing. All the work was now performed at a central location—the factory.

The work in Lowell's mills was both mechanized and specialized. Specialization meant the work was broken down into specific tasks, and workers repeatedly did the one task assigned to them in the course of a day. As machines took over labor from humans and people increasingly found themselves confined to the same repetitive step, the process of **deskilling** began.

The Boston Associates' mills, which each employed hundreds of workers, were located in company towns, where the factories and worker housing were owned by a single company. This gave the owners and their agents control over their workers. The most famous of these company towns was Lowell, Massachusetts. The new town was built on land the Boston Associates purchased in 1821 from the village of East Chelmsford at the falls of the Merrimack River, north of Boston. The mill buildings themselves were constructed of red brick with large windows to let in light. Company-owned boarding houses to shelter employees were constructed near the mills. The mill owners planted flowers and trees to maintain the appearance of a rural New England town and to forestall arguments, made by many, that factory work was unnatural and unwholesome.

In contrast to many smaller mills, the Boston Associates' enterprises avoided the Rhode Island system, preferring individual workers to families. These employees were not difficult to find. The competition New England farmers faced from farmers now settling in the West, and the growing scarcity of land in population-dense New England, had important implications for farmers' children. Realizing their chances of inheriting a large farm or receiving a substantial dowry were remote, these teenagers sought other employment opportunities, often at the urging of their parents. While young men could work at a variety of occupations, young women had more limited options. The textile mills provided suitable employment for the daughters of Yankee farm families.

Needing to reassure anxious parents that their daughters' virtue would be protected and hoping to avoid what they viewed as the problems of industrialization—filth and vice—the Boston Associates established strict rules governing the lives of these young workers. The women lived in company-owned boarding houses to which they paid a portion of their wages. They woke early at the sound of a bell and worked a twelve-hour day during which talking was forbidden. They could not swear or drink alcohol, and they were required to attend church on Sunday. Overseers at the mills and boarding-house keepers kept a close eye on the young women's behavior; workers who associated with people of questionable reputation or acted in ways that called their virtue into question lost their jobs and were evicted.

DEFINING "AMERICAN"

☸ *Michel Chevalier on Mill Worker Rules and Wages*

In the 1830s, the French government sent engineer and economist Michel Chevalier to study industrial and financial affairs in Mexico and the United States. In 1839, he published *Society, Manners, and Politics in the United States*, in which he recorded his impressions of the Lowell textile mills. In the excerpt below, Chevalier describes the rules and wages of the Lawrence Company in 1833.

> All persons employed by the Company must devote themselves assiduously to their duty during working-hours. They must be capable of doing the work which they undertake, or use all their efforts to this effect. They must on all occasions, both in their words and in their actions, show that they are penetrated by a laudable love of temperance and virtue, and animated by a sense of their moral and social obligations. The Agent of the Company shall endeavour to set to all a good example in this respect. Every individual who shall be notoriously dissolute, idle, dishonest, or intemperate, who shall be in the practice of absenting himself from divine service, or shall violate the Sabbath, or shall be addicted to gaming, shall be dismissed from the service of the Company. . . . All ardent spirits are banished from the Company's grounds, except when prescribed by a physician. All games of hazard and cards are prohibited within their limits and in the boarding-houses.
> Weekly wages were as follows:
> For picking and carding, $2.78 to $3.10
> For spinning, $3.00
> For weaving, $3.10 to $3.12
> For warping and sizing, $3.45 to $4.00
> For measuring and folding, $3.12

What kind of world were the factory owners trying to create with these rules? How do you think those who believed all white people were born free and equal would react to them?

Click and Explore

Visit the Textile Industry History (http://openstaxcollege.org/l/15textHistory) site to explore the mills of New England through its collection of history, images, and ephemera.

The mechanization of formerly handcrafted goods, and the removal of production from the home to the factory, dramatically increased output of goods. For example, in one nine-month period, the numerous Rhode Island women who spun yarn into cloth on hand looms in their homes produced a total of thirty-four thousand yards of fabrics of different types. In 1855, the women working in just one of Lowell's mechanized mills produced more than forty-three thousand yards.

The Boston Associates' cotton mills quickly gained a competitive edge over the smaller mills established by Samuel Slater and those who had imitated him. Their success prompted the Boston Associates to expand. In Massachusetts, in addition to Lowell, they built new mill towns in Chicopee, Lawrence, and Holyoke.

In New Hampshire, they built them in Manchester, Dover, and Nashua. And in Maine, they built a large mill in Saco on the Saco River. Other entrepreneurs copied them. By the time of the Civil War, 878 textile factories had been built in New England. All together, these factories employed more than 100,000 people and produced more than 940 million yards of cloth.

Success in New England was repeated elsewhere. Small mills, more like those in Rhode Island than those in northern Massachusetts, New Hampshire, and Maine, were built in New York, Delaware, and Pennsylvania. By midcentury, three hundred textile mills were located in and near Philadelphia. Many produced specialty goods, such as silks and printed fabrics, and employed skilled workers, including people working in their own homes. Even in the South, the region that otherwise relied on slave labor to produce the very cotton that fed the northern factory movement, more than two hundred textile mills were built. Most textiles, however, continued to be produced in New England before the Civil War.

Alongside the production of cotton and woolen cloth, which formed the backbone of the Industrial Revolution in the United States as in Britain, other crafts increasingly became mechanized and centralized in factories in the first half of the nineteenth century. Shoe making, leather tanning, papermaking, hat making, clock making, and gun making had all become mechanized to one degree or another by the time of the Civil War. Flour milling, because of the inventions of Oliver Evans (**Figure 1.5**), had become almost completely automated and centralized by the early decades of the nineteenth century. So efficient were Evans-style mills that two employees were able to do work that had originally required five, and mills using Evans's system spread throughout the mid-Atlantic states.

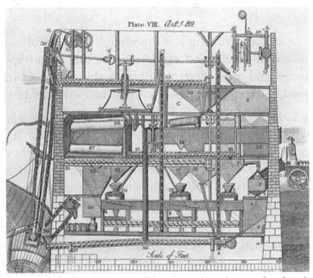

Figure 1.5   Oliver Evans was an American engineer and inventor, best known for developing ways to automate the flour milling process, which is illustrated here in a drawing from a 1785 instructional book called *The Young Mill-Wright & Miller's Guide*.

THE RISE OF CONSUMERISM

At the end of the eighteenth century, most American families lived in candlelit homes with bare floors and unadorned walls, cooked and warmed themselves over fireplaces, and owned few changes of clothing. All manufactured goods were made by hand and, as a result, were usually scarce and fairly expensive.

The automation of the manufacturing process changed that, making consumer goods that had once been thought of as luxury items widely available for the first time. Now all but the very poor could afford the necessities and some of the small luxuries of life. Rooms were lit by oil lamps, which gave brighter light than candles. Homes were heated by parlor stoves, which allowed for more privacy; people no longer needed to huddle together around the hearth. Iron cookstoves with multiple burners made it possible for housewives to prepare more elaborate meals. Many people could afford carpets and upholstered furniture, and even farmers could decorate their homes with curtains and wallpaper. Clocks, which had once been quite expensive, were now within the reach of most ordinary people.

THE WORK EXPERIENCE TRANSFORMED

As production became mechanized and relocated to factories, the experience of workers underwent significant changes. Farmers and artisans had controlled the pace of their labor and the order in which things were done. If an artisan wanted to take the afternoon off, he could. If a farmer wished to rebuild his fence on Thursday instead of on Wednesday, he could. They conversed and often drank during the workday. Indeed, journeymen were often promised alcohol as part of their wages. One member of the group might be asked to read a book or a newspaper aloud to the others. In the warm weather, doors and windows might be opened to the outside, and work stopped when it was too dark to see.

Work in factories proved to be quite different. Employees were expected to report at a certain time, usually early in the morning, and to work all day. They could not leave when they were tired or take breaks other than at designated times. Those who arrived late found their pay docked; five minutes' tardiness could result in several hours' worth of lost pay, and repeated tardiness could result in dismissal. The monotony of repetitive tasks made days particularly long. Hours varied according to the factory, but most factory employees toiled ten to twelve hours a day, six days a week. In the winter, when the sun set early, oil lamps were used to light the factory floor, and employees strained their eyes to see their work and coughed as the rooms filled with smoke from the lamps. In the spring, as the days began to grow longer, factories held "blowing-out" celebrations to mark the extinguishing of the oil lamps. These "blow-outs" often featured processions and dancing.

Freedom within factories was limited. Drinking was prohibited. Some factories did not allow employees to sit down. Doors and windows were kept closed, especially in textile factories where fibers could be easily disturbed by incoming breezes, and mills were often unbearably hot and humid in the summer. In the winter, workers often shivered in the cold. In such environments, workers' health suffered.

The workplace posed other dangers as well. The presence of cotton bales alongside the oil used to lubricate machines made fire a common problem in textile factories. Workplace injuries were also common. Workers' hands and fingers were maimed or severed when they were caught in machines; in some cases, their limbs or entire bodies were crushed. Workers who didn't die from such injuries almost certainly lost their jobs, and with them, their income. Corporal punishment of both children and adults was common in factories; where abuse was most extreme, children sometimes died as a result of injuries suffered at the hands of an overseer.

As the decades passed, working conditions deteriorated in many mills. Workers were assigned more machines to tend, and the owners increased the speed at which the machines operated. Wages were cut in many factories, and employees who had once labored for an hourly wage now found themselves reduced to piecework, paid for the amount they produced and not for the hours they toiled. Owners also reduced compensation for piecework. Low wages combined with regular periods of unemployment to make the lives of workers difficult, especially for those with families to support. In New York City in 1850, for example, the average male worker earned $300 a year; it cost approximately $600 a year to support a family of five.

WORKERS AND THE LABOR MOVEMENT

Many workers undoubtedly enjoyed some of the new wage opportunities factory work presented. For many of the young New England women who ran the machines in Waltham, Lowell, and elsewhere, the experience of being away from the family was exhilarating and provided a sense of solidarity among them. Though most sent a large portion of their wages home, having even a small amount of money of their own was a liberating experience, and many used their earnings to purchase clothes, ribbons, and other consumer goods for themselves.

The long hours, strict discipline, and low wages, however, soon led workers to organize to protest their working conditions and pay. In 1821, the young women employed by the Boston Manufacturing Company in Waltham went on strike for two days when their wages were cut. In 1824, workers in Pawtucket struck to protest reduced pay rates and longer hours, the latter of which had been achieved by cutting back the amount of time allowed for meals. Similar strikes occurred at Lowell and in other mill towns like Dover, New Hampshire, where the women employed by the Cocheco Manufacturing Company ceased working in December 1828 after their wages were reduced. In the 1830s, female mill operatives in Lowell formed the Lowell Factory Girls Association to organize strike activities in the face of wage cuts (**Figure 9.6**) and, later, established the Lowell Female Labor Reform Association to protest the twelve-hour workday. Even though strikes were rarely successful and workers usually were forced to accept reduced wages and increased hours, work stoppages as a form of labor protest represented the beginnings of the labor movement in the United States.

(a)   (b)

Figure 1.6 New England mill workers were often young women, as seen in this early tintype made ca. 1870 (a). When management proposed rent increases for those living in company boarding houses, female textile workers in Lowell responded by forming the Lowell Factory Girls Association—its constitution is shown in image (b)—in 1836 and organizing a "turn-out" or strike.

Critics of industrialization blamed it for the increased concentration of wealth in the hands of the few: the factory owners made vast profits while the workers received only a small fraction of the revenue from what they produced. Under the **labor theory of value**, said critics, the value of a product should accurately reflect the labor needed to produce it. Profits from the sale of goods produced by workers should be distributed so laborers recovered in the form of wages the value their effort had added to the finished product. While factory owners, who contributed the workspace, the machinery, and the raw materials needed to create a product, should receive a share of the profits, their share should not be greater than the value of their contribution. Workers should thus receive a much larger portion of the profits than they currently did, and factory owners should receive less.

In Philadelphia, New York, and Boston—all cities that experienced dizzying industrial growth during the nineteenth century—workers united to form political parties. Thomas Skidmore, from Connecticut, was the outspoken organizer of the **Working Men's Party**, which lodged a radical protest against the exploitation of workers that accompanied industrialization. Skidmore took his cue from Thomas Paine and the American Revolution to challenge the growing inequity in the United States. He argued that inequality originated in the unequal distribution of property through inheritance laws. In his 1829 treatise, *The Rights of Man to Property*, Skidmore called for the abolition of inheritance and the redistribution of property. The Working Men's Party also advocated the end of imprisonment for debt, a common practice whereby the debtor who could not pay was put in jail and his tools and property, if any, were confiscated. Skidmore's vision of radical equality extended to all; women and men, no matter their race, should be allowed to vote and receive property, he believed. Skidmore died in 1832 when a cholera epidemic swept New York City, but the state of New York did away with imprisonment for debt in the same year.

Worker activism became less common in the late 1840s and 1850s. As German and Irish immigrants poured into the United States in the decades preceding the Civil War, native-born laborers found themselves competing for jobs with new arrivals who were willing to work longer hours for less pay. In Lowell, Massachusetts, for example, the daughters of New England farmers encountered competition from the daughters of Irish farmers suffering the effects of the potato famine; these immigrant women were willing to work for far less and endure worse conditions than native-born women. Many of these native-born "daughters of freemen," as they referred to themselves, left the factories and returned to their families. Not all wage workers had this luxury, however. Widows with children to support and girls from destitute families had no choice but to stay and accept the faster pace and lower pay. Male German and Irish immigrants competed with native-born men. Germans, many of whom were skilled workers, took jobs in furniture making. The Irish provided a ready source of unskilled labor needed to lay railroad track and dig canals. American men with families to support grudgingly accepted low wages in order to keep their jobs. As work became increasingly deskilled, no worker was irreplaceable, and no one's job was safe.

1.2 A Vibrant Capitalist Republic

By the end of this section, you will be able to:
- Explain the process of selling western land
- Discuss the causes of the Panic of 1819
- Identify key American innovators and inventors

By the 1840s, the United States economy bore little resemblance to the import-and-export economy of colonial days. It was now a market economy, one in which the production of goods, and their prices, were unregulated by the government. Commercial centers, to which job seekers flocked, mushroomed. New York City's population skyrocketed. In 1790, it was 33,000; by 1820, it had reached 200,000; and by 1825, it had swelled to 270,000. New opportunities for wealth appeared to be available to anyone.

However, the expansion of the American economy made it prone to the boom-and-bust cycle. Market economies involve fluctuating prices for labor, raw materials, and consumer goods and depend on credit and financial instruments—any one of which can be the source of an imbalance and an economic downturn in which businesses and farmers default, wage workers lose their employment, and investors lose their assets. This happened for the first time in the United States in 1819, when waves of enthusiastic speculation (expectations of rapidly rising prices) in land and commodities gave way to drops in prices.

THE LAND OFFICE BUSINESS

In the early nineteenth century, people poured into the territories west of the long-settled eastern seaboard. Among them were speculators seeking to buy cheap parcels from the federal government in anticipation of a rise in prices. The Ohio Country in the Northwest Territory appeared to offer the best prospects for many in the East, especially New Englanders. The result was "Ohio fever," as thousands traveled there to reap the benefits of settling in this newly available territory (**Figure 1.7**).

Figure 1.7 Cartographer John Cary drew this map "exhibiting The Western Territory, Kentucky, Pennsylvania, Maryland, Virginia &c" for his 1808 atlas; it depicted the huge western territory that fascinated settlers in the early nineteenth century.

The federal government oversaw the orderly transfer of public land to citizens at public auctions. The Land Law of 1796 applied to the territory of Ohio after it had been wrested from Indians. Under this law, the United States would sell a minimum parcel of 640 acres for $2 an acre. The Land Law of 1800 further encouraged land sales in the Northwest Territory by reducing the minimum parcel size by half and enabling sales on credit, with the goal of stimulating settlement by ordinary farmers. The government created **land offices** to handle these sales and established them in the West within easy reach of prospective landowners. They could thus purchase land directly from the government, at the price the government had set. Buyers were given low interest rates, with payments that could be spread over four years. Surveyors marked off the parcels in straight lines, creating a landscape of checkerboard squares.

The future looked bright for those who turned their gaze on the land in the West. Surveying, settling, and farming, turning the wilderness into a profitable commodity, gave purchasers a sense of progress. A uniquely American story of settling the land developed: hardy individuals wielding an axe cleared it, built a log cabin, and turned the frontier into a farm that paved the way for mills and towns (**Figure 1.8**).

Figure 1.8 Thomas Cole, who painted *Home in the Woods* in 1847, was an American artist. Cole founded the Hudson River School, a style renowned for portrayals of landscapes and wilderness influenced by the emotional aesthetic known as romanticism. In what ways is this image realistic, and how is it idealized or romanticized?

MY STORY

✪ *A New Englander Heads West*

A native of Vermont, Gershom Flagg was one of thousands of New Englanders who caught "Ohio fever." In this letter to his brother, Azariah Flagg, dated August 3, 1817, he describes the hustle and bustle of the emerging commercial town of Cincinnati.

> DEAR BROTHER,
>
> Cincinnati is an incorporated City. It contained in 1815, 1,100 buildings of different descriptions among which are above 20 of Stone 250 of brick & 800 of Wood. The population in 1815 was 6,500. There are about 60 Mercantile stores several of which are wholesale. Here are a great share of Mechanics of all kinds.
>
> Here is one Woolen Factory four Cotton factories but not now in operation. A most stupendously large building of Stone is likewise erected immediately on the bank of the River for a steam Mill. It is nine stories high at the Waters edge & is 87 by 62 feet. It drives four pair of Stones besides various other Machinery as Wool carding &c &c. There is also a valuable Steam Saw Mill driving four saws also an inclined Wheel ox Saw Mill with two saws, one Glass Factory. The town is Rapidly increasing in Wealth & population. Here is a Branch of the United States Bank and three other banks & two Printing offices. The country around is rich. . . .
>
> That you may all be prospered in the world is the anxious wish of your affectionate Brother
> GERSHOM FLAGG

What caught Flagg's attention? From your reading of this letter and study of the engraving below (**Figure 1.9**), what impression can you take away of Cincinnati in 1817?

A View of CINCINNATI on the OHIO.

Figure 1.9 This engraving from *A Topographical Description of the State of Ohio, Indiana Territory, and Louisiana* (1812), by Jervis Cutler, presents a view of Cincinnati as it may have looked to Gershom Flagg.

Click and Explore

Learn more about settlement of and immigration to the Northwest Territory by exploring the National Park Service's **Historic Resource Study** (http://openstaxcollege.org/l/ 15LincMemorial) related to the Lincoln Boyhood National Memorial. According to the guide's maps, what lands were available for purchase?

THE PANIC OF 1819

The first major economic crisis in the United States after the War of 1812 was due, in large measure, to factors in the larger Atlantic economy. It was made worse, however, by land speculation and poor banking practices at home. British textile mills voraciously consumed American cotton, and the devastation of the Napoleonic Wars made Europe reliant on other American agricultural commodities such as wheat. This drove up both the price of American agricultural products and the value of the land on which staples such as cotton, wheat, corn, and tobacco were grown.

Many Americans were struck with "land fever." Farmers strove to expand their acreage, and those who lived in areas where unoccupied land was scarce sought holdings in the West. They needed money to purchase this land, however. Small merchants and factory owners, hoping to take advantage of this boom time, also sought to borrow money to expand their businesses. When existing banks refused to lend money to small farmers and others without a credit history, state legislatures chartered new banks to meet the demand. In one legislative session, Kentucky chartered forty-six. As loans increased, paper money from new state banks flooded the country, creating inflation that drove the price of land and goods still higher. This, in turn, encouraged even more people to borrow money with which to purchase land or to expand or start their own businesses. Speculators took advantage of this boom in the sale of land by purchasing property not to live on, but to buy cheaply and resell at exorbitant prices.

During the War of 1812, the Bank of the United States had suspended payments in **specie**, "hard money" usually in the form of gold and silver coins. When the war ended, the bank continued to issue only paper banknotes and to redeem notes issued by state banks with paper only. The newly chartered banks also adopted this practice, issuing banknotes in excess of the amount of specie in their vaults. This shaky economic scheme worked only so long as people were content to conduct business with paper money and refrain from demanding that banks instead give them the gold and silver that was supposed to back it. If large numbers of people, or banks that had loaned money to other banks, began to demand specie payments, the banking system would collapse, because there was no longer enough specie to support the amount of paper money the banks had put into circulation. So terrified were bankers that customers would demand gold and silver that an irate bank employee in Ohio stabbed a customer who had the audacity to ask for specie in exchange for the banknotes he held.

In an effort to bring stability to the nation's banking system, Congress chartered the Second Bank of the United States (a revival of Alexander Hamilton's national bank) in 1816. But this new institution only compounded the problem by making risky loans, opening branches in the South and West where land fever was highest, and issuing a steady stream of Bank of the United States notes, a move that increased inflation and speculation.

The inflated economic bubble burst in 1819, resulting in a prolonged economic depression or severe downturn in the economy called the Panic of 1819. It was the first economic depression experienced by the American public, who panicked as they saw the prices of agricultural products fall and businesses fail. Prices had already begun falling in 1815, at the end of the Napoleonic Wars, when Britain began to "dump" its surplus manufactured goods, the result of wartime overproduction, in American ports, where they were sold for low prices and competed with American-manufactured goods. In 1818, to make the economic situation worse, prices for American agricultural products began to fall both in the United States and in Europe; the overproduction of staples such as wheat and cotton coincided with the recovery of European agriculture, which reduced demand for American crops. Crop prices tumbled by as much 75 percent.

This dramatic decrease in the value of agricultural goods left farmers unable to pay their debts. As they defaulted on their loans, banks seized their property. However, because the drastic fall in agricultural prices had greatly reduced the value of land, the banks were left with farms they were unable to sell. Land speculators lost the value of their investments. As the countryside suffered, hard-hit farmers ceased to purchase manufactured goods. Factories responded by cutting wages or firing employees.

In 1818, the Second Bank of the United States needed specie to pay foreign investors who had loaned money to the United States to enable the country to purchase Louisiana. The bank began to call in the loans it had made and required that state banks pay their debts in gold and silver. State banks that could not collect loan payments from hard-pressed farmers could not, in turn, meet their obligations to the Second Bank of the United States. Severe consequences followed as banks closed their doors and businesses failed. Three-quarters of the work force in Philadelphia was unemployed, and charities were swamped by thousands of newly destitute people needing assistance. In states with imprisonment for debt, the prison population swelled. As a result, many states drafted laws to provide relief for debtors. Even those at the top of the social ladder were affected by the Panic of 1819. Thomas Jefferson, who had cosigned a loan for a friend, nearly lost Monticello when his acquaintance defaulted, leaving Jefferson responsible for the debt.

In an effort to stimulate the economy in the midst of the economic depression, Congress passed several acts modifying land sales. The Land Law of 1820 lowered the price of land to $1.25 per acre and allowed small parcels of eighty acres to be sold. The Relief Act of 1821 allowed Ohioans to return land to the government if they could not afford to keep it. The money they received in return was credited toward their debt. The act also extended the credit period to eight years. States, too, attempted to aid those faced with economic hard times by passing laws to prevent mortgage foreclosures so buyers could keep their homes. Americans made the best of the opportunities presented in business, in farming, or on the frontier, and by 1823 the Panic of 1819 had ended. The recovery provided ample evidence of the vibrant and resilient nature of the American people.

ENTREPRENEURS AND INVENTORS

The volatility of the U.S. economy did nothing to dampen the creative energies of its citizens in the years before the Civil War. In the 1800s, a frenzy of entrepreneurship and invention yielded many new products and machines. The republic seemed to be a laboratory of innovation, and technological advances appeared unlimited.

One of the most influential advancements of the early nineteenth century was the cotton engine or gin, invented by Eli Whitney and patented in 1794. Whitney, who was born in Massachusetts, had spent time in the South and knew that a device to speed up the production of cotton was desperately needed so cotton farmers could meet the growing demand for their crop. He hoped the cotton gin would render slavery obsolete. Whitney's seemingly simple invention cleaned the seeds from the raw cotton far more quickly and efficiently than could slaves working by hand (**Figure 1.10**). The raw cotton with seeds was placed in the cotton gin, and with the use of a hand crank, the seeds were extracted through a carding device that aligned the cotton fibers in strands for spinning.

Figure 1.10 *The First Cotton-Gin*, an 1869 drawing by William L. Sheppard, shows the first use of a cotton gin "at the close of the last century." African American slaves handle the gin while white men conduct business in the background. What do you think the artist was trying to convey with this image? (credit: Library of Congress)

Whitney also worked on **machine tools**, devices that cut and shaped metal to make standardized, interchangeable parts for other mechanical devices like clocks and guns. Whitney's machine tools to manufacture parts for muskets enabled guns to be manufactured and repaired by people other than skilled gunsmiths. His creative genius served as a source of inspiration for many other American inventors.

Another influential new technology of the early 1800s was the steamship engine, invented by Robert Fulton in 1807. Fulton's first steamship, the *Clermont*, used paddle wheels to travel the 150 miles from New York City to Albany in a record time of only thirty-two hours (**Figure 1.11**). Soon, a fleet of steamboats was traversing the Hudson River and New York Harbor, later expanding to travel every major American river including the mighty Mississippi. By the 1830s there were over one thousand of these vessels, radically changing water transportation by ending its dependence on the wind. Steamboats could travel faster and more cheaply than sailing vessels or keelboats, which floated downriver and had to be poled or towed upriver on the return voyage. Steamboats also arrived with much greater dependability. The steamboat facilitated the rapid economic development of the massive Mississippi River Valley and the settlement of the West.

Figure 1.11 Fulton's steamboat the *Clermont* transformed the speed, cost, and dependability of water transportation in the United States. (credit: Project Gutenberg Archives)

Virginia-born Cyrus McCormick wanted to replace the laborious process of using a scythe to cut and gather wheat for harvest. In 1831, he and the slaves on his family's plantation tested a horse-drawn mechanical reaper, and over the next several decades, he made constant improvements to it (**Figure 9.12**). More farmers began using it in the 1840s, and greater demand for the McCormick reaper led McCormick and his brother to establish the McCormick Harvesting Machine Company in Chicago, where labor was more readily available. By the 1850s, McCormick's mechanical reaper had enabled farmers to vastly increase their output. McCormick—and also John Deere, who improved on the design of plows—opened the prairies to agriculture. McCormick's bigger machine could harvest grain faster, and Deere's plow could cut through the thick prairie sod. Agriculture north of the Ohio River became the pantry that would lower food prices and feed the major cities in the East. In short order, Ohio, Indiana, and Illinois all become major agricultural states.

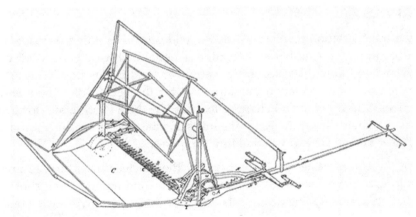

Figure 1.12 This sketch is from the 1845 patent for an improved grain reaper invented by Cyrus Hall McCormick. The reaper mechanized the labor-intensive use of scythes to harvest wheat.

Samuel Morse added the telegraph to the list of American innovations introduced in the years before the Civil War. Born in Massachusetts in 1791, Morse first gained renown as a painter before turning his attention to the development of a method of rapid communication in the 1830s. In 1838, he gave the first public demonstration of his method of conveying electric pulses over a wire, using the basis of what became known as Morse code. In 1843, Congress agreed to help fund the new technology by allocating $30,000 for a telegraph line to connect Washington, DC, and Baltimore along the route of the Baltimore and Ohio Railroad. In 1844, Morse sent the first telegraph message on the new link. Improved communication systems fostered the development of business, economics, and politics by allowing for dissemination of news at a speed previously unknown.

1.3 On the Move: The Transportation Revolution

By the end of this section, you will be able to:
- Describe the development of improved methods of nineteenth-century domestic transportation
- Identify the ways in which roads, canals, and railroads impacted Americans' lives in the nineteenth century

Americans in the early 1800s were a people on the move, as thousands left the eastern coastal states for opportunities in the West. Unlike their predecessors, who traveled by foot or wagon train, these settlers had new transport options. Their trek was made possible by the construction of roads, canals, and railroads, projects that required the funding of the federal government and the states.

New technologies, like the steamship and railroad lines, had brought about what historians call the transportation revolution. States competed for the honor of having the most advanced transport systems. People celebrated the transformation of the wilderness into an orderly world of improvement demonstrating the steady march of progress and the greatness of the republic. In 1817, John C. Calhoun of South Carolina looked to a future of rapid internal improvements, declaring, "Let us . . . bind the Republic together with a perfect system of roads and canals." Americans agreed that internal transportation routes would promote progress. By the eve of the Civil War, the United States had moved beyond roads and canals to a well-established and extensive system of railroads.

ROADS AND CANALS

One key part of the transportation revolution was the widespread building of roads and turnpikes. In 1811, construction began on the **Cumberland Road**, a national highway that provided thousands with a route from Maryland to Illinois. The federal government funded this important artery to the West, beginning the creation of a transportation infrastructure for the benefit of settlers and farmers. Other entities built turnpikes, which (as today) charged fees for use. New York State, for instance, chartered turnpike companies that dramatically increased the miles of state roads from one thousand in 1810 to four thousand by 1820. New York led the way in building turnpikes.

Canal mania swept the United States in the first half of the nineteenth century. Promoters knew these artificial rivers could save travelers immense amounts of time and money. Even short waterways, such as the two-and-a-half-mile canal going around the rapids of the Ohio River near Louisville, Kentucky, proved a huge leap forward, in this case by opening a water route from Pittsburgh to New Orleans. The preeminent example was the **Erie Canal** (**Figure 1.13**), which linked the Hudson River, and thus New York City and the Atlantic seaboard, to the Great Lakes and the Mississippi River Valley.

With its central location, large harbor, and access to the hinterland via the Hudson River, New York City already commanded the lion's share of commerce. Still, the city's merchants worried about losing ground to their competitors in Philadelphia and Baltimore. Their search for commercial advantage led to the dream of creating a water highway connecting the city's Hudson River to Lake Erie and markets in the West. The result was the Erie Canal. Chartered in 1817 by the state of New York, the canal took seven years to complete. When it opened in 1825, it dramatically decreased the cost of shipping while reducing the time to travel to the West. Soon $15 million worth of goods (more than $200 million in today's money) was being transported on the 363-mile waterway every year.

Figure 1.13 Although the Erie Canal was primarily used for commerce and trade, in *Pittsford on the Erie Canal* (1837), George Harvey portrays it in a pastoral, natural setting. Why do you think the painter chose to portray the canal this way?

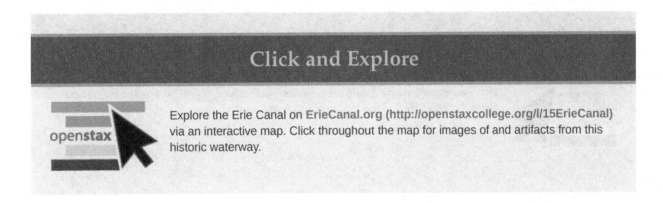

Click and Explore

Explore the Erie Canal on **ErieCanal.org (http://openstaxcollege.org/l/15ErieCanal)** via an interactive map. Click throughout the map for images of and artifacts from this historic waterway.

The success of the Erie Canal led to other, similar projects. The Wabash and Erie Canal, which opened in the early 1840s, stretched over 450 miles, making it the longest canal in North America (**Figure 1.14**). Canals added immensely to the country's sense of progress. Indeed, they appeared to be the logical next step in the process of transforming wilderness into civilization.

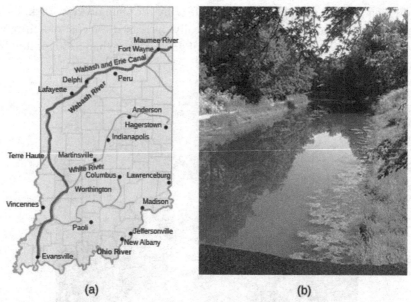

(a) (b)

Figure 9.14 This map (a) shows the route taken by the Wabash and Erie Canal through the state of Indiana. The canal began operation in 1843 and boats operated on it until the 1870s. Sections have since been restored, as shown in this 2007 photo (b) from Delphi, Indiana.

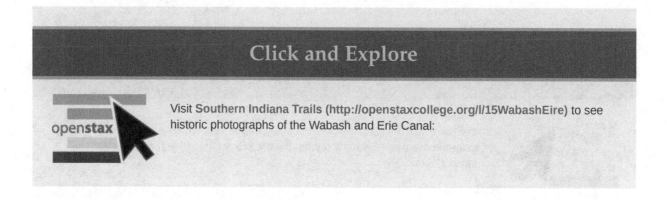

Click and Explore

Visit **Southern Indiana Trails (http://openstaxcollege.org/l/15WabashEire)** to see historic photographs of the Wabash and Erie Canal:

As with highway projects such as the Cumberland Road, many canals were federally sponsored, especially during the presidency of John Quincy Adams in the late 1820s. Adams, along with Secretary of State Henry Clay, championed what was known as the American System, part of which included plans for a broad range of internal transportation improvements. Adams endorsed the creation of roads and canals to facilitate commerce and develop markets for agriculture as well as to advance settlement in the West.

RAILROADS

Starting in the late 1820s, steam locomotives began to compete with horse-drawn locomotives. The railroads with steam locomotives offered a new mode of transportation that fascinated citizens, buoying their optimistic view of the possibilities of technological progress. The **Mohawk and Hudson Railroad** was the first to begin service with a steam locomotive. Its inaugural train ran in 1831 on a track outside Albany and covered twelve miles in twenty-five minutes. Soon it was traveling regularly between Albany and Schenectady.

Toward the middle of the century, railroad construction kicked into high gear, and eager investors quickly formed a number of railroad companies. As a railroad grid began to take shape, it stimulated a greater demand for coal, iron, and steel. Soon, both railroads and canals crisscrossed the states (**Figure**

1.15), providing a transportation infrastructure that fueled the growth of American commerce. Indeed, the transportation revolution led to development in the coal, iron, and steel industries, providing many Americans with new job opportunities.

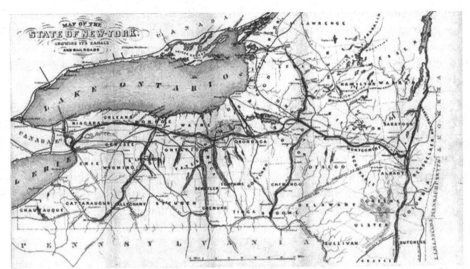

Figure 1.15 This 1853 map of the "Empire State" shows the extent of New York's canal and railroad networks. The entire country's transportation infrastructure grew dramatically during the first half of the nineteenth century.

AMERICANS ON THE MOVE

The expansion of roads, canals, and railroads changed people's lives. In 1786, it had taken a minimum of four days to travel from Boston, Massachusetts, to Providence, Rhode Island. By 1840, the trip took half a day on a train. In the twenty-first century, this may seem intolerably slow, but people at the time were amazed by the railroad's speed. Its average of twenty miles per hour was twice as fast as other available modes of transportation.

By 1840, more than three thousand miles of canals had been dug in the United States, and thirty thousand miles of railroad track had been laid by the beginning of the Civil War. Together with the hundreds of steamboats that plied American rivers, these advances in transportation made it easier and less expensive to ship agricultural products from the West to feed people in eastern cities, and to send manufactured goods from the East to people in the West. Without this ability to transport goods, the market revolution would not have been possible. Rural families also became less isolated as a result of the transportation revolution. Traveling circuses, menageries, peddlers, and itinerant painters could now more easily make their way into rural districts, and people in search of work found cities and mill towns within their reach.

1.4 A New Social Order: Class Divisions

By the end of this section, you will be able to:
- Identify the shared perceptions and ideals of each social class
- Assess different social classes' views of slavery

The profound economic changes sweeping the United States led to equally important social and cultural transformations. The formation of distinct classes, especially in the rapidly industrializing North, was one of the most striking developments. The unequal distribution of newly created wealth spurred new divisions along class lines. Each class had its own specific culture and views on the issue of slavery.

THE ECONOMIC ELITE

Economic elites gained further social and political ascendance in the United States due to a fast-growing economy that enhanced their wealth and allowed distinctive social and cultural characteristics to develop among different economic groups. In the major northern cities of Boston, New York, and Philadelphia, leading merchants formed an industrial capitalist elite. Many came from families that had been deeply engaged in colonial trade in tea, sugar, pepper, slaves, and other commodities and that were familiar with trade networks connecting the United States with Europe, the West Indies, and the Far East. These colonial merchants had passed their wealth to their children.

After the War of 1812, the new generation of merchants expanded their economic activities. They began to specialize in specific types of industry, spearheading the development of industrial capitalism based on factories they owned and on specific commercial services such as banking, insurance, and shipping. Junius Spencer Morgan (**Figure 1.16**), for example, rose to prominence as a banker. His success began in Boston, where he worked in the import business in the 1830s. He then formed a partnership with a London banker, George Peabody, and created Peabody, Morgan & Co. In 1864, he renamed the enterprise J. S. Morgan & Co. His son, J. P. Morgan, became a noted financier in the later nineteenth and early twentieth century.

Figure 1.16   Junius Spencer Morgan of Boston was one of the fathers of the American private banking system. (credit: Project Gutenberg Archives)

Click and Explore

Visit the **Internet Archive** (http://openstaxcollege.org/l/15Hunts) to see scanned pages from *Hunt's Merchant's Magazine and Commercial Review*. This monthly business review provided the business elite with important information about issues pertaining to trade and finance: commodity prices, new laws affecting business, statistics regarding imports and exports, and similar content. Choose three articles and decide how they might have been important to the northern business elite.

Members of the northern business elite forged close ties with each other to protect and expand their economic interests. Marriages between leading families formed a crucial strategy to advance economic advantage, and the homes of the northern elite became important venues for solidifying social bonds. Exclusive neighborhoods started to develop as the wealthy distanced themselves from the poorer urban residents, and cities soon became segregated by class.

Industrial elites created chambers of commerce to advance their interests; by 1858 there were ten in the United States. These networking organizations allowed top bankers and merchants to stay current on the economic activities of their peers and further strengthen the bonds among themselves. The elite also established social clubs to forge and maintain ties. The first of these, the Philadelphia Club, came into being in 1834. Similar clubs soon formed in other cities and hosted a range of social activities designed to further bind together the leading economic families. Many northern elites worked hard to ensure the transmission of their inherited wealth from one generation to the next. Politically, they exercised considerable power in local and state elections. Most also had ties to the cotton trade, so they were strong supporters of slavery.

The Industrial Revolution led some former artisans to reinvent themselves as manufacturers. These enterprising leaders of manufacturing differed from the established commercial elite in the North and South because they did not inherit wealth. Instead, many came from very humble working-class origins and embodied the dream of achieving upward social mobility through hard work and discipline. As the beneficiaries of the economic transformations sweeping the republic, these newly established manufacturers formed a new economic elite that thrived in the cities and cultivated its own distinct sensibilities. They created a culture that celebrated hard work, a position that put them at odds with southern planter elites who prized leisure and with other elite northerners who had largely inherited their wealth and status.

Peter Cooper provides one example of the new northern manufacturing class. Ever inventive, Cooper dabbled in many different moneymaking enterprises before gaining success in the glue business. He opened his Manhattan glue factory in the 1820s and was soon using his profits to expand into a host of other activities, including iron production. One of his innovations was the steam locomotive, which he invented in 1827 (**Figure 1.17**). Despite becoming one of the wealthiest men in New York City, Cooper lived simply. Rather than buying an ornate bed, for example, he built his own. He believed respectability came through hard work, not family pedigree.

Figure 1.17 Peter Cooper, who would go on to found the Cooper Union for the Advancement of Science and Art in New York City, designed and built the Tom Thumb, the first American-built steam locomotive, a replica of which is shown here.

Those who had inherited their wealth derided self-made men like Cooper, and he and others like him were excluded from the social clubs established by the merchant and financial elite of New York City. Self-made northern manufacturers, however, created their own organizations that aimed to promote upward mobility. The Providence Association of Mechanics and Manufacturers was formed in 1789 and promoted both industrial arts and education as a pathway to economic success. In 1859, Peter Cooper established the Cooper Union for the Advancement of Science and Art, a school in New York City dedicated to providing education in technology. Merit, not wealth, mattered most according to Cooper, and admission to the school was based solely on ability; race, sex, and family connections had no place. The best and brightest could attend Cooper Union tuition-free, a policy that remained in place until 2014.

THE MIDDLE CLASS

Not all enterprising artisans were so successful that they could rise to the level of the elite. However, many artisans and small merchants, who owned small factories and stores, did manage to achieve and maintain respectability in an emerging middle class. Lacking the protection of great wealth, members of the middle class agonized over the fear that they might slip into the ranks of wage laborers; thus they strove to maintain or improve their middle-class status and that of their children.

To this end, the middle class valued cleanliness, discipline, morality, hard work, education, and good manners. Hard work and education enabled them to rise in life. Middle-class children, therefore, did not work in factories. Instead they attended school and in their free time engaged in "self-improving" activities, such as reading or playing the piano, or they played with toys and games that would teach them the skills and values they needed to succeed in life. In the early nineteenth century, members of the middle class began to limit the number of children they had. Children no longer contributed economically to the household, and raising them "correctly" required money and attention. It therefore made sense to have fewer of them.

Middle-class women did not work for wages. Their job was to care for the children and to keep the house in a state of order and cleanliness, often with the help of a servant. They also performed the important tasks of cultivating good manners among their children and their husbands and of purchasing consumer goods; both activities proclaimed to neighbors and prospective business partners that their families were educated, cultured, and financially successful.

Northern business elites, many of whom owned or had invested in businesses like cotton mills that profited from slave labor, often viewed the institution of slavery with ambivalence. Most members of the middle class took a dim view of it, however, since it promoted a culture of leisure. Slavery stood as the antithesis of the middle-class view that dignity and respectability were achieved through work, and many members of this class became active in efforts to end it.

This class of upwardly mobile citizens promoted temperance, or abstinence from alcohol. They also gave their support to Protestant ministers like George Grandison Finney, who preached that all people possessed **free moral agency**, meaning they could change their lives and bring about their own salvation, a message that resonated with members of the middle class, who already believed their worldly efforts had led to their economic success.

THE WORKING CLASS

The Industrial Revolution in the United States created a new class of wage workers, and this working class also developed its own culture. They formed their own neighborhoods, living away from the oversight of bosses and managers. While industrialization and the market revolution brought some improvements to the lives of the working class, these sweeping changes did not benefit laborers as much as they did the middle class and the elites. The working class continued to live an often precarious existence. They suffered greatly during economic slumps, such as the Panic of 1819.

Although most working-class men sought to emulate the middle class by keeping their wives and children out of the work force, their economic situation often necessitated that others besides the male head of the family contribute to its support. Thus, working-class children might attend school for a few years or learn to read and write at Sunday school, but education was sacrificed when income was needed, and many working-class children went to work in factories. While the wives of wage laborers usually did not work for wages outside the home, many took in laundry or did piecework at home to supplement the family's income.

Although the urban working class could not afford the consumer goods that the middle class could, its members did exercise a great deal of influence over popular culture. Theirs was a festive public culture of release and escape from the drudgery of factory work, catered to by the likes of Phineas Taylor Barnum, the celebrated circus promoter and showman. Taverns also served an important function as places to forget the long hours and uncertain wages of the factories. Alcohol consumption was high among the working class, although many workers did take part in the temperance movement. It is little wonder that middle-class manufacturers attempted to abolish alcohol.

AMERICANA

✸ *P. T. Barnum and the Feejee Mermaid*

The Connecticut native P. T. Barnum catered to the demand for escape and cheap amusements among the working class. His American Museum in New York City opened in 1841 and achieved great success. Millions flocked to see Barnum's exhibits, which included a number of fantastic human and animal oddities, almost all of which were hoaxes. One exhibit in the 1840s featured the "Feejee Mermaid," which Barnum presented as proof of the existence of the mythical mermaids of the deep (**Figure 1.18**). In truth, the mermaid was a half-monkey, half-fish stitched together.

(a)   (b)

Figure 1.18 Spurious though they were, attractions such as the Feejee mermaid (a) from P. T. Barnum's American Museum in New York City (b) drew throngs of working-class wage earners in the middle of the nineteenth century.

Click and Explore

Visit **The Lost Museum** (http://openstaxcollege.org/l/15LostMuseum) to take a virtual tour of P. T. Barnum's incredible museum.

Wage workers in the North were largely hostile to the abolition of slavery, fearing it would unleash more competition for jobs from free blacks. Many were also hostile to immigration. The pace of immigration to the United States accelerated in the 1840s and 1850s as Europeans were drawn to the promise of employment and land in the United States. Many new members of the working class came from the ranks of these immigrants, who brought new foods, customs, and religions. The Roman Catholic population of the United States, fairly small before this period, began to swell with the arrival of the Irish and the Germans.

CHAPTER 2

Cotton is King: The Antebellum South, 1800–1860

Figure 2.1 *Bateaux à Vapeur Géant, la Nouvelle-Orléans 1853* (*Giant Steamboats at New Orleans, 1853*), by Hippolyte Sebron, shows how New Orleans, at the mouth of the Mississippi River, was the primary trading hub for the cotton that fueled the growth of the southern economy.

Chapter Outline

2.1 The Economics of Cotton
2.2 African Americans in the Antebellum United States
2.3 Wealth and Culture in the South
2.4 The Filibuster and the Quest for New Slave States

Introduction

Nine new slave states entered the Union between 1789 and 1860, rapidly expanding and transforming the South into a region of economic growth built on slave labor. In the image above (**Figure 2.1**), innumerable slaves load cargo onto a steamship in the Port of New Orleans, the commercial center of the antebellum South, while two well-dressed white men stand by talking. Commercial activity extends as far as the eye can see.

By the mid-nineteenth century, southern commercial centers like New Orleans had become home to the greatest concentration of wealth in the United States. While most white southerners did not own slaves, they aspired to join the ranks of elite slaveholders, who played a key role in the politics of both the South and the nation. Meanwhile, slavery shaped the culture and society of the South, which rested on a racial ideology of white supremacy and a vision of the United States as a white man's republic. Slaves endured the traumas of slavery by creating their own culture and using the Christian message of redemption to find hope for a world of freedom without violence.

2.1 The Economics of Cotton

By the end of this section, you will be able to:
- Explain the labor-intensive processes of cotton production
- Describe the importance of cotton to the Atlantic and American antebellum economy

In the **antebellum** era—that is, in the years before the Civil War—American planters in the South continued to grow Chesapeake tobacco and Carolina rice as they had in the colonial era. Cotton, however, emerged as the antebellum South's major commercial crop, eclipsing tobacco, rice, and sugar in economic importance. By 1860, the region was producing two-thirds of the world's cotton. In 1793, Eli Whitney revolutionized the production of cotton when he invented the **cotton gin**, a device that separated the seeds from raw cotton. Suddenly, a process that was extraordinarily labor-intensive when done by hand could be completed quickly and easily. American plantation owners, who were searching for a successful staple crop to compete on the world market, found it in cotton.

As a commodity, cotton had the advantage of being easily stored and transported. A demand for it already existed in the industrial textile mills in Great Britain, and in time, a steady stream of slave-grown American cotton would also supply northern textile mills. Southern cotton, picked and processed by American slaves, helped fuel the nineteenth-century Industrial Revolution in both the United States and Great Britain.

KING COTTON

Almost no cotton was grown in the United States in 1787, the year the federal constitution was written. However, following the War of 1812, a huge increase in production resulted in the so-called **cotton boom**, and by midcentury, cotton became the key **cash crop** (a crop grown to sell rather than for the farmer's sole use) of the southern economy and the most important American commodity. By 1850, of the 3.2 million slaves in the country's fifteen slave states, 1.8 million were producing cotton; by 1860, slave labor was producing over two billion pounds of cotton per year. Indeed, American cotton soon made up two-thirds of the global supply, and production continued to soar. By the time of the Civil War, South Carolina

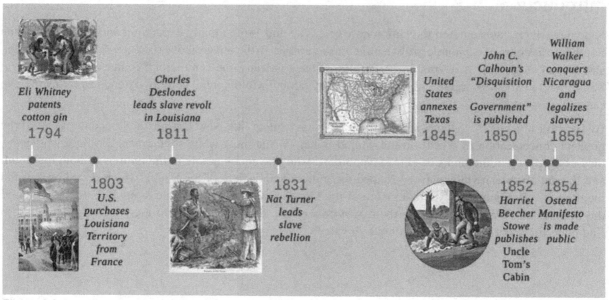

Figure 2.2

politician James Hammond confidently proclaimed that the North could never threaten the South because "cotton is king."

The crop grown in the South was a hybrid: *Gossypium barbadense*, known as Petit Gulf cotton, a mix of Mexican, Georgia, and Siamese strains. Petit Gulf cotton grew extremely well in different soils and climates. It dominated cotton production in the Mississippi River Valley—home of the new slave states of Louisiana, Mississippi, Arkansas, Tennessee, Kentucky, and Missouri—as well as in other states like Texas. Whenever new slave states entered the Union, white slaveholders sent armies of slaves to clear the land in order to grow and pick the lucrative crop. The phrase "to be sold down the river," used by Harriet Beecher Stowe in her 1852 novel *Uncle Tom's Cabin*, refers to this forced migration from the upper southern states to the Deep South, lower on the Mississippi, to grow cotton.

The slaves who built this cotton kingdom with their labor started by clearing the land. Although the Jeffersonian vision of the settlement of new U.S. territories entailed white yeoman farmers single-handedly carving out small independent farms, the reality proved quite different. Entire old-growth forests and cypress swamps fell to the axe as slaves labored to strip the vegetation to make way for cotton. With the land cleared, slaves readied the earth by plowing and planting. To ambitious white planters, the extent of new land available for cotton production seemed almost limitless, and many planters simply leapfrogged from one area to the next, abandoning their fields every ten to fifteen years after the soil became exhausted. Theirs was a world of mobility and restlessness, a constant search for the next area to grow the valuable crop. Slaves composed the vanguard of this American expansion to the West.

Cotton planting took place in March and April, when slaves planted seeds in rows around three to five feet apart. Over the next several months, from April to August, they carefully tended the plants. Weeding the cotton rows took significant energy and time. In August, after the cotton plants had flowered and the flowers had begun to give way to cotton bolls (the seed-bearing capsule that contains the cotton fiber), all the plantation's slaves—men, women, and children—worked together to pick the crop (**Figure 2.3**). On each day of cotton picking, slaves went to the fields with sacks, which they would fill as many times as they could. The effort was laborious, and a white "driver" employed the lash to make slaves work as quickly as possible.

Figure 2.3 In the late nineteenth century, J. N. Wilson captured this image of harvest time at a southern plantation. While the workers in this photograph are not slave laborers, the process of cotton harvesting shown here had changed little from antebellum times.

Cotton planters projected the amount of cotton they could harvest based on the number of slaves under their control. In general, planters expected a good "hand," or slave, to work ten acres of land and pick two hundred pounds of cotton a day. An overseer or master measured each individual slave's daily yield.

Great pressure existed to meet the expected daily amount, and some masters whipped slaves who picked less than expected.

Cotton picking occurred as many as seven times a season as the plant grew and continued to produce bolls through the fall and early winter. During the picking season, slaves worked from sunrise to sunset with a ten-minute break at lunch; many slaveholders tended to give them little to eat, since spending on food would cut into their profits. Other slaveholders knew that feeding slaves could increase productivity and therefore provided what they thought would help ensure a profitable crop. The slaves' day didn't end after they picked the cotton; once they had brought it to the gin house to be weighed, they then had to care for the animals and perform other chores. Indeed, slaves often maintained their own gardens and livestock, which they tended after working the cotton fields, in order to supplement their supply of food.

Sometimes the cotton was dried before it was ginned (put through the process of separating the seeds from the cotton fiber). The cotton gin allowed a slave to remove the seeds from fifty pounds of cotton a day, compared to one pound if done by hand. After the seeds had been removed, the cotton was pressed into bales. These bales, weighing about four hundred to five hundred pounds, were wrapped in burlap cloth and sent down the Mississippi River.

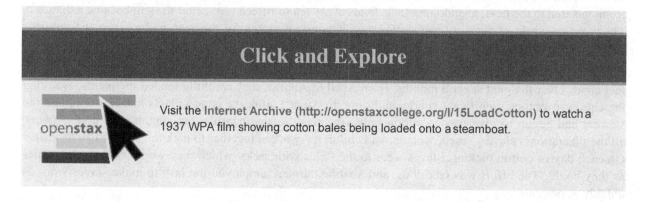

Click and Explore

Visit the Internet Archive (http://openstaxcollege.org/l/15LoadCotton) to watch a 1937 WPA film showing cotton bales being loaded onto a steamboat.

As the cotton industry boomed in the South, the Mississippi River quickly became the essential water highway in the United States. Steamboats, a crucial part of the transportation revolution thanks to their enormous freight-carrying capacity and ability to navigate shallow waterways, became a defining component of the cotton kingdom. Steamboats also illustrated the class and social distinctions of the antebellum age. While the decks carried precious cargo, ornate rooms graced the interior. In these spaces, whites socialized in the ship's saloons and dining halls while black slaves served them (**Figure 2.4**).

Figure 2.4 As in this depiction of the saloon of the Mississippi River steamboat *Princess*, elegant and luxurious rooms often occupied the interiors of antebellum steamships, whose decks were filled with cargo.

Investors poured huge sums into steamships. In 1817, only seventeen plied the waters of western rivers, but by 1837, there were over seven hundred steamships in operation. Major new ports developed at St. Louis, Missouri; Memphis, Tennessee; and other locations. By 1860, some thirty-five hundred vessels were steaming in and out of New Orleans, carrying an annual cargo made up primarily of cotton that amounted to $220 million worth of goods (approximately $6.5 billion in 2014 dollars).

New Orleans had been part of the French empire before the United States purchased it, along with the rest of the Louisiana Territory, in 1803. In the first half of the nineteenth century, it rose in prominence and importance largely because of the cotton boom, steam-powered river traffic, and its strategic position near the mouth of the Mississippi River. Steamboats moved down the river transporting cotton grown on plantations along the river and throughout the South to the port at New Orleans. From there, the bulk of American cotton went to Liverpool, England, where it was sold to British manufacturers who ran the cotton mills in Manchester and elsewhere. This lucrative international trade brought new wealth and new residents to the city. By 1840, New Orleans alone had 12 percent of the nation's total banking capital, and visitors often commented on the great cultural diversity of the city. In 1835, Joseph Holt Ingraham wrote: "Truly does New-Orleans represent every other city and nation upon earth. I know of none where is congregated so great a variety of the human species." Slaves, cotton, and the steamship transformed the city from a relatively isolated corner of North America in the eighteenth century to a thriving metropolis that rivaled New York in importance (**Figure 2.5**).

Figure 2.5 This print of *The Levee - New Orleans* (1884) shows the bustling port of New Orleans with bales of cotton waiting to be shipped. The sheer volume of cotton indicates its economic importance throughout the century.

THE DOMESTIC SLAVE TRADE

The South's dependence on cotton was matched by its dependence on slaves to harvest the cotton. Despite the rhetoric of the Revolution that "all men are created equal," slavery not only endured in the American republic but formed the very foundation of the country's economic success. Cotton and slavery occupied a central—and intertwined—place in the nineteenth-century economy.

In 1807, the U.S. Congress abolished the foreign slave trade, a ban that went into effect on January 1, 1808. After this date, importing slaves from Africa became illegal in the United States. While smuggling continued to occur, the end of the international slave trade meant that domestic slaves were in very high demand. Fortunately for Americans whose wealth depended upon the exploitation of slave labor, a fall in the price of tobacco had caused landowners in the Upper South to reduce their production of this crop and use more of their land to grow wheat, which was far more profitable. While tobacco was a labor-intensive crop that required many people to cultivate it, wheat was not. Former tobacco farmers in the older states of Virginia and Maryland found themselves with "surplus" slaves whom they were obligated to feed, clothe, and shelter. Some slaveholders responded to this situation by freeing slaves; far more decided to sell their excess bondsmen. Virginia and Maryland therefore took the lead in the **domestic slave trade**, the trading of slaves within the borders of the United States.

The domestic slave trade offered many economic opportunities for white men. Those who sold their slaves could realize great profits, as could the slave brokers who served as middlemen between sellers and buyers. Other white men could benefit from the trade as owners of warehouses and pens in which slaves were held, or as suppliers of clothing and food for slaves on the move. Between 1790 and 1859, slaveholders in Virginia sold more than half a million slaves. In the early part of this period, many of these slaves were sold to people living in Kentucky, Tennessee, and North and South Carolina. By the 1820s, however, people in Kentucky and the Carolinas had begun to sell many of their slaves as well. Maryland slave dealers sold at least 185,000 slaves. Kentucky slaveholders sold some seventy-one thousand individuals. Most of the slave traders carried these slaves further south to Alabama, Louisiana, and Mississippi. New Orleans, the hub of commerce, boasted the largest slave market in the United States and grew to become the nation's fourth-largest city as a result. Natchez, Mississippi, had the second-largest market. In Virginia, Maryland, the Carolinas, and elsewhere in the South, slave auctions happened every day.

All told, the movement of slaves in the South made up one of the largest forced internal migrations in the United States. In each of the decades between 1820 and 1860, about 200,000 people were sold and relocated. The 1800 census recorded over one million African Americans, of which nearly 900,000 were slaves. By 1860, the total number of African Americans increased to 4.4 million, and of that number, 3.95 million were held in bondage. For many slaves, the domestic slave trade incited the terror of being sold away from family and friends.

MY STORY

⊙ *Solomon Northup Remembers the New Orleans Slave Market*

Solomon Northup was a free black man living in Saratoga, New York, when he was kidnapped and sold into slavery in 1841. He later escaped and wrote a book about his experiences: *Twelve Years a Slave. Narrative of Solomon Northup, a Citizen of New-York, Kidnapped in Washington City in 1841 and Rescued in 1853* (the basis of a 2013 Academy Award–winning film). This excerpt derives from Northup's description of being sold in New Orleans, along with fellow slave Eliza and her children Randall and Emily.

> One old gentleman, who said he wanted a coachman, appeared to take a fancy to me. . . . The same man also purchased Randall. The little fellow was made to jump, and run across the floor, and perform many other feats, exhibiting his activity and condition. All the time the trade was going on, Eliza was crying aloud, and wringing her hands. She besought the man not to buy him, unless he also bought her self and Emily. . . . Freeman turned round to her, savagely, with his whip in his uplifted hand, ordering her to stop her noise, or he would flog her. He would not have such work—such snivelling; and unless she ceased that minute, he would take her to the yard and give her a hundred lashes. . . . Eliza shrunk before him, and tried to wipe away her tears, but it was all in vain. She wanted to be with her children, she said, the little time she had to live. All the frowns and threats of Freeman, could not wholly silence the afflicted mother.

What does Northup's narrative tell you about the experience of being a slave? How does he characterize Freeman, the slave trader? How does he characterize Eliza?

THE SOUTH IN THE AMERICAN AND WORLD MARKETS

The first half of the nineteenth century saw a market revolution in the United States, one in which industrialization brought changes to both the production and the consumption of goods. Some southerners of the time believed that their region's reliance on a single cash crop and its use of slaves to produce it gave the South economic independence and made it immune from the effects of these changes, but this was far from the truth. Indeed, the production of cotton brought the South more firmly into the larger American and Atlantic markets. Northern mills depended on the South for supplies of raw cotton that was then converted into textiles. But this domestic cotton market paled in comparison to the Atlantic market. About 75 percent of the cotton produced in the United States was eventually exported abroad. Exporting at such high volumes made the United States the undisputed world leader in cotton production. Between the years 1820 and 1860, approximately 80 percent of the global cotton supply was produced in the United States. Nearly all the exported cotton was shipped to Great Britain, fueling its burgeoning textile industry and making the powerful British Empire increasingly dependent on American cotton and southern slavery.

The power of cotton on the world market may have brought wealth to the South, but it also increased its economic dependence on other countries and other parts of the United States. Much of the corn and pork that slaves consumed came from farms in the West. Some of the inexpensive clothing, called "slops," and shoes worn by slaves were manufactured in the North. The North also supplied the furnishings found in the homes of both wealthy planters and members of the middle class. Many of the trappings of domestic life, such as carpets, lamps, dinnerware, upholstered furniture, books, and musical instruments—all the accoutrements of comfortable living for southern whites—were made in either the North or Europe. Southern planters also borrowed money from banks in northern cities, and in the southern summers, took advantage of the developments in transportation to travel to resorts at Saratoga, New York; Litchfield, Connecticut; and Newport, Rhode Island.

2.2 African Americans in the Antebellum United States

By the end of this section, you will be able to:
- Discuss the similarities and differences in the lives of slaves and free blacks
- Describe the independent culture and customs that slaves developed

In addition to cotton, the great commodity of the antebellum South was human chattel. Slavery was the cornerstone of the southern economy. By 1850, about 3.2 million slaves labored in the United States, 1.8 million of whom worked in the cotton fields. Slaves faced arbitrary power abuses from whites; they coped by creating family and community networks. Storytelling, song, and Christianity also provided solace and allowed slaves to develop their own interpretations of their condition.

LIFE AS A SLAVE

Southern whites frequently relied upon the idea of **paternalism**—the premise that white slaveholders acted in the best interests of slaves, taking responsibility for their care, feeding, discipline, and even their Christian morality—to justify the existence of slavery. This grossly misrepresented the reality of slavery, which was, by any measure, a dehumanizing, traumatizing, and horrifying human disaster and crime against humanity. Nevertheless, slaves were hardly passive victims of their conditions; they sought and found myriad ways to resist their shackles and develop their own communities and cultures.

Slaves often used the notion of paternalism to their advantage, finding opportunities within this system to engage in acts of resistance and win a degree of freedom and autonomy. For example, some slaves played into their masters' racism by hiding their intelligence and feigning childishness and ignorance. The slaves could then slow down the workday and sabotage the system in small ways by "accidentally" breaking tools, for example; the master, seeing his slaves as unsophisticated and childlike, would believe these incidents were accidents rather than rebellions. Some slaves engaged in more dramatic forms of resistance, such as poisoning their masters slowly. Other slaves reported rebellious slaves to their masters, hoping to gain preferential treatment. Slaves who informed their masters about planned slave rebellions could often expect the slaveholder's gratitude and, perhaps, more lenient treatment. Such expectations were always tempered by the individual personality and caprice of the master.

Slaveholders used both psychological coercion and physical violence to prevent slaves from disobeying their wishes. Often, the most efficient way to discipline slaves was to threaten to sell them. The lash, while the most common form of punishment, was effective but not efficient; whippings sometimes left slaves incapacitated or even dead. Slave masters also used punishment gear like neck braces, balls and chains, leg irons, and paddles with holes to produce blood blisters. Slaves lived in constant terror of both physical violence and separation from family and friends (**Figure 2.6**).

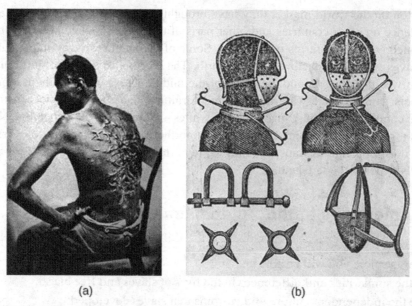

(a)   (b)

Figure 2.6 The original caption of this photograph of a slave's scarred back (a), taken in Baton Rouge, Louisiana, in 1863, reads as follows: "*Overseer Artayou Carrier whipped me. I was two months in bed sore from the whipping. My master come after I was whipped; he discharged the overseer. The very words of poor Peter, taken as he sat for his picture.*" Images like this one helped bolster the northern abolitionist message of the inhumanity of slavery. The drawing of an iron mask, collar, leg shackles, and spurs (b) demonstrates the various cruel and painful instruments used to restrain slaves.

Under southern law, slaves could not marry. Nonetheless, some slaveholders allowed marriages to promote the birth of children and to foster harmony on plantations. Some masters even forced certain slaves to form unions, anticipating the birth of more children (and consequently greater profits) from them. Masters sometimes allowed slaves to choose their own partners, but they could also veto a match. Slave couples always faced the prospect of being sold away from each other, and, once they had children, the horrifying reality that their children could be sold and sent away at any time.

Click and Explore

Browse a collection of first-hand narratives of slaves and former slaves at the National Humanities Center (http://openstaxcollege.org/l/15Enslavement) to learn more about the experience of slavery.

Slave parents had to show their children the best way to survive under slavery. This meant teaching them to be discreet, submissive, and guarded around whites. Parents also taught their children through the stories they told. Popular stories among slaves included tales of tricksters, sly slaves, or animals like Brer Rabbit, who outwitted their antagonists (**Figure 2.7**). Such stories provided comfort in humor and conveyed the slaves' sense of the wrongs of slavery. Slaves' work songs commented on the harshness of their life and often had double meanings—a literal meaning that whites would not find offensive and a deeper meaning for slaves.

Figure 2.7 Brer Rabbit, depicted here in an illustration from *Uncle Remus, His Songs and His Sayings: The Folk-Lore of the Old Plantation* (1881) by Joel Chandler Harris, was a trickster who outwitted his opponents.

African beliefs, including ideas about the spiritual world and the importance of African healers, survived in the South as well. Whites who became aware of non-Christian rituals among slaves labeled such practices as witchcraft. Among Africans, however, the rituals and use of various plants by respected slave healers created connections between the African past and the American South while also providing a sense of community and identity for slaves. Other African customs, including traditional naming patterns, the making of baskets, and the cultivation of certain native African plants that had been brought to the New World, also endured.

AMERICANA

✪ African Americans and Christian Spirituals

Many slaves embraced Christianity. Their masters emphasized a scriptural message of obedience to whites and a better day awaiting slaves in heaven, but slaves focused on the uplifting message of being freed from bondage.

The styles of worship in the Methodist and Baptist churches, which emphasized emotional responses to scripture, attracted slaves to those traditions and inspired some to become preachers. Spiritual songs that referenced the Exodus (the biblical account of the Hebrews' escape from slavery in Egypt), such as "Roll, Jordan, Roll," allowed slaves to freely express messages of hope, struggle, and overcoming adversity (Figure 2.8).

Figure 2.8 This version of "Roll, Jordan, Roll" was included in *Slave Songs of the United States*, the first published collection of African American music, which appeared in 1867.

What imagery might the Jordan River suggest to slaves working in the Deep South? What lyrics in this song suggest redemption and a better world ahead?

Click and Explore

Listen to a rendition of "Roll, Jordan, Roll" (http://openstaxcollege.org/l/15RollJordan) from the movie based on Solomon Northup's memoir and life.

THE FREE BLACK POPULATION

Complicating the picture of the antebellum South was the existence of a large free black population. In fact, more free blacks lived in the South than in the North; roughly 261,000 lived in slave states, while 226,000 lived in northern states without slavery. Most free blacks did not live in the Lower, or Deep South: the states of Alabama, Arkansas, Florida, Georgia, Louisiana, Mississippi, South Carolina, and Texas. Instead, the largest number lived in the upper southern states of Delaware, Maryland, Virginia, North Carolina, and later Kentucky, Missouri, Tennessee, and the District of Columbia.

Part of the reason for the large number of free blacks living in slave states were the many instances of manumission—the formal granting of freedom to slaves—that occurred as a result of the Revolution, when many slaveholders put into action the ideal that "all men are created equal" and freed their slaves. The transition in the Upper South to the staple crop of wheat, which did not require large numbers of slaves to produce, also spurred manumissions. Another large group of free blacks in the South had been free residents of Louisiana before the 1803 Louisiana Purchase, while still other free blacks came from Cuba and Haiti.

Most free blacks in the South lived in cities, and a majority of free blacks were lighter-skinned women, a reflection of the interracial unions that formed between white men and black women. Everywhere in the United States blackness had come to be associated with slavery, the station at the bottom of the social ladder. Both whites and those with African ancestry tended to delineate varying degrees of lightness in skin color in a social hierarchy. In the slaveholding South, different names described one's distance from blackness or whiteness: mulattos (those with one black and one white parent), quadroons (those with one black grandparent), and octoroons (those with one black great-grandparent) (**Figure 2.9**). Lighter-skinned blacks often looked down on their darker counterparts, an indication of the ways in which both whites and blacks internalized the racism of the age.

Figure 2.9 In this late eighteenth-century painting, a free woman of color stands with her quadroon daughter in New Orleans. Families with members that had widely varying ethnic characteristics were not uncommon at the time, especially in the larger cities.

Some free blacks in the South owned slaves of their own. Andrew Durnford, for example, was born in New Orleans in 1800, three years before the Louisiana Purchase. His father was white, and his mother was a free black. Durnford became an American citizen after the Louisiana Purchase, rising to prominence as a Louisiana sugar planter and slaveholder. William Ellison, another free black who amassed great wealth and power in the South, was born a slave in 1790 in South Carolina. After buying his freedom and that of his wife and daughter, he proceeded to purchase his own slaves, whom he then put to work manufacturing cotton gins. By the eve of the Civil War, Ellison had become one of the richest and largest slaveholders in the entire state.

The phenomenon of free blacks amassing large fortunes within a slave society predicated on racial difference, however, was exceedingly rare. Most free blacks in the South lived under the specter of slavery and faced many obstacles. Beginning in the early nineteenth century, southern states increasingly made manumission of slaves illegal. They also devised laws that divested free blacks of their rights, such as the right to testify against whites in court or the right to seek employment where they pleased. Interestingly, it was in the upper southern states that such laws were the harshest. In Virginia, for example, legislators made efforts to require free blacks to leave the state. In parts of the Deep South, free blacks were able to maintain their rights more easily. The difference in treatment between free blacks in the Deep South and those in the Upper South, historians have surmised, came down to economics. In the Deep South, slavery as an institution was strong and profitable. In the Upper South, the opposite was true. The anxiety of this economic uncertainty manifested in the form of harsh laws that targeted free blacks.

SLAVE REVOLTS

Slaves resisted their enslavement in small ways every day, but this resistance did not usually translate into mass uprisings. Slaves understood that the chances of ending slavery through rebellion were slim and would likely result in massive retaliation; many also feared the risk that participating in such actions would pose to themselves and their families. White slaveholders, however, constantly feared uprisings and took drastic steps, including torture and mutilation, whenever they believed that rebellions might be simmering. Gripped by the fear of insurrection, whites often imagined revolts to be in the works even when no uprising actually happened.

At least two major slave uprisings did occur in the antebellum South. In 1811, a major rebellion broke out in the sugar parishes of the booming territory of Louisiana. Inspired by the successful overthrow of the white planter class in Haiti, Louisiana slaves took up arms against planters. Perhaps as many five hundred slaves joined the rebellion, led by Charles Deslondes, a mixed-race slave driver on a sugar plantation owned by Manuel Andry.

The revolt began in January 1811 on Andry's plantation. Deslondes and other slaves attacked the Andry household, where they killed the slave master's son (although Andry himself escaped). The rebels then began traveling toward New Orleans, armed with weapons gathered at Andry's plantation. Whites mobilized to stop the rebellion, but not before Deslondes and the other rebelling slaves set fire to three plantations and killed numerous whites. A small white force led by Andry ultimately captured Deslondes, whose body was mutilated and burned following his execution. Other slave rebels were beheaded, and their heads placed on pikes along the Mississippi River.

The second rebellion, led by the slave Nat Turner, occurred in 1831 in Southampton County, Virginia. Turner had suffered not only from personal enslavement, but also from the additional trauma of having his wife sold away from him. Bolstered by Christianity, Turner became convinced that like Christ, he should lay down his life to end slavery. Mustering his relatives and friends, he began the rebellion August 22, killing scores of whites in the county. Whites mobilized quickly and within forty-eight hours had brought the rebellion to an end. Shocked by Nat Turner's Rebellion, Virginia's state legislature considered ending slavery in the state in order to provide greater security. In the end, legislators decided slavery would remain and that their state would continue to play a key role in the domestic slave trade.

SLAVE MARKETS

As discussed above, after centuries of slave trade with West Africa, Congress banned the further importation of slaves beginning in 1808. The domestic slave trade then expanded rapidly. As the cotton trade grew in size and importance, so did the domestic slave trade; the cultivation of cotton gave new life and importance to slavery, increasing the value of slaves. To meet the South's fierce demand for labor, American smugglers illegally transferred slaves through Florida and later through Texas. Many more slaves arrived illegally from Cuba; indeed, Cubans relied on the smuggling of slaves to prop up their finances. The largest number of slaves after 1808, however, came from the massive, legal internal slave market in which slave states in the Upper South sold enslaved men, women, and children to states in the Lower South. For slaves, the domestic trade presented the full horrors of slavery as children were ripped from their mothers and fathers and families destroyed, creating heartbreak and alienation.

Some slaveholders sought to increase the number of slave children by placing male slaves with fertile female slaves, and slave masters routinely raped their female slaves. The resulting births played an important role in slavery's expansion in the first half of the nineteenth century, as many slave children were born as a result of rape. One account written by a slave named William J. Anderson captures the horror of sexual exploitation in the antebellum South. Anderson wrote about how a Mississippi slaveholder divested a poor female slave of all wearing apparel, tied her down to stakes, and whipped her with a handsaw until he broke it over her naked body. In process of time he ravished [raped] her person, and became the father of a child by her. Besides, he always kept a colored Miss in the house with him. This is another curse of Slavery—concubinage and illegitimate connections—which is carried on to an alarming extent in the far South. A poor slave man who lives close by his wife, is permitted to visit her but very seldom, and other men, both white and colored, cohabit with her. It is undoubtedly the worst place of incest and bigamy in the world. A white man thinks nothing of putting a colored man out to carry the fore row [front row in field work], and carry on the same sport with the colored man's wife at the same time.

Anderson, a devout Christian, recognized and explains in his narrative that one of the evils of slavery is the way it undermines the family. Anderson was not the only critic of slavery to emphasize this point. Frederick Douglass, a Maryland slave who escaped to the North in 1838, elaborated on this dimension of slavery in his 1845 narrative. He recounted how slave masters had to sell their own children whom they had with slave women to appease the white wives who despised their offspring.

The selling of slaves was a major business enterprise in the antebellum South, representing a key part of the economy. White men invested substantial sums in slaves, carefully calculating the annual returns they could expect from a slave as well as the possibility of greater profits through natural increase. The domestic slave trade was highly visible, and like the infamous Middle Passage that brought captive Africans to the Americas, it constituted an equally disruptive and horrifying journey now called the **second middle passage**. Between 1820 and 1860, white American traders sold a million or more slaves in the domestic slave market. Groups of slaves were transported by ship from places like Virginia, a state that specialized in raising slaves for sale, to New Orleans, where they were sold to planters in the Mississippi Valley. Other slaves made the overland trek from older states like North Carolina to new and booming Deep South states like Alabama.

New Orleans had the largest slave market in the United States (**Figure 2.10**). Slaveholders brought their slaves there from the East (Virginia, Maryland, and the Carolinas) and the West (Tennessee and Kentucky) to be sold for work in the Mississippi Valley. The slave trade benefited whites in the Chesapeake and Carolinas, providing them with extra income: A healthy young male slave in the 1850s could be sold for $1,000 (approximately $30,000 in 2014 dollars), and a planter who could sell ten such slaves collected a windfall.

Figure 2.10 In *Sale of Estates, Pictures and Slaves in the Rotunda, New Orleans* (1853) by J. M. Starling, it is clear that slaves are considered property to be auctioned off, just like pictures or other items.

In fact, by the 1850s, the demand for slaves reached an all-time high, and prices therefore doubled. A slave who would have sold for $400 in the 1820s could command a price of $800 in the 1850s. The high price of slaves in the 1850s and the inability of natural increase to satisfy demands led some southerners to demand the reopening of the international slave trade, a movement that caused a rift between the Upper South and the Lower South. Whites in the Upper South who sold slaves to their counterparts in the Lower South worried that reopening the trade would lower prices and therefore hurt their profits.

MY STORY

✪ *John Brown on Slave Life in Georgia*

A slave named John Brown lived in Virginia, North Carolina, and Georgia before he escaped and moved to England. While there, he dictated his autobiography to someone at the British and Foreign Anti-Slavery Society, who published it in 1855.

> I really thought my mother would have died of grief at being obliged to leave her two children, her mother, and her relations behind. But it was of no use lamenting, the few things we had were put together that night, and we completed our preparations for being parted for life by kissing one another over and over again, and saying good bye till some of us little ones fell asleep. . . . And here I may as well tell what kind of man our new master was. He was of small stature, and thin, but very strong. He had sandy hair, a very red face, and chewed tobacco. His countenance had a very cruel expression, and his disposition was a match for it. He was, indeed, a very bad man, and used to flog us dreadfully. He would make his slaves work on one meal a day, until quite night, and after supper, set them to burn brush or spin cotton. We worked from four in the morning till twelve before we broke our fast, and from that time till eleven or twelve at night . . . we labored eighteen hours a day.
> —John Brown, *Slave Life in Georgia: A Narrative of the Life, Sufferings, and Escape of John Brown, A Fugitive Slave, Now in England*, 1855

What features of the domestic slave trade does Brown's narrative illuminate? Why do you think he brought his story to an antislavery society? How do you think people responded to this narrative?

Click and Explore

Read through several narratives at "Born in Slavery," part of the **American Memory** (http://openstaxcollege.org/l/15BornSlavery) collection at the Library of Congress. Do these narratives have anything in common? What differences can you find between them?

2.3 Wealth and Culture in the South

By the end of this section, you will be able to:
- Assess the distribution of wealth in the antebellum South
- Describe the southern culture of honor
- Identify the main proslavery arguments in the years prior to the Civil War

During the antebellum years, wealthy southern planters formed an elite master class that wielded most of the economic and political power of the region. They created their own standards of gentility and honor, defining ideals of southern white manhood and womanhood and shaping the culture of the South.

To defend the system of forced labor on which their economic survival and genteel lifestyles depended, elite southerners developed several proslavery arguments that they levied at those who would see the institution dismantled.

SLAVERY AND THE WHITE CLASS STRUCTURE

The South prospered, but its wealth was very unequally distributed. Upward social mobility did not exist for the millions of slaves who produced a good portion of the nation's wealth, while poor southern whites envisioned a day when they might rise enough in the world to own slaves of their own. Because of the cotton boom, there were more millionaires per capita in the Mississippi River Valley by 1860 than anywhere else in the United States. However, in that same year, only 3 percent of whites owned more than fifty slaves, and two-thirds of white households in the South did not own any slaves at all (**Figure 2.11**). Distribution of wealth in the South became less democratic over time; fewer whites owned slaves in 1860 than in 1840.

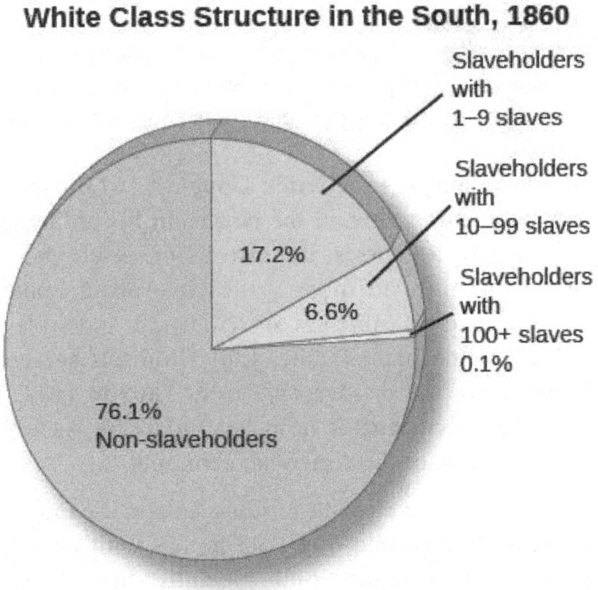

White Class Structure in the South, 1860

Slaveholders with 1–9 slaves

Slaveholders with 10–99 slaves

Slaveholders with 100+ slaves 0.1%

17.2%

6.6%

76.1% Non-slaveholders

Figure 2.11 As the wealth of the antebellum South increased, it also became more unequally distributed, and an ever-smaller percentage of slaveholders held a substantial number of slaves.

At the top of southern white society stood the planter elite, which comprised two groups. In the Upper South, an aristocratic gentry, generation upon generation of whom had grown up with slavery, held a privileged place. In the Deep South, an elite group of slaveholders gained new wealth from cotton. Some members of this group hailed from established families in the eastern states (Virginia and the Carolinas), while others came from humbler backgrounds. South Carolinian Nathaniel Heyward, a wealthy rice planter and member of the aristocratic gentry, came from an established family and sat atop the pyramid of southern slaveholders. He amassed an enormous estate; in 1850, he owned more than eighteen hundred slaves. When he died in 1851, he left an estate worth more than $2 million (approximately $63 million in 2014 dollars).

As cotton production increased, new wealth flowed to the cotton planters. These planters became the staunchest defenders of slavery, and as their wealth grew, they gained considerable political power.

One member of the planter elite was Edward Lloyd V, who came from an established and wealthy family of Talbot County, Maryland. Lloyd had inherited his position rather than rising to it through his own labors. His hundreds of slaves formed a crucial part of his wealth. Like many of the planter elite, Lloyd's plantation was a masterpiece of elegant architecture and gardens (**Figure 2.12**).

Figure 2.12 The grand house of Edward Lloyd V advertised the status and wealth of its owner. In its heyday, the Lloyd family's plantation boasted holdings of forty-two thousand acres and one thousand slaves.

One of the slaves on Lloyd's plantation was Frederick Douglass, who escaped in 1838 and became an abolitionist leader, writer, statesman, and orator in the North. In his autobiography, Douglass described the plantation's elaborate gardens and racehorses, but also its underfed and brutalized slave population. Lloyd provided employment opportunities to other whites in Talbot County, many of whom served as slave traders and the "slave breakers" entrusted with beating and overworking unruly slaves into submission. Like other members of the planter elite, Lloyd himself served in a variety of local and national political offices. He was governor of Maryland from 1809 to 1811, a member of the House of Representatives from 1807 to 1809, and a senator from 1819 to 1826. As a representative and a senator, Lloyd defended slavery as the foundation of the American economy.

Wealthy plantation owners like Lloyd came close to forming an American ruling class in the years before the Civil War. They helped shape foreign and domestic policy with one goal in view: to expand the power and reach of the cotton kingdom of the South. Socially, they cultivated a refined manner and believed whites, especially members of their class, should not perform manual labor. Rather, they created an identity for themselves based on a world of leisure in which horse racing and entertainment mattered greatly, and where the enslavement of others was the bedrock of civilization.

Below the wealthy planters were the yeoman farmers, or small landowners (**Figure 2.13**). Below yeomen were poor, landless whites, who made up the majority of whites in the South. These landless white men dreamed of owning land and slaves and served as slave overseers, drivers, and traders in the southern economy. In fact, owning land and slaves provided one of the only opportunities for upward social and economic mobility. In the South, living the American dream meant possessing slaves, producing cotton, and owning land.

Figure 2.13 In this painting by Felix Octavius Carr Darley, a yeoman farmer carrying a scythe follows his livestock down the road.

Despite this unequal distribution of wealth, non-slaveholding whites shared with white planters a common set of values, most notably a belief in white supremacy. Whites, whether rich or poor, were bound together by racism. Slavery defused class tensions among them, because no matter how poor they were, white southerners had race in common with the mighty plantation owners. Non-slaveholders accepted the rule of the planters as defenders of their shared interest in maintaining a racial hierarchy. Significantly, all whites were also bound together by the constant, prevailing fear of slave uprisings.

MY STORY

✪ *D. R. Hundley on the Southern Yeoman*

D. R. Hundley was a well-educated planter, lawyer, and banker from Alabama. Something of an amateur sociologist, he argued against the common northern assumption that the South was made up exclusively of two tiers of white residents: the very wealthy planter class and the very poor landless whites. In his 1860 book, *Social Relations in Our Southern States*, Hundley describes what he calls the "Southern Yeomen," a social group he insists is roughly equivalent to the middle-class farmers of the North.

> *But you have no Yeomen in the South, my dear Sir?* Beg your pardon, our dear Sir, but we have—hosts of them. *I thought you had only poor White Trash?* Yes, we dare say as much—and that the moon is made of green cheese! . . . Know, then, that the Poor Whites of the South constitute a separate class to themselves; the Southern Yeomen are as distinct from them as the Southern Gentleman is from the Cotton Snob. Certainly the Southern Yeomen are nearly always poor, at least so far as this world's goods are to be taken into account. As a general thing they own no slaves; and even in case they do, the wealthiest of them rarely possess more than from ten to fifteen. . . . The Southern Yeoman much resembles in his speech, religious opinions, household arrangements, indoor sports, and family traditions, the middle class farmers of the Northern States. He is fully as intelligent as the latter, and is on the whole much better versed in the lore of politics and the provisions of our Federal and State Constitutions. . . . [A]lthough not as a class pecuniarily interested in slave property, the Southern Yeomanry are almost unanimously pro-slavery in sentiment. Nor do we see how any honest, thoughtful person can reasonably find fault with them on this account.
> —D. R. Hundley, *Social Relations in Our Southern States*, 1860

What elements of social relations in the South is Hundley attempting to emphasize for his readers? In what respects might his position as an educated and wealthy planter influence his understanding of social relations in the South?

Because race bound all whites together as members of the master race, non-slaveholding whites took part in civil duties. They served on juries and voted. They also engaged in the daily rounds of maintaining slavery by serving on neighborhood patrols to ensure that slaves did not escape and that rebellions did not occur. The practical consequence of such activities was that the institution of slavery, and its perpetuation, became a source of commonality among different economic and social tiers that otherwise were separated by a gulf of difference.

Southern planters exerted a powerful influence on the federal government. Seven of the first eleven presidents owned slaves, and more than half of the Supreme Court justices who served on the court from its inception to the Civil War came from slaveholding states. However, southern white yeoman farmers generally did not support an active federal government. They were suspicious of the state bank and supported President Jackson's dismantling of the Second Bank of the United States. They also did not support taxes to create internal improvements such as canals and railroads; to them, government involvement in the economic life of the nation disrupted what they perceived as the natural workings of the economy. They also feared a strong national government might tamper with slavery.

Planters operated within a larger capitalist society, but the labor system they used to produce goods—that is, slavery—was similar to systems that existed before capitalism, such as feudalism and serfdom. Under capitalism, free workers are paid for their labor (by owners of capital) to produce commodities; the money from the sale of the goods is used to pay for the work performed. As slaves did not reap any earnings from their forced labor, some economic historians consider the antebellum plantation system a "pre-capitalist" system.

HONOR IN THE SOUTH

A complicated code of honor among privileged white southerners, dictating the beliefs and behavior of "gentlemen" and "ladies," developed in the antebellum years. Maintaining appearances and reputation was supremely important. It can be argued that, as in many societies, the concept of honor in the antebellum South had much to do with control over dependents, whether slaves, wives, or relatives. Defending their honor and ensuring that they received proper respect became preoccupations of whites in the slaveholding South. To question another man's assertions was to call his honor and reputation into question. Insults in the form of words or behavior, such as calling someone a coward, could trigger a rupture that might well end on the dueling ground (**Figure 2.14**). Dueling had largely disappeared in the antebellum North by the early nineteenth century, but it remained an important part of the southern code of honor through the Civil War years. Southern white men, especially those of high social status, settled their differences with duels, before which antagonists usually attempted reconciliation, often through the exchange of letters addressing the alleged insult. If the challenger was not satisfied by the exchange, a duel would often result.

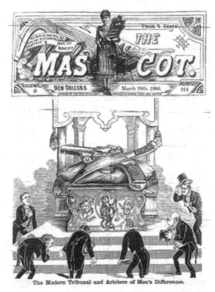

Figure 2.14 "The Modern Tribunal and Arbiter of Men's Differences," an illustration that appeared on the cover of *The Mascot*, a newspaper published in nineteenth-century New Orleans, reveals the importance of dueling in southern culture; it shows men bowing before an altar on which are laid a pistol and knife.

The dispute between South Carolina's James Hammond and his erstwhile friend (and brother-in-law) Wade Hampton II illustrates the southern culture of honor and the place of the duel in that culture. A strong friendship bound Hammond and Hampton together. Both stood at the top of South Carolina's society as successful, married plantation owners involved in state politics. Prior to his election as governor of the state in 1842, Hammond became sexually involved with each of Hampton's four teenage daughters, who were his nieces by marriage. "[A]ll of them rushing on every occasion into my arms," Hammond confided in his private diary, "covering me with kisses, lolling on my lap, pressing their bodies almost into mine . . . and permitting my hands to stray unchecked." Hampton found out about these dalliances, and in keeping with the code of honor, could have demanded a duel with Hammond. However, Hampton instead tried to use the liaisons to destroy his former friend politically. This effort proved disastrous for Hampton, because it represented a violation of the southern code of honor. "As matters now stand," Hammond wrote, "he [Hampton] is a convicted dastard who, not having nerve to redress his own wrongs, put forward bullies to do it for him. . . . To challenge me [to a duel] would be to throw himself upon my mercy for he knows I am not bound to meet him [for a duel]." Because Hampton's behavior marked him as a man who lacked honor, Hammond was no longer bound to meet Hampton in a duel even if Hampton were to demand one. Hammond's reputation, though tarnished, remained high in the esteem of South Carolinians, and the governor went on to serve as a U.S. senator from 1857 to 1860. As for the four Hampton daughters, they never married; their names were disgraced, not only by the whispered-about scandal but by their father's actions in response to it; and no man of honor in South Carolina would stoop so low as to marry them.

GENDER AND THE SOUTHERN HOUSEHOLD

The antebellum South was an especially male-dominated society. Far more than in the North, southern men, particularly wealthy planters, were patriarchs and sovereigns of their own household. Among the white members of the household, labor and daily ritual conformed to rigid gender delineations. Men represented their household in the larger world of politics, business, and war. Within the family, the patriarchal male was the ultimate authority. White women were relegated to the household and lived under the thumb and protection of the male patriarch. The ideal southern lady conformed to her prescribed gender role, a role that was largely domestic and subservient. While responsibilities and experiences varied across different social tiers, women's subordinate state in relation to the male patriarch remained the same.

Writers in the antebellum period were fond of celebrating the image of the ideal southern woman (**Figure 2.15**). One such writer, Thomas Roderick Dew, president of Virginia's College of William and Mary in the mid-nineteenth century, wrote approvingly of the virtue of southern women, a virtue he concluded derived from their natural weakness, piety, grace, and modesty. In his *Dissertation on the Characteristic Differences Between the Sexes*, he writes that southern women derive their power not by

> leading armies to combat, or of enabling her to bring into more formidable action the physical power which nature has conferred on her. No! It is but the better to perfect all those feminine graces, all those fascinating attributes, which render her the center of attraction, and which delight and charm all those who breathe the atmosphere in which she moves; and, in the language of Mr. Burke, would make ten thousand swords leap from their scabbards to avenge the insult that might be offered to her. By her very meekness and beauty does she subdue all around her.

Such popular idealizations of elite southern white women, however, are difficult to reconcile with their lived experience: in their own words, these women frequently described the trauma of childbirth, the loss of children, and the loneliness of the plantation.

Figure 2.15 This cover illustration from *Harper's Weekly* in 1861 shows the ideal of southern womanhood.

MY STORY

✿ *Louisa Cheves McCord's "Woman's Progress"*

Louisa Cheves McCord was born in Charleston, South Carolina, in 1810. A child of some privilege in the South, she received an excellent education and became a prolific writer. As the excerpt from her poem "Woman's Progress" indicates, some southern women also contributed to the idealization of southern white womanhood.

> Sweet Sister! stoop not thou to be a man!
> Man has his place as woman hers; and she
> As made to comfort, minister and help;
> Moulded for gentler duties, ill fulfils
> His jarring destinies. Her mission is
> To labour and to pray; to help, to heal,
> To soothe, to bear; patient, with smiles, to suffer;
> And with self-abnegation noble lose
> Her private interest in the dearer weal
> Of those she loves and lives for. Call not this—
> (The all-fulfilling of her destiny;
> She the world's soothing mother)—call it not,
> With scorn and mocking sneer, a drudgery.
> The ribald tongue profanes Heaven's holiest things,
> But holy still they are. The lowliest tasks
> Are sanctified in nobly acting them.
> Christ washed the apostles' feet, not thus cast shame
> Upon the God-like in him. Woman lives
> Man's constant prophet. If her life be true
> And based upon the instincts of her being,
> She is a living sermon of that truth
> Which ever through her gentle actions speaks,
> That life is given to labour and to love.
> —Louisa Susanna Cheves McCord, "Woman's Progress," 1853

What womanly virtues does Louisa Cheves McCord emphasize? How might her social status, as an educated southern woman of great privilege, influence her understanding of gender relations in the South?

For slaveholding whites, the male-dominated household operated to protect gendered divisions and prevalent gender norms; for slave women, however, the same system exposed them to brutality and frequent sexual domination. The demands on the labor of slave women made it impossible for them to perform the role of domestic caretaker that was so idealized by southern men. That slaveholders put them out into the fields, where they frequently performed work traditionally thought of as male, reflected little the ideal image of gentleness and delicacy reserved for white women. Nor did the slave woman's role as daughter, wife, or mother garner any patriarchal protection. Each of these roles and the relationships they defined was subject to the prerogative of a master, who could freely violate enslaved women's persons, sell off their children, or separate them from their families.

DEFENDING SLAVERY

With the rise of democracy during the Jacksonian era in the 1830s, slaveholders worried about the power of the majority. If political power went to a majority that was hostile to slavery, the South—and the honor of white southerners—would be imperiled. White southerners keen on preserving the institution of slavery bristled at what they perceived to be northern attempts to deprive them of their livelihood. Powerful southerners like South Carolinian John C. Calhoun (**Figure 2.16**) highlighted laws like the Tariff of

1828 as evidence of the North's desire to destroy the southern economy and, by extension, its culture. Such a tariff, he and others concluded, would disproportionately harm the South, which relied heavily on imports, and benefit the North, which would receive protections for its manufacturing centers. The tariff appeared to open the door for other federal initiatives, including the abolition of slavery. Because of this perceived threat to southern society, Calhoun argued that states could nullify federal laws. This belief illustrated the importance of the states' rights argument to the southern states. It also showed slaveholders' willingness to unite against the federal government when they believed it acted unjustly against their interests.

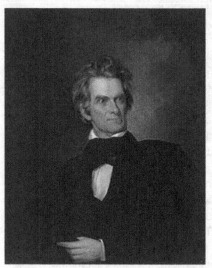

Figure 2.16 John C. Calhoun, shown here in a ca. 1845 portrait by George Alexander Healy, defended states' rights, especially the right of the southern states to protect slavery from a hostile northern majority.

As the nation expanded in the 1830s and 1840s, the writings of abolitionists—a small but vocal group of northerners committed to ending slavery—reached a larger national audience. White southerners responded by putting forth arguments in defense of slavery, their way of life, and their honor. Calhoun became a leading political theorist defending slavery and the rights of the South, which he saw as containing an increasingly embattled minority. He advanced the idea of a **concurrent majority**, a majority of a separate region (that would otherwise be in the minority of the nation) with the power to veto or disallow legislation put forward by a hostile majority.

Calhoun's idea of the concurrent majority found full expression in his 1850 essay "Disquisition on Government." In this treatise, he wrote about government as a necessary means to ensure the preservation of society, since society existed to "preserve and protect our race." If government grew hostile to society, then a concurrent majority had to take action, including forming a new government. "Disquisition on Government" advanced a profoundly anti-democratic argument. It illustrates southern leaders' intense suspicion of democratic majorities and their ability to effect legislation that would challenge southern interests.

Click and Explore

Go to the Internet Archive (http://openstaxcollege.org/l/15Disquisition) to read John C. Calhoun's "Disquisition on Government." Why do you think he proposed the creation of a concurrent majority?

White southerners reacted strongly to abolitionists' attacks on slavery. In making their defense of slavery, they critiqued wage labor in the North. They argued that the Industrial Revolution had brought about a new type of slavery—wage slavery—and that this form of "slavery" was far worse than the slave labor used on southern plantations. Defenders of the institution also lashed out directly at abolitionists such as William Lloyd Garrison for daring to call into question their way of life. Indeed, Virginians cited Garrison as the instigator of Nat Turner's 1831 rebellion.

The Virginian George Fitzhugh contributed to the defense of slavery with his book *Sociology for the South, or the Failure of Free Society* (1854). Fitzhugh argued that laissez-faire capitalism, as celebrated by Adam Smith, benefited only the quick-witted and intelligent, leaving the ignorant at a huge disadvantage. Slaveholders, he argued, took care of the ignorant—in Fitzhugh's argument, the slaves of the South. Southerners provided slaves with care from birth to death, he asserted; this offered a stark contrast to the wage slavery of the North, where workers were at the mercy of economic forces beyond their control. Fitzhugh's ideas exemplified southern notions of paternalism.

DEFINING "AMERICAN"

⊗ *George Fitzhugh's Defense of Slavery*

George Fitzhugh, a southern writer of social treatises, was a staunch supporter of slavery, not as a necessary evil but as what he argued was a necessary good, a way to take care of slaves and keep them from being a burden on society. He published *Sociology for the South, or the Failure of Free Society* in 1854, in which he laid out what he believed to be the benefits of slavery to both the slaves and society as a whole. According to Fitzhugh:

> [I]t is clear the Athenian democracy would not suit a negro nation, nor will the government of mere law suffice for the individual negro. He is but a grown up child and must be governed as a child . . . The master occupies towards him the place of parent or guardian. . . . The negro is improvident; will not lay up in summer for the wants of winter; will not accumulate in youth for the exigencies of age. He would become an insufferable burden to society. Society has the right to prevent this, and can only do so by subjecting him to domestic slavery.
> In the last place, the negro race is inferior to the white race, and living in their midst, they would be far outstripped or outwitted in the chase of free competition. . . . Our negroes are not only better off as to physical comfort than free laborers, but their moral condition is better.

What arguments does Fitzhugh use to promote slavery? What basic premise underlies his ideas? Can you think of a modern parallel to Fitzhugh's argument?

The North also produced defenders of slavery, including Louis Agassiz, a Harvard professor of zoology and geology. Agassiz helped to popularize **polygenism**, the idea that different human races came from separate origins. According to this formulation, no single human family origin existed, and blacks made up a race wholly separate from the white race. Agassiz's notion gained widespread popularity in the 1850s with the 1854 publication of George Gliddon and Josiah Nott's *Types of Mankind* and other books. The theory of polygenism codified racism, giving the notion of black inferiority the lofty mantle of science. One popular advocate of the idea posited that blacks occupied a place in evolution between the Greeks and chimpanzees (**Figure 2.17**).

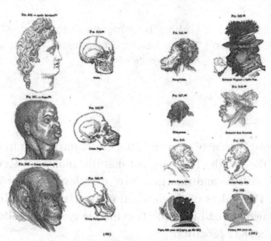

Figure 2.17 This 1857 illustration by an advocate of polygenism indicates that the "Negro" occupies a place between the Greeks and chimpanzees. What does this image reveal about the methods of those who advocated polygenism?

2.4 The Filibuster and the Quest for New Slave States

By the end of this section, you will be able to:
- Explain the expansionist goals of advocates of slavery
- Describe the filibuster expeditions undertaken during the antebellum era

Southern expansionists had spearheaded the drive to add more territory to the United States. They applauded the Louisiana Purchase and fervently supported Indian removal, the annexation of Texas, and the Mexican-American War. Drawing inspiration from the annexation of Texas, proslavery expansionists hoped to replicate that feat by bringing Cuba and other territories into the United States and thereby enlarging the American empire of slavery.

In the 1850s, the expansionist drive among white southerners intensified. Among southern imperialists, one way to push for the creation of an American empire of slavery was through the actions of filibusters—men who led unofficial military operations intended to seize land from foreign countries or foment revolution there. These unsanctioned military adventures were not part of the official foreign policy of the United States; American citizens simply formed themselves into private armies to forcefully annex new land without the government's approval.

An 1818 federal law made it a crime to undertake such adventures, which was an indication of both the reality of efforts at expansion through these illegal expeditions and the government's effort to create a U.S. foreign policy. Nonetheless, Americans continued to filibuster throughout the nineteenth century. In 1819, an expedition of two hundred Americans invaded Spanish Texas, intent on creating a republic modeled on the United States, only to be driven out by Spanish forces. Using force, taking action, and asserting white supremacy in these militaristic drives were seen by many as an ideal of American male vigor. President Jackson epitomized this military prowess as an officer in the Tennessee militia, where earlier in the century he had played a leading role in ending the Creek War and driving Indian peoples out of Alabama and Georgia. His reputation helped him to win the presidency in 1828 and again in 1832.

Filibustering plots picked up pace in the 1850s as the drive for expansion continued. Slaveholders looked south to the Caribbean, Mexico, and Central America, hoping to add new slave states. Spanish Cuba became the objective of many American slaveholders in the 1850s, as debate over the island dominated the national conversation. Many who urged its annexation believed Cuba had to be made part of the United States to prevent it from going the route of Haiti, with black slaves overthrowing their masters and creating another black republic, a prospect horrifying to many in the United States. Americans also feared that the British, who had an interest in the sugar island, would make the first move and snatch Cuba from the United States. Since Britain had outlawed slavery in its colonies in 1833, blacks on the island of Cuba would then be free.

Narisco López, a Cuban who wanted to end Spanish control of the island, gained American support. He tried five times to take the island, with his last effort occurring in the summer of 1851 when he led an armed group from New Orleans. Thousands came out to cheer his small force as they set off to wrest Cuba from the Spanish. Unfortunately for López and his supporters, however, the effort to take Cuba did not produce the hoped-for spontaneous uprising of the Cuban people. Spanish authorities in Cuba captured and executed López and the American filibusters.

Efforts to take Cuba continued under President Franklin Pierce, who had announced at his inauguration in 1853 his intention to pursue expansion. In 1854, American diplomats met in Ostend, Belgium, to find a way to gain Cuba. They wrote a secret memo, known as the **Ostend Manifesto** (thought to be penned by James Buchanan, who was elected president two years later), stating that if Spain refused to sell Cuba to the United States, the United States was justified in taking the island as a national security measure.

The contents of this memo were supposed to remain secret, but details were leaked to the public, leading the House of Representatives to demand a copy. Many in the North were outraged over what appeared to be a southern scheme, orchestrated by what they perceived as the Slave Power—a term they used to describe the disproportionate influence that elite slaveholders wielded—to expand slavery. European powers also reacted with anger. Southern annexationists, however, applauded the effort to take Cuba. The Louisiana legislature in 1854 asked the federal government to take decisive action, and John Quitman, a former Mississippi governor, raised money from slaveholders to fund efforts to take the island.

Click and Explore

Read an 1860 editorial titled Annexation of Cuba Made Easy (http://openstaxcollege.org/l/15AnnexCuba) from the online archives of *The New York Times*. Does the author support annexation? Why or why not?

Controversy around the Ostend Manifesto caused President Pierce to step back from the plan to take Cuba. After his election, President Buchanan, despite his earlier expansionist efforts, denounced filibustering as the action of pirates. Filibustering caused an even wider gulf between the North and the South (**Figure 2.18**).

Figure 2.18 *The "Ostend Doctrine"* (1856), by artist Louis Maurer and lithographer Nathaniel Currier, mocks James Buchanan by depicting him being robbed, just as many northerners believed slaveholders were attempting to rob Spain. The thugs robbing Buchanan use specific phrases from the Ostend Manifesto as they relieve him of his belongings.

Cuba was not the only territory in slaveholders' expansionist sights: some focused on Mexico and Central America. In 1855, Tennessee-born William Walker, along with an army of no more than sixty mercenaries, gained control of the Central American nation of Nicaragua. Previously, Walker had launched a successful invasion of Mexico, dubbing his conquered land the Republic of Sonora. In a relatively short period of time, Walker was dislodged from Sonora by Mexican authorities and forced to retreat back to the United States. His conquest of Nicaragua garnered far more attention, catapulting him into national popularity as the heroic embodiment of white supremacy (**Figure 2.19**).

(a)   (b)

Figure 2.19 Famed Civil War photographer Mathew Brady took this photograph (a) of "General" William Walker circa 1855–1860. Walker led a filibuster expedition and briefly conquered Nicaragua, fulfilling a dream of many pro-expansionist southern slaveholders. Cornelius Vanderbilt (b), the shipping tycoon who controlled much of the traffic across Nicaragua between the Atlantic and the Pacific, clashed with Walker and ultimately supported Costa Rica in its war against him.

Why Nicaragua? Nicaragua presented a tempting target because it provided a quick route from the Caribbean to the Pacific: Only twelve miles of land stood between the Pacific Ocean, the inland Lake

Nicaragua, and the river that drained into the Atlantic. Shipping from the East Coast to the West Coast of the United States had to travel either by land across the continent, south around the entire continent of South America, or through Nicaragua. Previously, American tycoon Cornelius Vanderbilt (**Figure 2.19**) had recognized the strategic importance of Nicaragua and worked with the Nicaraguan government to control shipping there. The filibustering of William Walker may have excited expansionist-minded southerners, but it greatly upset Vanderbilt's business interests in the region.

Walker clung to the racist, expansionist philosophies of the proslavery South. In 1856, Walker made slavery legal in Nicaragua—it had been illegal there for thirty years—in a move to gain the support of the South. He also reopened the slave trade. In 1856, he was elected president of Nicaragua, but in 1857, he was chased from the country. When he returned to Central America in 1860, he was captured by the British and released to Honduran authorities, who executed him by firing squad.

CHAPTER 3

A Nation on the Move: Westward Expansion, 1800–1860

Figure 3.1 In the first half of the nineteenth century, settlers began to move west of the Mississippi River in large numbers. In John Gast's *American Progress* (ca. 1872), the figure of Columbia, representing the United States and the spirit of democracy, makes her way westward, literally bringing light to the darkness as she advances.

Chapter Outline

3.1 Lewis and Clark

3.2 The Missouri Crisis

3.3 Independence for Texas

3.4 The Mexican-American War, 1846–1848

3.5 Free Soil or Slave? The Dilemma of the West

Introduction

After 1800, the United States militantly expanded westward across North America, confident of its right and duty to gain control of the continent and spread the benefits of its "superior" culture. In John Gast's *American Progress* (**Figure 3.1**), the white, blonde figure of Columbia—a historical personification of the United States—strides triumphantly westward with the Star of Empire on her head. She brings education, symbolized by the schoolbook, and modern technology, represented by the telegraph wire. White settlers follow her lead, driving the helpless natives away and bringing successive waves of technological progress in their wake. In the first half of the nineteenth century, the quest for control of the West led to the Louisiana Purchase, the annexation of Texas, and the Mexican-American War. Efforts to seize western territories from native peoples and expand the republic by warring with Mexico succeeded beyond expectations. Few nations ever expanded so quickly. Yet, this expansion led to debates about the fate of slavery in the West, creating tensions between North and South that ultimately led to the collapse of American democracy and a brutal civil war.

3.1 Lewis and Clark

By the end of this section, you will be able to:
- Explain the significance of the Louisiana Purchase
- Describe the terms of the Adams-Onís Treaty
- Describe the role played by the filibuster in American expansion

For centuries Europeans had mistakenly believed an all-water route across the North American continent existed. This "**Northwest Passage**" would afford the country that controlled it not only access to the interior of North America but also—more importantly—a relatively quick route to the Pacific Ocean and to trade with Asia. The Spanish, French, and British searched for years before American explorers took up the challenge of finding it. Indeed, shortly before Lewis and Clark set out on their expedition for the U.S. government, Alexander Mackenzie, an officer of the British North West Company, a fur trading outfit, had attempted to discover the route. Mackenzie made it to the Pacific and even believed (erroneously) he had discovered the headwaters of the Columbia River, but he could not find an easy water route with a minimum of difficult portages, that is, spots where boats must be carried overland.

Many Americans also dreamed of finding a Northwest Passage and opening the Pacific to American commerce and influence, including President Thomas Jefferson. In April 1803, Jefferson achieved his goal of purchasing the Louisiana Territory from France, effectively doubling the size of the United States. The purchase was made possible due to events outside the nation's control. With the success of the Haitian Revolution, an uprising of slaves against the French, France's Napoleon abandoned his quest to re-establish an extensive French Empire in America. As a result, he was amenable to selling off the vast Louisiana territory. President Jefferson quickly set out to learn precisely what he had bought and to assess its potential for commercial exploitation. Above all else, Jefferson wanted to exert U.S. control over the territory, an area already well known to French and British explorers. It was therefore vital for the United States to explore and map the land to pave the way for future white settlement.

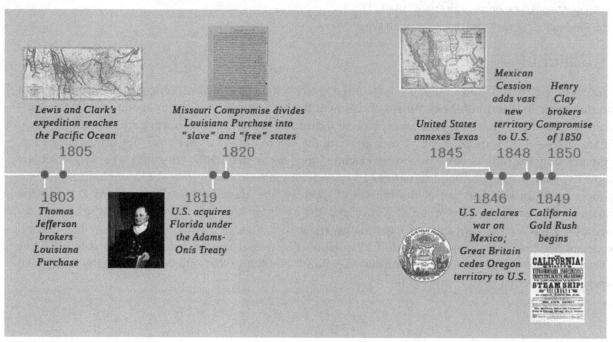

Figure 3.2

JEFFERSON'S CORPS OF DISCOVERY HEADS WEST

To head the expedition into the Louisiana territory, Jefferson appointed his friend and personal secretary, twenty-nine-year-old army captain Meriwether Lewis, who was instructed to form a **Corps of Discovery**. Lewis in turn selected William Clark, who had once been his commanding officer, to help him lead the group (**Figure 3.3**).

(a)   (b)

Figure 3.3   Charles Willson Peale, celebrated portraitist of the American Revolution, painted both William Clark (a) and Meriwether Lewis (b) in 1810 and 1807, respectively, after they returned from their expedition west.

Jefferson wanted to improve the ability of American merchants to access the ports of China. Establishing a river route from St. Louis to the Pacific Ocean was crucial to capturing a portion of the fur trade that had proven so profitable to Great Britain. He also wanted to legitimize American claims to the land against rivals, such as Great Britain and Spain. Lewis and Clark were thus instructed to map the territory through which they would pass and to explore all tributaries of the Missouri River. This part of the expedition struck fear into Spanish officials, who believed that Lewis and Clark would encroach on New Mexico, the northern part of New Spain. Spain dispatched four unsuccessful expeditions from Santa Fe to intercept the explorers. Lewis and Clark also had directives to establish friendly relationships with the western tribes, introducing them to American trade goods and encouraging warring groups to make peace. Establishing an overland route to the Pacific would bolster U.S. claims to the Pacific Northwest, first established in 1792 when Captain Robert Gray sailed his ship *Columbia* into the mouth of the river that now bears his vessel's name and forms the present-day border between Oregon and Washington. Finally, Jefferson, who had a keen interest in science and nature, ordered Lewis and Clark to take extensive notes on the geography, plant life, animals, and natural resources of the region into which they would journey.

After spending the winter of 1803–1804 encamped at the mouth of the Missouri River while the men prepared for their expedition, the corps set off in May 1804. Although the thirty-three frontiersmen, boatmen, and hunters took with them Alexander Mackenzie's account of his explorations and the best maps they could find, they did not have any real understanding of the difficulties they would face. Fierce storms left them drenched and freezing. Enormous clouds of gnats and mosquitos swarmed about their heads as they made their way up the Missouri River. Along the way they encountered (and killed) a variety of animals including elk, buffalo, and grizzly bears. One member of the expedition survived a rattlesnake bite. As the men collected minerals and specimens of plants and animals, the overly curious Lewis sampled minerals by tasting them and became seriously ill at one point. What they did not collect, they sketched and documented in the journals they kept. They also noted the customs of the Indian tribes who controlled the land and attempted to establish peaceful relationships with them in order to ensure that future white settlement would not be impeded.

Click and Explore

Read the journals of Lewis and Clark on the **University of Virginia** (http://openstaxcollege.org/l/15LandClark) website or on the **University of Nebraska–Lincoln** (http://openstaxcollege.org/l/15LandClark1) website, which also has footnotes, maps, and commentary. According to their writings, what challenges did the explorers confront?

The corps spent their first winter in the wilderness, 1804–1805, in a Mandan village in what is now North Dakota. There they encountered a reminder of France's former vast North American empire when they met a French fur trapper named Toussaint Charbonneau. When the corps left in the spring of 1805, Charbonneau accompanied them as a guide and interpreter, bringing his teenage Shoshone wife Sacagawea and their newborn son. Charbonneau knew the land better than the Americans, and Sacagawea proved invaluable in many ways, not least of which was that the presence of a young woman and her infant convinced many groups that the men were not a war party and meant no harm (**Figure 3.4**).

Figure 3.4 In this idealized image, Sacagawea leads Lewis and Clark through the Montana wilderness. In reality, she was still a teenager at the time and served as interpreter; she did not actually guide the party, although legend says she did. Kidnapped as a child, she would not likely have retained detailed memories about the place where she grew up.

The corps set about making friends with native tribes while simultaneously attempting to assert American power over the territory. Hoping to overawe the people of the land, Lewis would let out a blast of his air rifle, a relatively new piece of technology the Indians had never seen. The corps also followed native custom by distributing gifts, including shirts, ribbons, and kettles, as a sign of goodwill. The explorers presented native leaders with medallions, many of which bore Jefferson's image, and invited them to visit their new "ruler" in the East. These medallions or peace medals were meant to allow future explorers to identify friendly native groups. Not all efforts to assert U.S. control went peacefully; some Indians rejected the explorers' intrusion onto their land. An encounter with the Blackfoot turned hostile, for example, and members of the corps killed two Blackfoot men.

After spending eighteen long months on the trail and nearly starving to death in the Bitterroot Mountains of Montana, the Corps of Discovery finally reached the Pacific Ocean in 1805 and spent the winter of 1805–1806 in Oregon. They returned to St. Louis later in 1806 having lost only one man, who had died of appendicitis. Upon their return, Meriwether Lewis was named governor of the Louisiana Territory. Unfortunately, he died only three years later in circumstances that are still disputed, before he could write a complete account of what the expedition had discovered.

Although the Corps of Discovery failed to find an all-water route to the Pacific Ocean (for none existed), it nevertheless accomplished many of the goals Jefferson had set. The men traveled across the North American continent and established relationships with many Indian tribes, paving the way for fur traders like John Jacob Astor who later established trading posts solidifying U.S. claims to Oregon. Delegates of several tribes did go to Washington to meet the president. Hundreds of plant and animal specimens were collected, several of which were named for Lewis and Clark in recognition of their efforts. And the territory was now more accurately mapped and legally claimed by the United States. Nonetheless, most of the vast territory, home to a variety of native peoples, remained unknown to Americans (**Figure 3.5**).

Figure 3.5 This 1814 map of Lewis and Clark's path across North America from the Missouri River to the Pacific Ocean was based on maps and notes made by William Clark. Although most of the West still remained unknown, the expedition added greatly to knowledge of what lay west of the Mississippi. Most important, it allowed the United States to solidify its claim to the immense territory.

AMERICANA

⚙ *A Selection of Hats for the Fashionable Gentleman*

Beaver hats (**Figure 3.6**) were popular apparel in the eighteenth and nineteenth centuries in both Europe and the United States because they were naturally waterproof and bore a glossy sheen. Demand for beaver pelts (and for the pelts of sea otters, foxes, and martens) by hat makers, dressmakers, and tailors led many fur trappers into the wilderness in pursuit of riches. Beaver hats fell out of fashion in the 1850s when silk hats became the rage and beaver became harder to find. In some parts of the West, the animals had been hunted nearly to extinction.

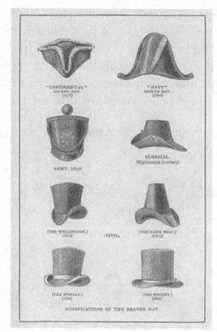

Figure 3.6 This illustration from *Castrologia, Or, The History and Traditions of the Canadian Beaver* shows a variety of beaver hat styles. Beaver pelts were also used to trim women's bonnets.

Are there any contemporary fashions or fads that likewise promise to alter the natural world?

SPANISH FLORIDA AND THE ADAMS-ONÍS TREATY

Despite the Lewis and Clark expedition, the boundaries of the Louisiana Purchase remained contested. Expansionists chose to believe the purchase included vast stretches of land, including all of Spanish Texas. The Spanish government disagreed, however. The first attempt to resolve this issue took place in February 1819 with the signing of the Adams-Onís Treaty, which was actually intended to settle the problem of Florida.

Spanish Florida had presented difficulties for its neighbors since the settlement of the original North American colonies, first for England and then for the United States. By 1819, American settlers no longer feared attack by Spanish troops garrisoned in Florida, but hostile tribes like the Creek and Seminole raided Georgia and then retreated to the relative safety of the Florida wilderness. These tribes also sheltered runaway slaves, often intermarrying with them and making them members of their tribes. Sparsely populated by Spanish colonists and far from both Mexico City and Madrid, the frontier in Florida proved next to impossible for the Spanish government to control.

In March 1818, General Andrew Jackson, frustrated by his inability to punish Creek and Seminole raiders, pursued them across the international border into Spanish Florida. Under Jackson's command, U.S. troops defeated the Creek and Seminole, occupied several Florida settlements, and executed two British citizens accused of acting against the United States. Outraged by the U.S. invasion of its territory, the Spanish government demanded that Jackson and his troops withdraw. In agreeing to the withdrawal, however, U.S. Secretary of State John Quincy Adams also offered to purchase the colony. Realizing that conflict between the United States and the Creeks and Seminoles would continue, Spain opted to cede the Spanish colony to its northern neighbor. The Adams-Onís Treaty, named for Adams and the Spanish ambassador, Luís de Onís, made the cession of Florida official while also setting the boundary between the United States and Mexico at the Sabine River (**Figure 3.7**). In exchange, Adams gave up U.S. claims to lands west of the Sabine and forgave Spain's $5 million debt to the United States.

The Adams-Onís Treaty

Figure 3.7   The red line indicates the border between U.S. and Spanish territory established by the Adams-Onís Treaty of 1819.

The Adams-Onís Treaty upset many American expansionists, who criticized Adams for not laying claim to all of Texas, which they believed had been included in the Louisiana Purchase. In the summer of 1819, James Long, a planter from Natchez, Mississippi, became a **filibuster**, or a private, unauthorized military adventurer, when he led three hundred men on an expedition across the Sabine River to take control of Texas. Long's men succeeded in capturing Nacogdoches, writing a Declaration of Independence (see below), and setting up a republican government. Spanish troops drove them out a month later. Returning in 1820 with a much smaller force, Long was arrested by the Spanish authorities, imprisoned, and killed. Long was but one of many nineteenth-century American filibusters who aimed at seizing territory in the Caribbean and Central America.

DEFINING "AMERICAN"

✿ *The Long Expedition's Declaration of Independence*

The Long Expedition's short-lived Republic of Texas was announced with the drafting of a Declaration of Independence in 1819. The declaration named settlers' grievances against the limits put on expansion by the Adams-Onís treaty and expressed their fears of Spain:

> The citizens of Texas have long indulged the hope, that in the adjustment of the boundaries of the Spanish possessions in America, and of the territories of the United States, that they should be included within the limits of the latter. The claims of the United States, long and strenuously urged, encouraged the hope. The recent [Adams-Onís] treaty between Spain and the United States of America has dissipated an illusion too long fondly cherished, and has roused the citizens of Texas . . . They have seen themselves . . . literally abandoned to the dominion of the crown of Spain and left a prey . . . to all those exactions which Spanish rapacity is fertile in devising. The citizens of Texas would have proved themselves unworthy of the age . . . unworthy of their ancestry, of the kindred of the republics of the American continent, could they have hesitated in this emergency . . . Spurning the fetters of colonial vassalage, disdaining to submit to the most atrocious despotism that ever disgraced the annals of Europe, they have resolved under the blessing of God to be free.

How did the filibusters view Spain? What do their actions say about the nature of American society and of U.S. expansion?

3.2 The Missouri Crisis

By the end of this section, you will be able to:
- Explain why the North and South differed over the admission of Missouri as a state
- Explain how the admission of new states to the Union threatened to upset the balance between free and slave states in Congress

Another stage of U.S. expansion took place when inhabitants of Missouri began petitioning for statehood beginning in 1817. The Missouri territory had been part of the Louisiana Purchase and was the first part of that vast acquisition to apply for statehood. By 1818, tens of thousands of settlers had flocked to Missouri, including slaveholders who brought with them some ten thousand slaves. When the status of the Missouri territory was taken up in earnest in the U.S. House of Representatives in early 1819, its admission to the Union proved to be no easy matter, since it brought to the surface a violent debate over whether slavery would be allowed in the new state.

Politicians had sought to avoid the issue of slavery ever since the 1787 Constitutional Convention arrived at an uneasy compromise in the form of the "three-fifths clause." This provision stated that the entirety of a state's free population and 60 percent of its enslaved population would be counted in establishing the number of that state's members in the House of Representatives and the size of its federal tax bill. Although slavery existed in several northern states at the time, the compromise had angered many northern politicians because, they argued, the "extra" population of slaves would give southern states more votes than they deserved in both the House and the Electoral College. Admitting Missouri as a slave state also threatened the tenuous balance between free and slave states in the Senate by giving slave states a two-vote advantage.

The debate about representation shifted to the morality of slavery itself when New York representative James Tallmadge, an opponent of slavery, attempted to amend the statehood bill in the House of Representatives. Tallmadge proposed that Missouri be admitted as a free state, that no more slaves be allowed to enter Missouri after it achieved statehood, and that all enslaved children born there after its admission be freed at age twenty-five. The amendment shifted the terms of debate by presenting slavery as an evil to be stopped.

Northern representatives supported the **Tallmadge Amendment**, denouncing slavery as immoral and opposed to the nation's founding principles of equality and liberty. Southerners in Congress rejected the amendment as an attempt to gradually abolish slavery—not just in Missouri but throughout the Union—by violating the property rights of slaveholders and their freedom to take their property wherever they wished. Slavery's apologists, who had long argued that slavery was a necessary evil, now began to perpetuate the idea that slavery was a positive good for the United States. They asserted that it generated wealth and left white men free to exercise their true talents instead of toiling in the soil, as the descendants of Africans were better suited to do. Slaves were cared for, supporters argued, and were better off exposed to the teachings of Christianity as slaves than living as free heathens in uncivilized Africa. Above all, the United States had a destiny, they argued, to create an empire of slavery throughout the Americas. These proslavery arguments were to be made repeatedly and forcefully as expansion to the West proceeded.

Most disturbing for the unity of the young nation, however, was that debaters divided along sectional lines, not party lines. With only a few exceptions, northerners supported the Tallmadge Amendment regardless of party affiliation, and southerners opposed it despite having party differences on other matters. It did not pass, and the crisis over Missouri led to strident calls of disunion and threats of civil war.

Congress finally came to an agreement, called the **Missouri Compromise**, in 1820. Missouri and Maine (which had been part of Massachusetts) would enter the Union at the same time, Maine as a free state, Missouri as a slave state. The Tallmadge Amendment was narrowly rejected, the balance between free and slave states was maintained in the Senate, and southerners did not have to fear that Missouri slaveholders would be deprived of their human property. To prevent similar conflicts each time a territory applied for statehood, a line coinciding with the southern border of Missouri (at latitude 36° 30') was drawn across the remainder of the Louisiana Territory (**Figure 3.8**). Slavery could exist south of this line but was forbidden north of it, with the obvious exception of Missouri.

The Missouri Compromise

Free States
Slave States
New States
Missouri Compromise Line

Figure 3.8 The Missouri Compromise resulted in the District of Maine, which had originally been settled in 1607 by the Plymouth Company and was a part of Massachusetts, being admitted to the Union as a free state and Missouri being admitted as a slave state.

MY STORY

☉ *Thomas Jefferson on the Missouri Crisis*

On April 22, 1820, Thomas Jefferson wrote to John Holmes to express his reaction to the Missouri Crisis, especially the open threat of disunion and war:

> I thank you, Dear Sir, for the copy you have been so kind as to send me of the letter to your constituents on the Missouri question. it is a perfect justification to them. I had for a long time ceased to read the newspapers or pay any attention to public affairs, confident they were in good hands, and content to be a passenger in our bark to the shore from which I am not distant. but this momentous question [over slavery in Missouri], like a fire bell in the night, awakened and filled me with terror. I considered it at once as the knell of the Union. it is hushed indeed for the moment. but this is a reprieve only, not a final sentence. a geographical line, coinciding with a marked principle, moral and political, once concieved [sic] and held up to the angry passions of men, will never be obliterated; and every new irritation will mark it deeper and deeper. I can say with conscious truth that there is not a man on earth who would sacrifice more than I would, to relieve us from this heavy reproach, in any practicable way. . . .
>
> I regret that I am now to die in the belief that the useless sacrifice of themselves, by the generation of 76. to acquire self government and happiness to their country, is to be thrown away by the unwise and unworthy passions of their sons, and that my only consolation is to be that I live not to weep over it. if they would but dispassionately weigh the blessings they will throw away against an abstract principle more likely to be effected by union than by scission, they would pause before they would perpetuate this act of suicide themselves and of treason against the hopes of the world. to yourself as the faithful advocate of union I tender the offering of my high esteem and respect.
> Th. Jefferson

How would you characterize the former president's reaction? What do you think he means by writing that the Missouri Compromise line "is a reprieve only, not a final sentence"?

Click and Explore

Access a collection of primary documents relating to the Missouri Compromise, including Missouri's application for admission into the Union and Jefferson's correspondence on the Missouri question, at the **Library of Congress (http://openstaxcollege.org/l/15MOComp)** website.

3.3 Independence for Texas

By the end of this section, you will be able to:
- Explain why American settlers in Texas sought independence from Mexico
- Discuss early attempts to make Texas independent of Mexico
- Describe the relationship between Anglo-Americans and Tejanos in Texas before and after independence

As the incursions of the earlier filibusters into Texas demonstrated, American expansionists had desired this area of Spain's empire in America for many years. After the 1819 Adams-Onís treaty established the boundary between Mexico and the United States, more American expansionists began to move into the northern portion of Mexico's province of Coahuila y Texas. Following Mexico's independence from Spain in 1821, American settlers immigrated to Texas in even larger numbers, intent on taking the land from the new and vulnerable Mexican nation in order to create a new American slave state.

AMERICAN SETTLERS MOVE TO TEXAS

After the 1819 Adams-Onís Treaty defined the U.S.-Mexico boundary, Spain began actively encouraging Americans to settle their northern province. Texas was sparsely settled, and the few Mexican farmers and ranchers who lived there were under constant threat of attack by hostile Indian tribes, especially the Comanche, who supplemented their hunting with raids in pursuit of horses and cattle.

To increase the non-Indian population in Texas and provide a buffer zone between its hostile tribes and the rest of Mexico, Spain began to recruit *empresarios*. An *empresario* was someone who brought settlers to the region in exchange for generous grants of land. Moses Austin, a once-prosperous entrepreneur reduced to poverty by the Panic of 1819, requested permission to settle three hundred English-speaking American residents in Texas. Spain agreed on the condition that the resettled people convert to Roman Catholicism.

On his deathbed in 1821, Austin asked his son Stephen to carry out his plans, and Mexico, which had won independence from Spain the same year, allowed Stephen to take control of his father's grant. Like Spain, Mexico also wished to encourage settlement in the state of Coahuila y Texas and passed colonization laws to encourage immigration. Thousands of Americans, primarily from slave states, flocked to Texas and quickly came to outnumber the **Tejanos**, the Mexican residents of the region. The soil and climate offered good opportunities to expand slavery and the cotton kingdom. Land was plentiful and offered at generous terms. Unlike the U.S. government, Mexico allowed buyers to pay for their land in installments and did not require a minimum purchase. Furthermore, to many whites, it seemed not only their God-given right but also their patriotic duty to populate the lands beyond the Mississippi River, bringing with them American slavery, culture, laws, and political traditions (**Figure 3.9**).

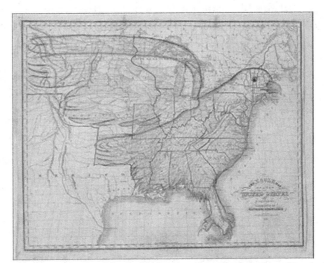

Figure 3.9 By the early 1830s, all the lands east of the Mississippi River had been settled and admitted to the Union as states. The land west of the river, though in this contemporary map united with the settled areas in the body of an eagle symbolizing the territorial ambitions of the United States, remained largely unsettled by white Americans. Texas (just southwest of the bird's tail feathers) remained outside the U.S. border.

THE TEXAS WAR FOR INDEPENDENCE

Many Americans who migrated to Texas at the invitation of the Mexican government did not completely shed their identity or loyalty to the United States. They brought American traditions and expectations with them (including, for many, the right to own slaves). For instance, the majority of these new settlers were Protestant, and though they were not required to attend the Catholic mass, Mexico's prohibition on the public practice of other religions upset them and they routinely ignored it.

Accustomed to representative democracy, jury trials, and the defendant's right to appear before a judge, the Anglo-American settlers in Texas also disliked the Mexican legal system, which provided for an initial hearing by an *alcalde*, an administrator who often combined the duties of mayor, judge, and law enforcement officer. The *alcalde* sent a written record of the proceeding to a judge in Saltillo, the state capital, who decided the outcome. Settlers also resented that at most two Texas representatives were allowed in the state legislature.

Their greatest source of discontent, though, was the Mexican government's 1829 abolition of slavery. Most American settlers were from southern states, and many had brought slaves with them. Mexico tried to accommodate them by maintaining the fiction that the slaves were indentured servants. But American slaveholders in Texas distrusted the Mexican government and wanted Texas to be a new U.S. slave state. The dislike of most for Roman Catholicism (the prevailing religion of Mexico) and a widely held belief in American racial superiority led them generally to regard Mexicans as dishonest, ignorant, and backward.

Belief in their own superiority inspired some Texans to try to undermine the power of the Mexican government. When *empresario* Haden Edwards attempted to evict people who had settled his land grant before he gained title to it, the Mexican government nullified its agreement with him. Outraged, Edwards and a small party of men took prisoner the *alcalde* of Nacogdoches. The Mexican army marched to the town, and Edwards and his troop then declared the formation of the Republic of Fredonia between the Sabine and Rio Grande Rivers. To demonstrate loyalty to their adopted country, a force led by Stephen Austin hastened to Nacogdoches to support the Mexican army. Edwards's revolt collapsed, and the revolutionaries fled Texas.

The growing presence of American settlers in Texas, their reluctance to abide by Mexican law, and their desire for independence caused the Mexican government to grow wary. In 1830, it forbade future U.S. immigration and increased its military presence in Texas. Settlers continued to stream illegally across the long border; by 1835, after immigration resumed, there were twenty thousand Anglo-Americans in Texas (**Figure 3.10**).

Figure 3.10   This 1833 map shows the extent of land grants made by Mexico to American settlers in Texas. Nearly all are in the eastern portion of the state, one factor that led to war with Mexico in 1846.

Fifty-five delegates from the Anglo-American settlements gathered in 1831 to demand the suspension of customs duties, the resumption of immigration from the United States, better protection from Indian tribes, the granting of promised land titles, and the creation of an independent state of Texas separate from Coahuila. Ordered to disband, the delegates reconvened in early April 1833 to write a constitution for an independent Texas. Surprisingly, General Antonio Lopez de Santa Anna, Mexico's new president, agreed to all demands, except the call for statehood (**Figure 3.11**). Coahuila y Texas made provisions for jury trials, increased Texas's representation in the state legislature, and removed restrictions on commerce.

Figure 3.11 This portrait of General Antonio Lopez de Santa Anna depicts the Mexican president and general in full military regalia.

Texans' hopes for independence were quashed in 1834, however, when Santa Anna dismissed the Mexican Congress and abolished all state governments, including that of Coahuila y Texas. In January 1835, reneging on earlier promises, he dispatched troops to the town of Anahuac to collect customs duties. Lawyer and soldier William B. Travis and a small force marched on Anahuac in June, and the fort surrendered. On October 2, Anglo-American forces met Mexican troops at the town of Gonzales; the Mexican troops fled and the Americans moved on to take San Antonio. Now more cautious, delegates to the Consultation of 1835 at San Felipe de Austin voted against declaring independence, instead drafting a statement, which became known as the Declaration of Causes, promising continued loyalty if Mexico returned to a constitutional form of government. They selected Henry Smith, leader of the Independence Party, as governor of Texas and placed Sam Houston, a former soldier who had been a congressman and governor of Tennessee, in charge of its small military force.

The Consultation delegates met again in March 1836. They declared their independence from Mexico and drafted a constitution calling for an American-style judicial system and an elected president and legislature. Significantly, they also established that slavery would not be prohibited in Texas. Many wealthy Tejanos supported the push for independence, hoping for liberal governmental reforms and economic benefits.

REMEMBER THE ALAMO!

Mexico had no intention of losing its northern province. Santa Anna and his army of four thousand had besieged San Antonio in February 1836. Hopelessly outnumbered, its two hundred defenders, under Travis, fought fiercely from their refuge in an old mission known as the Alamo (**Figure 3.12**). After ten days, however, the mission was taken and all but a few of the defenders were dead, including Travis and James Bowie, the famed frontiersman who was also a land speculator and slave trader. A few male survivors, possibly including the frontier legend and former Tennessee congressman Davy Crockett, were led outside the walls and executed. The few women and children inside the mission were allowed to leave with the only adult male survivor, a slave owned by Travis who was then freed by the Mexican Army. Terrified, they fled.

Figure 3.12   The *Fall of the Alamo*, painted by Theodore Gentilz fewer than ten years after this pivotal moment in the Texas Revolution, depicts the 1836 assault on the Alamo complex.

Although hungry for revenge, the Texas forces under Sam Houston nevertheless withdrew across Texas, gathering recruits as they went. Coming upon Santa Anna's encampment on the banks of San Jacinto River on April 21, 1836, they waited as the Mexican troops settled for an afternoon nap. Assured by Houston that "Victory is certain!" and told to "Trust in God and fear not!" the seven hundred men descended on a sleeping force nearly twice their number with cries of "Remember the Alamo!" Within fifteen minutes the Battle of San Jacinto was over. Approximately half the Mexican troops were killed, and the survivors, including Santa Anna, taken prisoner.

Santa Anna grudgingly signed a peace treaty and was sent to Washington, where he met with President Andrew Jackson and, under pressure, agreed to recognize an independent Texas with the Rio Grande River as its southwestern border. By the time the agreement had been signed, however, Santa Anna had been removed from power in Mexico. For that reason, the Mexican Congress refused to be bound by Santa Anna's promises and continued to insist that the renegade territory still belonged to Mexico.

Click and Explore

Visit the official **Alamo (http://openstaxcollege.org/l/15Alamo)** website to learn more about the battle of the Alamo and take a virtual tour of the old mission.

THE LONE STAR REPUBLIC

In September 1836, military hero Sam Houston was elected president of Texas, and, following the relentless logic of U.S. expansion, Texans voted in favor of annexation to the United States. This had been the dream of many settlers in Texas all along. They wanted to expand the United States west and saw Texas as the next logical step. Slaveholders there, such as Sam Houston, William B. Travis and James Bowie (the latter two of whom died at the Alamo), believed too in the destiny of slavery. Mindful of the vicious debates over Missouri that had led to talk of disunion and war, American politicians were reluctant to annex Texas or, indeed, even to recognize it as a sovereign nation. Annexation would almost certainly mean war with Mexico, and the admission of a state with a large slave population, though permissible under the Missouri Compromise, would bring the issue of slavery once again to the fore. Texas had no choice but to organize itself as the independent Lone Star Republic. To protect itself from Mexican attempts to reclaim it, Texas sought and received recognition from France, Great Britain, Belgium, and the Netherlands. The United States did not officially recognize Texas as an independent nation until March 1837, nearly a year after the final victory over the Mexican army at San Jacinto.

Uncertainty about its future did not discourage Americans committed to expansion, especially slaveholders, from rushing to settle in the Lone Star Republic, however. Between 1836 and 1846, its population nearly tripled. By 1840, nearly twelve thousand enslaved Africans had been brought to Texas by American slaveholders. Many new settlers had suffered financial losses in the severe financial depression of 1837 and hoped for a new start in the new nation. According to folklore, across the United States, homes and farms were deserted overnight, and curious neighbors found notes reading only "GTT" ("Gone to Texas"). Many Europeans, especially Germans, also immigrated to Texas during this period.

In keeping with the program of ethnic cleansing and white racial domination, as illustrated by the image at the beginning of this chapter, Americans in Texas generally treated both Tejano and Indian residents with utter contempt, eager to displace and dispossess them. Anglo-American leaders failed to return the support their Tejano neighbors had extended during the rebellion and repaid them by seizing their lands. In 1839, the republic's militia attempted to drive out the Cherokee and Comanche.

The impulse to expand did not lay dormant, and Anglo-American settlers and leaders in the newly formed Texas republic soon cast their gaze on the Mexican province of New Mexico as well. Repeating the tactics of earlier filibusters, a Texas force set out in 1841 intent on taking Santa Fe. Its members encountered an army of New Mexicans and were taken prisoner and sent to Mexico City. On Christmas Day, 1842, Texans avenged a Mexican assault on San Antonio by attacking the Mexican town of Mier. In August, another Texas army was sent to attack Santa Fe, but Mexican troops forced them to retreat. Clearly, hostilities between Texas and Mexico had not ended simply because Texas had declared its independence.

3.4 The Mexican-American War, 1846–1848

By the end of this section, you will be able to:
- Identify the causes of the Mexican-American War
- Describe the outcomes of the war in 1848, especially the Mexican Cession
- Describe the effect of the California Gold Rush on westward expansion

Tensions between the United States and Mexico rapidly deteriorated in the 1840s as American expansionists eagerly eyed Mexican land to the west, including the lush northern Mexican province of California. Indeed, in 1842, a U.S. naval fleet, incorrectly believing war had broken out, seized Monterey, California, a part of Mexico. Monterey was returned the next day, but the episode only added to the uneasiness with which Mexico viewed its northern neighbor. The forces of expansion, however, could not be contained, and American voters elected James Polk in 1844 because he promised to deliver more lands. President Polk fulfilled his promise by gaining Oregon and, most spectacularly, provoking a war with Mexico that ultimately fulfilled the wildest fantasies of expansionists. By 1848, the United States encompassed much of North America, a republic that stretched from the Atlantic to the Pacific.

JAMES K. POLK AND THE TRIUMPH OF EXPANSION

A fervent belief in expansion gripped the United States in the 1840s. In 1845, a New York newspaper editor, John O'Sullivan, introduced the concept of "manifest destiny" to describe the very popular idea of the special role of the United States in overspreading the continent—the divine right and duty of white Americans to seize and settle the American West, thus spreading Protestant, democratic values. In this climate of opinion, voters in 1844 elected James K. Polk, a slaveholder from Tennessee, because he vowed to annex Texas as a new slave state and take Oregon.

Annexing Oregon was an important objective for U.S. foreign policy because it appeared to be an area rich in commercial possibilities. Northerners favored U.S. control of Oregon because ports in the Pacific Northwest would be gateways for trade with Asia. Southerners hoped that, in exchange for their support of expansion into the northwest, northerners would not oppose plans for expansion into the southwest.

President Polk—whose campaign slogan in 1844 had been "Fifty-four forty or fight!"—asserted the United States' right to gain full control of what was known as Oregon Country, from its southern border at 42° latitude (the current boundary with California) to its northern border at 54° 40' latitude. According to an 1818 agreement, Great Britain and the United States held joint ownership of this territory, but the 1827 Treaty of Joint Occupation opened the land to settlement by both countries. Realizing that the British were not willing to cede all claims to the territory, Polk proposed the land be divided at 49° latitude (the current border between Washington and Canada). The British, however, denied U.S. claims to land north of the Columbia River (Oregon's current northern border) (**Figure 3.13**). Indeed, the British foreign secretary refused even to relay Polk's proposal to London. However, reports of the difficulty Great Britain would face defending Oregon in the event of a U.S. attack, combined with concerns over affairs at home and elsewhere in its empire, quickly changed the minds of the British, and in June 1846, Queen Victoria's government agreed to a division at the forty-ninth parallel.

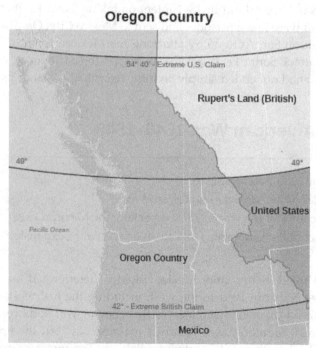

Figure 3.13 This map of the Oregon territory during the period of joint occupation by the United States and Great Britain shows the area whose ownership was contested by the two powers.

In contrast to the diplomatic solution with Great Britain over Oregon, when it came to Mexico, Polk and the American people proved willing to use force to wrest more land for the United States. In keeping with voters' expectations, President Polk set his sights on the Mexican state of California. After the mistaken capture of Monterey, negotiations about purchasing the port of San Francisco from Mexico broke off until September 1845. Then, following a revolt in California that left it divided in two, Polk attempted to purchase Upper California and New Mexico as well. These efforts went nowhere. The Mexican government, angered by U.S. actions, refused to recognize the independence of Texas.

Finally, after nearly a decade of public clamoring for the annexation of Texas, in December 1845 Polk officially agreed to the annexation of the former Mexican state, making the Lone Star Republic an additional slave state. Incensed that the United States had annexed Texas, however, the Mexican government refused to discuss the matter of selling land to the United States. Indeed, Mexico refused even to acknowledge Polk's emissary, John Slidell, who had been sent to Mexico City to negotiate. Not to be deterred, Polk encouraged Thomas O. Larkin, the U.S. consul in Monterey, to assist any American settlers and any **Californios**, the Mexican residents of the state, who wished to proclaim their independence from Mexico. By the end of 1845, having broken diplomatic ties with the United States over Texas and having grown alarmed by American actions in California, the Mexican government warily anticipated the next move. It did not have long to wait.

WAR WITH MEXICO, 1846–1848

Expansionistic fervor propelled the United States to war against Mexico in 1846. The United States had long argued that the Rio Grande was the border between Mexico and the United States, and at the end of the Texas war for independence Santa Anna had been pressured to agree. Mexico, however, refused to be bound by Santa Anna's promises and insisted the border lay farther north, at the Nueces River (**Figure 3.14**). To set it at the Rio Grande would, in effect, allow the United States to control land it had never occupied. In Mexico's eyes, therefore, President Polk violated its sovereign territory when he ordered U.S. troops into the disputed lands in 1846. From the Mexican perspective, it appeared the United States had invaded their nation.

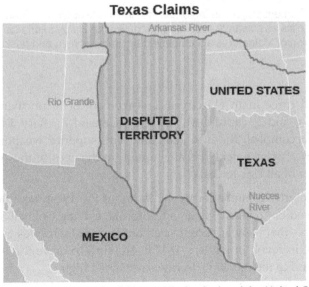

Figure 3.14 In 1845, when Texas joined the United States, Mexico insisted the United States had a right only to the territory northeast of the Nueces River. The United States argued in turn that it should have title to all land between the Nueces and the Rio Grande as well.

In January 1846, the U.S. force that was ordered to the banks of the Rio Grande to build a fort on the "American" side encountered a Mexican cavalry unit on patrol. Shots rang out, and sixteen U.S. soldiers were killed or wounded. Angrily declaring that Mexico "has invaded our territory and shed American blood upon American soil," President Polk demanded the United States declare war on Mexico. On May 12, Congress obliged.

The small but vocal antislavery faction decried the decision to go to war, arguing that Polk had deliberately provoked hostilities so the United States could annex more slave territory. Illinois representative Abraham Lincoln and other members of Congress issued the "Spot Resolutions" in which they demanded to know the precise spot on U.S. soil where American blood had been spilled. Many Whigs also denounced the war. Democrats, however, supported Polk's decision, and volunteers for the army came forward in droves from every part of the country except New England, the seat of abolitionist activity. Enthusiasm for the war was aided by the widely held belief that Mexico was a weak, impoverished country and that the Mexican people, perceived as ignorant, lazy, and controlled by a corrupt Roman Catholic clergy, would be easy to defeat. (**Figure 3.15**).

Figure 3.15 Anti-Catholic sentiment played an important role in the Mexican-American War. The American public widely regarded Roman Catholics as cowardly and vice-ridden, like the clergy in this ca. 1846 lithograph who are shown fleeing the Mexican town of Matamoros accompanied by pretty women and baskets full of alcohol. (credit: Library of Congress)

U.S. military strategy had three main objectives: 1) Take control of northern Mexico, including New Mexico; 2) seize California; and 3) capture Mexico City. General Zachary Taylor and his Army of the Center were assigned to accomplish the first goal, and with superior weapons they soon captured the Mexican city of Monterrey. Taylor quickly became a hero in the eyes of the American people, and Polk appointed him commander of all U.S. forces.

General Stephen Watts Kearny, commander of the Army of the West, accepted the surrender of Santa Fe, New Mexico, and moved on to take control of California, leaving Colonel Sterling Price in command. Despite Kearny's assurances that New Mexicans need not fear for their lives or their property, and in fact the region's residents rose in revolt in January 1847 in an effort to drive the Americans away. Although Price managed to put an end to the rebellion, tensions remained high.

Kearny, meanwhile, arrived in California to find it already in American hands through the joint efforts of California settlers, U.S. naval commander John D. Sloat, and John C. Fremont, a former army captain and son-in-law of Missouri senator Thomas Benton. Sloat, at anchor off the coast of Mazatlan, learned that war had begun and quickly set sail for California. He seized the town of Monterey in July 1846, less than a month after a group of American settlers led by William B. Ide had taken control of Sonoma and declared

California a republic. A week after the fall of Monterey, the navy took San Francisco with no resistance. Although some Californios staged a short-lived rebellion in September 1846, many others submitted to the U.S. takeover. Thus Kearny had little to do other than take command of California as its governor.

Leading the Army of the South was General Winfield Scott. Both Taylor and Scott were potential competitors for the presidency, and believing—correctly—that whoever seized Mexico City would become a hero, Polk assigned Scott the campaign to avoid elevating the more popular Taylor, who was affectionately known as "Old Rough and Ready."

Scott captured Veracruz in March 1847, and moving in a northwesterly direction from there (much as Spanish conquistador Hernán Cortés had done in 1519), he slowly closed in on the capital. Every step of the way was a hard-fought victory, however, and Mexican soldiers and civilians both fought bravely to save their land from the American invaders. Mexico City's defenders, including young military cadets, fought to the end. According to legend, cadet Juan Escutia's last act was to save the Mexican flag, and he leapt from the city's walls with it wrapped around his body. On September 14, 1847, Scott entered Mexico City's central plaza; the city had fallen (**Figure 3.16**). While Polk and other expansionists called for "all Mexico," the Mexican government and the United States negotiated for peace in 1848, resulting in the Treaty of Guadalupe Hidalgo.

Figure 3.16 In *General Scott's Entrance into Mexico* (1851), Carl Nebel depicts General Winfield Scott on a white horse entering Mexico City's Plaza de la Constitución as anxious residents of the city watch. One woman peers furtively from behind the curtain of an upstairs window. On the left, a man bends down to pick up a paving stone to throw at the invaders.

The Treaty of Guadalupe Hidalgo, signed in February 1848, was a triumph for American expansionism under which Mexico ceded nearly half its land to the United States. The **Mexican Cession**, as the conquest of land west of the Rio Grande was called, included the current states of California, New Mexico, Arizona, Nevada, Utah, and portions of Colorado and Wyoming. Mexico also recognized the Rio Grande as the border with the United States. Mexican citizens in the ceded territory were promised U.S. citizenship in the future when the territories they were living in became states. In exchange, the United States agreed to assume $3.35 million worth of Mexican debts owed to U.S. citizens, paid Mexico $15 million for the loss of its land, and promised to guard the residents of the Mexican Cession from Indian raids.

As extensive as the Mexican Cession was, some argued the United States should not be satisfied until it had taken all of Mexico. Many who were opposed to this idea were southerners who, while desiring the annexation of more slave territory, did not want to make Mexico's large mestizo (people of mixed Indian and European ancestry) population part of the United States. Others did not want to absorb a large group of Roman Catholics. These expansionists could not accept the idea of new U.S. territory filled with mixed-race, Catholic populations.

Click and Explore

Explore the **U.S.-Mexican War** (http://openstaxcollege.org/l/15MexAmWar) at PBS to read about life in the Mexican and U.S. armies during the war and to learn more about the various battles.

CALIFORNIA AND THE GOLD RUSH

The United States had no way of knowing that part of the land about to be ceded by Mexico had just become far more valuable than anyone could have imagined. On January 24, 1848, James Marshall discovered gold in the millrace of the sawmill he had built with his partner John Sutter on the south fork of California's American River. Word quickly spread, and within a few weeks all of Sutter's employees had left to search for gold. When the news reached San Francisco, most of its inhabitants abandoned the town and headed for the American River. By the end of the year, thousands of California's residents had gone north to the gold fields with visions of wealth dancing in their heads, and in 1849 thousands of people from around the world followed them (**Figure 3.17**). The Gold Rush had begun.

Figure 3.17 Word about the discovery of gold in California in 1848 quickly spread and thousands soon made their way to the West Coast in search of quick riches.

The fantasy of instant wealth induced a mass exodus to California. Settlers in Oregon and Utah rushed to the American River. Easterners sailed around the southern tip of South America or to Panama's Atlantic coast, where they crossed the Isthmus of Panama to the Pacific and booked ship's passage for San Francisco. As California-bound vessels stopped in South American ports to take on food and fresh water, hundreds of Peruvians and Chileans streamed aboard. Easterners who could not afford to sail to California crossed the continent on foot, on horseback, or in wagons. Others journeyed from as far away as Hawaii and Europe. Chinese people came as well, adding to the polyglot population in the California boomtowns (**Figure 3.18**).

Figure 3.18 This Currier & Ives lithograph from 1849 imagines the extreme lengths that people might go to in order to be part of the California Gold Rush. In addition to the men with picks and shovels trying to reach the ship from the dock, airships and rocket are shown flying overhead. (credit: Library of Congress)

Once in California, gathered in camps with names like Drunkard's Bar, Angel's Camp, Gouge Eye, and Whiskeytown, the "**forty-niners**" did not find wealth so easy to come by as they had first imagined. Although some were able to find gold by panning for it or shoveling soil from river bottoms into sieve-like contraptions called rockers, most did not. The placer gold, the gold that had been washed down the mountains into streams and rivers, was quickly exhausted, and what remained was deep below ground. Independent miners were supplanted by companies that could afford not only to purchase hydraulic mining technology but also to hire laborers to work the hills. The frustration of many a miner was expressed in the words of Sullivan Osborne. In 1857, Osborne wrote that he had arrived in California "full of high hopes and bright anticipations of the future" only to find his dreams "have long since perished." Although $550 million worth of gold was found in California between 1849 and 1850, very little of it went to individuals.

Observers in the gold fields also reported abuse of Indians by miners. Some miners forced Indians to work their claims for them; others drove Indians off their lands, stole from them, and even murdered them. Foreigners were generally disliked, especially those from South America. The most despised, however, were the thousands of Chinese migrants. Eager to earn money to send to their families in Hong Kong and southern China, they quickly earned a reputation as frugal men and hard workers who routinely took over diggings others had abandoned as worthless and worked them until every scrap of gold had been found. Many American miners, often spendthrifts, resented their presence and discriminated against them, believing the Chinese, who represented about 8 percent of the nearly 300,000 who arrived, were depriving them of the opportunity to make a living.

Click and Explore

Visit **The Chinese in California (http://openstaxcollege.org/l/15ChinaCA)** to learn more about the experience of Chinese migrants who came to California in the Gold Rush era.

In 1850, California imposed a tax on foreign miners, and in 1858 it prohibited all immigration from China. Those Chinese who remained in the face of the growing hostility were often beaten and killed, and some Westerners made a sport of cutting off Chinese men's queues, the long braids of hair worn down their backs (**Figure 3.19**). In 1882, Congress took up the power to restrict immigration by banning the further immigration of Chinese.

Figure 3.19 "Pacific Chivalry: Encouragement to Chinese Immigration," which appeared in *Harper's Weekly* in 1869, depicts a white man attacking a Chinese man with a whip as he holds him by the queue. Americans sometimes forcefully cut off the queues of Chinese immigrants. This could have serious consequences for the victim. Until 1911, all Chinese men were required by their nation's law to wear the queue as a sign of loyalty. Miners returning to China without it could be put to death. (credit: Library of Congress)

As people flocked to California in 1849, the population of the new territory swelled from a few thousand to about 100,000. The new arrivals quickly organized themselves into communities, and the trappings of "civilized" life—stores, saloons, libraries, stage lines, and fraternal lodges—began to appear. Newspapers were established, and musicians, singers, and acting companies arrived to entertain the gold seekers. The epitome of these Gold Rush boomtowns was San Francisco, which counted only a few hundred residents in 1846 but by 1850 had reached a population of thirty-four thousand (**Figure 3.20**). So quickly did the territory grow that by 1850 California was ready to enter the Union as a state. When it sought admission, however, the issue of slavery expansion and sectional tensions emerged once again.

Figure 3.20 This daguerreotype shows the bustling port of San Francisco in January 1851, just a few months after San Francisco became part of the new U.S. state of California. (credit: Library of Congress)

3.5 Free Soil or Slave? The Dilemma of the West

By the end of this section, you will be able to:
- Describe the terms of the Wilmot Proviso
- Discuss why the Free-Soil Party objected to the westward expansion of slavery
- Explain why sectional and political divisions in the United States grew
- Describe the terms of the Compromise of 1850

The 1848 treaty with Mexico did not bring the United States domestic peace. Instead, the acquisition of new territory revived and intensified the debate over the future of slavery in the western territories, widening the growing division between North and South and leading to the creation of new single-issue parties. Increasingly, the South came to regard itself as under attack by radical northern abolitionists, and many northerners began to speak ominously of a southern drive to dominate American politics for the purpose of protecting slaveholders' human property. As tensions mounted and both sides hurled accusations, national unity frayed. Compromise became nearly impossible and antagonistic sectional rivalries replaced the idea of a unified, democratic republic.

THE LIBERTY PARTY, THE WILMOT PROVISO, AND THE ANTISLAVERY MOVEMENT

Committed to protecting white workers by keeping slavery out of the lands taken from Mexico, Pennsylvania congressman David Wilmot attached to an 1846 revenue bill an amendment that would prohibit slavery in the new territory. The **Wilmot Proviso** was not entirely new. Other congressmen had drafted similar legislation, and Wilmot's language was largely copied from the 1787 Northwest Ordinance that had banned slavery in that territory. His ideas were very controversial in the 1840s, however, because his proposals would prevent American slaveholders from bringing what they viewed as their lawful property, their slaves, into the western lands. The measure passed the House but was defeated in the Senate. When Polk tried again to raise revenue the following year (to pay for lands taken from Mexico), the Wilmot Proviso was reintroduced, this time calling for the prohibition of slavery not only in the Mexican Cession but in all U.S. territories. The revenue bill passed, but without the proviso.

That Wilmot, a loyal Democrat, should attempt to counter the actions of a Democratic president hinted at the party divisions that were to come. The 1840s were a particularly active time in the creation and reorganization of political parties and constituencies, mainly because of discontent with the positions of the mainstream Whig and Democratic Parties in regard to slavery and its extension into the territories. The first new party, the small and politically weak **Liberty Party** founded in 1840, was a single-issue party, as were many of those that followed it. Its members were abolitionists who fervently believed slavery was evil and should be ended, and that this was best accomplished by political means.

The Wilmot Proviso captured the "antislavery" sentiments during and after the Mexican War. Antislavery advocates differed from the abolitionists. While abolitionists called for the end of slavery everywhere, antislavery advocates, for various reasons, did not challenge the presence of slavery in the states where it already existed. Those who supported antislavery fervently opposed its expansion westward because, they argued, slavery would degrade white labor and reduce its value, cast a stigma upon hard-working whites, and deprive them of a chance to advance economically. The western lands, they argued, should be open to white men only—small farmers and urban workers for whom the West held the promise of economic advancement. Where slavery was entrenched, according to antislavery advocates, there was little land left for small farmers to purchase, and such men could not compete fairly with slaveholders who held large farms and gangs of slaves. Ordinary laborers suffered also; no one would pay a white man a decent wage when a slave worked for nothing. When labor was associated with loss of freedom, antislavery supporters argued, all white workers carried a stigma that marked them as little better than slaves.

Wilmot opposed the extension of slavery into the Mexican Cession not because of his concern for African Americans, but because of his belief that slavery hurt white workers, and that lands acquired by the government should be used to better the position of white small farmers and laborers. Work was not simply something that people did; it gave them dignity, but in a slave society, labor had no dignity. In response to these arguments, southerners maintained that laborers in northern factories were treated worse than slaves. Their work was tedious and low paid. Their meager income was spent on inadequate food, clothing, and shelter. There was no dignity in such a life. In contrast, they argued, southern slaves were provided with a home, the necessities of life, and the protection of their masters. Factory owners did not care for or protect their employees in the same way.

THE FREE-SOIL PARTY AND THE ELECTION OF 1848

The Wilmot Proviso was an issue of great importance to the Democrats. Would they pledge to support it? At the party's New York State convention in Buffalo, Martin Van Buren's antislavery supporters—called **Barnburners** because they were likened to farmers who were willing to burn down their own barn to get rid of a rat infestation—spoke in favor of the proviso. Their opponents, known as Hunkers, refused to support it. Angered, the Barnburners organized their own convention, where they chose antislavery, pro–Wilmot Proviso delegates to send to the Democrats' national convention in Baltimore. In this way, the controversy over the expansion of slavery divided the Democratic Party.

At the national convention, both sets of delegates were seated—the pro-proviso ones chosen by the Barnburners and the anti-proviso ones chosen by the Hunkers. When it came time to vote for the party's presidential nominee, the majority of votes were for Lewis Cass, an advocate of popular sovereignty. Popular sovereignty was the belief that citizens should be able to decide issues based on the principle of majority rule; in this case, residents of a territory should have the right to decide whether slavery would be allowed in it. Theoretically, this doctrine would allow slavery to become established in any U.S. territory, including those from which it had been banned by earlier laws.

Disgusted by the result, the Barnburners united with antislavery Whigs and former members of the Liberty Party to form a new political party—the **Free-Soil Party**, which took as its slogan "Free Soil, Free Speech, Free Labor, and Free Men." The party had one real goal—to oppose the extension of slavery into the territories (**Figure 3.21**). In the minds of its members and many other northerners of the time, southern slaveholders had marshaled their wealth and power to control national politics for the purpose of protecting the institution of slavery and extending it into the territories. Many in the Free-Soil Party believed in this far-reaching conspiracy of the slaveholding elite to control both foreign affairs and domestic policies for their own ends, a cabal that came to be known as the **Slave Power**.

Figure 3.21 This political cartoon depicts Martin Van Buren and his son John, both Barnburners, forcing the slavery issue within the Democratic Party by "smoking out" fellow Democrat Lewis Cass on the roof. Their support of the Wilmot Proviso and the new Free-Soil Party is demonstrated by John's declaration, "That's you Dad! more 'Free-Soil.' We'll rat 'em out yet. Long life to Davy Wilmot." (credit: Library of Congress)

In the wake of the Mexican War, antislavery sentiment entered mainstream American politics when the new Free-Soil party promptly selected Martin Van Buren as its presidential candidate. For the first time, a national political party committed itself to the goal of stopping the expansion of slavery. The Democrats chose Lewis Cass, and the Whigs nominated General Zachary Taylor, as Polk had assumed they would. On Election Day, Democrats split their votes between Van Buren and Cass. With the strength of the Democratic vote diluted, Taylor won. His popularity with the American people served him well, and his status as a slaveholder helped him win the South.

Click and Explore

Visit the archives of the **Gilder Lehrman Institute (http://openstaxcollege.org/l/ 15GerritSmith)** to read an August 1848 letter from Gerrit Smith, a staunch abolitionist, regarding the Free-Soil candidate, Martin Van Buren. Smith played a major role in the Liberty Party and was their presidential candidate in 1848.

THE COMPROMISE OF 1850

The election of 1848 did nothing to quell the controversy over whether slavery would advance into the Mexican Cession. Some slaveholders, like President Taylor, considered the question a moot point because the lands acquired from Mexico were far too dry for growing cotton and therefore, they thought, no slaveholder would want to move there. Other southerners, however, argued that the question was not whether slaveholders *would* want to move to the lands of the Mexican Cession, but whether they *could* and still retain control of their slave property. Denying them the right to freely relocate with their lawful property was, they maintained, unfair and unconstitutional. Northerners argued, just as fervidly, that because Mexico had abolished slavery, no slaves currently lived in the Mexican Cession, and to introduce slavery there would extend it to a new territory, thus furthering the institution and giving the Slave Power more control over the United States. The strong current of antislavery sentiment—that is, the desire to protect white labor—only increased the opposition to the expansion of slavery into the West.

Most northerners, except members of the Free-Soil Party, favored popular sovereignty for California and the New Mexico territory. Many southerners opposed this position, however, for they feared residents of these regions might choose to outlaw slavery. Some southern politicians spoke ominously of secession from the United States. Free-Soilers rejected popular sovereignty and demanded that slavery be permanently excluded from the territories.

Beginning in January 1850, Congress worked for eight months on a compromise that might quiet the growing sectional conflict. Led by the aged Henry Clay, members finally agreed to the following:

1. California, which was ready to enter the Union, was admitted as a free state in accordance with its state constitution.
2. Popular sovereignty was to determine the status of slavery in New Mexico and Utah, even though Utah and part of New Mexico were north of the Missouri Compromise line.
3. The slave trade was banned in the nation's capital. Slavery, however, was allowed to remain.
4. Under a new fugitive slave law, those who helped runaway slaves or refused to assist in their return would be fined and possibly imprisoned.
5. The border between Texas and New Mexico was established.

The **Compromise of 1850** brought temporary relief. It resolved the issue of slavery in the territories for the moment and prevented secession. The peace would not last, however. Instead of relieving tensions between North and South, it had actually made them worse.

CHAPTER 4

Antebellum Idealism and Reform Impulses, 1820–1860

Figure 4.1 The masthead of *The Liberator*, by Hammatt Billings in 1850, highlights the religious aspect of antislavery crusades. *The Liberator* was an abolitionist newspaper published by William Lloyd Garrison, one of the leaders of the abolitionist movement in the United States.

Chapter Outline
4.1 An Awakening of Religion and Individualism
4.2 Antebellum Communal Experiments
4.3 Reforms to Human Health
4.4 Addressing Slavery
4.5 Women's Rights

Introduction

This masthead for the abolitionist newspaper *The Liberator* shows two Americas (**Figure 4.1**). On the left is the southern version where slaves are being sold; on the right, free blacks enjoy the blessing of liberty. Reflecting the role of evangelical Protestantism in reforms such as abolition, the image features Jesus as the central figure. The caption reads, "I come to break the bonds of the oppressor," and below the masthead, "Our country is the World, our Countrymen are all Mankind."

The reform efforts of the antebellum years, including abolitionism, aimed to perfect the national destiny and redeem the souls of individual Americans. A great deal of optimism, fueled by evangelical Protestantism revivalism, underwrote the moral crusades of the first half of the nineteenth century. Some reformers targeted what they perceived as the shallow, materialistic, and democratic market culture of the United States and advocated a stronger sense of individualism and self-reliance. Others dreamed of a more equal society and established their own idealistic communities. Still others, who viewed slavery as the most serious flaw in American life, labored to end the institution. Women's rights, temperance, health reforms, and a host of other efforts also came to the forefront during the heyday of reform in the 1830s and 1840s.

4.1 An Awakening of Religion and Individualism

By the end of this section, you will be able to:
- Explain the connection between evangelical Protestantism and the Second Great Awakening
- Describe the message of the transcendentalists

Protestantism shaped the views of the vast majority of Americans in the antebellum years. The influence of religion only intensified during the decades before the Civil War, as religious camp meetings spread the word that people could bring about their own salvation, a direct contradiction to the Calvinist doctrine of predestination. Alongside this religious fervor, transcendentalists advocated a more direct knowledge of the self and an emphasis on individualism. The writers and thinkers devoted to transcendentalism, as well as the reactions against it, created a trove of writings, an outpouring that has been termed the American Renaissance.

THE SECOND GREAT AWAKENING

The reform efforts of the antebellum era sprang from the Protestant revival fervor that found expression in what historians refer to as the **Second Great Awakening**. (The First Great Awakening of evangelical Protestantism had taken place in the 1730s and 1740s.) The Second Great Awakening emphasized an emotional religious style in which sinners grappled with their unworthy nature before concluding that they were born again, that is, turning away from their sinful past and devoting themselves to living a righteous, Christ-centered life. This emphasis on personal salvation, with its rejection of predestination (the Calvinist concept that God selected only a chosen few for salvation), was the religious embodiment of the Jacksonian celebration of the individual. Itinerant ministers preached the message of the awakening to hundreds of listeners at outdoors revival meetings (**Figure 4.3**).

Figure 4.2

Figure 4.3 This 1819 engraving by Jacques Gerard shows a Methodist camp meeting. Revivalist camp meetings held by itinerant Protestant ministers became a feature of nineteenth-century American life.

The burst of religious enthusiasm that began in Kentucky and Tennessee in the 1790s and early 1800s among Baptists, Methodists, and Presbyterians owed much to the uniqueness of the early decades of the republic. These years saw swift population growth, broad western expansion, and the rise of participatory democracy. These political and social changes made many people anxious, and the more egalitarian, emotional, and individualistic religious practices of the Second Great Awakening provided relief and comfort for Americans experiencing rapid change. The awakening soon spread to the East, where it had a profound impact on Congregationalists and Presbyterians. The thousands swept up in the movement believed in the possibility of creating a much better world. Many adopted **millennialism**, the fervent belief that the Kingdom of God would be established on earth and that God would reign on earth for a thousand years, characterized by harmony and Christian morality. Those drawn to the message of the Second Great Awakening yearned for stability, decency, and goodness in the new and turbulent American republic.

The Second Great Awakening also brought significant changes to American culture. Church membership doubled in the years between 1800 and 1835. Several new groups formed to promote and strengthen the message of religious revival. The American Bible Society, founded in 1816, distributed Bibles in an effort to ensure that every family had access to the sacred text, while the American Sunday School Union, established in 1824, focused on the religious education of children and published religious materials specifically for young readers. In 1825, the American Tract Society formed with the goal of disseminating the Protestant revival message in a flurry of publications.

Missionaries and circuit riders (ministers without a fixed congregation) brought the message of the awakening across the United States, including into the lives of slaves. The revival spurred many slaveholders to begin encouraging their slaves to become Christians. Previously, many slaveholders feared allowing their slaves to convert, due to a belief that Christians could not be enslaved and because of the fear that slaves might use Christian principles to oppose their enslavement. However, by the 1800s, Americans established a legal foundation for the enslavement of Christians. Also, by this time, slaveholders had come to believe that if slaves learned the "right" (that is, white) form of Christianity, then slaves would be more obedient and hardworking. Allowing slaves access to Christianity also served to ease the consciences of Christian slaveholders, who argued that slavery was divinely ordained, yet it was a faith that also required slaveholders to bring slaves to the "truth." Also important to this era was the creation of African American forms of worship as well as African American churches such as the African Methodist Episcopal Church, the first independent black Protestant church in the United States. Formed in the 1790s by Richard Allen, the African Methodist Episcopal Church advanced the African American effort to express their faith apart from white Methodists (**Figure 4.4**).

Figure 4.4 Charles Grandison Finney (a) was one of the best-known ministers of the Second Great Awakening. Richard Allen (b) created the first separate African American church, the African Methodist Episcopal Church, in the 1790s.

In the Northeast, Presbyterian minister Charles Grandison Finney rose to prominence as one of the most important evangelicals in the movement (**Figure 4.4**). Born in 1792 in western New York, Finney studied to be a lawyer until 1821, when he experienced a religious conversion and thereafter devoted himself to revivals. He led revival meetings in New York and Pennsylvania, but his greatest success occurred after he accepted a ministry in Rochester, New York, in 1830. At the time, Rochester was a boomtown because the Erie Canal had brought a lively shipping business.

The new middle class—an outgrowth of the Industrial Revolution—embraced Finney's message. It fit perfectly with their understanding of themselves as people shaping their own destiny. Workers also latched onto the message that they too could control their salvation, spiritually and perhaps financially as well. Western New York gained a reputation as the "burned over district," a reference to the intense flames of religious fervor that swept the area during the Second Great Awakening.

TRANSCENDENTALISM

Beginning in the 1820s, a new intellectual movement known as **transcendentalism** began to grow in the Northeast. In this context, to transcend means to go beyond the ordinary sensory world to grasp personal insights and gain appreciation of a deeper reality, and transcendentalists believed that all people could attain an understanding of the world that surpassed rational, sensory experience. Transcendentalists were critical of mainstream American culture. They reacted against the age of mass democracy in Jacksonian America—what Tocqueville called the "tyranny of majority"—by arguing for greater individualism against conformity. European romanticism, a movement in literature and art that stressed emotion over cold, calculating reason, also influenced transcendentalists in the United States, especially the transcendentalists' celebration of the uniqueness of individual feelings.

Ralph Waldo Emerson emerged as the leading figure of this movement (**Figure 4.5**). Born in Boston in 1803, Emerson came from a religious family. His father served as a Unitarian minister and, after graduating from Harvard Divinity School in the 1820s, Emerson followed in his father's footsteps. However, after his wife died in 1831, he left the clergy. On a trip to Europe in 1832, he met leading figures of romanticism who rejected the hyper-rationalism of the Enlightenment, emphasizing instead emotion and the sublime.

(a)   (b)

Figure 4.5 Ralph Waldo Emerson (a), shown here circa 1857, is considered the father of transcendentalism. This letter (b) from Emerson to Walt Whitman, another brilliant writer of the transcendentalist movement, demonstrates the closeness of a number of these writers.

When Emerson returned home the following year, he began giving lectures on his romanticism-influenced ideas. In 1836, he published "Nature," an essay arguing that humans can find their true spirituality in nature, not in the everyday bustling working world of Jacksonian democracy and industrial transformation. In 1841, Emerson published his essay "Self-Reliance," which urged readers to think for themselves and reject the mass conformity and mediocrity he believed had taken root in American life. In this essay, he wrote, "Whoso would be a man must be a nonconformist," demanding that his readers be true to themselves and not blindly follow a herd mentality. Emerson's ideas dovetailed with those of the French aristocrat, Alexis de Tocqueville, who wrote about the "tyranny of the majority" in his *Democracy in America*. Tocqueville, like Emerson, expressed concern that a powerful majority could overpower the will of individuals.

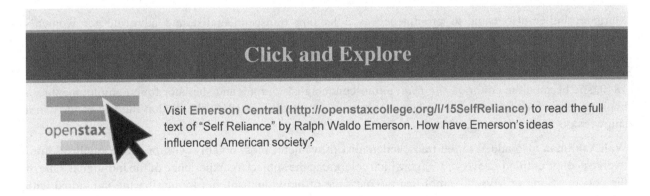

Click and Explore

Visit **Emerson Central** (http://openstaxcollege.org/l/15SelfReliance) to read the full text of "Self Reliance" by Ralph Waldo Emerson. How have Emerson's ideas influenced American society?

Emerson's ideas struck a chord with a class of literate adults who also were dissatisfied with mainstream American life and searching for greater spiritual meaning. Many writers were drawn to transcendentalism, and they started to express its ideas through new stories, poems, essays, and articles. The ideas of transcendentalism were able to permeate American thought and culture through a prolific print culture, which allowed magazines and journals to be widely disseminated.

Among those attracted to Emerson's ideas was his friend Henry David Thoreau, whom he encouraged to write about his own ideas. Thoreau placed a special emphasis on the role of nature as a gateway to the transcendentalist goal of greater individualism. In 1848, Thoreau gave a lecture in which he argued that individuals must stand up to governmental injustice, a topic he chose because of his disgust over the Mexican-American War and slavery. In 1849, he published his lecture "Civil Disobedience" and urged readers to refuse to support a government that was immoral. In 1854, he published *Walden; Or, Life in the Woods*, a book about the two years he spent in a small cabin on Walden Pond near Concord, Massachusetts (**Figure 4.6**). Thoreau had lived there as an experiment in living apart, but not too far apart, from his conformist neighbors.

(a)   (b)

Figure 4.6 Henry David Thoreau (a) argued that men had the right to resist authority if they deemed it unjust. "All men recognize the right of revolution; that is, the right to refuse allegiance to, and to resist, the government, when its tyranny or its inefficiency are great and unendurable." Thoreau's *Walden; or, Life in the Woods* (b) articulated his emphasis on the importance of nature as a gateway to greater individuality.

Margaret Fuller also came to prominence as a leading transcendentalist and advocate for women's equality. Fuller was a friend of Emerson and Thoreau, and other intellectuals of her day. Because she was a woman, she could not attend Harvard, as it was a male-only institution for undergraduate students until 1973. However, she was later granted the use of the library there because of her towering intellect. In 1840, she became the editor of *The Dial*, a transcendentalist journal, and she later found employment as a book reviewer for the *New York Tribune* newspaper. Tragically, in 1850, she died at the age of forty in a shipwreck off Fire Island, New York.

Walt Whitman also added to the transcendentalist movement, most notably with his 1855 publication of twelve poems, entitled *Leaves of Grass*, which celebrated the subjective experience of the individual. One of the poems, "Song of Myself," amplified the message of individualism, but by uniting the individual with all other people through a transcendent bond.

AMERICANA

⊗ *Walt Whitman's "Song of Myself"*

Walt Whitman (**Figure 4.7**) was a poet associated with the transcendentalists. His 1855 poem, "Song of Myself," shocked many when it was first published, but it has been called one of the most influential poems in American literature.

Figure 4.7 This steel engraving of Walt Whitman by Samuel Hollyer is from a lost daguerreotype by Gabriel Harrison, taken in 1854.

I CELEBRATE myself, and sing myself,
And what I assume you shall assume,
For every atom belonging to me as good belongs to you.
I loafe and invite my soul,
I lean and loafe at my ease observing a spear of summer grass.
My tongue, every atom of my blood, form'd from this soil, this air,
Born here of parents born here from parents the same, and their parents the same,
I, now thirty-seven years old in perfect health begin,
Hoping to cease not till death. . . .
And I say to mankind, Be not curious about God,
For I who am curious about each am not curious about God,
(No array of terms can say how much I am at peace about God and about death.)
I hear and behold God in every object, yet understand God not in the least,
Nor do I understand who there can be more wonderful than myself. . . .
I too am not a bit tamed, I too am untranslatable,
I sound my barbaric yawp over the roofs of the world. . . .
You will hardly know who I am or what I mean,
But I shall be good health to you nevertheless,
And filter and fibre your blood.
Failing to fetch me at first keep encouraged,
Missing me one place search another,
I stop somewhere waiting for you.

What images does Whitman use to describe himself and the world around him? What might have been shocking about this poem in 1855? Why do you think it has endured?

Some critics took issue with transcendentalism's emphasis on rampant individualism by pointing out the destructive consequences of compulsive human behavior. Herman Melville's novel *Moby Dick, Or, The Whale* emphasized the perils of individual obsession by telling the tale of Captain Ahab's single-minded quest to kill a white whale, Moby Dick, which had destroyed Ahab's original ship and caused him to lose one of his legs. Edgar Allan Poe, a popular author, critic, and poet, decried "the so-called poetry of the so-called transcendentalists." These American writers who questioned transcendentalism illustrate the underlying tension between individualism and conformity in American life.

4.2 Antebellum Communal Experiments

By the end of this section, you will be able to:
• Identify similarities and differences among utopian groups of the antebellum era
• Explain how religious utopian communities differed from nonreligious ones

Prior to 1815, in the years before the market and Industrial Revolution, most Americans lived on farms where they produced much of the foods and goods they used. This largely pre-capitalist culture centered on large family units whose members all lived in the same towns, counties, and parishes.

Economic forces unleashed after 1815, however, forever altered that world. More and more people now bought their food and goods in the thriving market economy, a shift that opened the door to a new way of life. These economic transformations generated various reactions; some people were nostalgic for what they viewed as simpler, earlier times, whereas others were willing to try new ways of living and working. In the early nineteenth century, experimental communities sprang up, created by men and women who hoped not just to create a better way of life but to recast American civilization, so that greater equality and harmony would prevail. Indeed, some of these reformers envisioned the creation of alternative ways of living, where people could attain perfection in human relations. The exact number of these societies is unknown because many of them were so short-lived, but the movement reached its apex in the 1840s.

RELIGIOUS UTOPIAN SOCIETIES

Most of those attracted to utopian communities had been profoundly influenced by evangelical Protestantism, especially the Second Great Awakening. However, their experience of revivalism had left them wanting to further reform society. The communities they formed and joined adhered to various socialist ideas and were considered radical, because members wanted to create a new social order, not reform the old.

German Protestant migrants formed several **pietistic** societies: communities that stressed transformative individual religious experience or piety over religious rituals and formality. One of the earliest of these, the Ephrata Cloister in Pennsylvania, was founded by a charismatic leader named Conrad Beissel in the 1730s. By the antebellum era, it was the oldest communal experiment in the United States. Its members devoted themselves to spiritual contemplation and a disciplined work regime while they awaited the millennium. They wore homespun rather than buying cloth or premade clothing, and encouraged celibacy. Although the Ephrata Cloister remained small, it served as an early example of the type of community that antebellum reformers hoped to create.

In 1805, a second German religious society, led by George Rapp, took root in Pennsylvania with several hundred members called Rappites who encouraged celibacy and adhered to the socialist principle of holding all goods in common (as opposed to allowing individual ownership). They not only built the town of Harmony but also produced surplus goods to sell to the outside world. In 1815, the group sold its Pennsylvanian holdings and moved to Indiana, establishing New Harmony on a twenty-thousand-acre plot along the Wabash River. In 1825, members returned to Pennsylvania, and established themselves in the town called Economy.

The **Shakers** provide another example of a community established with a religious mission. The Shakers started in England as an outgrowth of the Quaker religion in the middle of the eighteenth century. Ann Lee, a leader of the group in England, emigrated to New York in the 1770s, having experienced a profound religious awakening that convinced her that she was "mother in Christ." She taught that God was both male and female; Jesus embodied the male side, while Mother Ann (as she came to be known by her followers) represented the female side. To Shakers in both England and the United States, Mother Ann represented the completion of divine revelation and the beginning of the millennium of heaven on earth.

In practice, men and women in Shaker communities were held as equals—a radical departure at the time—and women often outnumbered men. Equality extended to the possession of material goods as well; no one could hold private property. Shaker communities aimed for self-sufficiency, raising food and making all that was necessary, including furniture that emphasized excellent workmanship as a substitute for worldly pleasure.

The defining features of the Shakers were their spiritual mysticism and their prohibition of sexual intercourse, which they held as an example of a lesser spiritual life and a source of conflict between women and men. Rapturous Shaker dances, for which the group gained notoriety, allowed for emotional release (**Figure 4.8**). The high point of the Shaker movement came in the 1830s, when about six thousand members populated communities in New England, New York, Ohio, Indiana, and Kentucky.

Figure 4.8   In this image of a Shaker dance from 1840, note the raised arms, indicating emotional expression.

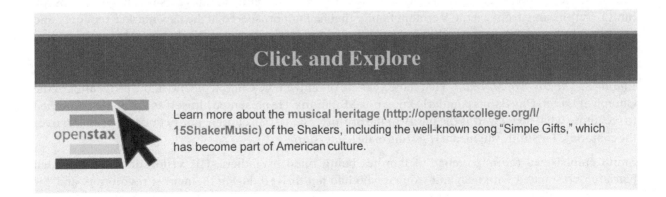

Click and Explore

Learn more about the **musical heritage** (http://openstaxcollege.org/l/15ShakerMusic) of the Shakers, including the well-known song "Simple Gifts," which has become part of American culture.

Another religious utopian experiment, the Oneida Community, began with the teachings of John Humphrey Noyes, a Vermonter who had graduated from Dartmouth, Andover Theological Seminary, and Yale. The Second Great Awakening exerted a powerful effect on him, and he came to believe in perfectionism, the idea that it is possible to be perfect and free of sin. Noyes claimed to have achieved this state of perfection in 1834.

Noyes applied his idea of perfection to relationships between men and women, earning notoriety for his unorthodox views on marriage and sexuality. Beginning in his home town of Putney, Vermont, he began to advocate what he called "complex marriage:" a form of communal marriage in which women and men who had achieved perfection could engage in sexual intercourse without sin. Noyes also promoted "male continence," whereby men would not ejaculate, thereby freeing women from pregnancy and the difficulty of determining paternity when they had many partners. Intercourse became fused with spiritual power among Noyes and his followers.

The concept of complex marriage scandalized the townspeople in Putney, so Noyes and his followers removed to Oneida, New York. Individuals who wanted to join the Oneida Community underwent a tough screening process to weed out those who had not reached a state of perfection, which Noyes believed promoted self-control, not out-of-control behavior. The goal was a balance between individuals in a community of love and respect. The perfectionist community Noyes envisioned ultimately dissolved in 1881, although the Oneida Community itself continues to this day (**Figure 4.9**).

Figure 4.9 The Oneida Community was a utopian experiment located in Oneida, New York, from 1848 to 1881.

The most successful religious utopian community to arise in the antebellum years was begun by Joseph Smith. Smith came from a large Vermont family that had not prospered in the new market economy and moved to the town of Palmyra, in the "burned over district" of western New York. In 1823, Smith claimed to have to been visited by the angel Moroni, who told him the location of a trove of golden plates or tablets. During the late 1820s, Smith translated the writing on the golden plates, and in 1830, he published his finding as *The Book of Mormon*. That same year, he organized the Church of Christ, the progenitor of the Church of Latter-Day Saints popularly known as **Mormons**. He presented himself as a prophet and aimed to recapture what he viewed as the purity of the primitive Christian church, purity that had been lost over the centuries. To Smith, this meant restoring male leadership.

Smith emphasized the importance of families being ruled by fathers. His vision of a reinvigorated patriarchy resonated with men and women who had not thrived during the market revolution, and his claims attracted those who hoped for a better future. Smith's new church placed great stress on work and discipline. He aimed to create a New Jerusalem where the church exercised oversight of its members.

Smith's claims of translating the golden plates antagonized his neighbors in New York. Difficulties with anti-Mormons led him and his followers to move to Kirtland, Ohio, in 1831. By 1838, as the United States experienced continued economic turbulence following the Panic of 1837, Smith and his followers were facing financial collapse after a series of efforts in banking and money-making ended in disaster. They moved to Missouri, but trouble soon developed there as well, as citizens reacted against the Mormons' beliefs. Actual fighting broke out in 1838, and the ten thousand or so Mormons removed to Nauvoo, Illinois, where they founded a new center of Mormonism.

By the 1840s, Nauvoo boasted a population of thirty thousand, making it the largest utopian community in the United States. Thanks to some important conversions to Mormonism among powerful citizens in Illinois, the Mormons had virtual autonomy in Nauvoo, which they used to create the largest armed force in the state. Smith also received further revelations there, including one that allowed male church leaders to practice polygamy. He also declared that all of North and South America would be the new Zion and announced that he would run for president in the 1844 election.

Smith and the Mormons' convictions and practices generated a great deal of opposition from neighbors in surrounding towns. Smith was arrested for treason (for destroying the printing press of a newspaper that criticized Mormonism), and while he was in prison, an anti-Mormon mob stormed into his cell and killed him. Brigham Young (**Figure 4.10**) then assumed leadership of the group, which he led to a permanent home in what is now Salt Lake City, Utah.

(a)   (b)

Figure 4.10 Carl Christian Anton Christensen depicts *The angel Moroni delivering the plates of the Book of Mormon to Joseph Smith*, circa 1886 (a). On the basis of these plates, Joseph Smith (b) founded the Church of Latter-Day Saints. Following Smith's death at the hands of a mob in Illinois, Brigham Young took control of the church and led them west to the Salt Lake Valley, which at that time was still part of Mexico.

SECULAR UTOPIAN SOCIETIES

Not all utopian communities were prompted by the religious fervor of the Second Great Awakening; some were outgrowths of the intellectual ideas of the time, such as romanticism with its emphasis on the importance of individualism over conformity. One of these, Brook Farm, took shape in West Roxbury, Massachusetts, in the 1840s. It was founded by George Ripley, a transcendentalist from Massachusetts. In the summer of 1841, this utopian community gained support from Boston-area thinkers and writers, an intellectual group that included many important transcendentalists. Brook Farm is best characterized as a community of intensely individualistic personalities who combined manual labor, such as the growing and harvesting food, with intellectual pursuits. They opened a school that specialized in the liberal arts rather than rote memorization and published a weekly journal called *The Harbinger*, which was "Devoted to Social and Political Progress" (**Figure 4.11**). Members of Brook Farm never totaled more than one hundred, but it won renown largely because of the luminaries, such as Emerson and Thoreau, whose names were attached to it. Nathaniel Hawthorne, a Massachusetts writer who took issue with some of the transcendentalists' claims, was a founding member of Brook Farm, and he fictionalized some of his experiences in his novel *The Blithedale Romance*. In 1846, a fire destroyed the main building of Brook Farm, and already hampered by financial problems, the Brook Farm experiment came to an end in 1847.

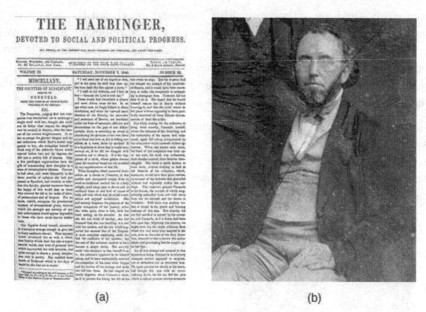

(a)   (b)

Figure 4.11 Brook Farm printed *The Harbinger* (a) to share its ideals more widely. George Ripley (b), who founded the farm, was burdened with a huge debt several years later when the community collapsed.

Robert Owen, a British industrialist, helped inspire those who dreamed of a more equitable world in the face of the changes brought about by industrialization. Owen had risen to prominence before he turned thirty by running cotton mills in New Lanark, Scotland; these were considered the most successful cotton mills in Great Britain. Owen was very uneasy about the conditions of workers, and he devoted both his life and his fortune to trying to create cooperative societies where workers would lead meaningful, fulfilled lives. Unlike the founders of many utopian communities, he did not gain inspiration from religion; his vision derived instead from his faith in human reason to make the world better.

When the Rappite community in Harmony, Indiana, decided to sell its holdings and relocate to Pennsylvania, Owen seized the opportunity to put his ideas into action. In 1825, he bought the twenty-thousand-acre parcel in Indiana and renamed it New Harmony (**Figure 4.12**). After only a few years, however, a series of bad decisions by Owen and infighting over issues like the elimination of private property led to the dissolution of the community. But Owen's ideas of cooperation and support inspired other "Owenite" communities in the United States, Canada, and Great Britain.

Figure 4.12 This 1838 engraving of New Harmony shows the ideal collective community that Robert Owen hoped to build.

A French philosopher who advocated the creation of a new type of utopian community, Charles Fourier also inspired American readers, notably Arthur Brisbane, who popularized Fourier's ideas in the United States. Fourier emphasized collective effort by groups of people or "associations." Members of the association would be housed in large buildings or "phalanxes," a type of communal living arrangement. Converts to Fourier's ideas about a new science of living published and lectured vigorously. They believed labor was a type of capital, and the more unpleasant the job, the higher the wages should be. Fourierists in the United States created some twenty-eight communities between 1841 and 1858, but by the late 1850s, the movement had run its course in the United States.

4.3 Reforms to Human Health

By the end of this section, you will be able to:
- Explain the different reforms aimed at improving the health of the human body
- Describe the various factions and concerns within the temperance movement

Antebellum reform efforts aimed at perfecting the spiritual and social worlds of individuals, and as an outgrowth of those concerns, some reformers moved in the direction of ensuring the health of American citizens. Many Americans viewed drunkenness as a major national problem, and the battle against alcohol and the many problems associated with it led many to join the temperance movement. Other reformers offered plans to increase physical well-being, instituting plans designed to restore vigor. Still others celebrated new sciences that would unlock the mysteries of human behavior and, by doing so, advance American civilization.

TEMPERANCE

According to many antebellum reformers, intemperance (drunkenness) stood as the most troubling problem in the United States, one that eroded morality, Christianity, and played a starring role in corrupting American democracy. Americans consumed huge quantities of liquor in the early 1800s, including gin, whiskey, rum, and brandy. Indeed, scholars agree that the rate of consumption of these drinks during the first three decades of the 1800s reached levels that have never been equaled in American history.

A variety of reformers created organizations devoted to **temperance**, that is, moderation or self-restraint. Each of these organizations had its own distinct orientation and target audience. The earliest ones were formed in the 1810s in New England. The Massachusetts Society for the Suppression of Intemperance and the Connecticut Society for the Reformation of Morals were both formed in 1813. Protestant ministers led both organizations, which enjoyed support from New Englanders who clung to the ideals of the Federalist Party and later the Whigs. These early temperance societies called on individuals to lead pious lives and avoid sin, including the sin of overindulging in alcohol. They called not for the eradication of drinking but for a more restrained and genteel style of imbibing.

AMERICANA

⚙ *The Drunkard's Progress*

This 1840 temperance illustration (**Figure 4.13**) charts the path of destruction for those who drink. The step-by-step progression reads:

> Step 1. A glass with a friend.
> Step 2. A glass to keep the cold out.
> Step 3. A glass too much.
> Step 4. Drunk and riotous.
> Step 5. The summit attained. Jolly companions. A confirmed drunkard.
> Step 6. Poverty and disease.
> Step 7. Forsaken by Friends.
> Step 8. Desperation and crime.
> Step 9. Death by suicide.

Figure 4.13   This 1846 image, *The Drunkards Progress. From the First Glass to the Grave* by Nathaniel Currier, shows the destruction that prohibitionists thought could result from drinking alcoholic beverages.

Who do you think was the intended audience for this engraving? How do you think different audiences (children, drinkers, nondrinkers) would react to the story it tells? Do you think it is an effective piece of propaganda? Why or why not?

In the 1820s, temperance gained ground largely through the work of Presbyterian minister Lyman Beecher. In 1825, Beecher delivered six sermons on temperance that were published the follow year as *Six Sermons on the Nature, Occasions, Signs, Evils, and Remedy of Intemperance*. He urged total abstinence from hard liquor and called for the formation of voluntary associations to bring forth a new day without spirits (whiskey, rum, gin, brandy). Lyman's work enjoyed a wide readership and support from leading Protestant ministers as well as the emerging middle class; temperance fit well with the middle-class ethic of encouraging hard work and a sober workforce.

In 1826, the American Temperance Society was formed, and by the early 1830s, thousands of similar societies had sprouted across the country. Members originally pledged to shun only hard liquor. By 1836, however, leaders of the temperance movement, including Beecher, called for a more comprehensive approach. Thereafter, most temperance societies advocated total abstinence; no longer would beer and wine be tolerated. Such total abstinence from alcohol is known as **teetotalism**.

Teetotalism led to disagreement within the movement and a loss of momentum for reform after 1836. However, temperance enjoyed a revival in the 1840s, as a new type of reformer took up the cause against alcohol. The engine driving the new burst of enthusiastic temperance reform was the Washington Temperance Society (named in deference to George Washington), which organized in 1840. The leaders of the Washingtonians came not from the ranks of Protestant ministers but from the working class. They aimed their efforts at confirmed alcoholics, unlike the early temperance advocates who mostly targeted the middle class.

Washingtonians welcomed the participation of women and children, as they cast alcohol as the destroyer of families, and those who joined the group took a public pledge of teetotalism. Americans flocked to the Washingtonians; as many as 600,000 had taken the pledge by 1844. The huge surge in membership had much to do with the style of this reform effort. The Washingtonians turned temperance into theater by dramatizing the plight of those who fell into the habit of drunkenness. Perhaps the most famous fictional drama put forward by the temperance movement was *Ten Nights in a Bar-Room* (1853), a novel that became the basis for popular theatrical productions. The Washingtonians also sponsored picnics and parades that drew whole families into the movement. The group's popularity quickly waned in the late 1840s and early 1850s, when questions arose about the effectiveness of merely taking a pledge. Many who had done so soon relapsed into alcoholism.

Still, by that time, temperance had risen to a major political issue. Reformers lobbied for laws limiting or prohibiting alcohol, and states began to pass the first temperance laws. The earliest, an 1838 law in Massachusetts, prohibited the sale of liquor in quantities less than fifteen gallons, a move designed to make it difficult for ordinary workmen of modest means to buy spirits. The law was repealed in 1840, but Massachusetts towns then took the initiative by passing local laws banning alcohol. In 1845, close to one hundred towns in the state went "dry."

An 1839 Mississippi law, similar to Massachusetts' original law, outlawed the sale of less than a gallon of liquor. Mississippi's law illustrates the national popularity of temperance; regional differences notwithstanding, citizens in northern and southern states agreed on the issue of alcohol. Nonetheless, northern states pushed hardest for outlawing alcohol. Maine enacted the first statewide prohibition law in 1851. New England, New York, and states in the Midwest passed local laws in the 1850s, prohibiting the sale and manufacture of intoxicating beverages.

REFORMS FOR THE BODY AND THE MIND

Beyond temperance, other reformers looked to ways to maintain and improve health in a rapidly changing world. Without professional medical organizations or standards, health reform went in many different directions; although the American Medical Association was formed in 1847, it did not have much power to oversee medical practices. Too often, quack doctors prescribed regimens and medicines that did far more harm that good.

Sylvester Graham stands out as a leading light among the health reformers in the antebellum years. A Presbyterian minister, Graham began his career as a reformer, lecturing against the evils of strong drink. He combined an interest in temperance with vegetarianism and sexuality into what he called a "Science of Human Life," calling for a regimented diet of more vegetables, fruits, and grain, and no alcohol, meat, or spices.

Graham advocated baths and cleanliness in general to preserve health; hydropathy, or water cures for various ailments, became popular in the United States in the 1840s and 1850s. He also viewed masturbation and excessive sex as a cause of disease and debility. His ideas led him to create what he believed to be a perfect food that would maintain health: the Graham cracker, which he invented in 1829. Followers of

Graham, known as Grahamites, established boardinghouses where lodgers followed the recommended strict diet and sexual regimen.

During the early nineteenth century, reformers also interested themselves in the workings of the mind in an effort to better understand the effects of a rapidly changing world awash with religious revivals and democratic movements. **Phrenology**—the mapping of the cranium to specific human attributes—stands as an early type of science, related to what would become psychology and devoted to understanding how the mind worked. Phrenologists believed that the mind contained thirty-seven "faculties," the strengths or weaknesses of which could be determined by a close examination of the size and shape of the cranium (**Figure 4.14**).

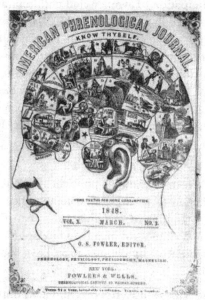

Figure 4.14 This March 1848 cover of the *American Phrenological Journal* illustrates the different faculties of the mind as envisioned by phrenologists.

Initially developed in Europe by Franz Joseph Gall, a German doctor, phrenology first came to the United States in the 1820s. In the 1830s and 1840s, it grew in popularity as lecturers crisscrossed the republic. It was sometimes used as an educational test, and like temperance, it also became a form of popular entertainment.

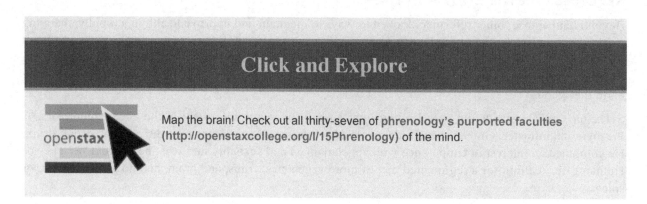

Click and Explore

Map the brain! Check out all thirty-seven of phrenology's purported faculties (http://openstaxcollege.org/l/15Phrenology) of the mind.

The popularity of phrenology offers us some insight into the emotional world of the antebellum United States. Its popularity speaks to the desire of those living in a rapidly changing society, where older ties to community and family were being challenged, to understand one another. It appeared to offer a way to quickly recognize an otherwise-unknown individual as a readily understood set of human faculties.

4.4 Addressing Slavery

By the end of this section, you will be able to:
- Identify the different approaches to reforming the institution of slavery
- Describe the abolitionist movement in the early to mid-nineteenth century

The issue of slavery proved especially combustible in the reform-minded antebellum United States. Those who hoped to end slavery had different ideas about how to do it. Some could not envision a biracial society and advocated sending blacks to Africa or the Caribbean. Others promoted the use of violence as the best method to bring American slavery to an end. Abolitionists, by contrast, worked to end slavery and to create a multiracial society of equals using moral arguments—moral suasion—to highlight the immorality of slavery. In keeping with the religious fervor of the era, abolitionists hoped to bring about a mass conversion in public opinion to end slavery.

"REFORMS" TO SLAVERY

An early and popular "reform" to slavery was **colonization**, or a movement advocating the displacement of African Americans out of the country, usually to Africa. In 1816, the Society for the Colonization of Free People of Color of America (also called the American Colonization Society or ACS) was founded with this goal. Leading statesmen including Thomas Jefferson endorsed the idea of colonization.

Members of the ACS did not believe that blacks and whites could live as equals, so they targeted the roughly 200,000 free blacks in the United States for relocation to Africa. For several years after the ACS's founding, they raised money and pushed Congress for funds. In 1819, they succeeded in getting $100,000 from the federal government to further the colonization project. The ACS played a major role in the creation of the colony of Liberia, on the west coast of Africa. The country's capital, Monrovia, was named in honor of President James Monroe. The ACS stands as an example of how white reformers, especially men of property and standing, addressed the issue of slavery. Their efforts stand in stark contrast with other reformers' efforts to deal with slavery in the United States.

Although rebellion stretches the definition of reform, another potential solution to slavery was its violent overthrow. Nat Turner's Rebellion, one of the largest slave uprisings in American history, took place in 1831, in Southampton County, Virginia. Like many slaves, Nat Turner was inspired by the evangelical Protestant fervor sweeping the republic. He preached to fellow slaves in Southampton County, gaining a reputation among them as a prophet. He organized them for rebellion, awaiting a sign to begin, until an eclipse in August signaled that the appointed time had come.

Turner and as many as seventy other slaves killed their masters and their masters' families, murdering a total of around sixty-five people (**Figure 4.15**). Turner eluded capture until late October, when he was tried, hanged, and then beheaded and quartered. Virginia put to death fifty-six other slaves whom they believed to have taken part in the rebellion. White vigilantes killed two hundred more as panic swept through Virginia and the rest of the South.

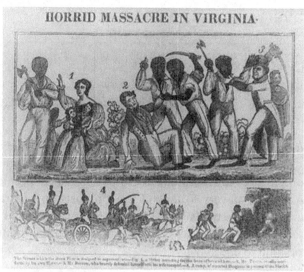

Figure 4.15 In *Horrid Massacre in Virginia*, circa 1831, the text on the bottom reads, "The Scenes which the above plate is designed to represent are Fig 1. a mother intreating for the lives of her children. -2. Mr. Travis, cruelly murdered by his own Slaves. -3. Mr. Barrow, who bravely defended himself until his wife escaped. -4. A comp. of mounted Dragoons in pursuit of the Blacks." From whose side do you think the illustrator is telling this story?

MY STORY

❂ *Nat Turner on His Battle against Slavery*

Thomas R. Gray was a lawyer in Southampton, Virginia, where he visited Nat Turner in jail. He published *The Confessions of Nat Turner, the leader of the late insurrection in Southampton, Va., as fully and voluntarily made to Thomas R. Gray* in November 1831, after Turner had been executed.

> For as the blood of Christ had been shed on this earth, and had ascended to heaven for the salvation of sinners, and was now returning to earth again in the form of dew . . . it was plain to me that the Saviour was about to lay down the yoke he had borne for the sins of men, and the great day of judgment was at hand. . . . And on the 12th of May, 1828, I heard a loud noise in the heavens, and the Spirit instantly appeared to me and said the Serpent was loosened, and Christ had laid down the yoke he had borne for the sins of men, and that I should take it on and fight against the Serpent, . . . *Ques.* Do you not find yourself mistaken now? *Ans.* Was not Christ crucified. And by signs in the heavens that it would make known to me when I should commence the great work—and on the appearance of the sign, (the eclipse of the sun last February) I should arise and prepare myself, and slay my enemies with their own weapons.

How did Turner interpret his fight against slavery? What did he mean by the "serpent?"

Nat Turner's Rebellion provoked a heated discussion in Virginia over slavery. The Virginia legislature was already in the process of revising the state constitution, and some delegates advocated for an easier manumission process. The rebellion, however, rendered that reform impossible. Virginia and other slave states recommitted themselves to the institution of slavery, and defenders of slavery in the South increasingly blamed northerners for provoking their slaves to rebel.

Literate, educated blacks, including David Walker, also favored rebellion. Walker was born a free black man in North Carolina in 1796. He moved to Boston in the 1820s, lectured on slavery, and promoted the first African American newspaper, *Freedom's Journal*. He called for blacks to actively resist slavery and to use violence if needed. He published *An Appeal to the Colored Citizens of the World* in 1829, denouncing the scheme of colonization and urging blacks to fight for equality in the United States, to take action   against racism. Walker died months after the publication of his *Appeal*, and debate continues to this day over the cause of his death. Many believe he was murdered. Walker became a symbol of hope to free people in the North and a symbol of the terrors of literate, educated blacks to the slaveholders of the South.

ABOLITIONISM

Abolitionists took a far more radical approach to the issue of the slavery by using moral arguments to advocate its immediate elimination. They publicized the atrocities committed under slavery and aimed to create a society characterized by equality of blacks and whites. In a world of intense religious fervor, they hoped to bring about a mass awakening in the United States of the sin of slavery, confident that they could transform the national conscience against the South's peculiar institution.

William Lloyd Garrison and Antislavery Societies

William Lloyd Garrison of Massachusetts distinguished himself as the leader of the **abolitionist** movement. Although he had once been in favor of colonization, he came to believe that such a scheme only deepened racism and perpetuated the sinful practices of his fellow Americans. In 1831, he founded the abolitionist newspaper *The Liberator*, whose first edition declared:

> I am aware that many object to the severity of my language; but is there not cause for severity? I will be as harsh as truth, and as uncompromising as justice. On this subject, I do not wish to think, or speak, or write, with moderation. No! No! Tell a man whose house is on fire to give a moderate alarm; tell him to moderately rescue his wife from the hands of the ravisher; tell the mother to gradually extricate her babe from the fire into which it has fallen;—but urge me not to use moderation in a cause like the present. I am in earnest—I will not equivocate—I will not excuse—I will not retreat a single inch—AND I WILL BE HEARD.

White Virginians blamed Garrison for stirring up slaves and instigating slave rebellions like Nat Turner's.

Garrison founded the New England Anti-Slavery Society in 1831, and the American Anti-Slavery Society (AASS) in 1833. By 1838, the AASS had 250,000 members, sometimes called Garrisonians. They rejected colonization as a racist scheme and opposed the use of violence to end slavery. Influenced by evangelical Protestantism, Garrison and other abolitionists believed in **moral suasion**, a technique of appealing to the conscience of the public, especially slaveholders. Moral suasion relied on dramatic narratives, often from former slaves, about the horrors of slavery, arguing that slavery destroyed families, as children were sold and taken away from their mothers and fathers (**Figure 4.16**). Moral suasion resonated with many women, who condemned the sexual violence against slave women and the victimization of southern white women by adulterous husbands.

(a)   (b)

Figure 4.16 These woodcuts of a chained and pleading slave, *Am I Not a Man and a Brother?* (a) and *Am I Not a Woman and a Sister?*, accompanied abolitionist John Greenleaf Whittier's antislavery poem, "Our Countrymen in Chains." Such images exemplified moral suasion: showing with pathos and humanity the moral wrongness of slavery.

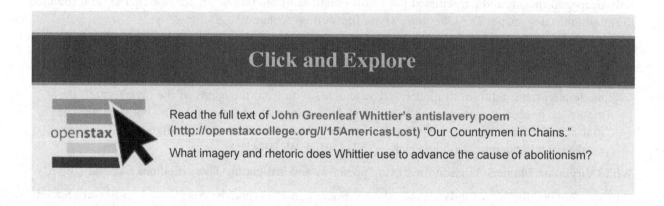

Click and Explore

Read the full text of **John Greenleaf Whittier's antislavery poem** (http://openstaxcollege.org/l/15AmericasLost) "Our Countrymen in Chains." What imagery and rhetoric does Whittier use to advance the cause of abolitionism?

Garrison also preached **immediatism**: the moral demand to take immediate action to end slavery. He wrote of equal rights and demanded that blacks be treated as equal to whites. He appealed to women and men, black and white, to join the fight. The abolition press, which produced hundreds of tracts, helped to circulate moral suasion. Garrison and other abolitionists also used the power of petitions, sending hundreds of petitions to Congress in the early 1830s, demanding an end to slavery. Since most newspapers published congressional proceedings, the debate over abolition petitions reached readers throughout the nation.

Although Garrison rejected the U.S. political system as a tool of slaveholders, other abolitionists believed mainstream politics could bring about their goal, and they helped create the Liberty Party in 1840. Its first candidate was James G. Birney, who ran for president that year. Birney epitomized the ideal and goals of the abolitionist movement. Born in Kentucky in 1792, Birney owned slaves and, searching for a solution to what he eventually condemned as the immorality of slavery, initially endorsed colonization. In the 1830s, however, he rejected colonization, freed his slaves, and began to advocate the immediate end of slavery. The Liberty Party did not generate much support and remained a fringe third party. Many of its supporters turned to the Free-Soil Party in the aftermath of the Mexican Cession.

The vast majority of northerners rejected abolition entirely. Indeed, abolition generated a fierce backlash in the United States, especially during the Age of Jackson, when racism saturated American culture. Anti-abolitionists in the North saw Garrison and other abolitionists as the worst of the worst, a threat to the republic that might destroy all decency and order by upending time-honored distinctions between blacks and whites, and between women and men. Northern anti-abolitionists feared that if slavery ended, the North would be flooded with blacks who would take jobs from whites.

Opponents made clear their resistance to Garrison and others of his ilk; Garrison nearly lost his life in 1835, when a Boston anti-abolitionist mob dragged him through the city streets. Anti-abolitionists tried to pass federal laws that made the distribution of abolitionist literature a criminal offense, fearing that such literature, with its engravings and simple language, could spark rebellious blacks to action. Their sympathizers in Congress passed a "gag rule" that forbade the consideration of the many hundreds of petitions sent to Washington by abolitionists. A mob in Illinois killed an abolitionist named Elijah Lovejoy in 1837, and the following year, ten thousand protestors destroyed the abolitionists' newly built Pennsylvania Hall in Philadelphia, burning it to the ground.

Frederick Douglass

Many escaped slaves joined the abolitionist movement, including Frederick Douglass. Douglass was born in Maryland in 1818, escaping to New York in 1838. He later moved to New Bedford, Massachusetts, with his wife. Douglass's commanding presence and powerful speaking skills electrified his listeners when he began to provide public lectures on slavery. He came to the attention of Garrison and others, who encouraged him to publish his story. In 1845, Douglass published *Narrative of the Life of Frederick Douglass, An American Slave Written by Himself*, in which he told about his life of slavery in Maryland (**Figure 4.17**). He identified by name the whites who had brutalized him, and for that reason, along with the mere act of publishing his story, Douglass had to flee the United States to avoid being murdered.

(a)   (b)

Figure 4.17 This 1856 ambrotype of Frederick Douglass (a) demonstrates an early type of photography developed on glass. Douglass was an escaped slave who was instrumental in the abolitionism movement. His slave narrative, told in *Narrative of the Life of Frederick Douglass, An American Slave Written by Himself* (b), followed a long line of similar narratives that demonstrated the brutality of slavery for northerners unfamiliar with the institution.

British abolitionist friends bought his freedom from his Maryland owner, and Douglass returned to the United States. He began to publish his own abolitionist newspaper, *North Star*, in Rochester, New York. During the 1840s and 1850s, Douglass labored to bring about the end of slavery by telling the story of his life and highlighting how slavery destroyed families, both black and white.

MY STORY

⚙ *Frederick Douglass on Slavery*

Most white slaveholders frequently raped female slaves. In this excerpt, Douglass explains the consequences for the children fathered by white masters and slave women.

> Slaveholders have ordained, and by law established, that the children of slave women shall in all cases follow the condition of their mothers . . . this is done too obviously to administer to their own lusts, and make a gratification of their wicked desires profitable as well as pleasurable . . . the slaveholder, in cases not a few, sustains to his slaves the double relation of master and father. . . .
>
> Such slaves [born of white masters] invariably suffer greater hardships . . . They are . . . a constant offence to their mistress . . . she is never better pleased than when she sees them under the lash, . . . The master is frequently compelled to sell this class of his slaves, out of deference to the feelings of his white wife; and, cruel as the deed may strike any one to be, for a man to sell his own children to human flesh-mongers, . . . for, unless he does this, he must not only whip them himself, but must stand by and see one white son tie up his brother, of but few shades darker . . . and ply the gory lash to his naked back.
>
> —Frederick Douglass, *Narrative of the Life of Frederick Douglass, An American Slave Written by Himself* (1845)

What moral complications did slavery unleash upon white slaveholders in the South, according to Douglass? What imagery does he use?

4.5 Women's Rights

By the end of this section, you will be able to:
- Explain the connections between abolition, reform, and antebellum feminism
- Describe the ways antebellum women's movements were both traditional and revolutionary

Women took part in all the antebellum reforms, from transcendentalism to temperance to abolition. In many ways, traditional views of women as nurturers played a role in encouraging their participation. Women who joined the cause of temperance, for example, amplified their accepted role as moral guardians of the home. Some women advocated a much more expansive role for themselves and their peers by educating children and men in solid republican principles. But it was their work in antislavery efforts that served as a springboard for women to take action against gender inequality. Many, especially northern women, came to the conclusion that they, like slaves, were held in shackles in a society dominated by men.

Despite the radical nature of their effort to end slavery and create a biracial society, most abolitionist men clung to traditional notions of proper gender roles. White and black women, as well as free black men, were forbidden from occupying leadership positions in the AASS. Because women were not allowed to join the men in playing leading roles in the organization, they formed separate societies, such as the Boston Female Anti-Slavery Society, the Philadelphia Female Anti-Slavery Society, and similar groups.

THE GRIMKÉ SISTERS

Two leading abolitionist women, Sarah and Angelina Grimké, played major roles in combining the fight to end slavery with the struggle to achieve female equality. The sisters had been born into a prosperous slaveholding family in South Carolina. Both were caught up in the religious fervor of the Second Great Awakening, and they moved to the North and converted to Quakerism.

In the mid-1830s, the sisters joined the abolitionist movement, and in 1837, they embarked on a public lecture tour, speaking about immediate abolition to "promiscuous assemblies," that is, to audiences of women and men. This public action thoroughly scandalized respectable society, where it was unheard of for women to lecture to men. William Lloyd Garrison endorsed the Grimké sisters' public lectures, but other abolitionists did not. Their lecture tour served as a turning point; the reaction against them propelled the question of women's proper sphere in society to the forefront of public debate.

THE DECLARATION OF RIGHTS AND SENTIMENTS

Participation in the abolitionist movement led some women to embrace feminism, the advocacy of women's rights. Lydia Maria Child, an abolitionist and feminist, observed, "The comparison between women and the colored race is striking . . . both have been kept in subjection by physical force." Other women, including Elizabeth Cady Stanton, Lucy Stone, and Susan B. Anthony, agreed (**Figure 4.18**).

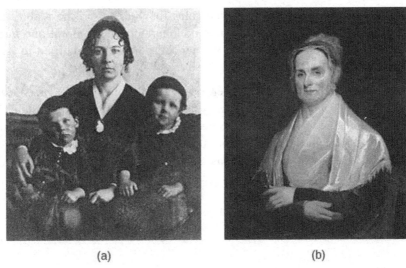

(a)   (b)

Figure 4.18 Elizabeth Cady Stanton (a) and Lucretia Mott (b) both emerged from the abolitionist movement as strong advocates of women's rights.

In 1848, about three hundred male and female feminists, many of them veterans of the abolition campaign, gathered at the **Seneca Falls** Convention in New York for a conference on women's rights that was organized by Lucretia Mott and Elizabeth Cady Stanton. It was the first of what became annual meetings that have continued to the present day. Attendees agreed to a "Declaration of Rights and Sentiments" based on the Declaration of Independence; it declared, "We hold these truths to be self-evident: that all men and women are created equal; that they are endowed by their Creator with certain inalienable rights; that among these are life, liberty, and the pursuit of happiness." "The history of mankind," the document continued, "is a history of repeated injuries and usurpations on the part of man toward woman, having in direct object the establishment of an absolute tyranny over her."

Click and Explore

Read the entire text of the **Declaration of Rights and Sentiments** (http://openstaxcollege.org/l/15SenecaFalls) in the Internet Modern History Sourcebook at Fordham University.

REPUBLICAN MOTHERHOOD IN THE ANTEBELLUM YEARS

Some northern female reformers saw new and vital roles for their sex in the realm of education. They believed in traditional gender roles, viewing women as inherently more moral and nurturing than men. Because of these attributes, the feminists argued, women were uniquely qualified to take up the roles of educators of children.

Catharine Beecher, the daughter of Lyman Beecher, pushed for women's roles as educators. In her 1845 book, *The Duty of American Women to Their Country*, she argued that the United States had lost its moral compass due to democratic excess. Both "intelligence and virtue" were imperiled in an age of riots and disorder. Women, she argued, could restore the moral center by instilling in children a sense of right and wrong. Beecher represented a northern, middle-class female sensibility. The home, especially the parlor, became the site of northern female authority.

CHAPTER 5

Troubled Times: the Tumultuous 1850s

Figure 5.1 In *Southern Chivalry: Argument versus Club's* (1856), by John Magee, South Carolinian Preston Brooks attacks Massachusetts senator Charles Sumner after his speech denouncing "border ruffians" pouring into Kansas from Missouri. For southerners, defending slavery meant defending southern honor.

Chapter Outline

Introduction

The heated sectional controversy between the North and the South reached new levels of intensity in the 1850s. Southerners and northerners grew ever more antagonistic as they debated the expansion of slavery in the West. The notorious confrontation between Representative Preston Brooks of South Carolina and Massachusetts senator Charles Sumner depicted in the image above (**Figure 5.1**), illustrates the contempt between extremists on both sides. The "Caning of Sumner" in May 1856 followed upon a speech given by Sumner two days earlier in which he condemned slavery in no uncertain terms, declaring: "[Admitting Kansas as a slave state] is the rape of a virgin territory, compelling it to the hateful embrace of slavery; and it may be clearly traced to a depraved longing for a new slave state, the hideous offspring of such a crime, in the hope of adding to the power of slavery in the national government." Sumner criticized proslavery legislators, particularly attacking a fellow senator and relative of Preston Brooks. Brooks responded by beating Sumner with a cane, a thrashing that southerners celebrated as a manly defense of gentlemanly honor and their way of life. The episode highlights the violent clash between pro- and antislavery factions in the 1850s, a conflict that would eventually lead to the traumatic unraveling of American democracy and civil war.

5.1 The Compromise of 1850

By the end of this section, you will be able to:
- Explain the contested issues that led to the Compromise of 1850
- Describe and analyze the reactions to the 1850 Fugitive Slave Act

At the end of the Mexican-American War, the United States gained a large expanse of western territory known as the Mexican Cession. The disposition of this new territory was in question; would the new states be slave states or free-soil states? In the long run, the Mexican-American War achieved what abolitionism alone had failed to do: it mobilized many in the North against slavery.

Antislavery northerners clung to the idea expressed in the 1846 Wilmot Proviso: slavery would not expand into the areas taken, and later bought, from Mexico. Though the proviso remained a proposal and never became a law, it defined the sectional division. The Free-Soil Party, which formed at the conclusion of the Mexican-American War in 1848 and included many members of the failed Liberty Party, made this position the centerpiece of all its political activities, ensuring that the issue of slavery and its expansion remained at the front and center of American political debate. Supporters of the Wilmot Proviso and members of the new Free-Soil Party did not want to abolish slavery in the states where it already existed; rather, Free-Soil advocates demanded that the western territories be kept free of slavery for the benefit of white laborers who might settle there. They wanted to protect white workers from having to compete with slave labor in the West. (Abolitionists, in contrast, looked to destroy slavery everywhere in the United States.) Southern extremists, especially wealthy slaveholders, reacted with outrage at this effort to limit slavery's expansion. They argued for the right to bring their slave property west, and they vowed to leave the Union if necessary to protect their way of life—meaning the right to own slaves—and ensure that the American empire of slavery would continue to grow.

BROKERING THE COMPROMISE

The issue of what to do with the western territories added to the republic by the Mexican Cession consumed Congress in 1850. Other controversial matters, which had been simmering over time, complicated the problem further. Chief among these issues were the slave trade in the District of

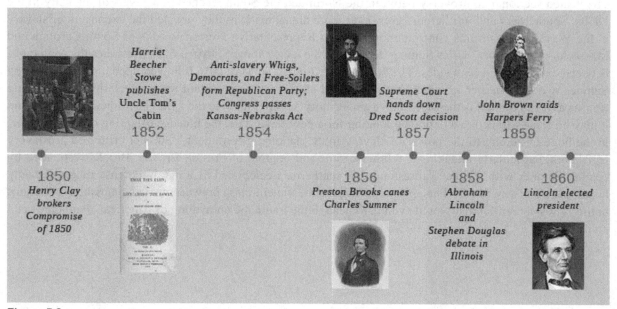

Figure 5.2

Columbia, which antislavery advocates hoped to end, and the fugitive slave laws, which southerners wanted to strengthen. The border between Texas and New Mexico remained contested because many Texans hoped to enlarge their state further, and, finally, the issue of California had not been resolved. California was the crown jewel of the Mexican Cession, and following the discovery of gold, it was flush with thousands of emigrants. By most estimates, however, it would be a free state, since the former Mexican ban on slavery still remained in force and slavery had not taken root in California. The map below (**Figure 5.3**) shows the disposition of land before the 1850 compromise.

Figure 5.3 This map shows the states and territories of the United States as they were in 1849–1850. (credit "User:Golbez"/Wikimedia Commons)

The presidential election of 1848 did little to solve the problems resulting from the Mexican Cession. Both the Whigs and the Democrats attempted to avoid addressing the issue of slavery publicly as much as possible. The Democrats nominated Lewis Cass of Michigan, a supporter of the idea of popular sovereignty, or letting the people in the territories decide the issue of whether or not to permit slavery based on majority rule. The Whigs nominated General Zachary Taylor, a slaveholder from Kentucky, who had achieved national prominence as a military hero in the Mexican-American War. Taylor did not take a personal stand on any issue and remained silent throughout the campaign. The fledgling Free-Soil Party put forward former president Martin Van Buren as their candidate. The Free-Soil Party attracted northern Democrats who supported the Wilmot Proviso, northern Whigs who rejected Taylor because he was a slaveholder, former members of the Liberty Party, and other abolitionists.

Both the Whigs and the Democrats ran different campaigns in the North and South. In the North, all three parties attempted to win voters with promises of keeping the territories free of slavery, while in the South, Whigs and Democrats promised to protect slavery in the territories. For southern voters, the slaveholder Taylor appeared the natural choice. In the North, the Free-Soil Party took votes away from Whigs and Democrats and helped to ensure Taylor's election in 1848.

As president, Taylor sought to defuse the sectional controversy as much as possible, and, above all else, to preserve the Union. Although Taylor was born in Virginia before relocating to Kentucky and owned more than one hundred slaves by the late 1840s, he did not push for slavery's expansion into the Mexican Cession. However, the California Gold Rush made California's statehood into an issue demanding immediate attention. In 1849, after California residents adopted a state constitution prohibiting slavery, President Taylor called on Congress to admit California and New Mexico as free states, a   move that infuriated southern defenders of slavery who argued for the right to bring their slave property wherever they chose. Taylor, who did not believe slavery could flourish in the arid lands of the Mexican Cession because the climate prohibited plantation-style farming, proposed that the Wilmot Proviso be applied to the entire area.

In Congress, Kentucky senator Henry Clay, a veteran of congressional conflicts, offered a series of resolutions addressing the list of issues related to slavery and its expansion. Clay's resolutions called for the admission of California as a free state; no restrictions on slavery in the rest of the Mexican Cession (a rejection of the Wilmot Proviso and the Free-Soil Party's position); a boundary between New Mexico and Texas that did not expand Texas (an important matter, since Texas allowed slavery and a larger Texas meant more opportunities for the expansion of slavery); payment of outstanding Texas debts from the Lone Star Republic days; and the end of the slave trade (but not of slavery) in the nation's capital, coupled with a more robust federal fugitive slave law. Clay presented these proposals as an omnibus bill, that is, one that would be voted on its totality.

Clay's proposals ignited a spirited and angry debate that lasted for eight months. The resolution calling for California to be admitted as a free state aroused the wrath of the aged and deathly ill John C. Calhoun, the elder statesman for the proslavery position. Calhoun, too sick to deliver a speech, had his friend Virginia senator James Mason present his assessment of Clay's resolutions and the current state of sectional strife.

In Calhoun's eyes, blame for the stalemate fell squarely on the North, which stood in the way of southern and American prosperity by limiting the zones where slavery could flourish. Calhoun called for a vigorous federal law to ensure that runaway slaves were returned to their masters. He also proposed a constitutional amendment specifying a dual presidency—one office that would represent the South and another for the North—a suggestion that hinted at the possibility of disunion. Calhoun's argument portrayed an embattled South faced with continued northern aggression—a line of reasoning that only furthered the sectional divide.

Several days after Mason delivered Calhoun's speech, Massachusetts senator Daniel Webster countered Calhoun in his "Seventh of March" speech. Webster called for national unity, famously declaring that he spoke "not as a Massachusetts man, not as a Northern man, but as an American." Webster asked southerners to end threats of disunion and requested that the North stop antagonizing the South by harping on the Wilmot Proviso. Like Calhoun, Webster also called for a new federal law to ensure the return of runaway slaves.

Webster's efforts to compromise led many abolitionist sympathizers to roundly denounce him as a traitor. Whig senator William H. Seward, who aspired to be president, declared that slavery—which he characterized as incompatible with the assertion in the Declaration of Independence that "all men are created equal"—would one day be extinguished in the United States. Seward's speech, in which he invoked the idea of a higher moral law than the Constitution, secured his reputation in the Senate as an advocate of abolition.

The speeches made in Congress were published in the nation's newspapers, and the American public followed the debates with great interest, anxious to learn how the issues of the day, especially the potential advance of slavery, would be resolved. Colorful reports of wrangling in Congress further piqued public interest. Indeed, it was not uncommon for arguments to devolve into fistfights or worse. One of the most astonishing episodes of the debate occurred in April 1850, when a quarrel erupted between Missouri Democratic senator Thomas Hart Benton, who by the time of the debate had become a critic of slavery (despite owning slaves), and Mississippi Democratic senator Henry S. Foote. When the burly Benton appeared ready to assault Foote, the Mississippi senator drew his pistol (**Figure 5.4**).

Figure 5.4 This 1850 print, *Scene in Uncle Sam's Senate*, depicts Mississippi senator Henry S. Foote taking aim at Missouri senator Thomas Hart Benton. In the print, Benton declares: "Get out of the way, and let the assassin fire! let the scoundrel use his weapon! I have no arm's! I did not come here to assassinate!" Foote responds, "I only meant to defend myself!" (credit: Library of Congress)

President Taylor and Henry Clay, whose resolutions had begun the verbal fireworks in the Senate, had no patience for each other. Clay had long harbored ambitions for the White House, and, for his part, Taylor resented Clay and disapproved of his resolutions. With neither side willing to budge, the government stalled on how to resolve the disposition of the Mexican Cession and the other issues of slavery. The drama only increased when on July 4, 1850, President Taylor became gravely ill, reportedly after eating an excessive amount of fruit washed down with milk. He died five days later, and Vice President Millard Fillmore became president. Unlike his predecessor, who many believed would be opposed to a compromise, Fillmore worked with Congress to achieve a solution to the crisis of 1850.

In the end, Clay stepped down as leader of the compromise effort in frustration, and Illinois senator Stephen Douglas pushed five separate bills through Congress, collectively composing the Compromise of 1850. First, as advocated by the South, Congress passed the Fugitive Slave Act, a law that provided federal money—or "bounties"—to slave-catchers. Second, to balance this concession to the South, Congress admitted California as a free state, a move that cheered antislavery advocates and abolitionists in the North. Third, Congress settled the contested boundary between New Mexico and Texas by favoring New Mexico and not allowing for an enlarged Texas, another outcome pleasing to the North. Fourth, antislavery advocates welcomed Congress's ban on the slave trade in Washington, DC, although slavery continued to thrive in the nation's capital. Finally, on the thorny issue of whether slavery would expand into the territories, Congress avoided making a direct decision and instead relied on the principle of popular sovereignty. This put the onus on residents of the territories to decide for themselves whether to allow slavery. Popular sovereignty followed the logic of American democracy; majorities in each territory would decide the territory's laws. The compromise, however, further exposed the sectional divide as votes on the bills divided along strict regional lines.

Most Americans breathed a sigh of relief over the deal brokered in 1850, choosing to believe it had saved the Union. Rather than resolving divisions between the North and the South, however, the compromise stood as a truce in an otherwise white-hot sectional conflict. Tensions in the nation remained extremely high; indeed, southerners held several conventions after the compromise to discuss ways to protect the South. At these meetings, extremists who called for secession found themselves in the minority, since most southerners committed themselves to staying in the Union—but only if slavery remained in the states where it already existed, and if no effort was made to block its expansion into areas where citizens wanted it, thereby applying the idea of popular sovereignty (**Figure 5.5**).

**States and Territories of the United States of America
September 9, 1850–March 2, 1853**

Figure 5.5 This map shows the states and territories of the United States as they were from 1850 to March 1853. (credit "User:Golbez"/Wikimedia Commons)

THE FUGITIVE SLAVE ACT AND ITS CONSEQUENCES

The hope that the Compromise of 1850 would resolve the sectional crisis proved short-lived when the Fugitive Slave Act turned into a major source of conflict. The federal law imposed heavy fines and prison sentences on northerners and midwesterners who aided runaway slaves or refused to join posses to catch fugitives. Many northerners felt the law forced them to act as slave-catchers against their will.

The law also established a new group of federal commissioners who would decide the fate of fugitives brought before them. In some instances, slave-catchers even brought in free northern blacks, prompting abolitionist societies to step up their efforts to prevent kidnappings (**Figure 5.6**). The commissioners had a financial incentive to send fugitives and free blacks to the slaveholding South, since they received ten dollars for every African American sent to the South and only five if they decided the person who came before them was actually free. The commissioners used no juries, and the alleged runaways could not testify in their own defense.

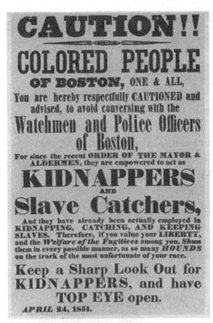

CAUTION!!

COLORED PEOPLE

OF BOSTON, ONE & ALL,

You are hereby respectfully CAUTIONED and advised, to avoid conversing with the

Watchmen and Police Officers of Boston,

For since the recent ORDER OF THE MAYOR & ALDERMEN, they are empowered to act as

KIDNAPPERS

AND

Slave Catchers,

And they have already been actually employed in KIDNAPPING, CATCHING, AND KEEPING SLAVES. Therefore, if you value your LIBERTY, and the *Welfare of the Fugitives* among you, Shun them in every possible manner, as so many *HOUNDS* on the track of the most unfortunate of your race.

Keep a Sharp Look Out for KIDNAPPERS, and have TOP EYE open.

APRIL 24, 1851.

Figure 5.6 This 1851 poster, written by Boston abolitionist Theodore Parker, warned that any black person, free or slave, risked kidnapping by slave-catchers.

The operation of the law further alarmed northerners and confirmed for many the existence of a "Slave Power"—that is, a minority of elite slaveholders who wielded a disproportionate amount of power over the federal government, shaping domestic and foreign policies to suit their interests. Despite southerners' repeated insistence on states' rights, the Fugitive Slave Act showed that slaveholders were willing to use the power of the federal government to bend people in other states to their will. While rejecting the use of federal power to restrict the expansion of slavery, proslavery southerners turned to the federal government to protect and promote the institution of slavery.

The actual number of runaway slaves who were not captured within a year of escaping remained very low, perhaps no more than one thousand per year in the early 1850s. Most stayed in the South, hiding in plain sight among free blacks in urban areas. Nonetheless, southerners feared the influence of a vast **Underground Railroad**: the network of northern whites and free blacks who sympathized with runaway slaves and provided safe houses and safe passage from the South. Quakers, who had long been troubled by slavery, were especially active in this network. It is unclear how many slaves escaped through the Underground Railroad, but historians believe that between 50,000 and 100,000 slaves used the network in their bids for freedom. Meanwhile, the 1850 Fugitive Slave Act greatly increased the perils of being captured. For many thousands of fugitives, escaping the United States completely by going to southern Ontario, Canada, where slavery had been abolished, offered the best chance of a better life beyond the reach of slaveholders.

Harriet Tubman, one of the thousands of slaves who made their escape through the Underground Railroad, distinguished herself for her efforts in helping other enslaved men and women escape. Born a slave in Maryland around 1822, Tubman, who suffered greatly under slavery but found solace in Christianity, made her escape in the late 1840s. She returned to the South more than a dozen times to lead other slaves, including her family and friends, along the Underground Railroad to freedom.

DEFINING "AMERICAN"

✹ *Harriet Tubman: An American Moses?*

Harriet Tubman (**Figure 5.7**) was a legendary figure in her own time and beyond. An escaped slave herself, she returned to the South thirteen times to help over three hundred slaves through the Underground Railroad to liberty in the North. In 1869, printer William J. Moses published Sarah H. Bradford's *Scenes in the Life of Harriet Tubman*. Bradford was a writer and biographer who had known Tubman's family for years. The excerpt below is from the beginning of her book, which she updated in 1886 under the title *Harriet, the Moses of Her People*.

Figure 5.7 This full-length portrait of Harriet Tubman hangs in the National Portrait Gallery of the Smithsonian.

> It is proposed in this little book to give a plain and unvarnished account of some scenes and adventures in the life of a woman who, though one of earth's lowly ones, and of dark-hued skin, has shown an amount of heroism in her character rarely possessed by those of any station in life. Her name (we say it advisedly and without exaggeration) deserves to be handed down to posterity side by side with the names of Joan of Arc, Grace Darling, and Florence Nightingale; for not one of these women has shown more courage and power of endurance in facing danger and death to relieve human suffering, than has this woman in her heroic and successful endeavors to reach and save all whom she might of her oppressed and suffering race, and to pilot them from the land of Bondage to the promised land of Liberty. Well has she been called "Moses," for she has been a leader and deliverer unto hundreds of her people.
> —Sarah H. Bradford, *Scenes in the Life of Harriet Tubman*

How does Bradford characterize Tubman? What language does Bradford use to tie religion into the fight for freedom?

The Fugitive Slave Act provoked widespread reactions in the North. Some abolitionists, such as Frederick Douglass, believed that standing up against the law necessitated violence. In Boston and elsewhere, abolitionists tried to protect fugitives from federal authorities. One case involved Anthony Burns, who had escaped slavery in Virginia in 1853 and made his way to Boston (**Figure 5.8**). When federal officials arrested Burns in 1854, abolitionists staged a series of mass demonstrations and a confrontation at the courthouse. Despite their best efforts, however, Burns was returned to Virginia when President Franklin Pierce supported the Fugitive Slave Act with federal troops. Boston abolitionists eventually bought Burns's freedom. For many northerners, however, the Burns incident, combined with Pierce's response, only amplified their sense of a conspiracy of southern power.

Figure 5.8 *Anthony Burns*, drawn ca. 1855 by an artist identified only as "Barry," shows a portrait of the fugitive slave surrounded by scenes from his life, including his escape from Virginia, his arrest in Boston, and his address to the court.

The most consequential reaction against the Fugitive Slave Act came in the form of a novel, *Uncle Tom's Cabin*. In it, author Harriet Beecher Stowe, born in Connecticut, made use of slaves' stories she had heard firsthand after marrying and moving to Ohio, then on the country's western frontier. Her novel first appeared as a series of stories in a Free-Soil newspaper, the *National Era*, in 1851 and was published as a book the following year. Stowe told the tale of slaves who were sold by their Kentucky master. While Uncle Tom is indeed sold down the river, young Eliza escapes with her baby (**Figure 5.9**). The story highlighted the idea that slavery was a sin because it destroyed families, ripping children from their parents and husbands and wives from one another. Stowe also emphasized the ways in which slavery corrupted white citizens. The cruelty of some of the novel's white slaveholders (who genuinely believe that slaves don't feel things the way that white people do) and the brutality of the slave dealer Simon Legree, who beats slaves and sexually exploits a slave woman, demonstrate the dehumanizing effect of the institution even on those who benefit from it.

Figure 5.9 This drawing from *Uncle Tom's Cabin*, captioned "Eliza comes to tell Uncle Tom that he is sold, and that she is running away to save her child," illustrates the ways in which Harriet Beecher Stowe's antislavery novel bolstered abolitionists' arguments against slavery.

Stowe's novel proved a runaway bestseller and was the most-read novel of the nineteenth century, inspiring multiple theatrical productions and musical compositions. It was translated into sixty languages and remains in print to this day. Its message about the evils of slavery helped convince many northerners of the righteousness of the cause of abolition. The novel also demonstrated the power of women to shape public opinion. Stowe and other American women believed they had a moral obligation to mold the conscience of the United States, even though they could not vote (**Figure 5.10**).

Figure 5.10 This photograph shows Harriet Beecher Stowe, the author of *Uncle Tom's Cabin*, in 1852. Stowe's work was an inspiration not only to abolitionists, but also to those who believed that women could play a significant role in upholding the nation's morality and shaping public opinion.

Click and Explore

Visit the **Documenting the American South** (http://openstaxcollege.org/l/ 15LeviCoffin) collection on the University of North Carolina at Chapel Hill website to read the memoirs of Levi Coffin, a prominent Quaker abolitionist who was known as the "president" of the Underground Railroad for his active role in helping slaves to freedom. The memoirs include the story of Eliza Harris, which inspired Harriet Beecher Stowe's famous character.

The backlash against the Fugitive Slave Act, fueled by *Uncle Tom's Cabin* and well-publicized cases like that of Anthony Burns, also found expression in personal liberty laws passed by eight northern state legislatures. These laws emphasized that the state would provide legal protection to anyone arrested as a fugitive slave, including the right to trial by jury. The personal liberty laws stood as a clear-cut example of the North's use of states' rights in opposition to federal power while providing further evidence to southerners that northerners had no respect for the Fugitive Slave Act or slaveholders' property rights.

Click and Explore

Go to an archived page from the **Michigan Department of Natural Resources** (http://openstaxcollege.org/l/15MIPFreedom) site to read the original text of Michigan's 1855 personal liberty laws. How do these laws refute the provisions of the federal Fugitive Slave Act of 1850?

5.2 The Kansas-Nebraska Act and the Republican Party

By the end of this section, you will be able to:
- Explain the political ramifications of the Kansas-Nebraska Act
- Describe the founding of the Republican Party

In the early 1850s, the United States' sectional crisis had abated somewhat, cooled by the Compromise of 1850 and the nation's general prosperity. In 1852, voters went to the polls in a presidential contest between Whig candidate Winfield Scott and Democratic candidate Franklin Pierce. Both men endorsed the Compromise of 1850. Though it was considered unseemly to hit the campaign trail, Scott did so—much to the benefit of Pierce, as Scott's speeches focused on forty-year-old battles during the War of 1812 and the weather. In New York, Scott, known as "Old Fuss and Feathers," talked about a thunderstorm that did not occur and greatly confused the crowd. In Ohio, a cannon firing to herald Scott's arrival killed a spectator.

Pierce was a supporter of the "Young America" movement of the Democratic Party, which enthusiastically anticipated extending democracy around the world and annexing additional territory for the United States. Pierce did not take a stance on the slavery issue. Helped by Scott's blunders and the fact that he had played no role in the bruising political battles of the past five years, Pierce won the election. The brief period of tranquility between the North and South did not last long, however; it came to an end in 1854 with the passage of the Kansas-Nebraska Act. This act led to the formation of a new political party, the Republican Party, that committed itself to ending the further expansion of slavery.

THE KANSAS-NEBRASKA ACT

The relative calm over the sectional issue was broken in 1854 over the issue of slavery in the territory of Kansas. Pressure had been building among northerners to organize the territory west of Missouri and Iowa, which had been admitted to the Union as a free state in 1846. This pressure came primarily from northern farmers, who wanted the federal government to survey the land and put it up for sale. Promoters of a transcontinental railroad were also pushing for this westward expansion.

Southerners, however, had long opposed the Wilmot Proviso's stipulation that slavery should not expand into the West. By the 1850s, many in the South were also growing resentful of the Missouri Compromise of 1820, which established the 36° 30' parallel as the geographical boundary of slavery on the north-south axis. Proslavery southerners now contended that popular sovereignty should apply to all territories, not just Utah and New Mexico. They argued for the right to bring their slave property wherever they chose.

Attitudes toward slavery in the 1850s were represented by a variety of regional factions. Throughout the South, slaveholders entrenched themselves in defense of their "way of life," which depended on the ownership of slaves. Since the 1830s, abolitionists, led by journalist and reformer William Lloyd Garrison, had cast slavery as a national sin and called for its immediate end. For three decades, the abolitionists remained a minority, but they had a significant effect on American society by bringing the evils of slavery into the public consciousness. By the 1850s, some abolitionists advocated the use of violence against those who owned slaves. In 1840, the Liberty Party, whose members came from the ranks of ministers, was founded; this group sought to work within the existing political system, a strategy Garrison and others rejected. Meanwhile, the Free-Soil Party committed itself to ensuring that white laborers would find work in newly acquired territories and not have to compete with unpaid slaves.

It is important to note that, even among those who opposed the expansion of slavery in the West, very different attitudes toward slavery existed. Some antislavery northerners wanted the West to be the best country for poor whites to go and seek opportunity. They did not want white workers to have to compete with slave labor, a contest that they believed demeaned white labor. Radical abolitionists, in contrast, envisioned the end of all slavery, and a society of equality between blacks and whites. Others opposed slavery in principle, but believed that the best approach was colonization; that is, settling freed slaves in a colony in Africa.

The growing political movement to address the issue of slavery stiffened the resolve of southern slaveholders to defend themselves and their society at all costs. Prohibiting slavery's expansion, they argued, ran counter to basic American property rights. As abolitionists fanned the flames of antislavery sentiment, southerners solidified their defense of their enormous investment in human chattel. Across the country, people of all political stripes worried that the nation's arguments would cause irreparable rifts in the country (**Figure 5.11**).

Figure 5.11 In this 1850 political cartoon, the artist takes aim at abolitionists, the Free-Soil Party, Southern states' rights activists, and others he believes risk the health of the Union.

As these different factions were agitating for the settlement of Kansas and Nebraska, leaders of the Democratic Party in 1853 and 1854 sought to bind their party together in the aftermath of intraparty fights over the distribution of patronage jobs. Illinois Democratic senator Stephen Douglas believed he had found a solution—the Kansas-Nebraska bill—that would promote party unity and also satisfy his colleagues from the South, who detested the Missouri Compromise line. In January 1854, Douglas introduced the bill (**Figure 5.12**). The act created two territories: Kansas, directly west of Missouri; and Nebraska, west of Iowa. The act also applied the principle of popular sovereignty, dictating that the people of these territories would decide for themselves whether to adopt slavery. In a concession crucial to many southerners, the proposed bill would also repeal the 36° 30' line from the Missouri Compromise. Douglas hoped his bill would increase his political capital and provide a step forward on his quest for the presidency. Douglas also wanted the territory organized in hopes of placing the eastern terminus of a transcontinental railroad in Chicago, rather than St. Louis or New Orleans.

Figure 5.12 This 1855 map shows the new territories of Kansas and Nebraska, complete with proposed routes of the transcontinental railroad.

After heated debates, Congress narrowly passed the Kansas-Nebraska Act. (In the House of Representatives, the bill passed by a mere three votes: 113 to 110.) This move had major political consequences. The Democrats divided along sectional lines as a result of the bill, and the Whig party, in decline in the early 1850s, found its political power slipping further. Most important, the Kansas-Nebraska Act gave rise to the **Republican Party**, a new political party that attracted northern Whigs, Democrats who shunned the Kansas-Nebraska Act, members of the Free-Soil Party, and assorted abolitionists. Indeed, with the formation of the Republican Party, the Free-Soil Party ceased to exist.

The new Republican Party pledged itself to preventing the spread of slavery into the territories and railed against the Slave Power, infuriating the South. As a result, the party became a solidly northern political organization. As never before, the U.S. political system was polarized along sectional fault lines.

BLEEDING KANSAS

In 1855 and 1856, pro- and antislavery activists flooded Kansas with the intention of influencing the popular-sovereignty rule of the territories. Proslavery Missourians who crossed the border to vote in Kansas became known as **border ruffians**; these gained the advantage by winning the territorial elections, most likely through voter fraud and illegal vote counting. (By some estimates, up to 60 percent of the votes cast in Kansas were fraudulent.) Once in power, they wrote a proslavery constitution, known as the Lecompton Constitution because President Pierce approved it at Lecompton, Kansas.

DEFINING "AMERICAN"

☼ *The Lecompton Constitution*

Kansas was home to no fewer than four state constitutions in its early years. Its first constitution, the Topeka Constitution, would have made Kansas a free-soil state. A proslavery legislature, however, created the 1857 Lecompton Constitution to enshrine the institution of slavery in the new Kansas-Nebraska territories. In January 1858, Kansas voters defeated the proposed Lecompton Constitution, excerpted below, with an overwhelming margin of 10,226 to 138.

> ARTICLE VII.—SLAVERY
> SECTION 1. The right of property is before and higher than any constitutional sanction, and the right of the owner of a slave to such slave and its increase is the same and as inviolable as the right of the owner of any property whatever.
> SEC. 2. The Legislature shall have no power to pass laws for the emancipation of slaves without the consent of the owners, or without paying the owners previous to their emancipation a full equivalent in money for the slaves so emancipated. They shall have no power to prevent immigrants to the State from bringing with them such persons as are deemed slaves by the laws of any one of the United States or Territories, so long as any person of the same age or description shall be continued in slavery by the laws of this State: Provided, That such person or slave be the bona fide property of such immigrants.

How are slaves defined in the 1857 Kansas constitution? How does this constitution safeguard the rights of slaveholders?

The majority in Kansas, however, were Free-Soilers who seethed at the border ruffians' co-opting of the democratic process (**Figure 5.13**). Many had come from New England to ensure a numerical advantage over the border ruffians. The New England Emigrant Aid Society, a northern antislavery group, helped fund these efforts to halt the expansion of slavery into Kansas and beyond.

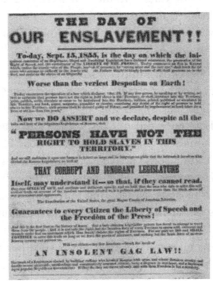

Figure 5.13 This full-page editorial ran in the Free-Soiler *Kansas Tribune* on September 15, 1855, the day Kansas' Act to Punish Offences against Slave Property of 1855 went into effect. This law made it punishable by death to aid or abet a fugitive slave, and it called for punishment of no less than two years for anyone who might: "print, publish, write, circulate, or cause to be introduced into this Territory . . . [any materials] . . . containing any denial of the right of persons to hold slaves in this Territory."

Click and Explore

Go to the Kansas Historical Society's **Kansapedia** (http://openstaxcollege.org/l/ 15KSConst) to read the four different state constitutions that Kansas had during its early years as a United States Territory. What can you deduce about the authors of each constitution?

In 1856, clashes between antislavery Free-Soilers and border ruffians came to a head in Lawrence, Kansas. The town had been founded by the New England Emigrant Aid Society, which funded antislavery settlement in the territory and were determined that Kansas should be a free-soil state. Proslavery emigrants from Missouri were equally determined that no "abolitionist tyrants" or "negro thieves" would control the territory. In the spring of 1856, several of Lawrence's leading antislavery citizens were indicted for treason, and federal marshal Israel Donaldson called for a posse to help make arrests. He did not have trouble finding volunteers from Missouri. When the posse, which included Douglas County sheriff Samuel Jones, arrived outside Lawrence, the antislavery town's "committee of safety" agreed on a policy of nonresistance. Most of those who were indicted fled. Donaldson arrested two men without incident and dismissed the posse.

However, Jones, who had been shot during an earlier confrontation in the town, did not leave. On May 21, falsely claiming that he had a court order to do so, Jones took command of the posse and rode into town armed with rifles, revolvers, cutlasses and bowie knives. At the head of the procession, two flags flew: an American flag and a flag with a crouching tiger. Other banners followed, bearing the words "Southern rights" and "The Superiority of the White Race." In the rear were five artillery pieces, which were dragged to the center of town. The posse smashed the presses of the two newspapers, *Herald of Freedom* and the *Kansas Free State*, and burned down the deserted Free State Hotel (**Figure 5.14**). When the posse finally left, Lawrence residents found themselves unharmed but terrified.

The next morning, a man named John Brown and his sons, who were on their way to provide Lawrence with reinforcements, heard the news of the attack. Brown, a strict, God-fearing Calvinist and staunch abolitionist, once remarked that "God had raised him up on purpose to break the jaws of the wicked." Disappointed that the citizens of Lawrence did not resist the "slave hounds" of Missouri, Brown opted not to go to Lawrence, but to the homes of proslavery settlers near Pottawatomie Creek in Kansas. The group of seven, including Brown's four sons, arrived on May 24, 1856, and announced they were the "Northern Army" that had come to serve justice. They burst into the cabin of proslavery Tennessean James Doyle and marched him and two of his sons off, sparing the youngest at the desperate request of Doyle's wife, Mahala. One hundred yards down the road, Owen and Salmon Brown hacked their captives to death with broadswords and John Brown shot a bullet into Doyle's forehead. Before the night was done, the Browns visited two more cabins and brutally executed two other proslavery settlers. None of those executed owned any slaves or had had anything to do with the raid on Lawrence.

Brown's actions precipitated a new wave of violence. All told, the guerilla warfare between proslavery "border ruffians" and antislavery forces, which would continue and even escalate during the Civil War, resulted in over 150 deaths and significant property loss. The events in Kansas served as an extreme reply to Douglas's proposition of popular sovereignty. As the violent clashes increased, Kansas became known as "**Bleeding Kansas**." Antislavery advocates' use of force carved out a new direction for some who opposed slavery. Distancing themselves from William Lloyd Garrison and other pacifists, Brown and fellow abolitionists believed the time had come to fight slavery with violence.

Figure 5.14 This undated image shows the aftermath of the sacking of Lawrence, Kansas, by border ruffians. Shown are the ruins of the Free State Hotel.

The violent hostilities associated with Bleeding Kansas were not limited to Kansas itself. It was the controversy over Kansas that prompted the caning of Charles Sumner, introduced at the beginning of this chapter with the political cartoon *Southern Chivalry: Argument versus Club's* (**Figure 5.1**). Note the title of the cartoon; it lampoons the southern ideal of chivalry, the code of behavior that Preston Brooks believed he was following in his attack on Sumner. In Sumner's "Crime against Kansas" speech he went much further than politics, filling his verbal attack with allusions to sexuality by singling out fellow senator Andrew Butler from South Carolina, a zealous supporter of slavery and Brooks's uncle. Sumner insulted Butler by comparing slavery to prostitution, declaring, "Of course he [Butler] has chosen a mistress to whom he has made his vows, and who, though ugly to others, is always lovely to him; though polluted in the sight of the world, is chaste in his sight. I mean the harlot Slavery." Because Butler was aged, it was his nephew, Brooks, who sought satisfaction for Sumner's attack on his family and southern honor. Brooks did not challenge Sumner to a duel; by choosing to beat him with a cane instead, he made it clear that he did not consider Sumner a gentleman. Many in the South rejoiced over Brooks's defense of slavery, southern society, and family honor, sending him hundreds of canes to replace the one he had broken assaulting Sumner. The attack by Brooks left Sumner incapacitated physically and mentally for a long period of time. Despite his injuries, the people of Massachusetts reelected him.

THE PRESIDENTIAL ELECTION OF 1856

The electoral contest in 1856 took place in a transformed political landscape. A third political party appeared: the anti-immigrant **American Party**, a formerly secretive organization with the nickname "the Know-Nothing Party" because its members denied knowing anything about it. By 1856, the American or Know-Nothing Party had evolved into a national force committed to halting further immigration. Its members were especially opposed to the immigration of Irish Catholics, whose loyalty to the Pope, they believed, precluded their loyalty to the United States. On the West Coast, they opposed the entry of immigrant laborers from China, who were thought to be too foreign to ever assimilate into a white America.

The election also featured the new Republican Party, which offered John C. Fremont as its candidate. Republicans accused the Democrats of trying to nationalize slavery through the use of popular sovereignty in the West, a view captured in the 1856 political cartoon *Forcing Slavery Down the Throat of a Free Soiler* (**Figure 5.15**). The cartoon features the image of a Free-Soiler settler tied to the Democratic Party platform while Senator Douglas (author of the Kansas-Nebraska Act) and President Pierce force a slave down his throat. Note that the slave cries out "Murder!!! Help—neighbors help, O my poor Wife and Children," a reference to the abolitionists' argument that slavery destroyed families.

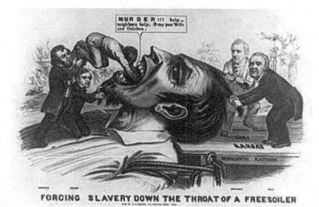

FORCING SLAVERY DOWN THE THROAT OF A FREESOILER

Figure 5.15 This 1856 political cartoon, *Forcing Slavery Down the Throat of a Free Soiler*, by John Magee, shows Republican resentment of the Democratic platform—here represented as an actual platform—of expanding slavery into new western territories.

The Democrats offered James Buchanan as their candidate. Buchanan did not take a stand on either side of the issue of slavery; rather, he attempted to please both sides. His qualification, in the minds of many, was that he was out of the country when the Kansas-Nebraska Act was passed. In the above political cartoon, Buchanan, along with Democratic senator Lewis Cass, holds down the Free-Soil advocate. Buchanan won the election, but Fremont garnered more than 33 percent of the popular vote, an impressive return for a new party. The Whigs had ceased to exist and had been replaced by the Republican Party. Know-Nothings also transferred their allegiance to the Republicans because the new party also took an anti-immigrant stance, a move that further boosted the new party's standing. (The Democrats courted the Catholic immigrant vote.) The Republican Party was a thoroughly northern party; no southern delegate voted for Fremont.

5.3 The Dred Scott Decision and Sectional Strife

By the end of this section, you will be able to:
• Explain the importance of the Supreme Court's Dred Scott ruling
• Discuss the principles of the Republican Party as expressed by Abraham Lincoln in 1858

As president, Buchanan confronted a difficult and volatile situation. The nation needed a strong personality to lead it, and Buchanan did not possess this trait. The violence in Kansas demonstrated that applying popular sovereignty—the democratic principle of majority rule—to the territory offered no solution to the national battle over slavery. A decision by the Supreme Court in 1857, which concerned the slave Dred Scott, only deepened the crisis.

DRED SCOTT

In 1857, several months after President Buchanan took the oath of office, the Supreme Court ruled in *Dred Scott v. Sandford*. Dred Scott (**Figure 5.16**), born a slave in Virginia in 1795, had been one of the thousands forced to relocate as a result of the massive internal slave trade and taken to Missouri, where slavery had been adopted as part of the Missouri Compromise. In 1820, Scott's owner took him first to Illinois and then to the Wisconsin territory. However, both of those regions were part of the Northwest Territory, where the 1787 Northwest Ordinance had prohibited slavery. When Scott returned to Missouri, he attempted to buy his freedom. After his owner refused, he sought relief in the state courts, arguing that by virtue of having lived in areas where slavery was banned, he should be free.

Figure 5.16 This 1888 portrait by Louis Schultze shows Dred Scott, who fought for his freedom through the American court system.

In a complicated set of legal decisions, a jury found that Scott, along with his wife and two children, were free. However, on appeal from Scott's owner, the state Superior Court reversed the decision, and the Scotts remained slaves. Scott then became the property of John Sanford (his name was misspelled as "Sandford" in later court documents), who lived in New York. He continued his legal battle, and because the issue involved Missouri and New York, the case fell under the jurisdiction of the federal court. In 1854, Scott lost in federal court and appealed to the United States Supreme Court.

In 1857, the Supreme Court—led by Chief Justice Roger Taney, a former slaveholder who had freed his slaves—handed down its decision. On the question of whether Scott was free, the Supreme Court decided he remained a slave. The court then went beyond the specific issue of Scott's freedom to make a sweeping and momentous judgment about the status of blacks, both free and slave. Per the court, blacks could never be citizens of the United States. Further, the court ruled that Congress had no authority to stop or limit the spread of slavery into American territories. This proslavery ruling explicitly made the Missouri Compromise unconstitutional; implicitly, it made Douglas's popular sovereignty unconstitutional.

DEFINING "AMERICAN"

⚙ *Roger Taney on Dred Scott v. Sandford*

In 1857, the United States Supreme Court ended years of legal battles when it ruled that Dred Scott, a slave who had resided in several free states, should remain a slave. The decision, written by Chief Justice Roger Taney, also stated that blacks could not be citizens and that Congress had no power to limit the spread of slavery. The excerpt below is from Taney's decision.

> A free negro of the African race, whose ancestors were brought to this country and sold as slaves, is not a "citizen" within the meaning of the Constitution of the United States. . . .
> The only two clauses in the Constitution which point to this race treat them as persons whom it was morally lawfully to deal in as articles of property and to hold as slaves. . . .
> Every citizen has a right to take with him into the Territory any article of property which the Constitution of the United States recognises as property. . . .
> The Constitution of the United States recognises slaves as property, and pledges the Federal Government to protect it. And Congress cannot exercise any more authority over property of that description than it may constitutionally exercise over property of any other kind. . . .
> Prohibiting a citizen of the United States from taking with him his slaves when he removes to the Territory . . . is an exercise of authority over private property which is not warranted by the Constitution, and the removal of the plaintiff [Dred Scott] by his owner to that Territory gave him no title to freedom.

How did the Supreme Court define Dred Scott? How did the court interpret the Constitution on this score?

The Dred Scott decision infuriated Republicans by rendering their goal—to prevent slavery's spread into the territories—unconstitutional. To Republicans, the decision offered further proof of the reach of the South's Slave Power, which now apparently extended even to the Supreme Court. The decision also complicated life for northern Democrats, especially Stephen Douglas, who could no longer sell popular sovereignty as a symbolic concession to southerners from northern voters. Few northerners favored slavery's expansion westward.

THE LINCOLN-DOUGLAS DEBATES

The turmoil in Kansas, combined with the furor over the Dred Scott decision, provided the background for the 1858 senatorial contest in Illinois between Democratic senator Stephen Douglas and Republican hopeful Abraham Lincoln (**Figure 5.17**). Lincoln and Douglas engaged in seven debates before huge crowds that met to hear the two men argue the central issue of slavery and its expansion. Newspapers throughout the United States published their speeches. Whereas Douglas already enjoyed national recognition, Lincoln remained largely unknown before the debates. These appearances provided an opportunity for him to raise his profile with both northerners and southerners.

(a)   (b)

Figure 5.17 In 1858, Abraham Lincoln (a) debated Stephen Douglas (b) seven times in the Illinois race for the U.S. Senate. Although Douglas won the seat, the debates propelled Lincoln into the national political spotlight.

Douglas portrayed the Republican Party as an abolitionist effort—one that aimed to bring about **miscegenation**, or race-mixing through sexual relations or marriage. The "black Republicans," Douglas declared, posed a dangerous threat to the Constitution. Indeed, because Lincoln declared the nation could not survive if the slave state–free state division continued, Douglas claimed the Republicans aimed to destroy what the founders had created.

For his part, Lincoln said: "A house divided against itself cannot stand. I believe this government cannot endure permanently half Slave and half Free. I do not expect the Union to be dissolved—I do not expect the house to fall—but I do expect it will cease to be divided. It will become all one thing, or all the other. Either the opponents of slavery will arrest the further spread of it, and place it where the public mind shall rest in the belief that it is in the course of ultimate extinction: or its advocates will push it forward till it shall became alike lawful in all the States—old as well as new, North as well as South." Lincoln interpreted the Dred Scott decision and the Kansas-Nebraska Act as efforts to nationalize slavery: that is, to make it legal everywhere from New England to the Midwest and beyond.

DEFINING "AMERICAN"

☉ *The Lincoln-Douglas Debates*

On August 21, 1858, Abraham Lincoln and Stephen Douglas met in Ottawa, Illinois, for the first of seven debates. People streamed into Ottawa from neighboring counties and from as far away as Chicago. Reporting on the event was strictly partisan, with each of the candidates' supporters claiming victory for their candidate. In this excerpt, Lincoln addresses the issues of equality between blacks and whites.

> [A]nything that argues me into his idea of perfect social and political equality with the negro, is but a specious and fantastic arrangement of words, . . . I have no purpose, directly or indirectly, to interfere with the institution of slavery in the States where it exists. I believe I have no lawful right to do so, and I have no inclination to do so. I have no purpose to introduce political and social equality between the white and the black races. There is a physical difference between the two, which, in my judgment, will probably forever forbid their living together upon the footing of perfect equality, . . . I, as well as Judge Douglas, am in favor of the race to which I belong having the superior position. . . . [N]otwithstanding all this, there is no reason in the world why the negro is not entitled to all the natural rights enumerated in the Declaration of Independence, the right to life, liberty, and the pursuit of happiness. I hold that he is as much entitled to these as the white man. . . . [I]n the right to eat the bread, without the leave of anybody else, which his own hand earns, he is my equal and the equal of Judge Douglas, and the equal of every living man.
> —Lincoln's speech on August 21, 1858, in Ottawa, Illinois

How would you characterize Lincoln's position on equality between blacks and whites? What types of equality exist, according to Lincoln?

Click and Explore

Go to the **Lincoln Home National Historic Site** (http://openstaxcollege.org/l/15LincDoug) on the National Park Service's website to read excerpts from and full texts of the debates. Then, visit **The Lincoln/Douglas Debates of 1858** (http://openstaxcollege.org/l/15LincDoug2) on the Northern Illinois University website to read different newspaper accounts of the debates. Do you see any major differences in the way the newspapers reported the debates? How does the commentary vary, and why?

During the debates, Lincoln demanded that Douglas explain whether or not he believed that the 1857 Supreme Court decision in the Dred Scott case trumped the right of a majority to prevent the expansion of slavery under the principle of popular sovereignty. Douglas responded to Lincoln during the second debate at Freeport, Illinois. In what became known as the **Freeport Doctrine**, Douglas adamantly upheld popular sovereignty, declaring: "It matters not what way the Supreme Court may hereafter decide as to the abstract question whether slavery may or may not go into a territory under the Constitution, the people have the lawful means to introduce it or exclude it as they please." The Freeport Doctrine antagonized southerners and caused a major rift in the Democratic Party. The doctrine did help Douglas in Illinois, however, where most voters opposed the further expansion of slavery. The Illinois legislature selected Douglas over Lincoln for the senate, but the debates had the effect of launching Lincoln into the national spotlight. Lincoln had argued that slavery was morally wrong, even as he accepted the racism inherent in slavery. He warned that Douglas and the Democrats would nationalize slavery through the policy of popular sovereignty. Though Douglas had survived the election challenge from Lincoln, his Freeport Doctrine undermined the Democratic Party as a national force.

5.4 John Brown and the Election of 1860

By the end of this section, you will be able to:
- Describe John Brown's raid on Harpers Ferry and its results
- Analyze the results of the election of 1860

Events in the late 1850s did nothing to quell the country's sectional unrest, and compromise on the issue of slavery appeared impossible. Lincoln's 1858 speeches during his debates with Douglas made the Republican Party's position well known; Republicans opposed the extension of slavery and believed a Slave Power conspiracy sought to nationalize the institution. They quickly gained political momentum and took control of the House of Representatives in 1858. Southern leaders were divided on how to respond to Republican success. Southern extremists, known as **"Fire-Eaters,"** openly called for secession. Others, like Mississippi senator Jefferson Davis, put forward a more moderate approach by demanding constitutional protection of slavery.

JOHN BROWN

In October 1859, the radical abolitionist John Brown and eighteen armed men, both blacks and whites, attacked the federal arsenal in **Harpers Ferry**, Virginia. They hoped to capture the weapons there and distribute them among slaves to begin a massive uprising that would bring an end to slavery. Brown had already demonstrated during the 1856 Pottawatomie attack in Kansas that he had no patience for the nonviolent approach preached by pacifist abolitionists like William Lloyd Garrison. Born in Connecticut in 1800, Brown (**Figure 5.18**) spent much of his life in the North, moving from Ohio to Pennsylvania and then upstate New York as his various business ventures failed. To him, slavery appeared an unacceptable evil that must be purged from the land, and like his Puritan forebears, he believed in using the sword to defeat the ungodly.

Figure 5.18 John Brown, shown here in a photograph from 1859, was a radical abolitionist who advocated the violent overthrow of slavery.

Brown had gone to Kansas in the 1850s in an effort to stop slavery, and there, he had perpetrated the killings at Pottawatomie. He told other abolitionists of his plan to take Harpers Ferry Armory and initiate a massive slave uprising. Some abolitionists provided financial support, while others, including Frederick Douglass, found the plot suicidal and refused to join. On October 16, 1859, Brown's force easily took control of the federal armory, which was unguarded (**Figure 5.19**). However, his vision of a mass uprising failed completely. Very few slaves lived in the area to rally to Brown's side, and the group found themselves holed up in the armory's engine house with townspeople taking shots at them. Federal troops, commanded by Colonel Robert E. Lee, soon captured Brown and his followers. On December 2, Brown was hanged by the state of Virginia for treason.

Figure 5.19 John Brown's raid on Harpers Ferry represented the radical abolitionist's attempt to start a revolt that would ultimately end slavery. This 1859 illustration, captioned "Harper's Ferry insurrection—Interior of the Engine-House, just before the gate is broken down by the storming party—Col. Washington and his associates as captives, held by Brown as hostages," is from *Frank Leslie's Illustrated Magazine*. Do you think this image represents a southern or northern version of the raid? How are the characters in the scene depicted?

Click and Explore

Visit the **Avalon Project** (http://openstaxcollege.org/l/15JohnBrown) on Yale Law School's website to read the impassioned speech that Henry David Thoreau delivered on October 30, 1859, arguing against the execution of John Brown. How does Thoreau characterize Brown? What does he ask of his fellow citizens?

John Brown's raid on Harpers Ferry generated intense reactions in both the South and the North. Southerners grew especially apprehensive of the possibility of other violent plots. They viewed Brown as a terrorist bent on destroying their civilization, and support for secession grew. Their anxiety led several southern states to pass laws designed to prevent slave rebellions. It seemed that the worst fears of the South had come true: A hostile majority would stop at nothing to destroy slavery. Was it possible, one resident of Maryland asked, to "live under a government, a majority of whose subjects or citizens regard John Brown as a martyr and Christian hero?" Many antislavery northerners did in fact consider Brown a martyr to the cause, and those who viewed slavery as a sin saw easy comparisons between him and Jesus Christ.

THE ELECTION OF 1860

The election of 1860 triggered the collapse of American democracy when the elevation of Abraham Lincoln to the presidency inspired secessionists in the South to withdraw their states from the Union.

Lincoln's election owed much to the disarray in the Democratic Party. The Dred Scott decision and the Freeport Doctrine had opened up huge sectional divisions among Democrats. Though Brown did not intend it, his raid had furthered the split between northern and southern Democrats. Fire-Eaters vowed to prevent a northern Democrat, especially Illinois's Stephen Douglas, from becoming their presidential candidate. These proslavery zealots insisted on a southern Democrat.

The Democratic nominating convention met in April 1860 in Charleston, South Carolina. However, it broke up after northern Democrats, who made up a majority of delegates, rejected Jefferson Davis's efforts to protect slavery in the territories. These northern Democratic delegates knew that supporting Davis on this issue would be very unpopular among the people in their states. A second conference, held in Baltimore, further illustrated the divide within the Democratic Party. Northern Democrats nominated Stephen Douglas, while southern Democrats, who met separately, put forward Vice President John Breckinridge from Kentucky. The Democratic Party had fractured into two competing sectional factions.

By offering two candidates for president, the Democrats gave the Republicans an enormous advantage. Also hoping to prevent a Republican victory, pro-Unionists from the border states organized the Constitutional Union Party and put up a fourth candidate, John Bell, for president, who pledged to end slavery agitation and preserve the Union but never fully explained how he'd accomplish this objective. In a pro-Lincoln political cartoon of the time (**Figure 5.20**), the presidential election is presented as a baseball game. Lincoln stands on home plate. A skunk raises its tail at the other candidates. Holding his nose, southern Democrat John Breckinridge holds a bat labeled "Slavery Extension" and declares "I guess I'd better leave for Kentucky, for I smell something strong around here, and begin to think, that we are completely skunk'd."

Figure 5.20 *The national game. Three "outs" and one "run"* (1860), by Currier and Ives, shows the two Democratic candidates and one Constitutional Union candidate who lost the 1860 election to Republican Lincoln, shown at right.

The Republicans nominated Lincoln, and in the November election, he garnered a mere 40 percent of the popular vote, though he won every northern state except New Jersey. (Lincoln's name was blocked from even appearing on many southern states' ballots by southern Democrats.) More importantly, Lincoln did gain a majority in the Electoral College (**Figure 5.21**). The Fire-Eaters, however, refused to accept the results. With South Carolina leading the way, Fire-Eaters in southern states began to withdraw formally from the United States in 1860. South Carolinian Mary Boykin Chesnut wrote in her diary about the reaction to the Lincoln's election. "Now that the black radical Republicans have the power," she wrote,

"I suppose they will Brown us all." Her statement revealed many southerners' fear that with Lincoln as President, the South could expect more mayhem like the John Brown raid.

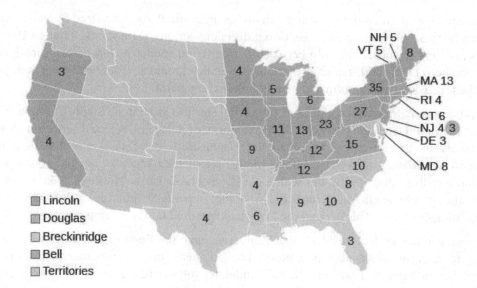

Figure 5.21 This map shows the disposition of electoral votes for the election of 1860. The votes were divided along almost perfect sectional lines.

CHAPTER 6

The Civil War, 1860–1865

Figure 6.1 This photograph by John Reekie, entitled, "A burial party on the battle-field of Cold Harbor," drives home the brutality and devastation wrought by the Civil War. Here, in April 1865, African Americans collect the bones of soldiers killed in Virginia during General Ulysses S. Grant's Wilderness Campaign of May–June 1864.

Chapter Outline

6.1 The Origins and Outbreak of the Civil War

6.2 Early Mobilization and War

6.3 1863: The Changing Nature of the War

6.4 The Union Triumphant

Introduction

In May 1864, General Ulysses S. Grant ordered the Union's Army of the Potomac to cross the Rapidan River in Virginia. Grant knew that Confederate general Robert E. Lee would defend the Confederate capital at Richmond at all costs, committing troops that might otherwise be sent to the Shenandoah or the Deep South to stop Union general William Tecumseh Sherman from capturing Atlanta, a key Confederate city. For two days, the Army of the Potomac fought Lee's troops in the Wilderness, a wooded area along the Rapidan River. Nearly ten thousand Confederate soldiers were killed or wounded, as were more than seventeen thousand Union troops. A few weeks later, the armies would meet again at the Battle of Cold Harbor, where another fifteen thousand men would be wounded or killed. As in many battles, the bodies of those who died were left on the field where they fell. A year later, African Americans, who were often called upon to perform menial labor for the Union army (**Figure 6.1**), collected the skeletal remains of the dead for a proper burial. The state of the graves of many Civil War soldiers partly inspired the creation of Memorial Day, a day set aside for visiting and decorating the graves of the dead.

6.1 The Origins and Outbreak of the Civil War

By the end of this section, you will be able to:
- Explain the major events that occurred during the Secession Crisis
- Describe the creation and founding principles of the Confederate States of America

The 1860 election of Abraham Lincoln was a turning point for the United States. Throughout the tumultuous 1850s, the Fire-Eaters of the southern states had been threatening to leave the Union. With Lincoln's election, they prepared to make good on their threats. Indeed, the Republican president-elect appeared to be their worst nightmare. The Republican Party committed itself to keeping slavery out of the territories as the country expanded westward, a position that shocked southern sensibilities. Meanwhile, southern leaders suspected that Republican abolitionists would employ the violent tactics of John Brown to deprive southerners of their slave property. The threat posed by the Republican victory in the election of 1860 spurred eleven southern states to leave the Union to form the Confederate States of America, a new republic dedicated to maintaining and expanding slavery. The Union, led by President Lincoln, was unwilling to accept the departure of these states and committed itself to restoring the country. Beginning in 1861 and continuing until 1865, the United States engaged in a brutal Civil War that claimed the lives of over 600,000 soldiers. By 1863, the conflict had become not only a war to save the Union, but also a war to end slavery in the United States. Only after four years of fighting did the North prevail. The Union was preserved, and the institution of slavery had been destroyed in the nation.

THE CAUSES OF THE CIVIL WAR

Lincoln's election sparked the southern secession fever into flame, but it did not cause the Civil War. For decades before Lincoln took office, the sectional divisions in the country had been widening. Both the Northern and southern states engaged in inflammatory rhetoric and agitation, and violent emotions ran strong on both sides. Several factors played into the ultimate split between the North and the South.

One key irritant was the question of slavery's expansion westward. The debate over whether new states would be slave or free reached back to the controversy over statehood for Missouri beginning in 1819

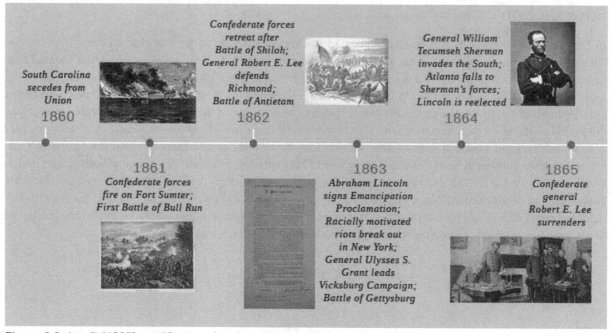

Figure 6.2 (credit "1865": modification of work by "Alaskan Dude"/Wikimedia Commons)

and Texas in the 1830s and early 1840s. This question arose again after the Mexican-American War (1846–1848), when the government debated whether slavery would be permitted in the territories taken from Mexico. Efforts in Congress to reach a compromise in 1850 fell back on the principle of popular sovereignty—letting the people in the new territories south of the 1820 Missouri Compromise line decide whether to allow slavery. This same principle came to be applied to the Kansas-Nebraska territories in 1854, a move that added fuel to the fire of sectional conflict by destroying the Missouri Compromise boundary and leading to the birth of the Republican Party. In the end, popular sovereignty proved to be no solution at all. This was especially true in "Bleeding Kansas" in the mid-1850s, as pro- and antislavery forces battled each another in an effort to gain the upper hand.

The small but very vocal abolitionist movement further contributed to the escalating tensions between the North and the South. Since the 1830s, abolitionists, led by journalist and reformer William Lloyd Garrison, had cast slavery as a national sin and called for its immediate end. For three decades, the abolitionists—a minority even within the antislavery movement—had had a significant effect on American society by bringing the evils of slavery into the public consciousness. By the 1850s, some of the most radical abolitionists, such as John Brown, had resorted to violence in their efforts to destroy the institution of slavery.

The formation of the Liberty Party (1840), the Free-Soil Party (1848), and the Republican Party (1854), all of which strongly opposed the spread of slavery to the West, brought the question solidly into the political arena. Although not all those who opposed the westward expansion of slavery had a strong abolitionist bent, the attempt to limit slaveholders' control of their human property stiffened the resolve of southern leaders to defend their society at all costs. Prohibiting slavery's expansion, they argued, ran counter to fundamental American property rights. Across the country, people of all political stripes worried that the nation's arguments would cause irreparable rifts in the country.

Despite the ruptures and tensions, by the 1860s, some hope of healing the nation still existed. Before Lincoln took office, John Crittenden, a senator from Kentucky who had helped form the Constitutional Union Party during the 1860 presidential election, attempted to diffuse the explosive situation by offering six constitutional amendments and a series of resolutions, known as the **Crittenden Compromise**. Crittenden's goal was to keep the South from seceding, and his strategy was to transform the Constitution to explicitly protect slavery forever. Specifically, Crittenden proposed an amendment that would restore the 36°30 ⌐ line from the Missouri Compromise and extend it all the way to the Pacific Ocean, protecting and ensuring slavery south of the line while prohibiting it north of the line (**Figure 6.3**). He further proposed an amendment that would prohibit Congress from abolishing slavery anywhere it already existed or from interfering with the interstate slave trade.

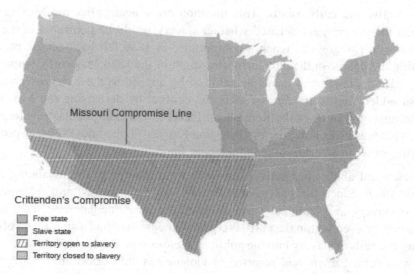

Figure 6.3 Crittenden's Compromise would protect slavery in all states where it already existed. More importantly, however, it proposed to allow the western expansion of slavery into states below the Missouri Compromise line.

Republicans, including President-elect Lincoln, rejected Crittenden's proposals because they ran counter to the party's goal of keeping slavery out of the territories. The southern states also rejected Crittenden's attempts at compromise, because it would prevent slaveholders from taking their human chattel north of the 36°30ʹ line. On December 20, 1860, only a few days after Crittenden's proposal was introduced in Congress, South Carolina began the march towards war when it seceded from the United States. Three more states of the Deep South—Mississippi, Florida, and Alabama—seceded before the U.S. Senate rejected Crittenden's proposal on January 16, 1861. Georgia, Louisiana, and Texas joined them in rapid succession on January 19, January 26, and February 1, respectively (**Figure 6.4**). In many cases, these secessions occurred after extremely divided conventions and popular votes. A lack of unanimity prevailed in much of the South.

Figure 6.4 Georgia's Ordinance of Secession and those of the other Deep South states were all based on that of South Carolina, which was drafted just a month after Abraham Lincoln was elected.

THE CREATION OF THE CONFEDERATE STATES OF AMERICA

The seven Deep South states that seceded quickly formed a new government. In the opinion of many Southern politicians, the federal Constitution that united the states as one nation was a contract by which individual states had agreed to be bound. However, they maintained, the states had not sacrificed their autonomy and could withdraw their consent to be controlled by the federal government. In their eyes, their actions were in keeping with the nature of the Constitution and the social contract theory of government that had influenced the founders of the American Republic.

The new nation formed by these men would not be a federal union, but a confederation. In a confederation, individual member states agree to unite under a central government for some purposes, such as defense, but to retain autonomy in other areas of government. In this way, states could protect themselves, and slavery, from interference by what they perceived to be an overbearing central government. The constitution of the Confederate States of America (CSA), or the **Confederacy**, drafted at a convention in Montgomery, Alabama, in February 1861, closely followed the 1787 Constitution. The only real difference between the two documents centered on slavery. The Confederate Constitution declared that the new nation existed to defend and perpetuate racial slavery, and the leadership of the slaveholding class. Specifically, the constitution protected the interstate slave trade, guaranteed that slavery would exist in any new territory gained by the Confederacy, and, perhaps most importantly, in Article One, Section Nine, declared that "No . . . law impairing or denying the right of property in negro slaves shall be passed." Beyond its focus on slavery, the Confederate Constitution resembled the 1787 U.S. Constitution. It allowed for a Congress composed of two chambers, a judicial branch, and an executive branch with a president to serve for six years.

The convention delegates chose Jefferson Davis of Mississippi to lead the new provisional government as president and Alexander Stephens of Georgia to serve as vice president until elections could be held in the spring and fall of 1861. By that time, four new states—Virginia, Arkansas, Tennessee, and North Carolina—had joined the CSA. As 1861 progressed, the Confederacy claimed Missouri and Kentucky, even though no ordinance of secession had been approved in those states. Southern nationalism ran high, and the Confederacy, buoyed by its sense of purpose, hoped that their new nation would achieve eminence in the world.

By the time Lincoln reached Washington, DC, in February 1861, the CSA had already been established. The new president confronted an unprecedented crisis. A conference held that month with delegates from the Southern states failed to secure a promise of peace or to restore the Union. On inauguration day, March 4, 1861, the new president repeated his views on slavery: "I have no purpose, directly or indirectly, to interfere with the institution of slavery in the States where it exists. I believe I have no lawful right to do so, and I have no inclination to do so." His recognition of slavery in the South did nothing to mollify slaveholders, however, because Lincoln also pledged to keep slavery from expanding into the new western territories. Furthermore, in his inaugural address, Lincoln made clear his commitment to maintaining federal power against the secessionists working to destroy it. Lincoln declared that the Union could not be dissolved by individual state actions, and, therefore, secession was unconstitutional.

Click and Explore

Read Lincoln's entire inaugural address (http://openstaxcollege.org/l/ 15LincAddress) at the Yale Avalon project's website. How would Lincoln's audience have responded to this speech?

FORT SUMTER

President Lincoln made it clear to Southern secessionists that he would fight to maintain federal property and to keep the Union intact. Other politicians, however, still hoped to avoid the use of force to resolve the crisis. In February 1861, in an effort to entice the rebellious states to return to the Union without resorting to force, Thomas Corwin, a representative from Ohio, introduced a proposal to amend the Constitution in the House of Representatives. His was but one of several measures proposed in January and February 1861, to head off the impending conflict and save the United States. The proposed amendment would have made it impossible for Congress to pass any law abolishing slavery. The proposal passed the House on February 28, 1861, and the Senate passed the proposal on March 2, 1861. It was then sent to the states to be ratified. Once ratified by three-quarters of state legislatures, it would become law. In his inaugural address, Lincoln stated that he had no objection to the amendment, and his predecessor James Buchanan had supported it. By the time of Lincoln's inauguration, however, seven states had already left the Union. Of the remaining states, Ohio ratified the amendment in 1861, and Maryland and Illinois did so in 1862. Despite this effort at reconciliation, the Confederate states did not return to the Union.

Indeed, by the time of the Corwin amendment's passage through Congress, Confederate forces in the Deep South had already begun to take over federal forts. The loss of **Fort Sumter**, in the harbor of Charleston, South Carolina, proved to be the flashpoint in the contest between the new Confederacy and the federal government. A small Union garrison of fewer than one hundred soldiers and officers held the fort, making it a vulnerable target for the Confederacy. Fire-Eaters pressured Jefferson Davis to take Fort Sumter and thereby demonstrate the Confederate government's resolve. Some also hoped that the Confederacy would gain foreign recognition, especially from Great Britain, by taking the fort in the South's most important Atlantic port. The situation grew dire as local merchants refused to sell food to the fort's Union soldiers, and by mid-April, the garrison's supplies began to run out. President Lincoln let it be known to Confederate leaders that he planned to resupply the Union forces. His strategy was clear: The decision to start the war would rest squarely on the Confederates, not on the Union. On April 12, 1861, Confederate forces in Charleston began a bombardment of Fort Sumter (**Figure 6.5**). Two days later, the Union soldiers there surrendered.

Figure 6.5 The Confederacy's attack on Fort Sumter, depicted here in an 1861 lithograph by Currier and Ives, stoked pro-war sentiment on both sides of the conflict.

The attack on Fort Sumter meant war had come, and on April 15, 1861, Lincoln called upon loyal states to supply armed forces to defeat the rebellion and regain Fort Sumter. Faced with the need to choose between the Confederacy and the Union, border states and those of the Upper South, which earlier had been reluctant to dissolve their ties with the United States, were inspired to take action. They quickly voted for secession. A convention in Virginia that had been assembled earlier to consider the question of secession voted to join the Confederacy on April 17, two days after Lincoln called for troops. Arkansas left the Union on May 6 along with Tennessee one day later. North Carolina followed on May 20.

Not all residents of the border states and the Upper South wished to join the Confederacy, however. Pro-Union feelings remained strong in Tennessee, especially in the eastern part of the state where slaves were few and consisted largely of house servants owned by the wealthy. The state of Virginia—home of revolutionary leaders and presidents such as George Washington, Thomas Jefferson, James Madison, and James Monroe—literally was split on the issue of secession. Residents in the north and west of the state, where few slaveholders resided, rejected secession. These counties subsequently united to form "West Virginia," which entered the Union as a free state in 1863. The rest of Virginia, including the historic lands along the Chesapeake Bay that were home to such early American settlements as Jamestown and Williamsburg, joined the Confederacy. The addition of this area gave the Confederacy even greater hope and brought General Robert E. Lee, arguably the best military commander of the day, to their side. In addition, the secession of Virginia brought Washington, DC, perilously close to the Confederacy, and fears that the border state of Maryland would also join the CSA, thus trapping the U.S. capital within Confederate territories, plagued Lincoln.

The Confederacy also gained the backing of the Five Civilized Tribes, as they were called, in the Indian Territory. The Five Civilized Tribes comprised the Choctaws, Chickasaws, Creeks, Seminoles, and Cherokees. The tribes supported slavery and many members owned slaves. These Indian slaveholders, who had been forced from their lands in Georgia and elsewhere in the Deep South during the presidency of Andrew Jackson, now found unprecedented common cause with white slaveholders. The CSA even allowed them to send delegates to the Confederate Congress.

While most slaveholding states joined the Confederacy, four crucial slave states remained in the Union (**Figure 6.6**). Delaware, which was technically a slave state despite its tiny slave population, never voted to secede. Maryland, despite deep divisions, remained in the Union as well. Missouri became the site of vicious fighting and the home of pro-Confederate guerillas but never joined the Confederacy. Kentucky declared itself neutral, although that did little to stop the fighting that occurred within the state. In all, these four states deprived the Confederacy of key resources and soldiers.

Figure 6.6 This map illustrates the southern states that seceded from the Union and formed the Confederacy in 1861, at the outset of the Civil War.

6.2 Early Mobilization and War

By the end of this section, you will be able to:
- Assess the strengths and weaknesses of the Confederacy and the Union
- Explain the strategic importance of the Battle of Bull Run and the Battle of Shiloh

In 1861, enthusiasm for war ran high on both sides. The North fought to restore the Union, which Lincoln declared could never be broken. The Confederacy, which by the summer of 1861 consisted of eleven states, fought for its independence from the United States. The continuation of slavery was a central issue in the war, of course, although abolitionism and western expansion also played roles, and Northerners and Southerners alike flocked eagerly to the conflict. Both sides thought it would be over quickly. Militarily, however, the North and South were more equally matched than Lincoln had realized, and it soon became clear that the war effort would be neither brief nor painless. In 1861, Americans in both the North and South romanticized war as noble and positive. Soon the carnage and slaughter would awaken them to the horrors of war.

THE FIRST BATTLE OF BULL RUN

After the fall of Fort Sumter on April 15, 1861, Lincoln called for seventy-five thousand volunteers from state militias to join federal forces. His goal was a ninety-day campaign to put down the Southern rebellion. The response from state militias was overwhelming, and the number of Northern troops exceeded the requisition. Also in April, Lincoln put in place a naval blockade of the South, a move that gave tacit recognition of the Confederacy while providing a legal excuse for the British and the French to trade with Southerners. The Confederacy responded to the blockade by declaring that a state of war existed with the United States. This official pronouncement confirmed the beginning of the Civil War. Men rushed to enlist, and the Confederacy turned away tens of thousands who hoped to defend the new nation.

Many believed that a single, heroic battle would decide the contest. Some questioned how committed Southerners really were to their cause. Northerners hoped that most Southerners would not actually fire on the American flag. Meanwhile, Lincoln and military leaders in the North hoped a quick blow to the South, especially if they could capture the Confederacy's new capital of Richmond, Virginia, would end the rebellion before it went any further. On July 21, 1861, the two armies met near Manassas, Virginia, along Bull Run Creek, only thirty miles from Washington, DC. So great was the belief that this would be a climactic Union victory that many Washington socialites and politicians brought picnic lunches to a nearby area, hoping to witness history unfolding before them. At the First Battle of Bull Run, also known as First Manassas, some sixty thousand troops assembled, most of whom had never seen combat, and each side sent eighteen thousand into the fray. The Union forces attacked first, only to be pushed back. The Confederate forces then carried the day, sending the Union soldiers and Washington, DC, onlookers scrambling back from Virginia and destroying Union hopes of a quick, decisive victory. Instead, the war would drag on for four long, deadly years (**Figure 6.7**).

Figure 6.7 The First Battle of Bull Run, which many Northerners thought would put a quick and decisive end to the South's rebellion, ended with a Confederate victory.

BALANCE SHEET: THE UNION AND THE CONFEDERACY

As it became clearer that the Union would not be dealing with an easily quashed rebellion, the two sides assessed their strengths and weaknesses. At the onset on the war, in 1861 and 1862, they stood as relatively equal combatants.

The Confederates had the advantage of being able to wage a defensive war, rather than an offensive one. They had to protect and preserve their new boundaries, but they did not have to be the aggressors against the Union. The war would be fought primarily in the South, which gave the Confederates the advantages of the knowledge of the terrain and the support of the civilian population. Further, the vast coastline from Texas to Virginia offered ample opportunities to evade the Union blockade. And with the addition of the Upper South states, especially Virginia, North Carolina, Tennessee, and Arkansas, the Confederacy gained a much larger share of natural resources and industrial might than the Deep South states could muster.

Still, the Confederacy had disadvantages. The South's economy depended heavily on the export of cotton, but with the naval blockade, the flow of cotton to England, the region's primary importer, came to an end. The blockade also made it difficult to import manufactured goods. Although the secession of the Upper South added some industrial assets to the Confederacy, overall, the South lacked substantive industry or an extensive railroad infrastructure to move men and supplies. To deal with the lack of commerce and the resulting lack of funds, the Confederate government began printing paper money, leading to runaway inflation (**Figure 6.8**). The advantage that came from fighting on home territory quickly turned to a disadvantage when Confederate armies were defeated and Union forces destroyed Southern farms and towns, and forced Southern civilians to take to the road as refugees. Finally, the population of the South stood at fewer than nine million people, of whom nearly four million were black slaves, compared to over twenty million residents in the North. These limited numbers became a major factor as the war dragged on and the death toll rose.

Figure 6.8 The Confederacy started printing paper money at an accelerated rate, causing runaway inflation and an economy in which formerly well-off people were unable to purchase food.

The Union side held many advantages as well. Its larger population, bolstered by continued immigration from Europe throughout the 1860s, gave it greater manpower reserves to draw upon. The North's greater industrial capabilities and extensive railroad grid made it far better able to mobilize men and supplies for the war effort. The Industrial Revolution and the transportation revolution, beginning in the 1820s and continuing over the next several decades, had transformed the North. Throughout the war, the North was able to produce more war materials and move goods more quickly than the South. Furthermore, the farms of New England, the Mid-Atlantic, the Old Northwest, and the prairie states supplied Northern civilians and Union troops with abundant food throughout the war. Food shortages and hungry civilians were common in the South, where the best land was devoted to raising cotton, but not in the North.

Unlike the South, however, which could hunker down to defend itself and needed to maintain relatively short supply lines, the North had to go forth and conquer. Union armies had to establish long supply lines, and Union soldiers had to fight on unfamiliar ground and contend with a hostile civilian population off the battlefield. Furthermore, to restore the Union—Lincoln's overriding goal, in 1861—the United States, after defeating the Southern forces, would then need to pacify a conquered Confederacy, an area of over half a million square miles with nearly nine million residents. In short, although it had better resources and a larger population, the Union faced a daunting task against the well-positioned Confederacy.

MILITARY STALEMATE

The military forces of the Confederacy and the Union battled in 1861 and early 1862 without either side gaining the upper hand. The majority of military leaders on both sides had received the same military education and often knew one another personally, either from their time as students at West Point or as commanding officers in the Mexican-American War. This familiarity allowed them to anticipate each other's strategies. Both sides believed in the use of concentrated armies charged with taking the capital city of the enemy. For the Union, this meant the capture of the Confederate capital in Richmond, Virginia, whereas Washington, DC, stood as the prize for Confederate forces. After hopes of a quick victory faded at Bull Run, the months dragged on without any major movement on either side (**Figure 6.9**).

Figure 6.9 As this cartoon indicates, the fighting strategy at the beginning of the war included watchful waiting by the leaders of the North and South.

General George B. McClellan, the **general in chief** of the army, responsible for overall control of Union land forces, proved especially reluctant to engage in battle with the Confederates. In direct command of the **Army of the Potomac**, the Union fighting force operating outside Washington, DC, McClellan believed, incorrectly, that Confederate forces were too strong to defeat and was reluctant to risk his troops in battle. His cautious nature made him popular with his men but not with the president or Congress. By 1862, however, both President Lincoln and the new Secretary of War Edwin Stanton had tired of waiting. The Union put forward a new effort to bolster troop strength, enlisting one million men to serve for three-year stints in the Army of the Potomac. In January 1862, Lincoln and Stanton ordered McClellan to invade the Confederacy with the goal of capturing Richmond.

To that end, General McClellan slowly moved 100,000 soldiers of the Army of the Potomac toward Richmond but stopped a few miles outside the city. As he did so, a Confederate force led by Thomas "Stonewall" Jackson moved north to take Washington, DC. To fend off Jackson's attack, somewhere between one-quarter and one-third of McClellan's soldiers, led by Major General Irvin McDowell, returned to defend the nation's capital, a move that Jackson hoped would leave the remaining troops near Richmond more vulnerable. Having succeeding in drawing off a sizable portion of the Union force, he joined General Lee to launch an attack on McClellan's remaining soldiers near Richmond. From June 25 to July 1, 1862, the two sides engaged in the brutal Seven Days Battles that killed or wounded almost twenty thousand Confederate and ten thousand Union soldiers. McClellan's army finally returned north, having failed to take Richmond.

General Lee, flush from his success at keeping McClellan out of Richmond, tried to capitalize on the Union's failure by taking the fighting northward. He moved his forces into northern Virginia, where, at the Second Battle of Bull Run, the Confederates again defeated the Union forces. Lee then pressed into Maryland, where his troops met the much larger Union forces near Sharpsburg, at Antietam Creek. The ensuing one-day battle on September 17, 1862, led to a tremendous loss of life. Although there are varying opinions about the total number of deaths, eight thousand soldiers were killed or wounded, more than on any other single day of combat. Once again, McClellan, mistakenly believing that the Confederate troops outnumbered his own, held back a significant portion of his forces. Lee withdrew from the field first, but McClellan, fearing he was outnumbered, refused to pursue him.

The Union army's inability to destroy Lee's army at Antietam made it clear to Lincoln that McClellan would never win the war, and the president was forced to seek a replacement. Lincoln wanted someone who could deliver a decisive Union victory. He also personally disliked McClellan, who referred to the president as a "baboon" and a "gorilla," and constantly criticized his decisions. Lincoln chose General Ambrose E. Burnside to replace McClellan as commander of the Army of the Potomac, but Burnside's efforts to push into Virginia failed in December 1862, as Confederates held their position at Fredericksburg and devastated Burnside's forces with heavy artillery fire. The Union's defeat at Fredericksburg harmed morale in the North but bolstered Confederate spirits. By the end of 1862, the Confederates were still holding their ground in Virginia. Burnside's failure led Lincoln to make another change in leadership, and Joseph "Fighting Joe" Hooker took over command of the Army of the Potomac in January 1863.

General Ulysses S. Grant's **Army of the West**, operating in Kentucky, Tennessee, and the Mississippi River Valley, had been more successful. In the western campaign, the goal of both the Union and the Confederacy was to gain control of the major rivers in the west, especially the Mississippi. If the Union could control the Mississippi, the Confederacy would be split in two. The fighting in this campaign initially centered in Tennessee, where Union forces commanded by Grant pushed Confederate troops back and gained control of the state. The major battle in the western theater took place at Pittsburgh Landing, Tennessee, on April 6 and 7, 1862. Grant's army was camped on the west side of the Tennessee River near a small log church called Shiloh, which gave the battle its name. On Sunday morning, April 6, Confederate forces under General Albert Sidney Johnston attacked Grant's encampment with the goal of separating them from their supply line on the Tennessee River and driving them into the swamps on the river's western side, where they could be destroyed. Union general William Tecumseh Sherman tried to rally the Union forces as Grant, who had been convalescing from an injured leg when the attack began and was unable to walk without crutches, called for reinforcements and tried to mount a defense. Many of Union troops fled in terror.

Unfortunately for the Confederates, Johnston was killed on the afternoon of the first day. Leadership of the Southern forces fell to General P. G. T. Beauregard, who ordered an assault at the end of that day. This assault was so desperate that one of the two attacking columns did not even have ammunition. Heavily reinforced Union forces counterattacked the next day, and the Confederate forces were routed. Grant had maintained the Union foothold in the western part of the Confederacy. The North could now concentrate on its efforts to gain control of the Mississippi River, splitting the Confederacy in two and depriving it of its most important water route.

Click and Explore

Read a first-hand account (http://openstaxcollege.org/l/15HMStanley) from a Confederate soldier at the Battle at Shiloh, followed by the perspective of a Union soldier (http://openstaxcollege.org/l/15CFBoyd) at the same battle.

In the spring and summer of 1862, the Union was successful in gaining control of part of the Mississippi River. In April 1862, the Union navy under Admiral David Farragut fought its way past the forts that guarded New Orleans and fired naval guns upon the below-sea-level city. When it became obvious that New Orleans could no longer be defended, Confederate major general Marshall Lovell sent his artillery upriver to Vicksburg, Mississippi. Armed civilians in New Orleans fought the Union forces that entered the city. They also destroyed ships and military supplies that might be used by the Union. Upriver, Union naval forces also bombarded Fort Pillow, forty miles from Memphis, Tennessee, a Southern industrial center and one of the largest cities in the Confederacy. On June 4, 1862, the Confederate defenders abandoned the fort. On June 6, Memphis fell to the Union after the ships defending it were destroyed.

6.3 1863: The Changing Nature of the War

By the end of this section, you will be able to:
- Explain what is meant by the term "total war" and provide examples
- Describe mobilization efforts in the North and the South
- Explain why 1863 was a pivotal year in the war

Wars have their own logic; they last far longer than anyone anticipates at the beginning of hostilities. As they drag on, the energy and zeal that marked the entry into warfare often wane, as losses increase and people on both sides suffer the tolls of war. The American Civil War is a case study of this characteristic of modern war.

Although Northerners and Southerners both anticipated that the battle between the Confederacy and the Union would be settled quickly, it soon became clear to all that there was no resolution in sight. The longer the war continued, the more it began to affect life in both the North and the South. Increased need for manpower, the issue of slavery, and the ongoing challenges of keeping the war effort going changed the way life on both sides as the conflict progressed.

MASS MOBILIZATION

By late 1862, the course of the war had changed to take on the characteristics of **total war**, in which armies attempt to demoralize the enemy by both striking military targets and disrupting their opponent's ability to wage war through destruction of their resources. In this type of war, armies often make no distinction between civilian and military targets. Both the Union and Confederate forces moved toward total war, although neither side ever entirely abolished the distinction between military and civilian. Total war also requires governments to mobilize all resources, extending their reach into their citizens' lives as never before. Another reality of war that became apparent in 1862 and beyond was the influence of combat on the size and scope of government. Both the Confederacy and the Union governments had to continue to grow in order to manage the logistics of recruiting men and maintaining, feeding, and equipping an army.

Confederate Mobilization

The Confederate government in Richmond, Virginia, exercised sweeping powers to ensure victory, in stark contradiction to the states' rights sentiments held by many Southern leaders. The initial emotional outburst of enthusiasm for war in the Confederacy waned, and the Confederate government instituted a military draft in April 1862. Under the terms of the draft, all men between the ages of eighteen and thirty-five would serve three years. The draft had a different effect on men of different socioeconomic classes. One loophole permitted men to hire substitutes instead of serving in the Confederate army. This provision favored the wealthy over the poor, and led to much resentment and resistance. Exercising its power over the states, the Confederate Congress denied state efforts to circumvent the draft.

In order to fund the war, the Confederate government also took over the South's economy. The government ran Southern industry and built substantial transportation and industrial infrastructure to make the weapons of war. Over the objections of slaveholders, it impressed slaves, seizing these workers from their owners and forcing them to work on fortifications and rail lines. Concerned about the resistance to and unhappiness with the government measures, in 1862, the Confederate Congress gave President Davis the power to suspend the writ of **habeas corpus**, the right of those arrested to be brought before a judge or court to determine whether there is cause to hold the prisoner. With a stated goal of bolstering national security in the fledgling republic, this change meant that the Confederacy could arrest and detain indefinitely any suspected enemy without giving a reason. This growth of the Confederate central government stood as a glaring contradiction to the earlier states' rights argument of pro-Confederate advocates.

The war efforts were costing the new nation dearly. Nevertheless, the Confederate Congress heeded the pleas of wealthy plantation owners and refused to place a tax on slaves or cotton, despite the Confederacy's desperate need for the revenue that such a tax would have raised. Instead, the Confederacy drafted a taxation plan that kept the Southern elite happy but in no way met the needs of the war. The government also resorted to printing immense amounts of paper money, which quickly led to runaway inflation. Food prices soared, and poor, white Southerners faced starvation. In April 1863, thousands of hungry people rioted in Richmond, Virginia (**Figure 6.10**). Many of the rioters were mothers who could not feed their children. The riot ended when President Davis threatened to have Confederate forces open fire on the crowds.

Figure 6.10 Rampant inflation in the 1860s made food too expensive for many Southerners, leading to widespread starvation.

One of the reasons that the Confederacy was so economically devastated was its ill-advised gamble that cotton sales would continue during the war. The government had high hopes that Great Britain and France, which both used cotton as the raw material in their textile mills, would ensure the South's economic strength—and therefore victory in the war—by continuing to buy. Furthermore, the Confederate government hoped that Great Britain and France would make loans to their new nation in order to ensure the continued flow of raw materials. These hopes were never realized. Great Britain in particular did not wish to risk war with the United States, which would have meant the invasion of Canada. The United States was also a major source of grain for Britain and an important purchaser of British goods. Furthermore, the blockade made Southern trade with Europe difficult. Instead, Great Britain, the major consumer of American cotton, found alternate sources in India and Egypt, leaving the South without the income or alliance it had anticipated.

Dissent within the Confederacy also affected the South's ability to fight the war. Confederate politicians disagreed over the amount of power that the central government should be allowed to exercise. Many states' rights advocates, who favored a weak central government and supported the sovereignty of individual states, resented President Davis's efforts to conscript troops, impose taxation to pay for the war, and requisition necessary resources. Governors in the Confederate states often proved reluctant to provide supplies or troops for the use of the Confederate government. Even Jefferson Davis's vice president Alexander Stephens opposed conscription, the seizure of slave property to work for the Confederacy, and suspension of habeas corpus. Class divisions also divided Confederates. Poor whites resented the ability of wealthy slaveholders to excuse themselves from military service. Racial tensions plagued the

South as well. On those occasions when free blacks volunteered to serve in the Confederate army, they were turned away, and enslaved African Americans were regarded with fear and suspicion, as whites whispered among themselves about the possibility of slave insurrections.

Union Mobilization

Mobilization for war proved to be easier in the North than it was in the South. During the war, the federal government in Washington, DC, like its Southern counterpart, undertook a wide range of efforts to ensure its victory over the Confederacy. To fund the war effort and finance the expansion of Union infrastructure, Republicans in Congress drastically expanded government activism, impacting citizens' everyday lives through measures such as new types of taxation. The government also contracted with major suppliers of food, weapons, and other needed materials. Virtually every sector of the Northern economy became linked to the war effort.

In keeping with their longstanding objective of keeping slavery out of the newly settled western territories, the Republicans in Congress (the dominant party) passed several measures in 1862. First, the Homestead Act provided generous inducements for Northerners to relocate and farm in the West. Settlers could lay claim to 160 acres of federal land by residing on the property for five years and improving it. The act not only motivated free-labor farmers to move west, but it also aimed to increase agricultural output for the war effort. The federal government also turned its attention to creating a transcontinental railroad to facilitate the movement of people and goods across the country. Congress chartered two companies, the Union Pacific and the Central Pacific, and provided generous funds for these two businesses to connect the country by rail.

The Republican emphasis on free labor, rather than slave labor, also influenced the 1862 Land Grant College Act, commonly known as the Morrill Act after its author, Vermont Republican senator Justin Smith Morrill. The measure provided for the creation of agricultural colleges, funded through federal grants, to teach the latest agricultural techniques. Each state in the Union would be granted thirty thousand acres of federal land for the use of these institutions of higher education.

Congress paid for the war using several strategies. They levied a tax on the income of the wealthy, as well as a tax on all inheritances. They also put high tariffs in place. Finally, they passed two National Bank Acts, one in 1863 and one in 1864, calling on the U.S. Treasury to issue war bonds and on Union banks to buy the bonds. A Union campaign to convince individuals to buy the bonds helped increase sales. The Republicans also passed the Legal Tender Act of 1862, calling for paper money—known as **greenbacks**—to be printed **Figure 6.11**). Some $150 million worth of greenbacks became legal tender, and the Northern economy boomed, although high inflation also resulted.

Figure 6.11 The Union began printing these paper "greenbacks" to use as legal tender as one of its strategies for funding the war effort.

Like the Confederacy, the Union turned to conscription to provide the troops needed for the war. In March 1863, Congress passed the Enrollment Act, requiring all unmarried men between the ages of twenty   and twenty-five, and all married men between the ages of thirty-five and forty-five—including immigrants who had filed for citizenship—to register with the Union to fight in the Civil War. All who registered were subject to military service, and draftees were selected by a lottery system (**Figure 6.12**). As in the South, a loophole in the law allowed individuals to hire substitutes if they could afford it. Others could avoid enlistment by paying $300 to the federal government. In keeping with the Supreme Court decision in *Dred Scott v. Sandford*, African Americans were not citizens and were therefore exempt from the draft.

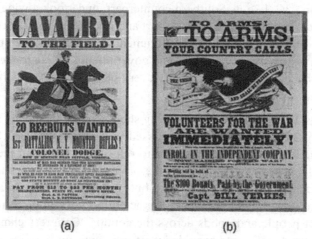

(a)   (b)

Figure 6.12 The Union tried to provide additional incentives for soldiers, in the form of bounties, to enlist without waiting for the draft, as shown in recruitment posters (a) and (b).

Like the Confederacy, the Union also took the step of suspending habeas corpus rights, so those suspected of pro-Confederate sympathies could be arrested and held without being given the reason. Lincoln had selectively suspended the writ of habeas corpus in the slave state of Maryland, home to many Confederate sympathizers, in 1861 and 1862, in an effort to ensure that the Union capital would be safe. In March 1863, he signed into law the Habeas Corpus Suspension Act, giving him the power to detain suspected Confederate operatives throughout the Union. The Lincoln administration also closed down three hundred newspapers as a national security measure during the war.

In both the North and the South, the Civil War dramatically increased the power of the belligerent governments. Breaking all past precedents in American history, both the Confederacy and the Union employed the power of their central governments to mobilize resources and citizens.

Women's Mobilization

As men on both sides mobilized for the war, so did women. In both the North and the South, women were forced to take over farms and businesses abandoned by their husbands as they left for war. Women organized themselves into ladies' aid societies to sew uniforms, knit socks, and raise money to purchase necessities for the troops. In the South, women took wounded soldiers into their homes to nurse. In the North, women volunteered for the United States Sanitary Commission, which formed in June 1861. They inspected military camps with the goal of improving cleanliness and reducing the number of soldiers who died from disease, the most common cause of death in the war. They also raised money to buy medical supplies and helped with the injured. Other women found jobs in the Union army as cooks and laundresses. Thousands volunteered to care for the sick and wounded in response to a call by reformer Dorothea Dix, who was placed in charge of the Union army's nurses. According to rumor, Dix sought respectable women over the age of thirty who were "plain almost to repulsion in dress" and thus could be trusted not to form romantic liaisons with soldiers. Women on both sides also acted as spies and, disguised as men, engaged in combat.

EMANCIPATION

Early in the war, President Lincoln approached the issue of slavery cautiously. While he disapproved of slavery personally, he did not believe that he had the authority to abolish it. Furthermore, he feared that making the abolition of slavery an objective of the war would cause the border slave states to join the Confederacy. His one objective in 1861 and 1862 was to restore the Union.

DEFINING "AMERICAN"

⚙ *Lincoln's Evolving Thoughts on Slavery*

President Lincoln wrote the following letter to newspaper editor Horace Greeley on August 22, 1862. In it, Lincoln states his position on slavery, which is notable for being a middle-of-the-road stance. Lincoln's later public speeches on the issue take the more strident antislavery tone for which he is remembered.

> I would save the Union. I would save it the shortest way under the Constitution. The sooner the national authority can be restored the nearer the Union will be "the Union as it was." If there be those who would not save the Union unless they could at the same time save Slavery, I do not agree with them. If there be those who would not save the Union unless they could at the same time destroy Slavery, I do not agree with them. My paramount object in this struggle is to save the Union, and is not either to save or destroy Slavery. If I could save the Union without freeing any slave, I would do it, and if I could save it by freeing all the slaves, I would do it, and if I could save it by freeing some and leaving others alone, I would also do that. What I do about Slavery and the colored race, I do because I believe it helps to save this Union, and what I forbear, I forbear because I do not believe it would help to save the Union. I shall do less whenever I shall believe what I am doing hurts the cause, and I shall do more whenever I shall believe doing more will help the cause. I shall try to correct errors when shown to be errors; and I shall adopt new views so fast as they shall appear to be true views. I have here stated my purpose according to my view of official duty, and I intend no modification of my oft-expressed personal wish that all men, everywhere, could be free. Yours, A. LINCOLN.

How would you characterize Lincoln's public position in August 1862? What was he prepared to do for slaves, and under what conditions?

Since the beginning of the war, thousands of slaves had fled to the safety of Union lines. In May 1861, Union general Benjamin Butler and others labeled these refugees from slavery **contrabands**. Butler reasoned that since Southern states had left the United States, he was not obliged to follow federal fugitive slave laws. Slaves who made it through the Union lines were shielded by the U.S. military and not returned to slavery. The intent was not only to assist slaves but also to deprive the South of a valuable source of manpower.

Congress began to define the status of these ex-slaves in 1861 and 1862. In August 1861, legislators approved the Confiscation Act of 1861, empowering the Union to seize property, including slaves, used by the Confederacy. The Republican-dominated Congress took additional steps, abolishing slavery in Washington, DC, in April 1862. Congress passed a second Confiscation Act in July 1862, which extended freedom to runaway slaves and those captured by Union armies. In that month, Congress also addressed the issue of slavery in the West, banning the practice in the territories. This federal law made the 1846 Wilmot Proviso and the dreams of the Free-Soil Party a reality. However, even as the Union government took steps to aid individual slaves and to limit the practice of slavery, it passed no measure to address the institution of slavery as a whole.

Lincoln moved slowly and cautiously on the issue of abolition. His primary concern was the cohesion of the Union and the bringing of the Southern states back into the fold. However, as the war dragged on and many thousands of contrabands made their way north, Republicans in Congress continued to call for the end of slavery. Throughout his political career, Lincoln's plans for former slaves had been to send them to

Liberia. As late as August 1862, he had hoped to interest African Americans in building a colony for former slaves in Central America, an idea that found favor neither with black leaders nor with abolitionists, and thus was abandoned by Lincoln. Responding to Congressional demands for an end to slavery, Lincoln presented an ultimatum to the Confederates on September 22, 1862, shortly after the Confederate retreat at Antietam. He gave the Confederate states until January 1, 1863, to rejoin the Union. If they did, slavery would continue in the slave states. If they refused to rejoin, however, the war would continue and all slaves would be freed at its conclusion. The Confederacy took no action. It had committed itself to maintaining its independence and had no interest in the president's ultimatum.

On January 1, 1863, Lincoln made good on his promise and signed the **Emancipation Proclamation**. It stated "That on the first day of January, in the year of our Lord one thousand eight hundred and sixty-three, all persons held as slaves within any State or designated part of a State, the people whereof shall then be in rebellion against the United States, shall be then, thenceforward, and forever free." The proclamation did not immediately free the slaves in the Confederate states. Although they were in rebellion against the United States, the lack of the Union army's presence in such areas meant that the president's directive could not be enforced. The proclamation also did not free slaves in the border states, because these states were not, by definition, in rebellion. Lincoln relied on his powers as commander-in-chief in issuing the Emancipation Proclamation. He knew the proclamation could be easily challenged in court, but by excluding the territories still outside his control, slaveholders and slave governments could not sue him. Moreover, slave states in the Union, such as Kentucky, could not sue because the proclamation did not apply to them. Slaveholders in Kentucky knew full well that if the institution were abolished throughout the South, it would not survive in a handful of border territories. Despite the limits of the proclamation, Lincoln dramatically shifted the objective of the war increasingly toward ending slavery. The Emancipation Proclamation became a monumental step forward on the road to changing the character of the United States.

Click and Explore

Read through the full text of the **Emancipation Proclamation** (http://openstaxcollege.org/l/15Emancipation) at the National Archives website.

The proclamation generated quick and dramatic reactions. The news created euphoria among slaves, as it signaled the eventual end of their bondage. Predictably, Confederate leaders raged against the proclamation, reinforcing their commitment to fight to maintain slavery, the foundation of the Confederacy. In the North, opinions split widely on the issue. Abolitionists praised Lincoln's actions, which they saw as the fulfillment of their long campaign to strike down an immoral institution. But other Northerners, especially Irish, working-class, urban dwellers loyal to the Democratic Party and others with racist beliefs, hated the new goal of emancipation and found the idea of freed slaves repugnant. At its core, much of this racism had an economic foundation: Many Northerners feared competing with emancipated slaves for scarce jobs.

In New York City, the Emancipation Proclamation, combined with unhappiness over the Union draft, which began in March 1863, fanned the flames of white racism. Many New Yorkers supported the Confederacy for business reasons, and, in 1861, the city's mayor actually suggested that New York City leave the Union. On July 13, 1863, two days after the first draft lottery took place, this racial hatred erupted into violence. A volunteer fire company whose commander had been drafted initiated a riot, and the violence spread quickly across the city. The rioters chose targets associated either with the Union army or with African Americans. An armory was destroyed, as was a Brooks Brothers' store, which supplied uniforms to the army. White mobs attacked and killed black New Yorkers and destroyed an African American orphanage (**Figure 6.13**). On the fourth day of the riots, federal troops dispatched by Lincoln arrived in the city and ended the violence. Millions of dollars in property had been destroyed. More than one hundred people died, approximately one thousand were left injured, and about one-fifth of the city's African American population fled New York in fear.

Figure 6.13 The race riots in New York showed just how divided the North was on the issue of equality, even as the North went to war with the South over the issue of slavery.

UNION ADVANCES

The war in the west continued in favor of the North in 1863. At the start of the year, Union forces controlled much of the Mississippi River. In the spring and summer of 1862, they had captured New Orleans—the most important port in the Confederacy, through which cotton harvested from all the Southern states was exported—and Memphis. Grant had then attempted to capture Vicksburg, Mississippi, a commercial center on the bluffs above the Mississippi River. Once Vicksburg fell, the Union would have won complete control over the river. A military bombardment that summer failed to force a Confederate surrender. An assault by land forces also failed in December 1862.

In April 1863, the Union began a final attempt to capture Vicksburg. On July 3, after more than a month of a Union siege, during which Vicksburg's residents hid in caves to protect themselves from the bombardment and ate their pets to stay alive, Grant finally achieved his objective. The trapped Confederate forces surrendered. The Union had succeeded in capturing Vicksburg and splitting the Confederacy (**Figure 6.14**). This victory inflicted a serious blow to the Southern war effort.

Figure 6.14 In this illustration, Union gun boats fire on Vicksburg in the campaign that helped the Union take control of the Mississippi River.

As Grant and his forces pounded Vicksburg, Confederate strategists, at the urging of General Lee, who had defeated a larger Union army at Chancellorsville, Virginia, in May 1863, decided on a bold plan to invade the North. Leaders hoped this invasion would force the Union to send troops engaged in the Vicksburg campaign east, thus weakening their power over the Mississippi. Further, they hoped the aggressive action of pushing north would weaken the Union's resolve to fight. Lee also hoped that a significant Confederate victory in the North would convince Great Britain and France to extend support to Jefferson Davis's government and encourage the North to negotiate peace.

Beginning in June 1863, General Lee began to move the Army of Northern Virginia north through Maryland. The Union army—the Army of the Potomac—traveled east to end up alongside the Confederate forces. The two armies met at Gettysburg, Pennsylvania, where Confederate forces had gone to secure supplies. The resulting battle lasted three days, July 1–3 (**Figure 6.15**) and remains the biggest and costliest battle ever fought in North America. The climax of the Battle of Gettysburg occurred on the third day. In the morning, after a fight lasting several hours, Union forces fought back a Confederate attack on Culp's Hill, one of the Union's defensive positions. To regain a perceived advantage and secure victory, Lee ordered a frontal assault, known as Pickett's Charge (for Confederate general George Pickett), against the center of the Union lines on Cemetery Ridge. Approximately fifteen thousand Confederate soldiers took part, and more than half lost their lives, as they advanced nearly a mile across an open field to attack the entrenched Union forces. In all, more than a third of the Army of Northern Virginia had been lost, and on the evening of July 4, Lee and his men slipped away in the rain. General George Meade did not pursue them. Both sides suffered staggering losses. Total casualties numbered around twenty-three thousand for the Union and some twenty-eight thousand among the Confederates. With its defeats at Gettysburg and Vicksburg, both on the same day, the Confederacy lost its momentum. The tide had turned in favor of the Union in both the east and the west.

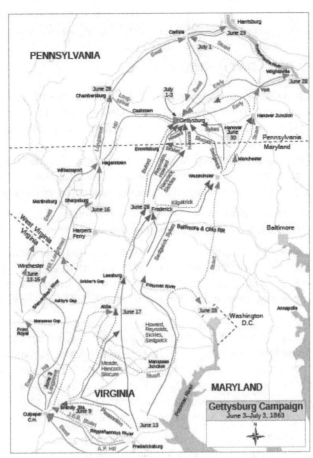

Figure 6.15 As this map indicates, the battlefield at Gettysburg was the farthest north that the Confederate army advanced. (credit: Hal Jesperson)

Following the Battle of Gettysburg, the bodies of those who had fallen were hastily buried. Attorney David Wills, a resident of Gettysburg, campaigned for the creation of a national cemetery on the site of the battlefield, and the governor of Pennsylvania tasked him with creating it. President Lincoln was invited to attend the cemetery's dedication. After the featured orator had delivered a two-hour speech, Lincoln addressed the crowd for several minutes. In his speech, known as the **Gettysburg Address**, which he had finished writing while a guest in David Wills' home the day before the dedication, Lincoln invoked the Founding Fathers and the spirit of the American Revolution. The Union soldiers who had died at Gettysburg, he proclaimed, had died not only to preserve the Union, but also to guarantee freedom and equality for all.

DEFINING "AMERICAN"

⚙ *Lincoln's Gettysburg Address*

Several months after the battle at Gettysburg, Lincoln traveled to Pennsylvania and, speaking to an audience at the dedication of the new Soldiers' National Ceremony near the site of the battle, he delivered his now-famous Gettysburg Address to commemorate the turning point of the war and the soldiers whose sacrifices had made it possible. The two-minute speech was politely received at the time, although press reactions split along party lines. Upon receiving a letter of congratulations from Massachusetts politician and orator William Everett, whose speech at the ceremony had lasted for two hours, Lincoln said he was glad to know that his brief address, now virtually immortal, was not "a total failure."

> Four score and seven years ago our fathers brought forth on this continent, a new nation, conceived in Liberty, and dedicated to the proposition that all men are created equal.
>
> Now we are engaged in a great civil war, testing whether that nation, or any nation so conceived and so dedicated, can long endure. We are met on a great battle-field of that war. We have come to dedicate a portion of that field, as a final resting place for those who here gave their lives that that nation might live. It is altogether fitting and proper that we should do this.
>
> It is for us the living . . . to be here dedicated to the great task remaining before us—that from these honored dead we take increased devotion to that cause for which they gave the last full measure of devotion—that we here highly resolve that these dead shall not have died in vain—that this nation, under God, shall have a new birth of freedom—and that government of the people, by the people, for the people, shall not perish from the earth.
>
> —Abraham Lincoln, Gettysburg Address, November 19, 1863

What did Lincoln mean by "a new birth of freedom"? What did he mean when he said "a government of the people, by the people, for the people, shall not perish from the earth"?

Click and Explore

Acclaimed filmmaker Ken Burns has created a **documentary** (http://openstaxcollege.org/l/15Address) about a small boys' school in Vermont where students memorize the Gettysburg Address. It explores the value the address has in these boys' lives, and why the words still matter.

6.4 The Union Triumphant

By the end of this section, you will be able to:
- Describe the reasons why many Americans doubted that Abraham Lincoln would be reelected
- Explain how the Union forces overpowered the Confederacy

By the outset of 1864, after three years of war, the Union had mobilized its resources for the ongoing struggle on a massive scale. The government had overseen the construction of new railroad lines and for the first time used standardized rail tracks that allowed the North to move men and materials with greater ease. The North's economy had shifted to a wartime model. The Confederacy also mobilized, perhaps to a greater degree than the Union, its efforts to secure independence and maintain slavery. Yet the Confederacy experienced ever-greater hardships after years of war. Without the population of the North, it faced a shortage of manpower. The lack of industry, compared to the North, undercut the ability to sustain and wage war. Rampant inflation as well as food shortages in the South lowered morale.

THE RELATIONSHIP WITH EUROPE

From the beginning of the war, the Confederacy placed great hope in being recognized and supported by Great Britain and France. European intervention in the conflict remained a strong possibility, but when it did occur, it was not in a way anticipated by either the Confederacy or the Union.

Napoleon III of France believed the Civil War presented an opportunity for him to restore a French empire in the Americas. With the United States preoccupied, the time seemed ripe for action. Napoleon's target was Mexico, and in 1861, a large French fleet took Veracruz. The French then moved to capture Mexico City, but the advance came to an end when Mexican forces defeated the French in 1862. Despite this setback, France eventually did conquer Mexico, establishing a regime that lasted until 1867. Rather than coming to the aid of the Confederacy, France used the Civil War to provide a pretext for efforts to reestablish its former eighteenth-century colonial holdings.

Still, the Confederacy had great confidence that it would find an ally in Great Britain despite the antislavery sentiment there. Southerners hoped Britain's dependence on cotton for its textile mills would keep the country on their side. The fact that the British proved willing to build and sell ironclad ships intended to smash through the Union naval blockade further raised Southern hopes. The Confederacy purchased two of these armored blockade runners, the CSS *Florida* and the CSS *Alabama*. Both were destroyed during the war.

The Confederacy's staunch commitment to slavery eventually worked against British recognition and support, since Great Britain had abolished slavery in 1833. The 1863 Emancipation Proclamation ended any doubts the British had about the goals of the Union cause. In the aftermath of the proclamation, many in Great Britain cheered for a Union victory. Ultimately, Great Britain, like France, disappointed the Confederacy's hope of an alliance, leaving the outnumbered and out-resourced states that had left the Union to fend for themselves.

AFRICAN AMERICAN SOLDIERS

At the beginning of the war, in 1861 and 1862, Union forces had used contrabands, or escaped slaves, for manual labor. The Emancipation Proclamation, however, led to the enrollment of African American men as Union soldiers. Huge numbers, former slaves as well as free blacks from the North, enlisted, and by the end of the war in 1865, their numbers had swelled to over 190,000. Racism among whites in the Union army ran deep, however, fueling the belief that black soldiers could never be effective or trustworthy. The Union also feared for the fate of captured black soldiers. Although many black soldiers saw combat duty, these factors affected the types of tasks assigned to them. Many black regiments were limited to hauling supplies, serving as cooks, digging trenches, and doing other types of labor, rather than serving on the battlefield (**Figure 6.16**).

Figure 6.16 This 1865 daguerreotype illustrates three of the Union's distinct advantages: African American soldiers, a stream of cannons and supplies, and an extensive railroad grid. (credit: Library of Congress)

African American soldiers also received lower wages than their white counterparts: ten dollars per month, with three dollars deducted for clothing. White soldiers, in contrast, received thirteen dollars monthly, with no deductions. Abolitionists and their Republican supporters in Congress worked to correct this discriminatory practice, and in 1864, black soldiers began to receive the same pay as white soldiers plus retroactive pay to 1863 (**Figure 6.17**).

Figure 6.17 African American and white soldiers of the Union army pose together in this photograph, although in reality, black soldiers were often kept separate and given only menial jobs.

For their part, African American soldiers welcomed the opportunity to prove themselves. Some 85 percent were former slaves who were fighting for the liberation of all slaves and the end of slavery. When given the opportunity to serve, many black regiments did so heroically. One such regiment, the Fifty-Fourth Regiment of Massachusetts Volunteers, distinguished itself at Fort Wagner in South Carolina by fighting valiantly against an entrenched Confederate position. They willingly gave their lives for the cause.

The Confederacy, not surprisingly, showed no mercy to African American troops. In April 1864, Southern forces attempted to take Fort Pillow in Tennessee from the Union forces that had captured it in 1862.

Confederate troops under Major General Nathan Bedford Forrest, the future founder of the Ku Klux Klan, quickly overran the fort, and the Union defenders surrendered. Instead of taking the African American soldiers prisoner, as they did the white soldiers, the Confederates executed them. The massacre outraged the North, and the Union refused to engage in any future exchanges of prisoners with the Confederacy.

THE CAMPAIGNS OF 1864 AND 1865

In the final years of the war, the Union continued its efforts on both the eastern and western fronts while bringing the war into the Deep South. Union forces increasingly engaged in total war, not distinguishing between military and civilian targets. They destroyed everything that lay in their path, committed to breaking the will of the Confederacy and forcing an end to the war. General Grant, mastermind of the Vicksburg campaign, took charge of the war effort. He understood the advantage of having large numbers of soldiers at his disposal and recognized that Union soldiers could be replaced, whereas the Confederates, whose smaller population was feeling the strain of the years of war, could not. Grant thus pushed forward relentlessly, despite huge losses of men. In 1864, Grant committed his forces to destroying Lee's army in Virginia.

In the Virginia campaign, Grant hoped to use his larger army to his advantage. But at the Battle of the Wilderness, fought from May 5 to May 7, Confederate forces stopped Grant's advance. Rather than retreating, he pushed forward. At the Battle of Spotsylvania on May 8 through 12, Grant again faced determined Confederate resistance, and again his advance was halted. As before, he renewed the Union campaign. At the Battle of Cold Harbor in early June, Grant had between 100,000 and 110,000 soldiers, whereas the Confederates had slightly more than half that number. Again, the Union advance was halted, if only momentarily, as Grant awaited reinforcements. An attack on the Confederate position on June 3 resulted in heavy casualties for the Union, and nine days later, Grant led his army away from Cold Harbor to Petersburg, Virginia, a rail center that supplied Richmond. The immense losses that Grant's forces suffered severely hurt Union morale. The war seemed unending, and with the tremendous loss of life, many in the North began to question the war and desire peace. Undaunted by the changing opinion in the North and hoping to destroy the Confederate rail network in the Upper South, however, Grant laid siege to Petersburg for nine months. As the months wore on, both sides dug in, creating miles of trenches and gun emplacements.

The other major Union campaigns of 1864 were more successful and gave President Lincoln the advantage that he needed to win reelection in November. In August 1864, the Union navy captured Mobile Bay. General Sherman invaded the Deep South, advancing slowly from Tennessee into Georgia, confronted at every turn by the Confederates, who were commanded by Johnston. When President Davis replaced Johnston with General John B. Hood, the Confederates made a daring but ultimately costly direct attack on the Union army that failed to drive out the invaders. Atlanta fell to Union forces on September 2, 1864. The fall of Atlanta held tremendous significance for the war-weary Union and helped to reverse the North's sinking morale. In keeping with the logic of total war, Sherman's forces cut a swath of destruction to Savannah. On **Sherman's March to the Sea**, the Union army, seeking to demoralize the South, destroyed everything in its path, despite strict instructions regarding the preservation of civilian property. Although towns were left standing, houses and barns were burned. Homes were looted, food was stolen, crops were destroyed, orchards were burned, and livestock was killed or confiscated. Savannah fell on December 21, 1864—a Christmas gift for Lincoln, Sherman proclaimed. In 1865, Sherman's forces invaded South Carolina, capturing Charleston and Columbia. In Columbia, the state capital, the Union army burned slaveholders' homes and destroyed much of the city. From South Carolina, Sherman's force moved north in an effort to join Grant and destroy Lee's army.

MY STORY

☉ *Dolly Sumner Lunt on Sherman's March to the Sea*

The following account is by Dolly Sumner Lunt, a widow who ran her Georgia cotton plantation after the death of her husband. She describes General Sherman's march to Savannah, where he enacted the policy of total war by burning and plundering the landscape to inhibit the Confederates' ability to keep fighting.

> Alas! little did I think while trying to save my house from plunder and fire that they were forcing my boys [slaves] from home at the point of the bayonet. One, Newton, jumped into bed in his cabin, and declared himself sick. Another crawled under the floor,—a lame boy he was,—but they pulled him out, placed him on a horse, and drove him off. Mid, poor Mid! The last I saw of him, a man had him going around the garden, looking, as I thought, for my sheep, as he was my shepherd. Jack came crying to me, the big tears coursing down his cheeks, saying they were making him go. I said: 'Stay in my room.'

> But a man followed in, cursing him and threatening to shoot him if he did not go; so poor Jack had to yield. . . .

> Sherman himself and a greater portion of his army passed my house that day. All day, as the sad moments rolled on, were they passing not only in front of my house, but from behind; they tore down my garden palings, made a road through my back-yard and lot field, driving their stock and riding through, tearing down my fences and desolating my home—wantonly doing it when there was no necessity for it. . . .

> About ten o'clock they had all passed save one, who came in and wanted coffee made, which was done, and he, too, went on. A few minutes elapsed, and two couriers riding rapidly passed back. Then, presently, more soldiers came by, and this ended the passing of Sherman's army by my place, leaving me poorer by thirty thousand dollars than I was yesterday morning. And a much stronger Rebel!

According to this account, what was the reaction of slaves to the arrival of the Union forces? What did the Union forces do with the slaves? For Lunt, did the strategy of total war work as planned?

THE ELECTION OF 1864

Despite the military successes for the Union army in 1863, in 1864, Lincoln's status among many Northern voters plummeted. Citing the suspension of the writ of habeas corpus, many saw him as a dictator, bent on grabbing power while senselessly and uncaringly drafting more young men into combat. Arguably, his greatest liability, however, was the Emancipation Proclamation and the enlistment of African American soldiers. Many whites in the North found this deeply offensive, since they still believed in racial inequality. The 1863 New York City Draft Riots illustrated the depth of white anger.

Northern Democrats railed against Lincoln and the war. Republicans labeled these vocal opponents of the President **Copperheads,** a term that many antiwar Democrats accepted. As the anti-Lincoln poster below illustrates, his enemies tried to paint him as an untrustworthy and suspect leader (**Figure 6.18**). It seemed to most in the North that the Democratic candidate, General George B. McClellan, who did not support abolition and was replaced with another commander by Lincoln, would win the election.

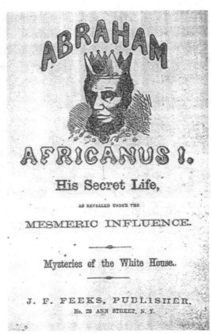

Figure 6.18 Anti-Lincoln sentiment in the North ran high in 1864, and many believed he would not be reelected president that year.

The Republican Party also split over the issue of reelecting Lincoln. Those who found him timid and indecisive, and favored extending full rights to African Americans, as well as completely refashioning the South after its defeat, earned the name Radicals. A moderate faction of Republicans opposed the Radicals. For his part, Lincoln did not align himself with either group.

The tide of the election campaign turned in favor of Lincoln, however, in the fall of 1864. Above all else, Union victories, including the fall of Atlanta in September and General Philip Sheridan's successes in the Shenandoah Valley of Virginia, bolstered Lincoln's popularity and his reelection bid. In November 1864, despite earlier forecasts to the contrary, Lincoln was reelected. Lincoln won all but three states—New Jersey and the border states of Delaware and Kentucky. To the chagrin of his opponent, McClellan, even Union army troops voted overwhelmingly for the incumbent President.

THE WAR ENDS

By the spring of 1865, it had become clear to both sides that the Confederacy could not last much longer. Most of its major cities, ports, and industrial centers—Atlanta, Savannah, Charleston, Columbia, Mobile, New Orleans, and Memphis—had been captured. In April 1865, Lee had abandoned both Petersburg and Richmond. His goal in doing so was to unite his depleted army with Confederate forces commanded by General Johnston. Grant effectively cut him off. On April 9, 1865, Lee surrendered to Grant at Appomattox Court House in Virginia (**Figure 6.19**). By that time, he had fewer than 35,000 soldiers, while Grant had some 100,000. Meanwhile, Sherman's army proceeded to North Carolina, where General Johnston surrendered on April 19, 1865. The Civil War had come to an end. The war had cost the lives of more than 600,000 soldiers. Many more had been wounded. Thousands of women were left widowed. Children were left without fathers, and many parents were deprived of a source of support in their old age. In some areas, where local volunteer units had marched off to battle, never to return, an entire generation of young women was left without marriage partners. Millions of dollars' worth of property had been destroyed, and towns and cities were laid to waste. With the conflict finally over, the very difficult work of reconciling North and South and reestablishing the United States lay ahead.

Figure 6.19 Vastly outnumbered by the Union army, the Confederate general Robert E. Lee (seated at the left) surrendered to Ulysses S. Grant at Appomattox Courthouse. (credit: "Alaskan Dude"/Wikimedia Commons)

CHAPTER 7

The Era of Reconstruction, 1865–1877

Figure 7.1 In this political cartoon by Thomas Nast, which appeared in *Harper's Weekly* in October 1874, the "White League" shakes hands with the Ku Klux Klan over a shield that shows a couple weeping over a baby. In the background, a schoolhouse burns, and a lynched freedman is shown hanging from a tree. Above the shield, which is labeled "Worse than Slavery," the text reads, "The Union as It Was: This Is a White Man's Government."

Chapter Outline

7.1 Restoring the Union
7.2 Congress and the Remaking of the South, 1865–1866
7.3 Radical Reconstruction, 1867–1872
7.4 The Collapse of Reconstruction

Introduction

Few times in U.S. history have been as turbulent and transformative as the Civil War and the twelve years that followed. Between 1865 and 1877, one president was murdered and another impeached. The Constitution underwent major revision with the addition of three amendments. The effort to impose Union control and create equality in the defeated South ignited a fierce backlash as various terrorist and vigilante organizations, most notably the Ku Klux Klan, battled to maintain a pre–Civil War society in which whites held complete power. These groups unleashed a wave of violence, including lynching and arson, aimed at freed blacks and their white supporters. Historians refer to this era as Reconstruction, when an effort to remake the South faltered and ultimately failed.

The above political cartoon (**Figure 7.1**) expresses the anguish many Americans felt in the decade after the Civil War. The South, which had experienced catastrophic losses during the conflict, was reduced to political dependence and economic destitution. This humiliating condition led many southern whites to vigorously contest Union efforts to transform the South's racial, economic, and social landscape. Supporters of equality grew increasingly dismayed at Reconstruction's failure to undo the old system, which further compounded the staggering regional and racial inequalities in the United States.

7.1 Restoring the Union

By the end of this section, you will be able to:
- Describe Lincoln's plan to restore the Union at the end of the Civil War
- Discuss the tenets of Radical Republicanism
- Analyze the success or failure of the Thirteenth Amendment

The end of the Civil War saw the beginning of the **Reconstruction** era, when former rebel Southern states were integrated back into the Union. President Lincoln moved quickly to achieve the war's ultimate goal: reunification of the country. He proposed a generous and non-punitive plan to return the former Confederate states speedily to the United States, but some Republicans in Congress protested, considering the president's plan too lenient to the rebel states that had torn the country apart. The greatest flaw of Lincoln's plan, according to this view, was that it appeared to forgive traitors instead of guaranteeing civil rights to former slaves. President Lincoln oversaw the passage of the Thirteenth Amendment abolishing slavery, but he did not live to see its ratification.

THE PRESIDENT'S PLAN

From the outset of the rebellion in 1861, Lincoln's overriding goal had been to bring the Southern states quickly back into the fold in order to restore the Union (**Figure 7.3**). In early December 1863, the president began the process of reunification by unveiling a three-part proposal known as the **ten percent plan** that outlined how the states would return. The ten percent plan gave a general pardon to all Southerners except high-ranking Confederate government and military leaders; required 10 percent of the 1860 voting population in the former rebel states to take a binding oath of future allegiance to the United States and the emancipation of slaves; and declared that once those voters took those oaths, the restored Confederate states would draft new state constitutions.

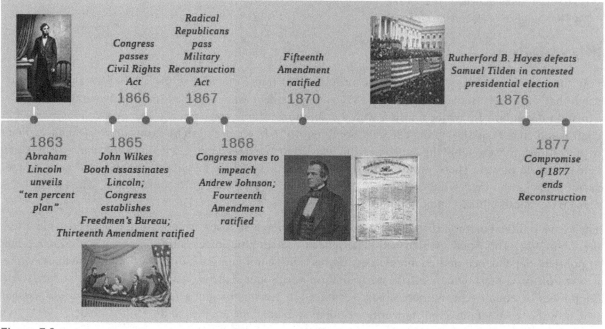

Figure 7.2

THE "RAIL SPLITTER" AT WORK REPAIRING THE UNION.

(a)   (b)

Figure 7.3 Thomas Le Mere took this albumen silver print (a) of Abraham Lincoln in April 1863. Le Mere thought a standing pose of Lincoln would be popular. In this political cartoon from 1865 (b), Lincoln and his vice president, Andrew Johnson, endeavor to sew together the torn pieces of the Union.

Lincoln hoped that the leniency of the plan—90 percent of the 1860 voters did not have to swear allegiance to the Union or to emancipation—would bring about a quick and long-anticipated resolution and make emancipation more acceptable everywhere. This approach appealed to some in the moderate wing of the Republican Party, which wanted to put the nation on a speedy course toward reconciliation. However, the proposal instantly drew fire from a larger faction of Republicans in Congress who did not want to deal moderately with the South. These members of Congress, known as **Radical Republicans**, wanted to remake the South and punish the rebels. Radical Republicans insisted on harsh terms for the defeated Confederacy and protection for former slaves, going far beyond what the president proposed.

In February 1864, two of the Radical Republicans, Ohio senator Benjamin Wade and Maryland representative Henry Winter Davis, answered Lincoln with a proposal of their own. Among other stipulations, the Wade-Davis Bill called for a majority of voters and government officials in Confederate states to take an oath, called the **Ironclad Oath**, swearing that they had never supported the Confederacy or made war against the United States. Those who could not or would not take the oath would be unable to take part in the future political life of the South. Congress assented to the Wade-Davis Bill, and it went to Lincoln for his signature. The president refused to sign, using the pocket veto (that is, taking no action) to kill the bill. Lincoln understood that no Southern state would have met the criteria of the Wade-Davis Bill, and its passage would simply have delayed the reconstruction of the South.

THE THIRTEENTH AMENDMENT

Despite the 1863 Emancipation Proclamation, the legal status of slaves and the institution of slavery remained unresolved. To deal with the remaining uncertainties, the Republican Party made the abolition of slavery a top priority by including the issue in its 1864 party platform. The platform read: "That as slavery was the cause, and now constitutes the strength of this Rebellion, and as it must be, always and everywhere, hostile to the principles of Republican Government, justice and the National safety demand its utter and complete extirpation from the soil of the Republic; and that, while we uphold and maintain the acts and proclamations by which the Government, in its own defense, has aimed a deathblow at this gigantic evil, we are in favor, furthermore, of such an amendment to the Constitution, to be made by the people in conformity with its provisions, as shall terminate and forever prohibit the existence of Slavery within the limits of the jurisdiction of the United States." The platform left no doubt about the intention to abolish slavery.

The president, along with the Radical Republicans, made good on this campaign promise in 1864 and 1865. A proposed constitutional amendment passed the Senate in April 1864, and the House of Representatives concurred in January 1865. The amendment then made its way to the states, where it swiftly gained the necessary support, including in the South. In December 1865, the Thirteenth Amendment was officially ratified and added to the Constitution. The first amendment added to the Constitution since 1804, it overturned a centuries-old practice by permanently abolishing slavery.

Click and Explore

Explore a comprehensive collection of documents, images, and ephemera related to Abraham Lincoln (http://openstaxcollege.org/l/15Lincoln) on the Library of Congress website.

President Lincoln never saw the final ratification of the Thirteenth Amendment. On April 14, 1865, the Confederate supporter and well-known actor John Wilkes Booth shot Lincoln while he was attending a play, *Our American Cousin*, at Ford's Theater in Washington. The president died the next day (**Figure 7.4**). Booth had steadfastly defended the Confederacy and white supremacy, and his act was part of a larger conspiracy to eliminate the heads of the Union government and keep the Confederate fight going. One of Booth's associates stabbed and wounded Secretary of State William Seward the night of the assassination. Another associate abandoned the planned assassination of Vice President Andrew Johnson at the last moment. Although Booth initially escaped capture, Union troops shot and killed him on April 26, 1865, in a Maryland barn. Eight other conspirators were convicted by a military tribunal for participating in the conspiracy, and four were hanged. Lincoln's death earned him immediate martyrdom, and hysteria spread throughout the North. To many Northerners, the assassination suggested an even greater conspiracy than what was revealed, masterminded by the unrepentant leaders of the defeated Confederacy. Militant Republicans would use and exploit this fear relentlessly in the ensuing months.

Figure 7.4 In *The Assassination of President Lincoln* (1865), by Currier and Ives, John Wilkes Booth shoots Lincoln in the back of the head as he sits in the theater box with his wife, Mary Todd Lincoln, and their guests, Major Henry R. Rathbone and Clara Harris.

ANDREW JOHNSON AND THE BATTLE OVER RECONSTRUCTION

Lincoln's assassination elevated Vice President Andrew Johnson, a Democrat, to the presidency. Johnson had come from very humble origins. Born into extreme poverty in North Carolina and having never attended school, Johnson was the picture of a self-made man. His wife had taught him how to read and he had worked as a tailor, a trade he had been apprenticed to as a child. In Tennessee, where he had moved as a young man, he gradually rose up the political ladder, earning a reputation for being a skillful stump speaker and a staunch defender of poor southerners. He was elected to serve in the House of Representatives in the 1840s, became governor of Tennessee the following decade, and then was elected a U.S. senator just a few years before the country descended into war. When Tennessee seceded, Johnson remained loyal to the Union and stayed in the Senate. As Union troops marched on his home state of North Carolina, Lincoln appointed him governor of the then-occupied state of Tennessee, where he served until being nominated by the Republicans to run for vice president on a Lincoln ticket. The nomination of Johnson, a Democrat and a slaveholding southerner, was a pragmatic decision made by concerned Republicans. It was important for them to show that the party supported all loyal men, regardless of their origin or political persuasion. Johnson appeared an ideal choice, because his nomination would bring with it the support of both pro-Southern elements and the War Democrats who rejected the conciliatory stance of the Copperheads, the northern Democrats who opposed the Civil War.

Unexpectedly elevated to the presidency in 1865, this formerly impoverished tailor's apprentice and unwavering antagonist of the wealthy southern planter class now found himself tasked with administering the restoration of a destroyed South. Lincoln's position as president had been that the secession of the Southern states was never legal; that is, they had not succeeded in leaving the Union, therefore they still had certain rights to self-government as states. In keeping with Lincoln's plan, Johnson desired to quickly reincorporate the South back into the Union on lenient terms and heal the wounds of the nation. This position angered many in his own party. The northern Radical Republican plan for Reconstruction looked to overturn southern society and specifically aimed at ending the plantation system. President Johnson quickly disappointed Radical Republicans when he rejected their idea that the federal government could provide voting rights for freed slaves. The initial disagreements between the president and the Radical Republicans over how best to deal with the defeated South set the stage for further conflict.

In fact, President Johnson's Proclamation of Amnesty and Reconstruction in May 1865 provided sweeping "amnesty and pardon" to rebellious Southerners. It returned to them their property, with the notable exception of their former slaves, and it asked only that they affirm their support for the Constitution of the United States. Those Southerners excepted from this amnesty included the Confederate political leadership, high-ranking military officers, and persons with taxable property worth more than $20,000. The inclusion of this last category was specifically designed to make it clear to the southern planter class that they had a unique responsibility for the outbreak of hostilities. But it also satisfied Johnson's desire to exact vengeance on a class of people he had fought politically for much of his life. For this class of wealthy Southerners to regain their rights, they would have to swallow their pride and request a personal pardon from Johnson himself.

For the Southern states, the requirements for readmission to the Union were also fairly straightforward. States were required to hold individual state conventions where they would repeal the ordinances of secession and ratify the Thirteenth Amendment. By the end of 1865, a number of former Confederate leaders were in the Union capital looking to claim their seats in Congress. Among them was Alexander Stephens, the vice president of the Confederacy, who had spent several months in a Boston jail after the war. Despite the outcries of Republicans in Congress, by early 1866 Johnson announced that all former Confederate states had satisfied the necessary requirements. According to him, nothing more needed to be done; the Union had been restored.

Understandably, Radical Republicans in Congress did not agree with Johnson's position. They, and their northern constituents, greatly resented his lenient treatment of the former Confederate states, and especially the return of former Confederate leaders like Alexander Stephens to Congress. They refused to acknowledge the southern state governments he allowed. As a result, they would not permit senators and representatives from the former Confederate states to take their places in Congress.

Instead, the Radical Republicans created a joint committee of representatives and senators to oversee Reconstruction. In the 1866 congressional elections, they gained control of the House, and in the ensuing years they pushed for the dismantling of the old southern order and the complete reconstruction of the South. This effort put them squarely at odds with President Johnson, who remained unwilling to compromise with Congress, setting the stage for a series of clashes.

7.2 Congress and the Remaking of the South, 1865–1866

By the end of this section, you will be able to:
- Describe the efforts made by Congress in 1865 and 1866 to bring to life its vision of Reconstruction
- Explain how the Fourteenth Amendment transformed the Constitution

President Johnson and Congress's views on Reconstruction grew even further apart as Johnson's presidency progressed. Congress repeatedly pushed for greater rights for freed people and a far more thorough reconstruction of the South, while Johnson pushed for leniency and a swifter reintegration. President Johnson lacked Lincoln's political skills and instead exhibited a stubbornness and confrontational approach that aggravated an already difficult situation.

THE FREEDMEN'S BUREAU

Freed people everywhere celebrated the end of slavery and immediately began to take steps to improve their own condition by seeking what had long been denied to them: land, financial security, education, and the ability to participate in the political process. They wanted to be reunited with family members, grasp the opportunity to make their own independent living, and exercise their right to have a say in their own government.

However, they faced the wrath of defeated but un-reconciled southerners who were determined to keep blacks an impoverished and despised underclass. Recognizing the widespread devastation in the

South and the dire situation of freed people, Congress created the Bureau of Refugees, Freedmen, and Abandoned Lands in March 1865, popularly known as the **Freedmen's Bureau**. Lincoln had approved of the bureau, giving it a charter for one year.

The Freedmen's Bureau engaged in many initiatives to ease the transition from slavery to freedom. It delivered food to blacks and whites alike in the South. It helped freed people gain labor contracts, a significant step in the creation of wage labor in place of slavery. It helped reunite families of freedmen, and it also devoted much energy to education, establishing scores of public schools where freed people and poor whites could receive both elementary and higher education. Respected institutions such as Fisk University, Hampton University, and Dillard University are part of the legacy of the Freedmen's Bureau.

In this endeavor, the Freedmen's Bureau received support from Christian organizations that had long advocated for abolition, such as the American Missionary Association (AMA). The AMA used the knowledge and skill it had acquired while working in missions in Africa and with American Indian groups to establish and run schools for freed slaves in the postwar South. While men and women, white and black, taught in these schools, the opportunity was crucially important for participating women (**Figure 7.5**). At the time, many opportunities, including admission to most institutes of higher learning, remained closed to women. Participating in these schools afforded these women the opportunities they otherwise may have been denied. Additionally, the fact they often risked life and limb to work in these schools in the South demonstrated to the nation that women could play a vital role in American civic life.

Figure 7.5 The Freedmen's Bureau, as shown in this 1866 illustration from *Frank Leslie's Illustrated Newspaper*, created many schools for black elementary school students. Many of the teachers who provided instruction in these southern schools, though by no means all, came from northern states.

The schools that the Freedmen's Bureau and the AMA established inspired great dismay and resentment among the white populations in the South and were sometimes targets of violence. Indeed, the Freedmen's Bureau's programs and its very existence were sources of controversy. Racists and others who resisted this type of federal government activism denounced it as both a waste of federal money and a foolish effort that encouraged laziness among blacks. Congress renewed the bureau's charter in 1866, but President Johnson, who steadfastly believed that the work of restoring the Union had been completed, vetoed the re-chartering. Radical Republicans continued to support the bureau, igniting a contest between Congress and the president that intensified during the next several years. Part of this dispute involved conflicting visions of the proper role of the federal government. Radical Republicans believed in the constructive power of the federal government to ensure a better day for freed people. Others, including Johnson, denied that the government had any such role to play.

AMERICANA

✿ *The Freedmen's Bureau*

The image below (Figure 7.6) shows a campaign poster for Hiester Clymer, who ran for governor of Pennsylvania in 1866 on a platform of white supremacy.

Figure 7.6 The caption of this image reads, "The Freedman's Bureau! An agency to keep the Negro in idleness at the expense of the white man. Twice vetoed by the President, and made a law by Congress. Support Congress & you support the Negro. Sustain the President & you protect the white man."

The image in the foreground shows an indolent black man wondering, "Whar is de use for me to work as long as dey make dese appropriations." White men toil in the background, chopping wood and plowing a field. The text above them reads, "In the sweat of thy face shall thou eat bread. . . . The white man must work to keep his children and pay his taxes." In the middle background, the Freedmen's Bureau looks like the Capitol, and the pillars are inscribed with racist assumptions of things blacks value, like "rum," "idleness," and "white women." On the right are estimates of the costs of the Freedmen's Bureau and the bounties (fees for enlistment) given to both white and black Union soldiers.

What does this poster indicate about the political climate of the Reconstruction era? How might different people have received this image?

BLACK CODES

In 1865 and 1866, as Johnson announced the end of Reconstruction, southern states began to pass a series of discriminatory state laws collectively known as **black codes**. While the laws varied in both content and severity from state to state, the goal of the laws remained largely consistent. In effect, these codes were designed to maintain the social and economic structure of racial slavery in the absence of slavery itself. The laws codified white supremacy by restricting the civic participation of freed slaves—depriving them of the right to vote, the right to serve on juries, the right to own or carry weapons, and, in some cases, even the right to rent or lease land.

A chief component of the black codes was designed to fulfill an important economic need in the postwar South. Slavery had been a pillar of economic stability in the region before the war. To maintain agricultural production, the South had relied on slaves to work the land. Now the region was faced with the daunting prospect of making the transition from a slave economy to one where labor was purchased on the open market. Not surprisingly, planters in the southern states were reluctant to make such a transition. Instead, they drafted black laws that would re-create the antebellum economic structure with the façade of a free-labor system.

Black codes used a variety of tactics to tie freed slaves to the land. To work, the freed slaves were forced to sign contracts with their employer. These contracts prevented blacks from working for more than one employer. This meant that, unlike in a free labor market, blacks could not positively influence wages and conditions by choosing to work for the employer who gave them the best terms. The predictable outcome was that freed slaves were forced to work for very low wages. With such low wages, and no ability to supplement income with additional work, workers were reduced to relying on loans from their employers. The debt that these workers incurred ensured that they could never escape from their condition. Those former slaves who attempt to violate these contracts could be fined or beaten. Those who refused to sign contracts at all could be arrested for vagrancy and then made to work for no wages, essentially being reduced to the very definition of a slave.

The black codes left no doubt that the former breakaway Confederate states intended to maintain white supremacy at all costs. These draconian state laws helped spur the congressional Joint Committee on Reconstruction into action. Its members felt that ending slavery with the Thirteenth Amendment did not go far enough. Congress extended the life of the Freedmen's Bureau to combat the black codes and in April 1866 passed the first Civil Rights Act, which established the citizenship of African Americans. This was a significant step that contradicted the Supreme Court's 1857 Dred Scott decision, which declared that blacks could never be citizens. The law also gave the federal government the right to intervene in state affairs to protect the rights of citizens, and thus, of African Americans. President Johnson, who continued to insist that restoration of the United States had already been accomplished, vetoed the 1866 Civil Rights Act. However, Congress mustered the necessary votes to override his veto. Despite the Civil Rights Act, the black codes endured, forming the foundation of the racially discriminatory Jim Crow segregation policies that impoverished generations of African Americans.

THE FOURTEENTH AMENDMENT

Questions swirled about the constitutionality of the Civil Rights Act of 1866. The Supreme Court, in its 1857 decision forbidding black citizenship, had interpreted the Constitution in a certain way; many argued that the 1866 statute, alone, could not alter that interpretation. Seeking to overcome all legal questions, Radical Republicans drafted another constitutional amendment with provisions that followed those of the 1866 Civil Rights Act. In July 1866, the Fourteenth Amendment went to state legislatures for ratification.

The Fourteenth Amendment stated, "All persons born or naturalized in the United States and subject to the jurisdiction thereof, are citizens of the United States and of the State wherein they reside." It gave citizens equal protection under both the state and federal law, overturning the Dred Scott decision. It eliminated the three-fifths compromise of the 1787 Constitution, whereby slaves had been counted as three-fifths of a free white person, and it reduced the number of House representatives and Electoral College electors for any state that denied suffrage to any adult male inhabitant, black or white. As Radical Republicans had proposed in the Wade-Davis bill, individuals who had "engaged in insurrection or rebellion [against] . . . or given aid or comfort to the enemies [of]" the United States were barred from holding political (state or federal) or military office unless pardoned by two-thirds of Congress.

The amendment also answered the question of debts arising from the Civil War by specifying that all debts incurred by fighting to defeat the Confederacy would be honored. Confederate debts, however, would not: "[N]either the United States nor any State shall assume or pay any debt or obligation incurred in aid of insurrection or rebellion against the United States, or any claim for the loss or emancipation of any slave; but all such debts, obligations and claims shall be held illegal and void." Thus, claims by former slaveholders requesting compensation for slave property had no standing. Any state that ratified the Fourteenth Amendment would automatically be readmitted. Yet, all former Confederate states refused to ratify the amendment in 1866.

President Johnson called openly for the rejection of the Fourteenth Amendment, a move that drove a further wedge between him and congressional Republicans. In late summer of 1866, he gave a series of speeches, known as the "swing around the circle," designed to gather support for his mild version of

Reconstruction. Johnson felt that ending slavery went far enough; extending the rights and protections of citizenship to freed people, he believed, went much too far. He continued to believe that blacks were inferior to whites. The president's "swing around the circle" speeches to gain support for his program and derail the Radical Republicans proved to be a disaster, as hecklers provoked Johnson to make damaging statements. Radical Republicans charged that Johnson had been drunk when he made his speeches. As a result, Johnson's reputation plummeted.

Click and Explore

Read the text of the Fourteenth Amendment (http://openstaxcollege.org/l/ 15Fourteena) and then view the original document (http://openstaxcollege.org/l/ 15Fourteenb) at Our Documents.

7.3 Radical Reconstruction, 1867–1872

By the end of this section, you will be able to:
- Explain the purpose of the second phase of Reconstruction and some of the key legislation put forward by Congress
- Describe the impeachment of President Johnson
- Discuss the benefits and drawbacks of the Fifteenth Amendment

During the Congressional election in the fall of 1866, Republicans gained even greater victories. This was due in large measure to the northern voter opposition that had developed toward President Johnson because of the inflexible and overbearing attitude he had exhibited in the White House, as well as his missteps during his 1866 speaking tour. Leading Radical Republicans in Congress included Massachusetts senator Charles Sumner (the same senator whom proslavery South Carolina representative Preston Brooks had thrashed with his cane in 1856 during the Bleeding Kansas crisis) and Pennsylvania representative Thaddeus Stevens. These men and their supporters envisioned a much more expansive change in the South. Sumner advocated integrating schools and giving black men the right to vote while disenfranchising many southern voters. For his part, Stevens considered that the southern states had forfeited their rights as states when they seceded, and were no more than conquered territory that the federal government could organize as it wished. He envisioned the redistribution of plantation lands and U.S. military control over the former Confederacy.

Their goals included the transformation of the South from an area built on slave labor to a free-labor society. They also wanted to ensure that freed people were protected and given the opportunity for a better life. Violent race riots in Memphis, Tennessee, and New Orleans, Louisiana, in 1866 gave greater urgency to the second phase of Reconstruction, begun in 1867.

THE RECONSTRUCTION ACTS

The 1867 Military Reconstruction Act, which encompassed the vision of Radical Republicans, set a new direction for Reconstruction in the South. Republicans saw this law, and three supplementary laws passed by Congress that year, called the Reconstruction Acts, as a way to deal with the disorder in the South. The

1867 act divided the ten southern states that had yet to ratify the Fourteenth Amendment into five military districts (Tennessee had already been readmitted to the Union by this time and so was excluded from these acts). Martial law was imposed, and a Union general commanded each district. These generals and twenty thousand federal troops stationed in the districts were charged with protecting freed people. When a supplementary act extended the right to vote to all freed men of voting age (21 years old), the military in each district oversaw the elections and the registration of voters. Only after new state constitutions had been written and states had ratified the Fourteenth Amendment could these states rejoin the Union. Predictably, President Johnson vetoed the Reconstruction Acts, viewing them as both unnecessary and unconstitutional. Once again, Congress overrode Johnson's vetoes, and by the end of 1870, all the southern states under military rule had ratified the Fourteenth Amendment and been restored to the Union (**Figure 7.7**).

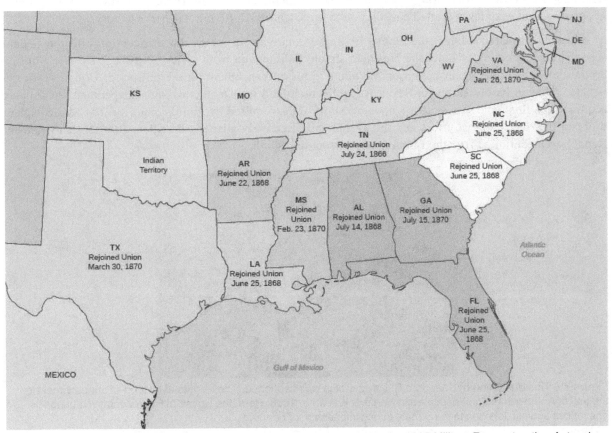

Figure 7.7 The map above shows the five military districts established by the 1867 Military Reconstruction Act and the date each state rejoined the Union. Tennessee was not included in the Reconstruction Acts as it had already been readmitted to the Union at the time of their passage.

THE IMPEACHMENT OF PRESIDENT JOHNSON

President Johnson's relentless vetoing of congressional measures created a deep rift in Washington, DC, and neither he nor Congress would back down. Johnson's prickly personality proved to be a liability, and many people found him grating. Moreover, he firmly believed in white supremacy, declaring in his 1868 State of the Union address, "The attempt to place the white population under the domination of persons of color in the South has impaired, if not destroyed, the kindly relations that had previously existed between them; and mutual distrust has engendered a feeling of animosity which leading in some instances to collision and bloodshed, has prevented that cooperation between the two races so essential to the success of industrial enterprise in the southern states." The president's racism put him even further at odds with those in Congress who wanted to create full equality between blacks and whites.

The Republican majority in Congress by now despised the president, and they wanted to prevent him from interfering in congressional Reconstruction. To that end, Radical Republicans passed two laws of dubious constitutionality. The Command of the Army Act prohibited the president from issuing military orders except through the commanding general of the army, who could not be relieved or reassigned without the consent of the Senate. The Tenure of Office Act, which Congress passed in 1867, required the president to gain the approval of the Senate whenever he appointed or removed officials. Congress had passed this act to ensure that Republicans who favored Radical Reconstruction would not be barred or stripped of their jobs. In August 1867, President Johnson removed Secretary of War Edwin M. Stanton, who had aligned himself with the Radical Republicans, without gaining Senate approval. He replaced Stanton with Ulysses S. Grant, but Grant resigned and sided with the Republicans against the president. Many Radical Republicans welcomed this blunder by the president as it allowed them to take action to remove Johnson from office, arguing that Johnson had openly violated the Tenure of Office Act. The House of Representatives quickly drafted a resolution to impeach him, a first in American history.

In impeachment proceedings, the House of Representatives serves as the prosecution and the Senate acts as judge, deciding whether the president should be removed from office (**Figure 7.8**). The House brought eleven counts against Johnson, all alleging his encroachment on the powers of Congress. In the Senate, Johnson barely survived. Seven Republicans joined the Democrats and independents to support acquittal; the final vote was 35 to 19, one vote short of the required two-thirds majority. The Radicals then dropped the impeachment effort, but the events had effectively silenced President Johnson, and Radical Republicans continued with their plan to reconstruct the South.

Figure 7.8 This illustration by Theodore R. Davis, which was captioned "The Senate as a court of impeachment for the trial of Andrew Johnson," appeared in *Harper's Weekly* in 1868. Here, the House of Representatives brings its grievances against Johnson to the Senate during impeachment hearings.

THE FIFTEENTH AMENDMENT

In November 1868, Ulysses S. Grant, the Union's war hero, easily won the presidency in a landslide victory. The Democratic nominee was Horatio Seymour, but the Democrats carried the stigma of disunion. The Republicans, in their campaign, blamed the devastating Civil War and the violence of its aftermath on the rival party, a strategy that southerners called "waving the bloody shirt."

Though Grant did not side with the Radical Republicans, his victory allowed the continuance of the Radical Reconstruction program. In the winter of 1869, Republicans introduced another constitutional amendment, the third of the Reconstruction era. When Republicans had passed the Fourteenth Amendment, which addressed citizenship rights and equal protections, they were unable to explicitly ban states from withholding the franchise based on race. With the Fifteenth Amendment, they sought to correct this major weakness by finally extending to black men the right to vote. The amendment directed that "[t]he right of citizens of the United States to vote shall not be denied or abridged by the United States or by any State on account of race, color, or previous condition of servitude." Unfortunately, the new amendment had weaknesses of its own. As part of a compromise to ensure the passage of the amendment with the broadest possible support, drafters of the amendment specifically excluded language that addressed literacy tests and poll taxes, the most common ways blacks were traditionally disenfranchised in both the North and the South. Indeed, Radical Republican leader Charles Sumner of Massachusetts, himself an ardent supporter of legal equality without exception to race, refused to vote for the amendment precisely because it did not address these obvious loopholes.

Despite these weaknesses, the language of the amendment did provide for universal manhood suffrage—the right of all men to vote—and crucially identified black men, including those who had been slaves, as deserving the right to vote. This, the third and final of the Reconstruction amendments, was ratified in 1870 (**Figure 7.9**). With the ratification of the Fifteenth Amendment, many believed that the process of restoring the Union was safely coming to a close and that the rights of freed slaves were finally secure. African American communities expressed great hope as they celebrated what they understood to be a national confirmation of their unqualified citizenship.

Figure 7.9 *The Fifteenth Amendment. Celebrated May 19th, 1870*, a commemorative print by Thomas Kelly, celebrates the passage of the Fifteenth Amendment with a series of vignettes highlighting black rights and those who championed them. Portraits include Ulysses S. Grant, Abraham Lincoln, and John Brown, as well as black leaders Martin Delany, Frederick Douglass, and Hiram Revels. Vignettes include the celebratory parade for the amendment's passage, "The Ballot Box is open to us," and "Our representative Sits in the National Legislature."

Click and Explore

Visit the Library of Congress (http://openstaxcollege.org/l/15Fifteen) to take a closer look at *The Fifteenth Amendment* by Thomas Kelly. Examine each individual vignette and the accompanying text. Why do you think Kelly chose these to highlight?

WOMEN'S SUFFRAGE

While the Fifteenth Amendment may have been greeted with applause in many corners, leading women's rights activists, who had been campaigning for decades for the right to vote, saw it as a major disappointment. More dispiriting still was the fact that many women's rights activists, such as Susan

B. Anthony and Elizabeth Cady Stanton, had played a large part in the abolitionist movement leading up to the Civil War. Following the war, women and men, white and black, formed the American Equal Rights Association (AERA) for the expressed purpose of securing "equal Rights to all American citizens, especially the right of suffrage, irrespective of race, color or sex." Two years later, with the adoption of the Fourteenth Amendment, section 2 of which specifically qualified the liberties it extended to "male citizens," it seemed as though the progress made in support of civil rights was not only passing women by but was purposely codifying their exclusion. As Congress debated the language of the Fifteenth Amendment, some held out hope that it would finally extend the franchise to women. Those hopes were dashed when Congress adopted the final language.

The consequence of these frustrated hopes was the effective split of a civil rights movement that had once been united in support of African Americans and women. Seeing this split occur, Frederick Douglass, a great admirer of Stanton, struggled to argue for a piecemeal approach that should prioritize the franchise for black men if that was the only option. He insisted that his support for women's right to vote was sincere, but that getting black men the right to vote was "of the most urgent necessity." "The government of this country loves women," he argued. "They are the sisters, mothers, wives and daughters of our rulers; but the negro is loathed. . . . The negro needs suffrage to protect his life and property, and to ensure him respect and education."

These appeals were largely accepted by women's rights leaders and AERA members like Lucy Stone and Henry Browne Blackwell, who believed that more time was needed to bring about female suffrage. Others demanded immediate action. Among those who pressed forward despite the setback were Stanton and Anthony. They felt greatly aggrieved at the fact that other abolitionists, with whom they had worked closely for years, did not demand that women be included in the language of the amendments. Stanton argued that the women's vote would be necessary to counter the influence of uneducated freedmen in the South and the waves of poor European immigrants arriving in the East.

In 1869, Stanton and Anthony helped organize the National Woman Suffrage Association (NWSA), an organization dedicated to ensuring that women gained the right to vote immediately, not at some future, undetermined date. Some women, including Virginia Minor, a member of the NWSA, took action by trying to register to vote; Minor attempted this in St. Louis, Missouri, in 1872. When election officials turned her away, Minor brought the issue to the Missouri state courts, arguing that the Fourteenth Amendment ensured that she was a citizen with the right to vote. This legal effort to bring about women's suffrage eventually made its way to the Supreme Court, which declared in 1874 that "the constitution of the United States does not confer the right of suffrage upon any one," effectively dismissing Minor's claim.

DEFINING "AMERICAN"

✪ *Constitution of the National Woman Suffrage Association*

Despite the Fifteenth Amendment's failure to guarantee female suffrage, women did gain the right to vote in western territories, with the Wyoming Territory leading the way in 1869. One reason for this was a belief that giving women the right to vote would provide a moral compass to the otherwise lawless western frontier. Extending the right to vote in western territories also provided an incentive for white women to emigrate to the West, where they were scarce. However, Susan B. Anthony, Elizabeth Cady Stanton, and others believed that immediate action on the national front was required, leading to the organization of the NWSA and its resulting constitution.

ARTICLE 1.—This organization shall be called the National Woman Suffrage Association.

ARTICLE 2.—The object of this Association shall be t o secure STATE and NATIONAL protection for women citizens in the exercise of their right to vote.

ARTICLE 3.—All citizens of the United States subscribing to this Constitution, and contributing not less than one dollar annually, shall be considered members of the Association, with the right to participate in its deliberations.

ARTICLE 4.—The officers of this Association shall be a President, Vice-Presidents from each of the States and Territories, Corresponding and Recording Secretaries, a Treasurer, an Executive Committee of not less than five, and an Advisory Committee consisting of one or more persons from each State and Territory.

ARTICLE 5.—All Woman Suffrage Societies throughout the country shall be welcomed as auxiliaries; and their accredited officers or duly appointed representatives shall be recognized as members of the National Association.
OFFICERS OF THE NATIONAL WOMAN SUFFRAGE ASSOCIATION.

PRESIDENT.
SUSAN B. ANTHONY, Rochester, N. Y.

How was the NWSA organized? How would the fact that it operated at the national level, rather than at the state or local level, help it to achieve its goals?

BLACK POLITICAL ACHIEVEMENTS

Black voter registration in the late 1860s and the ratification of the Fifteenth Amendment finally brought what Lincoln had characterized as "a new birth of freedom." **Union Leagues**, fraternal groups founded in the North that promoted loyalty to the Union and the Republican Party during the Civil War, expanded into the South after the war and were transformed into political clubs that served both political and civic functions. As centers of the black communities in the South, the leagues became vehicles for the dissemination of information, acted as mediators between members of the black community and the white establishment, and served other practical functions like helping to build schools and churches for the community they served. As extensions of the Republican Party, these leagues worked to enroll newly enfranchised black voters, campaign for candidates, and generally help the party win elections (**Figure 7.10**).

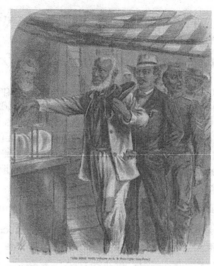

Figure 7.10 *The First Vote*, by Alfred R. Waud, appeared in *Harper's Weekly* in 1867. The Fifteenth Amendment gave black men the right to vote for the first time.

The political activities of the leagues launched a great many African Americans and former slaves into politics throughout the South. For the first time, blacks began to hold political office, and several were elected to the U.S. Congress. In the 1870s, fifteen members of the House of Representatives and two senators were black. The two senators, Blanche K. Bruce and Hiram Revels, were both from Mississippi, the home state of former U.S. senator and later Confederate president Jefferson Davis. Hiram Revels (**Figure 7.11**), was a freeborn man from North Carolina who rose to prominence as a minister in the African Methodist Episcopal Church and then as a Mississippi state senator in 1869. The following year he was elected by the state legislature to fill one of Mississippi's two U.S. Senate seats, which had been vacant since the war. His arrival in Washington, DC, drew intense interest: as the *New York Times* noted, when "the colored Senator from Mississippi, was sworn in and admitted to his seat this afternoon . . . there was not an inch of standing or sitting room in the galleries, so densely were they packed. . . . When the Vice-President uttered the words, 'The Senator elect will now advance and take the oath,' a pin might have been heard drop."

Figure 7.11 Hiram Revels served as a preacher throughout the Midwest before settling in Mississippi in 1866. When he was elected by the Mississippi state legislature in 1870, he became the country's first African American senator.

DEFINING "AMERICAN"

✿ *Senator Revels on Segregated Schools in Washington, DC*

Hiram R. Revels became the first African American to serve in the U.S. Senate in 1870. In 1871, he gave the following speech about Washington's segregated schools before Congress.

> Will establishing such [desegregated] schools as I am now advocating in this District harm our white friends? . . . By some it is contended that if we establish mixed schools here a great insult will be given to the white citizens, and that the white schools will be seriously damaged. . . . When I was on a lecturing tour in the state of Ohio . . . [o]ne of the leading gentlemen connected with the schools in that town came to see me. . . . He asked me, "Have you been to New England, where they have mixed schools?" I replied, "I have sir." "Well," said he, "please tell me this: does not social equality result from mixed schools?" "No, sir; very far from it," I responded. "Why," said he, "how can it be otherwise?" I replied, "I will tell you how it can be otherwise, and how it is otherwise. Go to the schools and you see there white children and colored children seated side by side, studying their lessons, standing side by side and reciting their lessons, and perhaps in walking to school they may walk together; but that is the last of it. The white children go to their homes; the colored children go to theirs; and on the Lord's day you will see those colored children in colored churches, and the white family, you will see the white children there, and the colored children at entertainments given by persons of their color." I aver, sir, that mixed schools are very far from bringing about social equality."

According to Senator Revels's speech, what is "social equality" and why is it important to the issue of desegregated schools? Does Revels favor social equality or social segregation? Did social equality exist in the United States in 1871?

Though the fact of their presence was dramatic and important, as the *New York Times* description above demonstrates, the few African American representatives and senators who served in Congress during Reconstruction represented only a tiny fraction of the many hundreds, possibly thousands, of blacks who served in a great number of capacities at the local and state levels. The South during the early 1870s brimmed with freed slaves and freeborn blacks serving as school board commissioners, county commissioners, clerks of court, board of education and city council members, justices of the peace, constables, coroners, magistrates, sheriffs, auditors, and registrars. This wave of local African American political activity contributed to and was accompanied by a new concern for the poor and disadvantaged in the South. The southern Republican leadership did away with the hated black codes, undid the work of white supremacists, and worked to reduce obstacles confronting freed people.

Reconstruction governments invested in infrastructure, paying special attention to the rehabilitation of the southern railroads. They set up public education systems that enrolled both white and black students. They established or increased funding for hospitals, orphanages, and asylums for the insane. In some states, the state and local governments provided the poor with basic necessities like firewood and even bread. And to pay for these new services and subsidies, the governments levied taxes on land and property, an action that struck at the heart of the foundation of southern economic inequality. Indeed, the land tax compounded the existing problems of white landowners, who were often cash-poor, and contributed to resentment of what southerners viewed as another northern attack on their way of life.

White southerners reacted with outrage at the changes imposed upon them. The sight of once-enslaved blacks serving in positions of authority as sheriffs, congressmen, and city council members stimulated great resentment at the process of Reconstruction and its undermining of the traditional social and economic foundations of the South. Indignant southerners referred to this period of reform as a time of "negro misrule." They complained of profligate corruption on the part of vengeful freed slaves and greedy northerners looking to fill their pockets with the South's riches. Unfortunately for the great many honest reformers, southerners did have a handful of real examples of corruption they could point to, such as legislators using state revenues to buy hams and perfumes or giving themselves inflated   salaries.

Such examples, however, were relatively few and largely comparable to nineteenth-century corruption across the country. Yet these powerful stories, combined with deep-seated racial animosity toward blacks in the South, led to Democratic campaigns to "redeem" state governments. Democrats across the South leveraged planters' economic power and wielded white vigilante violence to ultimately take back state political power from the Republicans. By the time President Grant's attentions were being directed away from the South and toward the Indian Wars in the West in 1876, power in the South had largely been returned to whites and Reconstruction was effectively abandoned. By the end of 1876, only South Carolina, Louisiana, and Florida still had Republican governments.

The sense that the South had been unfairly sacrificed to northern vice and black vengeance, despite a wealth of evidence to the contrary, persisted for many decades. So powerful and pervasive was this narrative that by the time D. W. Griffith released his 1915 motion picture, *The Birth of a Nation*, whites around the country were primed to accept the fallacy that white southerners were the frequent victims of violence and violation at the hands of unrestrained blacks. The reality is that the opposite was true. White southerners orchestrated a sometimes violent and generally successful counterrevolution against Reconstruction policies in the South beginning in the 1860s. Those who worked to change and modernize the South typically did so under the stern gaze of exasperated whites and threats of violence. Black Republican officials in the South were frequently terrorized, assaulted, and even murdered with impunity by organizations like the Ku Klux Klan. When not ignoring the Fourteenth and Fifteenth Amendments altogether, white leaders often used trickery and fraud at the polls to get the results they wanted. As Reconstruction came to a close, these methods came to define southern life for African Americans for nearly a century afterward.

7.4 The Collapse of Reconstruction

By the end of this section, you will be able to:
* Explain the reasons for the collapse of Reconstruction
* Describe the efforts of white southern "redeemers" to roll back the gains of Reconstruction

The effort to remake the South generated a brutal reaction among southern whites, who were committed to keeping blacks in a subservient position. To prevent blacks from gaining economic ground and to maintain cheap labor for the agricultural economy, an exploitative system of sharecropping spread throughout the South. Domestic terror organizations, most notably the Ku Klux Klan, employed various methods (arson, whipping, murder) to keep freed people from voting and achieving political, social, or economic equality with whites.

BUILDING BLACK COMMUNITIES

The degraded status of black men and women had placed them outside the limits of what antebellum southern whites considered appropriate gender roles and familial hierarchies. Slave marriages did not enjoy legal recognition. Enslaved men were humiliated and deprived of authority and of the ability to protect enslaved women, who were frequently exposed to the brutality and sexual domination of white masters and vigilantes alike. Slave parents could not protect their children, who could be bought, sold, put to work, brutally disciplined, and abused without their consent; parents, too, could be sold away from their children (**Figure 7.12**). Moreover, the division of labor idealized in white southern society, in which men worked the land and women performed the role of domestic caretaker, was null and void where slaves were concerned. Both slave men and women were made to perform hard labor in the fields.

Figure 7.12 After emancipation, many fathers who had been sold from their families as slaves—a circumstance illustrated in the engraving above, which shows a male slave forced to leave his wife and children—set out to find those lost families and rebuild their lives.

In the Reconstruction era, African Americans embraced the right to enjoy the family bonds and the expression of gender norms they had been systematically denied. Many thousands of freed black men who had been separated from their families as slaves took to the road to find their long-lost spouses and children and renew their bonds. In one instance, a journalist reported having interviewed a freed slave who traveled over six hundred miles on foot in search of the family that was taken from him while in bondage. Couples that had been spared separation quickly set out to legalize their marriages, often by way of the Freedmen's Bureau, now that this option was available. Those who had no families would sometimes relocate to southern towns and cities, so as to be part of the larger black community where churches and other mutual aid societies offered help and camaraderie.

SHARECROPPING

Most freed people stayed in the South on the lands where their families and loved ones had worked for generations as slaves. They hungered to own and farm their own lands instead of the lands of white plantation owners. In one case, former slaves on the Sea Islands off the coast of South Carolina initially had hopes of owning the land they had worked for many decades after General Sherman directed that freed people be granted title to plots of forty acres.

The Freedmen's Bureau provided additional cause for such hopes by directing that leases and titles to lands in the South be made available to former slaves. However, these efforts ran afoul of President Johnson. In 1865, he ordered the return of land to white landowners, a setback for those freed people, such as those on the South Carolina Sea Islands, who had begun to cultivate the land as their own. Ultimately, there was no redistribution of land in the South.

The end of slavery meant the transition to wage labor. However, this conversion did not entail a new era of economic independence for former slaves. While they no longer faced relentless toil under the lash, freed people emerged from slavery without any money and needed farm implements, food, and other basic necessities to start their new lives. Under the **crop-lien system**, store owners extended credit to farmers under the agreement that the debtors would pay with a portion of their future harvest. However, the creditors charged high interest rates, making it even harder for freed people to gain economic independence.

Throughout the South, **sharecropping** took root, a crop-lien system that worked to the advantage of landowners. Under the system, freed people rented the land they worked, often on the same plantations where they had been slaves. Some landless whites also became sharecroppers. Sharecroppers paid their landlords with the crops they grew, often as much as half their harvest. Sharecropping favored the landlords and ensured that freed people could not attain independent livelihoods. The year-to-year leases meant no incentive existed to substantially improve the land, and high interest payments siphoned additional money away from the farmers. Sharecroppers often became trapped in a never-ending cycle of debt, unable to buy their own land and unable to stop working for their creditor because of what they owed. The consequences of sharecropping affected the entire South for many generations, severely limiting economic development and ensuring that the South remained an agricultural backwater.

THE "INVISIBLE EMPIRE OF THE SOUTH"

Paramilitary white-supremacist terror organizations in the South helped bring about the collapse of Reconstruction, using violence as their primary weapon. The "Invisible Empire of the South," or **Ku Klux Klan**, stands as the most notorious. The Klan was founded in 1866 as an oath-bound fraternal order of Confederate veterans in Tennessee, with former Confederate General Nathan Bedford Forrest as its first leader. The organization—its name likely derived from *kuklos*, a Greek word meaning circle—devised elaborate rituals and grandiose names for its ranking members: Grand Wizard, Grand Dragon, Grand Titan, and Grand Cyclops. Soon, however, this fraternal organization evolved into a vigilante terrorist group that vented southern whites' collective frustration over the loss of the war and the course of Radical Reconstruction through acts of intimidation and violence.

The Klan terrorized newly freed blacks to deter them from exercising their citizenship rights and freedoms. Other anti-black vigilante groups around the South began to adopt the Klan name and perpetrate acts of unspeakable violence against anyone they considered a tool of Reconstruction. Indeed, as historians have noted, Klan units around the South operated autonomously and with a variety of motives. Some may have sincerely believed they were righting wrongs, others merely satisfying their lurid desires for violence. Nor was the Klan the only racist vigilante organization. Other groups, like the Red Shirts from Mississippi and the Knights of the White Camelia and the White League, both from Louisiana, also sprang up at this time. The Klan and similar organizations also worked as an extension of the Democratic Party to win elections.

Despite the great variety in Klan membership, on the whole, the group tended to direct its attention toward persecuting freed people and people they considered **carpetbaggers**, a term of abuse applied to northerners accused of having come to the South to acquire wealth through political power at the expense of southerners. The colorful term captured the disdain of southerners for these people, reflecting the common assumption that these men, sensing great opportunity, packed up all their worldly possessions in carpetbags, a then-popular type of luggage, and made their way to the South. Implied in this definition is the notion that these men came from little and were thus shiftless wanderers motivated only by the desire for quick money. In reality, these northerners tended to be young, idealistic, often well-educated men who responded to northern campaigns urging them to lead the modernization of the South. But the image of them as swindlers taking advantage of the South at its time of need resonated with a white southern population aggrieved by loss and economic decline. Southern whites who supported Reconstruction, known as **scalawags**, also generated great hostility as traitors to the South. They, too, became targets of the Klan and similar groups.

The Klan seized on the pervasive but largely fictional narrative of the northern carpetbagger as a powerful tool for restoring white supremacy and overturning Republican state governments in the South (**Figure 7.13**). To preserve a white-dominated society, Klan members punished blacks for attempting to improve their station in life or acting "uppity." To prevent freed people from attaining an education, the Klan burned public schools. In an effort to stop blacks from voting, the Klan murdered, whipped, and otherwise intimidated freed people and their white supporters. It wasn't uncommon for Klan members to intimidate Union League members and Freedmen's Bureau workers. The Klan even perpetrated acts of political assassination, killing a sitting U.S. congressman from Arkansas and three state congressmen from South Carolina.

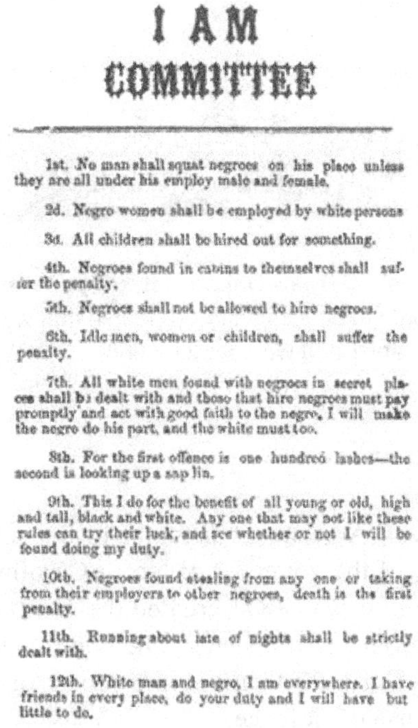

I AM
COMMITTEE

1st. No man shall squat negroes on his place unless they are all under his employ male and female.

2d. Negro women shall be employed by white persons

3d. All children shall be hired out for something.

4th. Negroes found in cabins to themselves shall suffer the penalty.

5th. Negroes shall not be allowed to hire negroes.

6th. Idle men, women or children, shall suffer the penalty.

7th. All white men found with negroes in secret places shall be dealt with and those that hire negroes must pay promptly and act with good faith to the negro, I will make the negro do his part, and the white must too.

8th. For the first offence is one hundred lashes—the second is looking up a sap lin.

9th. This I do for the benefit of all young or old, high and tall, black and white. Any one that may not like these rules can try their luck, and see whether or not I will be found doing my duty.

10th. Negroes found stealing from any one or taking from their employers to other negroes, death is the first penalty.

11th. Running about late of nights shall be strictly dealt with.

12th. White man and negro, I am everywhere. I have friends in every place, do your duty and I will have but little to do.

Figure 7.13 The Ku Klux Klan posted circulars such as this 1867 West Virginia broadside to warn blacks and white sympathizers of the power and ubiquity of the Klan.

Klan tactics included riding out to victims' houses, masked and armed, and firing into the homes or burning them down (**Figure 7.14**). Other tactics relied more on the threat of violence, such as happened in Mississippi when fifty masked Klansmen rode out to a local schoolteacher's house to express their displeasure with the school tax and to suggest that she consider leaving. Still other tactics intimidated through imaginative trickery. One such method was to dress up as ghosts of slain Confederate soldiers and stage stunts designed to convince their victims of their supernatural abilities.

Figure 7.14 This illustration by Frank Bellew, captioned "Visit of the Ku-Klux," appeared in *Harper's Weekly* in 1872. A hooded Klansman surreptitiously points a rifle at an unaware black family in their home.

Regardless of the method, the general goal of reinstating white supremacy as a foundational principle and returning the South to a situation that largely resembled antebellum conditions remained a constant.   The

Klan used its power to eliminate black economic independence, decimate blacks' political rights, reclaim white dominance over black women's bodies and black men's masculinity, tear apart black communities, and return blacks to earlier patterns of economic and political subservience and social deference. In this, they were largely successful.

Click and Explore

Visit Freedmen's Bureau Online (http://openstaxcollege.org/l/15Freedmen) to view digitized records of attacks on freed people that were reported in Albany, Georgia, between January 1 and October 31, 1868.

The president and Congress, however, were not indifferent to the violence, and they worked to bring it to an end. In 1870, at the insistence of the governor of North Carolina, President Grant told Congress to investigate the Klan. In response, Congress in 1871 created the Joint Select Committee to Inquire into the Condition of Affairs in the Late Insurrectionary States. The committee took testimony from freed people in the South, and in 1872, it published a thirteen-volume report on the tactics the Klan used to derail democracy in the South through the use of violence.

MY STORY

☮ Abram Colby on the Methods of the Ku Klux Klan

The following statements are from the October 27, 1871, testimony of fifty-two-year-old former slave Abram Colby, which the joint select committee investigating the Klan took in Atlanta, Georgia. Colby had been elected to the lower house of the Georgia State legislature in 1868.

> On the 29th of October, they came to my house and broke my door open, took me out of my bed and took me to the woods and whipped me three hours or more and left me in the woods for dead. They said to me, "Do you think you will ever vote another damned Radical ticket?" I said, "I will not tell you a lie." They said, "No; don't tell a lie." . . . I said, "If there was an election to-morrow, I would vote the Radical ticket." They set in and whipped me a thousand licks more, I suppose. . . .
>
> They said I had influence with the negroes of other counties, and had carried the negroes against them. About two days before they whipped me they offered me $5,000 to turn and go with them, and said they would pay me $2,500 cash if I would turn and let another man go to the legislature in my place. . . .
>
> I would have come before the court here last week, but I knew it was no use for me to try to get Ku-Klux condemned by Ku-Klux, and I did not come. Mr. Saunders, a member of the grand jury here last week, is the father of one of the very men I knew whipped me. . . .
>
> They broke something inside of me, and the doctor has been attending to me for more than a year. Sometimes I cannot get up and down off my bed, and my left hand is not of much use to me.
>
> —Abram Colby testimony, Joint Select Committee Report, 1872

Why did the Klan target Colby? What methods did they use?

Congress also passed a series of three laws designed to stamp out the Klan. Passed in 1870 and 1871, the Enforcement Acts or "Force Acts" were designed to outlaw intimidation at the polls and to give the federal government the power to prosecute crimes against freed people in federal rather than state courts. Congress believed that this last step, a provision in the third Enforcement Act, also called the Ku Klux Klan Act, was necessary in order to ensure that trials would not be decided by white juries in southern states friendly to the Klan. The act also allowed the president to impose martial law in areas controlled by the Klan and gave President Grant the power to suspend the writ of habeas corpus, a continuation of the wartime power granted to President Lincoln. The suspension meant individuals suspected of engaging in Klan activity could be jailed indefinitely.

President Grant made frequent use of the powers granted to him by Congress, especially in South Carolina, where federal troops imposed martial law in nine counties in an effort to derail Klan activities. However, the federal government faced entrenched local organizations and a white population firmly opposed to Radical Reconstruction. Changes came slowly or not at all, and disillusionment set in. After 1872, federal government efforts to put down paramilitary terror in the South waned.

"REDEEMERS" AND THE END OF RECONSTRUCTION

While the president and Congress may have seen the Klan and other clandestine white supremacist, terrorist organizations as a threat to stability and progress in the South, many southern whites saw them as an instrument of order in a world turned upside down. Many white southerners felt humiliated by the process of Radical Reconstruction and the way Republicans had upended southern society, placing blacks in positions of authority while taxing large landowners to pay for the education of former slaves. Those committed to rolling back the tide of Radical Reconstruction in the South called themselves **redeemers**, a label that expressed their desire to redeem their states from northern control and to restore the antebellum social order whereby blacks were kept safely under the boot heel of whites. They represented the Democratic Party in the South and worked tirelessly to end what they saw as an era of "negro misrule." By 1877, they had succeeded in bringing about the "redemption" of the South, effectively destroying the dream of Radical Reconstruction.

Although Ulysses S. Grant won a second term in the presidential election of 1872, the Republican grip on national political power began to slip in the early 1870s. Three major events undermined Republican control. First, in 1873, the United States experienced the start of a long economic downturn, the result of economic instability in Europe that spread to the United States. In the fall of 1873, the bank of Jay Cooke & Company failed to meet its financial obligations and went bankrupt, setting off a panic in American financial markets. An economic depression ensued, which Democrats blamed on Republicans and which lasted much of the decade.

Second, the Republican Party experienced internal squabbles and divided into two factions. Some Republicans began to question the expansive role of the federal government, arguing for limiting the size and scope of federal initiatives. These advocates, known as Liberal Republicans because they followed classical liberalism in championing small government, formed their own breakaway party. Their ideas changed the nature of the debate over Reconstruction by challenging reliance on federal government help to bring about change in the South. Now some Republicans argued for downsizing Reconstruction efforts.

Third, the Grant administration became mired in scandals, further tarnishing the Republicans while giving Democrats the upper hand. One scandal arose over the siphoning off of money from excise taxes on whiskey. The "Whiskey Ring," as it was called, involved people at the highest levels of the Grant administration, including the president's personal secretary, Orville Babcock. Another scandal entangled Crédit Mobilier of America, a construction company and part of the important French Crédit Mobilier banking company. The Union Pacific Railroad company, created by the federal government during the Civil War to construct a transcontinental railroad, paid Crédit Mobilier to build the railroad. However, Crédit Mobilier used the funds it received to buy Union Pacific Railroad bonds and resell them at a huge profit. Some members of Congress, as well as Vice President Schuyler Colfax, had accepted funds from

Crédit Mobilier in return for forestalling an inquiry. When the scam became known in 1872, Democratic opponents of Reconstruction pointed to Crédit Mobilier as an example of corruption in the Republican-dominated federal government and evidence that smaller government was better.

The Democratic Party in the South made significant advances in the 1870s in its efforts to wrest political control from the Republican-dominated state governments. The Ku Klux Klan, as well as other paramilitary groups in the South, often operated as military wings of the Democratic Party in former Confederate states. In one notorious episode following a contested 1872 gubernatorial election in Louisiana, as many as 150 freedmen loyal to the Republican Party were killed at the Colfax courthouse by armed members of the Democratic Party, even as many of them tried to surrender (**Figure 7.15**).

Figure 7.15 In this illustration by Charles Harvey Weigall, captioned "The Louisiana Murders—Gathering the Dead and Wounded" and published in *Harper's Weekly* in 1873, survivors of the Colfax Massacre tend to those involved in the conflict. The dead and wounded all appear to be black, and two white men on horses watch over them. Another man stands with a gun pointed at the survivors.

In other areas of the South, the Democratic Party gained control over state politics. Texas came under Democratic control by 1873, and in the following year Alabama and Arkansas followed suit. In national politics, too, the Democrats gained ground—especially during the 1874 elections, when they recaptured control of the House of Representatives for the first time since before the Civil War. Every other southern state, with the exception of Florida, South Carolina, and Louisiana—the states where federal troops remained a force—also fell to the Democratic Party and the restoration of white supremacy. Southerners everywhere celebrated their "redemption" from Radical Republican rule.

THE CONTESTED ELECTION OF 1876

By the time of the 1876 presidential election, Reconstruction had come to an end in most southern states. In Congress, the political power of the Radical Republicans had waned, although some continued their efforts to realize the dream of equality between blacks and whites. One of the last attempts to do so was the passage of the 1875 Civil Rights Act, which required equality in public places and on juries. This law was challenged in court, and in 1883 the Supreme Court ruled it unconstitutional, arguing that the Thirteenth and Fourteenth Amendments did not prohibit discrimination by private individuals. By the 1870s, the Supreme Court had also undercut the letter and the spirit of the Fourteenth Amendment by interpreting it as affording freed people only limited federal protection from the Klan and other terror groups.

The country remained bitterly divided, and this was reflected in the contested election of 1876. While Grant wanted to run for a third term, scandals and Democratic successes in the South dashed those hopes. Republicans instead selected Rutherford B. Hayes, the three-time governor of Ohio. Democrats nominated Samuel Tilden, the reform governor of New York, who was instrumental in ending the Tweed Ring and Tammany Hall corruption in New York City. The November election produced an apparent Democratic victory, as Tilden carried the South and large northern states with a 300,000-vote advantage in the popular vote. However, disputed returns from Louisiana, South Carolina, Florida, and Oregon, whose electoral votes totaled twenty, threw the election into doubt.

Hayes could still win if he gained those twenty electoral votes. As the Constitution did not provide a method to determine the validity of disputed votes, the decision fell to Congress, where Republicans controlled the Senate and Democrats controlled the House of Representatives. In late January 1877, Congress tried to break the deadlock by creating a special electoral commission composed of five senators, five representatives, and five justices of the Supreme Court. The congressional delegation represented both parties equally, with five Democrats and five Republicans. The court delegation had two Democrats, two Republicans, and one independent—David Davis, who resigned from the Supreme Court (and from the commission) when the Illinois legislature elected him to the Senate. After Davis's resignation, President Grant selected a Republican to take his place, tipping the scales in favor of Hayes. The commission then awarded the disputed electoral votes and the presidency to Hayes, voting on party lines, 8 to 7 (**Figure 7.16**). The Democrats called foul, threatening to hold up the commission's decision in the courts.

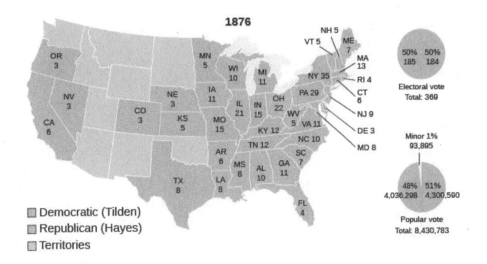

Figure 7.16 This map illustrates the results of the presidential election of 1876. Tilden, the Democratic candidate, swept the South, with the exception of the contested states of Florida, Louisiana, and South Carolina.

In what became known as the **Compromise of 1877**, Republican Senate leaders worked with the Democratic leadership so they would support Hayes and the commission's decision. The two sides agreed that one Southern Democrat would be appointed to Hayes's cabinet, Democrats would control federal patronage (the awarding of government jobs) in their areas in the South, and there would be a commitment to generous internal improvements, including federal aid for the Texas and Pacific Railway. Perhaps most important, all remaining federal troops would be withdrawn from the South, a move that effectively ended Reconstruction. Hayes believed that southern leaders would obey and enforce the Reconstruction-era constitutional amendments that protected the rights of freed people. His trust was soon proved to be misguided, much to his dismay, and he devoted a large part of his life to securing rights for freedmen. For their part, the Democrats took over the remaining southern states, creating what became known as the "Solid South"—a region that consistently voted in a bloc for the Democratic Party.

CHAPTER 8

Go West Young Man! Westward Expansion, 1840-1900

Figure 8.1 Widely held rhetoric of the nineteenth century suggested to Americans that it was their divine right and responsibility to settle the West with Protestant democratic values. Newspaper editor Horace Greely, who coined the phrase "Go west, young man," encouraged Americans to fulfill this dream. Artists of the day depicted this western expansion in idealized landscapes that bore little resemblance to the difficulties of life on the trail.

Chapter Outline

Introduction

In the middle of the nineteenth century, farmers in the "Old West"—the land across the Allegheny Mountains in Pennsylvania—began to hear about the opportunities to be found in the "New West." They had long believed that the land west of the Mississippi was a great desert, unfit for human habitation. But now, the federal government was encouraging them to join the migratory stream westward to this unknown land. For a variety of reasons, Americans increasingly felt compelled to fulfill their "Manifest Destiny," a phrase that came to mean that they were expected to spread across the land given to them by God and, most importantly, spread predominantly American values to the frontier (**Figure 8.1**).

With great trepidation, hundreds, and then hundreds of thousands, of settlers packed their lives into wagons and set out, following the Oregon, California, and Santa Fe Trails, to seek a new life in the West. Some sought open lands and greater freedom to fulfill the democratic vision originally promoted by Thomas Jefferson and experienced by their ancestors. Others saw economic opportunity. Still others believed it was their job to spread the word of God to the "heathens" on the frontier. Whatever their motivation, the great migration was underway. The American pioneer spirit was born.

8.1 The Westward Spirit

By the end of this section, you will be able to:
- Explain the evolution of American views about westward migration in the mid-nineteenth century
- Analyze the ways in which the federal government facilitated Americans' westward migration in the mid-nineteenth century

While a small number of settlers had pushed westward before the mid-nineteenth century, the land west of the Mississippi was largely unexplored. Most Americans, if they thought of it at all, viewed this territory as an arid wasteland suitable only for Indians whom the federal government had displaced from eastern lands in previous generations. The reflections of early explorers who conducted scientific treks throughout the West tended to confirm this belief. Major Stephen Harriman Long, who commanded an expedition through Missouri and into the Yellowstone region in 1819–1820, frequently described the Great Plains as a arid and useless region, suitable as nothing more than a "great American desert." But, beginning in the 1840s, a combination of economic opportunity and ideological encouragement changed the way Americans thought of the West. The federal government offered a number of incentives, making it viable for Americans to take on the challenge of seizing these rough lands from others and subsequently taming them. Still, most Americans who went west needed some financial security at the outset of their journey; even with government aid, the truly poor could not make the trip. The cost of moving an entire family westward, combined with the risks as well as the questionable chances of success, made the move prohibitive for most. While the economic Panic of 1837 led many to question the promise of urban America, and thus turn their focus to the promise of commercial farming in the West, the Panic also resulted in many lacking the financial resources to make such a commitment. For most, the dream to "Go west, young man" remained unfulfilled.

While much of the basis for westward expansion was economic, there was also a more philosophical reason, which was bound up in the American belief that the country—and the "heathens" who populated it—was destined to come under the civilizing rule of Euro-American settlers and their superior technology, most notably railroads and the telegraph. While the extent to which that belief was a heartfelt   motivation

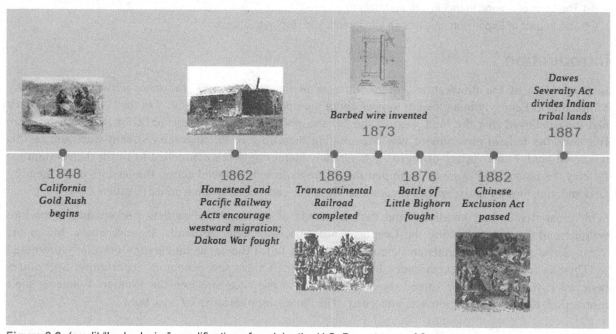

Figure 8.2 (credit "barbed wire": modification of work by the U.S. Department of Commerce)

held by most Americans, or simply a rationalization of the conquests that followed, remains debatable, the clashes—both physical and cultural—that followed this western migration left scars on the country that are still felt today.

MANIFEST DESTINY

The concept of **Manifest Destiny** found its roots in the long-standing traditions of territorial expansion upon which the nation itself was founded. This phrase, which implies divine encouragement for territorial expansion, was coined by magazine editor John O'Sullivan in 1845, when he wrote in the *United States Magazine and Democratic Review* that "it was our manifest destiny to overspread the continent allotted by Providence for the free development of our multiplying millions." Although the context of O'Sullivan's original article was to encourage expansion into the newly acquired Texas territory, the spirit it invoked would subsequently be used to encourage westward settlement throughout the rest of the nineteenth century. Land developers, railroad magnates, and other investors capitalized on the notion to encourage westward settlement for their own financial benefit. Soon thereafter, the federal government encouraged this inclination as a means to further develop the West during the Civil War, especially at its outset, when concerns over the possible expansion of slavery deeper into western territories was a legitimate fear.

The idea was simple: Americans were destined—and indeed divinely ordained—to expand democratic institutions throughout the continent. As they spread their culture, thoughts, and customs, they would, in the process, "improve" the lives of the native inhabitants who might otherwise resist Protestant institutions and, more importantly, economic development of the land. O'Sullivan may have coined the phrase, but the concept had preceded him: Throughout the 1800s, politicians and writers had stated the belief that the United States was destined to rule the continent. O'Sullivan's words, which resonated in the popular press, matched the economic and political goals of a federal government increasingly committed to expansion.

Manifest Destiny justified in Americans' minds their right and duty to govern any other groups they encountered during their expansion, as well as absolved them of any questionable tactics they employed in the process. While the commonly held view of the day was of a relatively empty frontier, waiting for the arrival of the settlers who could properly exploit the vast resources for economic gain, the reality was quite different. Hispanic communities in the Southwest, diverse Indian tribes throughout the western states, as well as other settlers from Asia and Western Europe already lived in many parts of the country. American expansion would necessitate a far more complex and involved exchange than simply filling empty space.

Still, in part as a result of the spark lit by O'Sullivan and others, waves of Americans and recently arrived immigrants began to move west in wagon trains. They travelled along several identifiable trails: first the Oregon Trail, then later the Santa Fe and California Trails, among others. The Oregon Trail is the most famous of these western routes. Two thousand miles long and barely passable on foot in the early nineteenth century, by the 1840s, wagon trains were a common sight. Between 1845 and 1870, considered to be the height of migration along the trail, over 400,000 settlers followed this path west from Missouri (**Figure 8.3**).

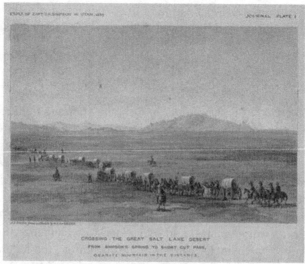

Figure 8.3 Hundreds of thousands of people travelled west on the Oregon, California, and Santa Fe Trails, but their numbers did not ensure their safety. Illness, starvation, and other dangers—both real and imagined— made survival hard. (credit: U.S. National Archives and Records Administration)

DEFINING "AMERICAN"

◉ *Who Will Set Limits to Our Onward March?*

America is destined for better deeds. It is our unparalleled glory that we have no reminiscences of battle fields, but in defense [sic] of humanity, of the oppressed of all nations, of the rights of conscience, the rights of personal enfranchisement. Our annals describe no scenes of horrid carnage, where men were led on by hundreds of thousands to slay one another, dupes and victims to emperors, kings, nobles, demons in the human form called heroes. We have had patriots to defend our homes, our liberties, but no aspirants to crowns or thrones; nor have the American people ever suffered themselves to be led on by wicked ambition to depopulate the land, to spread desolation far and wide, that a human being might be placed on a seat of supremacy. . . .

The expansive future is our arena, and for our history. We are entering on its untrodden space, with the truths of God in our minds, beneficent objects in our hearts, and with a clear conscience unsullied by the past. We are the nation of human progress, and who will, what can, set limits to our onward march? Providence is with us, and no earthly power can.

—John O'Sullivan, 1839

Think about how this quotation resonated with different groups of Americans at the time. When looked at through today's lens, the actions of the westward-moving settlers were fraught with brutality and racism. At the time, however, many settlers felt they were at the pinnacle of democracy, and that with no aristocracy or ancient history, America was a new world where anyone could succeed. Even then, consider how the phrase "anyone" was restricted by race, gender, and nationality.

Click and Explore

Visit **Across the Plains in '64** (http://openstaxcollege.org/l/iowaoregon) to follow one family making their way westward from Iowa to Oregon. Click on a few of the entries and see how the author describes their journey, from the expected to the surprising.

FEDERAL GOVERNMENT ASSISTANCE

To assist the settlers in their move westward and transform the migration from a trickle into a steady flow, Congress passed two significant pieces of legislation in 1862: the Homestead Act and the Pacific Railway Act. Born largely out of President Abraham Lincoln's growing concern that a potential Union defeat in the early stages of the Civil War might result in the expansion of slavery westward, Lincoln hoped that such laws would encourage the expansion of a "free soil" mentality across the West.

The Homestead Act allowed any head of household, or individual over the age of twenty-one—including unmarried women—to receive a parcel of 160 acres for only a nominal filing fee. All that recipients were required to do in exchange was to "improve the land" within a period of five years of taking possession. The standards for improvement were minimal: Owners could clear a few acres, build small houses or barns, or maintain livestock. Under this act, the government transferred over 270 million acres of public domain land to private citizens.

The Pacific Railway Act was pivotal in helping settlers move west more quickly, as well as move their farm products, and later cattle and mining deposits, back east. The first of many railway initiatives, this act commissioned the Union Pacific Railroad to build new track west from Omaha, Nebraska, while the Central Pacific Railroad moved east from Sacramento, California. The law provided each company with ownership of all public lands within two hundred feet on either side of the track laid, as well as additional land grants and payment through load bonds, prorated on the difficulty of the terrain it crossed. Because of these provisions, both companies made a significant profit, whether they were crossing hundreds of miles of open plains, or working their way through the Sierra Nevada Mountains of California. As a result, the nation's first transcontinental railroad was completed when the two companies connected their tracks at Promontory Point, Utah, in the spring of 1869. Other tracks, including lines radiating from this original one, subsequently created a network that linked all corners of the nation (**Figure 8.4**).

Figure 8.4 The "Golden Spike" connecting the country by rail was driven into the ground in Promontory Point, Utah, in 1869. The completion of the first transcontinental railroad dramatically changed the tenor of travel in the country, as people were able to complete in a week a route that had previously taken months.

In addition to legislation designed to facilitate western settlement, the U.S. government assumed an active role on the ground, building numerous forts throughout the West to protect and assist settlers during their migration. Forts such as Fort Laramie in Wyoming (built in 1834) and Fort Apache in Arizona (1870) served as protection from nearby Indians as well as maintained peace between potential warring tribes. Others located throughout Colorado and Wyoming became important trading posts for miners and fur trappers. Those built in Kansas, Nebraska, and the Dakotas served primarily to provide relief for farmers during times of drought or related hardships. Forts constructed along the California coastline provided protection in the wake of the Mexican-American War as well as during the American Civil War. These locations subsequently serviced the U.S. Navy and provided important support for growing Pacific trade routes. Whether as army posts constructed for the protection of white settlers and to maintain peace among Indian tribes, or as trading posts to further facilitate the development of the region, such forts proved to be vital contributions to westward migration.

WHO WERE THE SETTLERS?

In the nineteenth century, as today, it took money to relocate and start a new life. Due to the initial cost of relocation, land, and supplies, as well as months of preparing the soil, planting, and subsequent harvesting before any produce was ready for market, the original wave of western settlers along the Oregon Trail in the 1840s and 1850s consisted of moderately prosperous, white, native-born farming families of the East. But the passage of the Homestead Act and completion of the first transcontinental railroad meant that, by 1870, the possibility of western migration was opened to Americans of more modest means. What started as a trickle became a steady flow of migration that would last until the end of the century.

Nearly 400,000 settlers had made the trek westward by the height of the movement in 1870. The vast majority were men, although families also migrated, despite incredible hardships for women with young children. More recent immigrants also migrated west, with the largest numbers coming from Northern Europe and Canada. Germans, Scandinavians, and Irish were among the most common. These ethnic groups tended to settle close together, creating strong rural communities that mirrored the way of life they had left behind. According to U.S. Census Bureau records, the number of Scandinavians living in the United States during the second half of the nineteenth century exploded, from barely 18,000 in 1850 to over 1.1 million in 1900. During that same time period, the German-born population in the United States grew from 584,000 to nearly 2.7 million and the Irish-born population grew from 961,000 to 1.6 million. As they moved westward, several thousand immigrants established homesteads in the Midwest, primarily in Minnesota and Wisconsin, where, as of 1900, over one-third of the population was foreign-born, and in North Dakota, whose immigrant population stood at 45 percent at the turn of the century. Compared to

European immigrants, those from China were much less numerous, but still significant. More than 200,000 Chinese arrived in California between 1876 and 1890, albeit for entirely different reasons related to the Gold Rush.

In addition to a significant European migration westward, several thousand African Americans migrated west following the Civil War, as much to escape the racism and violence of the Old South as to find new economic opportunities. They were known as **exodusters**, referencing the biblical flight from Egypt, because they fled the racism of the South, with most of them headed to Kansas from Kentucky, Tennessee, Louisiana, Mississippi, and Texas. Over twenty-five thousand exodusters arrived in Kansas in 1879–1880 alone. By 1890, over 500,000 blacks lived west of the Mississippi River. Although the majority of black migrants became farmers, approximately twelve thousand worked as cowboys during the Texas cattle drives. Some also became "Buffalo Soldiers" in the wars against Indians. "Buffalo Soldiers" were African Americans allegedly so-named by various Indian tribes who equated their black, curly hair with that of the buffalo. Many had served in the Union army in the Civil War and were now organized into six, all-black cavalry and infantry units whose primary duties were to protect settlers from Indian attacks during the westward migration, as well as to assist in building the infrastructure required to support western settlement (**Figure 8.5**).

Figure 8.5 "Buffalo Soldiers," the first peacetime all-black regiments in the U.S. Army, protected settlers from Indian attacks. These soldiers also served as some of the country's first national park rangers.

Click and Explore

The **Oxford African American Studies Center** (http://openstaxcollege.org/l/ homesteads) features photographs and stories about black homesteaders. From exodusters to all-black settlements, the essay describes the largely hidden role that African Americans played in western expansion.

While white easterners, immigrants, and African Americans were moving west, several hundred thousand Hispanics had already settled in the American Southwest prior to the U.S. government seizing the land during its war with Mexico (1846–1848). The Treaty of Guadalupe Hidalgo, which ended the war in 1848, granted American citizenship to those who chose to stay in the United States, as the land switched from Mexican to U.S. ownership. Under the conditions of the treaty, Mexicans retained the right to their language, religion, and culture, as well as the property they held. As for citizenship, they could choose one of three options: 1) declare their intent to live in the United States but retain Mexican citizenship; 2) become U.S. citizens with all rights under the constitution; or 3) leave for Mexico. Despite such guarantees, within one generation, these new Hispanic American citizens found their culture under attack, and legal protection of their property all but non-existent.

8.2 Homesteading: Dreams and Realities

By the end of this section, you will be able to:
- Identify the challenges that farmers faced as they settled west of the Mississippi River
- Describe the unique experiences of women who participated in westward migration

As settlers and homesteaders moved westward to improve the land given to them through the Homestead Act, they faced a difficult and often insurmountable challenge. The land was difficult to farm, there were few building materials, and harsh weather, insects, and inexperience led to frequent setbacks. The prohibitive prices charged by the first railroad lines made it expensive to ship crops to market or have goods sent out. Although many farms failed, some survived and grew into large "bonanza" farms that hired additional labor and were able to benefit enough from economies of scale to grow profitable. Still, small family farms, and the settlers who worked them, were hard-pressed to do more than scrape out a living in an unforgiving environment that comprised arid land, violent weather shifts, and other challenges (**Figure 8.6**).

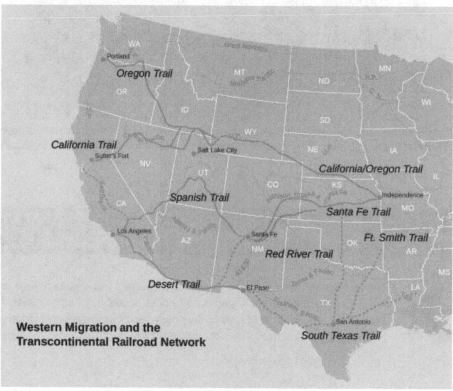

Figure 8.6 This map shows the trails (orange) used in westward migration and the development of railroad lines (blue) constructed after the completion of the first transcontinental railroad.

THE DIFFICULT LIFE OF THE PIONEER FARMER

Of the hundreds of thousands of settlers who moved west, the vast majority were homesteaders. These pioneers, like the Ingalls family of *Little House on the Prairie* book and television fame (see inset below), were seeking land and opportunity. Popularly known as "sodbusters," these men and women in the Midwest faced a difficult life on the frontier. They settled throughout the land that now makes up the Midwestern states of Wisconsin, Minnesota, Kansas, Nebraska, and the Dakotas. The weather and environment were bleak, and settlers struggled to eke out a living. A few unseasonably rainy years had led would-be settlers to believe that the "great desert" was no more, but the region's typically low rainfall and harsh temperatures made crop cultivation hard. Irrigation was a requirement, but finding water and building adequate systems proved too difficult and expensive for many farmers. It was not until 1902 and the passage of the Newlands Reclamation Act that a system finally existed to set aside funds from the sale of public lands to build dams for subsequent irrigation efforts. Prior to that, farmers across the Great Plains relied primarily on dry-farming techniques to grow corn, wheat, and sorghum, a practice that many continued in later years. A few also began to employ windmill technology to draw water, although both the drilling and construction of windmills became an added expense that few farmers could afford.

AMERICANA

❂ *The Enduring Appeal of Little House on the Prairie*

The story of western migration and survival has remained a touchstone of American culture, even today. The television show *Frontier Life* on PBS is one example, as are countless other modern-day evocations of the settlers. Consider the enormous popularity of the *Little House* series. The books, originally published in the 1930s and 1940s, have been in print continuously. The television show, *Little House on the Prairie*, ran for over a decade and was hugely successful (and was said to be President Ronald Reagan's favorite show). The books, although fictional, were based on Laura Ingalls Wilder's own childhood, as she travelled west with her family via covered wagon, stopping in Kansas, Wisconsin, South Dakota, and beyond (Figure 8.7).

(a)

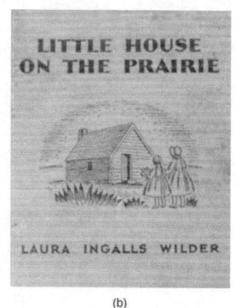
(b)

Figure 8.7 Laura Ingalls Wilder (a) is the celebrated author of the *Little House* series, which began in 1932 with the publication of *Little House in the Big Woods*. The third, and best known, book in the series, *Little House on the Prairie* (b), was published just three years later.

Wilder wrote of her stories, "As you read my stories of long ago I hope you will remember that the things that are truly worthwhile and that will give you happiness are the same now as they were then. Courage and kindness, loyalty, truth, and helpfulness are always the same and always needed." While Ingalls makes the point that her stories underscore traditional values that remain the same over time, this is not necessarily the only thing that made these books so popular. Perhaps part of their appeal is that they are adventure stories, with wild weather, wild animals, and wild Indians all playing a role. Does this explain their ongoing popularity? What other factors might make these stories appealing so long after they were originally written?

The first houses built by western settlers were typically made of mud and sod with thatch roofs, as there was little timber for building. Rain, when it arrived, presented constant problems for these **sod houses**, with mud falling into food, and vermin, most notably lice, scampering across bedding (**Figure 8.8**). Weather patterns not only left the fields dry, they also brought tornadoes, droughts, blizzards, and insect swarms. Tales of swarms of locusts were commonplace, and the crop-eating insects would at times cover the ground six to twelve inches deep. One frequently quoted Kansas newspaper reported a locust swarm in 1878 during which the insects devoured "everything green, stripping the foliage off the bark and from the tender twigs of the fruit trees, destroying every plant that is good for food or pleasant to the eye, that man has planted."

Figure 8.8 Sod houses were common in the Midwest as settlers moved west. There was no lumber to gather and no stones with which to build. These mud homes were vulnerable to weather and vermin, making life incredibly hard for the newly arrived homesteaders.

Farmers also faced the ever-present threat of debt and farm foreclosure by the banks. While land was essentially free under the Homestead Act, all other farm necessities cost money and were initially difficult to obtain in the newly settled parts of the country where market economies did not yet fully reach. Horses, livestock, wagons, wells, fencing, seed, and fertilizer were all critical to survival, but often hard to come by as the population initially remained sparsely settled across vast tracts of land. Railroads charged notoriously high rates for farm equipment and livestock, making it difficult to procure goods or make a profit on anything sent back east. Banks also charged high interest rates, and, in a cycle that replayed itself year after year, farmers would borrow from the bank with the intention of repaying their debt after the harvest. As the number of farmers moving westward increased, the market price of their produce steadily declined, even as the value of the actual land increased. Each year, hard-working farmers produced ever-larger crops, flooding the markets and subsequently driving prices down even further. Although some understood the economics of supply and demand, none could overtly control such forces.

Eventually, the arrival of a more extensive railroad network aided farmers, mostly by bringing much-needed supplies such as lumber for construction and new farm machinery. While John Deere sold a steel-faced plow as early as 1838, it was James Oliver's improvements to the device in the late 1860s that transformed life for homesteaders. His new, less expensive "chilled plow" was better equipped to cut through the shallow grass roots of the Midwestern terrain, as well as withstand damage from rocks just below the surface. Similar advancements in hay mowers, manure spreaders, and threshing machines greatly improved farm production for those who could afford them. Where capital expense became a significant factor, larger commercial farms—known as "**bonanza farms**"—began to develop. Farmers in Minnesota, North Dakota, and South Dakota hired migrant farmers to grow wheat on farms in excess of twenty thousand acres each. These large farms were succeeding by the end of the century, but small family farms continued to suffer. Although the land was nearly free, it cost close to $1000 for the necessary supplies to start up a farm, and many would-be landowners lured westward by the promise of cheap land became migrant farmers instead, working other peoples' land for a wage. The frustration of small farmers grew, ultimately leading to a revolt of sorts, discussed in a later chapter.

AN EVEN MORE CHALLENGING LIFE: A PIONEER WIFE

Although the West was numerically a male-dominated society, homesteading in particular encouraged the presence of women, families, and a domestic lifestyle, even if such a life was not an easy one. Women faced all the physical hardships that men encountered in terms of weather, illness, and danger, with the added complication of childbirth. Often, there was no doctor or midwife providing assistance, and many women died from treatable complications, as did their newborns. While some women could find employment in the newly settled towns as teachers, cooks, or seamstresses, they originally did not enjoy many rights. They could not sell property, sue for divorce, serve on juries, or vote. And for the vast majority of women, their work was not in towns for money, but on the farm. As late as 1900, a typical farm wife could expect to devote nine hours per day to chores such as cleaning, sewing, laundering, and preparing food. Two additional hours per day were spent cleaning the barn and chicken coop, milking the cows, caring for the chickens, and tending the family garden. One wife commented in 1879, "[We are] not much better than slaves. It is a weary, monotonous round of cooking and washing and mending and as a result the insane asylum is a third filled with wives of farmers."

Despite this grim image, the challenges of farm life eventually empowered women to break through some legal and social barriers. Many lived more equitably as partners with their husbands than did their eastern counterparts, helping each other through both hard times and good. If widowed, a wife typically took over responsibility for the farm, a level of management that was very rare back east, where the farm would fall to a son or other male relation. Pioneer women made important decisions and were considered by their husbands to be more equal partners in the success of the homestead, due to the necessity that all members had to work hard and contribute to the farming enterprise for it to succeed. Therefore, it is not surprising that the first states to grant women's rights, including the right to vote, were those in the Pacific Northwest and Upper Midwest, where women pioneers worked the land side by side with men. Some women seemed to be well suited to the challenges that frontier life presented them. Writing to her Aunt Martha from their homestead in Minnesota in 1873, Mary Carpenter refused to complain about the hardships of farm life: "I try to trust in God's promises, but we can't expect him to work miracles nowadays. Nevertheless, all that is expected of us is to do the best we can, and that we shall certainly endeavor to do. Even if we do freeze and starve in the way of duty, it will not be a dishonorable death."

8.3 Making a Living in Gold and Cattle

By the end of this section, you will be able to:
- Identify the major discoveries and developments in western gold, silver, and copper mining in the mid-nineteenth century
- Explain why the cattle industry was paramount to the development of the West and how it became the catalyst for violent range wars

Although homestead farming was the primary goal of most western settlers in the latter half of the nineteenth century, a small minority sought to make their fortunes quickly through other means. Specifically, gold (and, subsequently, silver and copper) prospecting attracted thousands of miners looking to "get rich quick" before returning east. In addition, ranchers capitalized on newly available railroad lines to move longhorn steers that populated southern and western Texas. This meat was highly sought after in eastern markets, and the demand created not only wealthy ranchers but an era of cowboys and cattle drives that in many ways defines how we think of the West today. Although neither miners nor ranchers intended to remain permanently in the West, many individuals from both groups ultimately stayed and settled there, sometimes due to the success of their gamble, and other times due to their abject failure.

THE CALIFORNIA GOLD RUSH AND BEYOND

The allure of gold has long sent people on wild chases; in the American West, the possibility of quick riches was no different. The search for gold represented an opportunity far different from the slow plod that homesteading farmers faced. The discovery of gold at Sutter's Mill in Coloma, California, set a pattern for such strikes that was repeated again and again for the next decade, in what collectively became known as the **California Gold Rush**. In what became typical, a sudden disorderly rush of prospectors descended upon a new discovery site, followed by the arrival of those who hoped to benefit from the strike by preying off the newly rich. This latter group of camp followers included saloonkeepers, prostitutes, store owners, and criminals, who all arrived in droves. If the strike was significant in size, a town of some magnitude might establish itself, and some semblance of law and order might replace the vigilante justice that typically grew in the small and short-lived mining outposts.

The original Forty-Niners were individual prospectors who sifted gold out of the dirt and gravel through "panning" or by diverting a stream through a sluice box (**Figure 8.9**). To varying degrees, the original California Gold Rush repeated itself throughout Colorado and Nevada for the next two decades. In 1859, Henry T. P. Comstock, a Canadian-born fur trapper, began gold mining in Nevada with other prospectors but then quickly found a blue-colored vein that proved to be the first significant silver discovery in the United States. Within twenty years, the **Comstock Lode**, as it was called, yielded more than $300 million in shafts that reached hundreds of feet into the mountain. Subsequent mining in Arizona and Montana yielded copper, and, while it lacked the glamour of gold, these deposits created huge wealth for those who exploited them, particularly with the advent of copper wiring for the delivery of electricity and telegraph communication.

(a)   (b)

Figure 8.9 The first gold prospectors in the 1850s and 1860s worked with easily portable tools that allowed anyone to follow their dream and strike it rich (a). It didn't take long for the most accessible minerals to be stripped, making way for large mining operations, including hydraulic mining, where high-pressure water jets removed sediment and rocks (b).

By the 1860s and 1870s, however, individual efforts to locate precious metals were less successful. The lowest-hanging fruit had been picked, and now it required investment capital and machinery to dig mine shafts that could reach remaining ore. With a much larger investment, miners needed a larger strike to be successful. This shift led to larger businesses underwriting mining operations, which eventually led to the development of greater urban stability and infrastructure. Denver, Colorado, was one of several cities that became permanent settlements, as businesses sought a stable environment to use as a base for their mining ventures.

For miners who had not yet struck it rich, this development was not a good one. They were now paid a daily or weekly wage to work underground in very dangerous conditions. They worked in shafts where the temperature could rise to above one hundred degrees Fahrenheit, and where poor ventilation might lead to long-term lung disease. They coped with shaft fires, dynamite explosions, and frequent cave-ins. By some historical accounts, close to eight thousand miners died on the frontier during this period, with over three times that number suffering crippling injuries. Some miners organized into unions and led strikes for better conditions, but these efforts were usually crushed by state militias.

Eventually, as the ore dried up, most mining towns turned into ghost towns. Even today, a visit through the American West shows old saloons and storefronts, abandoned as the residents moved on to their next shot at riches. The true lasting impact of the early mining efforts was the resulting desire of the U.S. government to bring law and order to the "Wild West" in order to more efficiently extract natural resources and encourage stable growth in the region. As more Americans moved to the region to seek permanent settlement, as opposed to brief speculative ventures, they also sought the safety and support that government order could bring. Nevada was admitted to the Union as a state in 1864, with Colorado following in 1876, then North Dakota, South Dakota, Montana, and Washington in 1889; and Idaho and Wyoming in 1890.

THE CATTLE KINGDOM

While the cattle industry lacked the romance of the Gold Rush, the role it played in western expansion should not be underestimated. For centuries, wild cattle roamed the Spanish borderlands. At the end of the Civil War, as many as five million longhorn steers could be found along the Texas frontier, yet few settlers had capitalized on the opportunity to claim them, due to the difficulty of transporting them to eastern markets. The completion of the first transcontinental railroad and subsequent railroad lines changed the game dramatically. Cattle ranchers and eastern businessmen realized that it was profitable to round up the wild steers and transport them by rail to be sold in the East for as much as thirty to fifty dollars per head. These ranchers and businessmen began the rampant speculation in the cattle industry that made, and lost, many fortunes.

So began the impressive cattle drives of the 1860s and 1870s. The famous Chisholm Trail provided a quick path from Texas to railroad terminals in Abilene, Wichita, and Dodge City, Kansas, where cowboys would receive their pay. These "cowtowns," as they became known, quickly grew to accommodate the needs of cowboys and the cattle industry. Cattlemen like Joseph G. McCoy, born in Illinois, quickly realized that the railroad offered a perfect way to get highly sought beef from Texas to the East. McCoy chose Abilene as a locale that would offer cowboys a convenient place to drive the cattle, and went about building stockyards, hotels, banks, and more to support the business. He promoted his services and encouraged cowboys to bring their cattle through Abilene for good money; soon, the city had grown into a bustling western city, complete with ways for the cowboys to spend their hard-earned pay (**Figure 8.10**).

Figure 8.10 Cattle drives were an integral part of western expansion. Cowboys worked long hours in the saddle, driving hardy longhorns to railroad towns that could ship the meat back east.

Between 1865 and 1885, as many as forty thousand cowboys roamed the Great Plains, hoping to work for local ranchers. They were all men, typically in their twenties, and close to one-third of them were Hispanic or African American. It is worth noting that the stereotype of the American cowboy—and indeed the cowboys themselves—borrowed much from the Mexicans who had long ago settled those lands. The saddles, lassos, chaps, and lariats that define cowboy culture all arose from the Mexican ranchers who had used them to great effect before the cowboys arrived.

Life as a cowboy was dirty and decidedly unglamorous. The terrain was difficult; conflicts with Native Americans, especially in Indian Territory (now Oklahoma), were notoriously deadly. But the longhorn cattle were hardy stock, and could survive and thrive while grazing along the long trail, so cowboys braved the trip for the promise of steady employment and satisfying wages. Eventually, however, the era of the free range ended. Ranchers developed the land, limiting grazing opportunities along the trail, and in 1873, the new technology of barbed wire allowed ranchers to fence off their lands and cattle claims. With the end of the free range, the cattle industry, like the mining industry before it, grew increasingly dominated by eastern businessmen. Capital investors from the East expanded rail lines and invested in ranches, ending the reign of the cattle drives.

AMERICANA

⊙ *Barbed Wire and a Way of Life Gone*

Called the "devil's rope" by Indians, barbed wire had a profound impact on the American West. Before its invention, settlers and ranchers alike were stymied by a lack of building materials to fence off land. Communal grazing and long cattle drives were the norm. But with the invention of barbed wire, large cattle ranchers and their investors were able to cheaply and easily parcel off the land they wanted—whether or not it was legally theirs to contain. As with many other inventions, several people "invented" barbed wire around the same time. In 1873, it was Joseph Glidden, however, who claimed the winning design and patented it. Not only did it spell the end of the free range for settlers and cowboys, it kept more land away from Indian tribes, who had never envisioned a culture that would claim to own land (Figure 8.11).

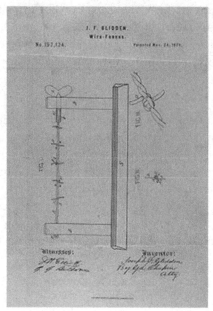

Figure 8.11 Joseph Glidden's invention of barbed wire in 1873 made him rich, changing the face of the American West forever. (credit: modification of work by the U.S. Department of Commerce)

In the early twentieth century, songwriter Cole Porter would take a poem by a Montana poet named Bob Fletcher and convert it into a cowboy song called, "Don't Fence Me In." As the lyrics below show, the song gave voice to the feeling that, as the fences multiplied, the ethos of the West was forever changed:

> Oh, give me land, lots of land, under starry skies above
> Don't fence me in
> Let me ride thru the wide-open country that I love
> Don't fence me in . . .
> Just turn me loose
> Let me straddle my old saddle underneath the western skies
> On my cayuse
> Let me wander over yonder till I see the mountains rise
> I want to ride to the ridge where the west commences
> Gaze at the moon until I lose my senses
> I can't look at hobbles and I can't stand fences
> Don't fence me in.

VIOLENCE IN THE WILD WEST: MYTH AND REALITY

The popular image of the Wild West portrayed in books, television, and film has been one of violence and mayhem. The lure of quick riches through mining or driving cattle meant that much of the West did indeed consist of rough men living a rough life, although the violence was exaggerated and even glorified in the dime store novels of the day. The exploits of Wyatt Earp, Doc Holiday, and others made for good stories, but the reality was that western violence was more isolated than the stories might suggest. These clashes often occurred as people struggled for the scarce resources that could make or break their chance at riches, or as they dealt with the sudden wealth or poverty that prospecting provided.

Where sporadic violence did erupt, it was concentrated largely in mining towns or during range wars among large and small cattle ranchers. Some mining towns were indeed as rough as the popular stereotype. Men, money, liquor, and disappointment were a recipe for violence. Fights were frequent, deaths were commonplace, and frontier justice reigned. The notorious mining town of Bodie, California, had twenty-nine murders between 1877 and 1883, which translated to a murder rate higher than any other city at that time, and only one person was ever convicted of a crime. The most prolific gunman of the day was John Wesley Hardin, who allegedly killed over twenty men in Texas in various gunfights, including one victim he killed in a hotel for snoring too loudly (**Figure 8.12**).

Figure 8.12 The towns that sprouted up around gold strikes existed first and foremost as places for the men who struck it rich to spend their money. Stores, saloons, and brothels were among the first businesses to arrive. The combination of lawlessness, vice, and money often made for a dangerous mix.

Ranching brought with it its own dangers and violence. In the Texas cattle lands, owners of large ranches took advantage of their wealth and the new invention of barbed wire to claim the prime grazing lands and few significant watering holes for their herds. Those seeking only to move their few head of cattle to market grew increasingly frustrated at their inability to find even a blade of grass for their meager herds. Eventually, frustration turned to violence, as several ranchers resorted to vandalizing the barbed wire fences to gain access to grass and water for their steers. Such vandalism quickly led to cattle rustling, as these cowboys were not averse to leading a few of the rancher's steers into their own herds as they left.

One example of the violence that bubbled up was the infamous **Fence Cutting War** in Clay County, Texas (1883–1884). There, cowboys began destroying fences that several ranchers erected along public lands: land they had no right to enclose. Confrontations between the cowboys and armed guards hired by the ranchers resulted in three deaths—hardly a "war," but enough of a problem to get the governor's attention. Eventually, a special session of the Texas legislature addressed the problem by passing laws to outlaw fence cutting, but also forced ranchers to remove fences illegally erected along public lands, as well as to place gates for passage where public areas adjoined private lands.

An even more violent confrontation occurred between large ranchers and small farmers in Johnson County, Wyoming, where cattle ranchers organized a "lynching bee" in 1891–1892 to make examples of cattle rustlers. Hiring twenty-two "invaders" from Texas to serve as hired guns, the ranch owners and their foremen hunted and subsequently killed the two rustlers best known for organizing the owners of the smaller Wyoming farms. Only the intervention of federal troops, who arrested and then later released the invaders, allowing them to return to Texas, prevented a greater massacre.

While there is much talk—both real and mythical—of the rough men who lived this life, relatively few women experienced it. While homesteaders were often families, gold speculators and cowboys tended to be single men in pursuit of fortune. The few women who went to these wild outposts were typically prostitutes, and even their numbers were limited. In 1860, in the Comstock Lode region of Nevada, for example, there were reportedly only thirty women total in a town of twenty-five hundred men. Some of the "painted ladies" who began as prostitutes eventually owned brothels and emerged as businesswomen in their own right; however, life for these young women remained a challenging one as western settlement progressed. A handful of women, numbering no more than six hundred, braved both the elements and male-dominated culture to become teachers in several of the more established cities in the West. Even fewer arrived to support husbands or operate stores in these mining towns.

As wealthy men brought their families west, the lawless landscape began to change slowly. Abilene, Kansas, is one example of a lawless town, replete with prostitutes, gambling, and other vices, transformed when middle-class women arrived in the 1880s with their cattle baron husbands. These women began to organize churches, school, civic clubs, and other community programs to promote family values. They fought to remove opportunities for prostitution and all the other vices that they felt threatened the values that they held dear. Protestant missionaries eventually joined the women in their efforts, and, while they were not widely successful, they did bring greater attention to the problems. As a response, the U.S. Congress passed both the Comstock Law (named after its chief proponent, anti-obscenity crusader Anthony Comstock) in 1873 to ban the spread of "lewd and lascivious literature" through the mail and the subsequent Page Act of 1875 to prohibit the transportation of women into the United States for employment as prostitutes. However, the "houses of ill repute" continued to operate and remained popular throughout the West despite the efforts of reformers.

Click and Explore

Take a look at the **National Cowboy and Western Heritage Museum** (http://openstaxcollege.org/l/natcowboy) to determine whether this site's portrayal of cowboy culture matches or contradicts the history shared in this chapter.

8.4 The Loss of American Indian Life and Culture

By the end of this section, you will be able to:
- Describe the methods that the U.S. government used to address the "Indian threat" during the settlement of the West
- Explain the process of "Americanization" as it applied to Indians in the nineteenth century

As American settlers pushed westward, they inevitably came into conflict with Indian tribes that had long been living on the land. Although the threat of Indian attacks was quite slim and nowhere proportionate to the number of U.S. Army actions directed against them, the occasional attack—often one of retaliation—was enough to fuel the popular fear of the "savage" Indians. The clashes, when they happened, were indeed brutal, although most of the brutality occurred at the hands of the settlers. Ultimately, the settlers, with the support of local militias and, later, with the federal government behind them, sought to eliminate the tribes from the lands they desired. The result was devastating for the Indian tribes, which lacked the weapons and group cohesion to fight back against such well-armed forces. The Manifest Destiny of the settlers spelled the end of the Indian way of life.

CLAIMING LAND, RELOCATING LANDOWNERS

Back east, the popular vision of the West was of a vast and empty land. But of course this was an exaggerated depiction. On the eve of westward expansion, as many as 250,000 Indians, representing a variety of tribes, populated the Great Plains. Previous wars against these tribes in the early nineteenth century, as well as the failure of earlier treaties, had led to a general policy of the forcible removal of many tribes in the eastern United States. The Indian Removal Act of 1830 resulted in the infamous "Trail of Tears," which saw nearly fifty thousand Seminole, Choctaw, Chickasaw, and Creek Indians relocated west of the Mississippi River to what is now Oklahoma between 1831 and 1838. Building upon such a history, the U.S. government was prepared, during the era of western settlement, to deal with tribes that settlers viewed as obstacles to expansion.

As settlers sought more land for farming, mining, and cattle ranching, the first strategy employed to deal with the perceived Indian threat was to negotiate settlements to move tribes out of the path of white settlers. In 1851, the chiefs of most of the Great Plains tribes agreed to the First Treaty of Fort Laramie. This agreement established distinct tribal borders, essentially codifying the reservation system. In return for annual payments of $50,000 to the tribes (originally guaranteed for fifty years, but later revised to last for only ten) as well as the hollow promise of noninterference from westward settlers, Indians agreed to stay clear of the path of settlement. Due to government corruption, many annuity payments never reached the tribes, and some reservations were left destitute and near starving. In addition, within a decade, as the pace and number of western settlers increased, even designated reservations became prime locations for farms and mining. Rather than negotiating new treaties, settlers—oftentimes backed by local or state militia units—simply attacked the tribes out of fear or to force them from the land. Some Indians resisted, only to then face massacres.

In 1862, frustrated and angered by the lack of annuity payments and the continuous encroachment on their reservation lands, Dakota Sioux Indians in Minnesota rebelled in what became known as the Dakota War, killing the white settlers who moved onto their tribal lands. Over one thousand white settlers were captured or killed in the attack, before an armed militia regained control. Of the four hundred Sioux captured by U.S. troops, 303 were sentenced to death, but President Lincoln intervened, releasing all but thirty-eight of the men. The thirty-eight who were found guilty were hanged in the largest mass execution in the country's history, and the rest of the tribe was banished. Settlers in other regions responded to news of this raid with fear and aggression. In Colorado, Arapahoe and Cheyenne tribes fought back against land encroachment; white militias then formed, decimating even some of the tribes that were willing to cooperate. One of the more vicious examples was near Sand Creek, Colorado, where Colonel John Chivington led a militia raid upon a camp in which the leader had already negotiated a peaceful settlement. The camp was flying both the American flag and the white flag of surrender when Chivington's troops murdered close to one hundred people, the majority of them women and children, in what became known as the **Sand Creek Massacre**. For the rest of his life, Chivington would proudly display his collection of nearly one hundred Indian scalps from that day. Subsequent investigations by the U.S. Army condemned Chivington's tactics and their results; however, the raid served as a model for some settlers who sought any means by which to eradicate the perceived Indian threat.

Hoping to forestall similar uprisings and all-out Indian wars, the U.S. Congress commissioned a committee to investigate the causes of such incidents. The subsequent report of their findings led to the passage of two additional treaties: the Second Treaty of Fort Laramie and the Treaty of Medicine Lodge Creek, both designed to move the remaining tribes to even more remote reservations. The Second Treaty of Fort Laramie moved the remaining Sioux to the Black Hills in the Dakota Territory and the Treaty of Medicine Lodge Creek moved the Cheyenne, Arapaho, Kiowa, and Comanche to "Indian Territory," later to become the State of Oklahoma.

The agreements were short-lived, however. With the subsequent discovery of gold in the Black Hills, settlers seeking their fortune began to move upon the newly granted Sioux lands with support from U.S. cavalry troops. By the middle of 1875, thousands of white prospectors were illegally digging and panning in the area. The Sioux protested the invasion of their territory and the violation of sacred ground. The government offered to lease the Black Hills or to pay $6 million if the Indians were willing to sell the land. When the tribes refused, the government imposed what it considered a fair price for the land, ordered the Indians to move, and in the spring of 1876, made ready to force them onto the reservation.

In the Battle of Little Bighorn, perhaps the most famous battle of the American West, a Sioux chieftain, Sitting Bull, urged Indians from all neighboring tribes to join his men in defense of their lands (**Figure 8.13**). At the Little Bighorn River, the U.S. Army's Seventh Cavalry, led by Colonel George Custer, sought a showdown. Driven by his own personal ambition, on June 25, 1876, Custer foolishly attacked what he thought was a minor Indian encampment. Instead, it turned out to be the main Sioux force. The Sioux warriors—nearly three thousand in strength—surrounded and killed Custer and 262 of his men and support units, in the single greatest loss of U.S. troops to an Indian attack in the era of westward expansion. Eyewitness reports of the attack indicated that the victorious Sioux bathed and wrapped Custer's body in the tradition of a chieftain burial; however, they dismembered many other soldiers' corpses in order for a few distant observers from Major Marcus Reno's wounded troops and Captain Frederick Benteen's company to report back to government officials about the ferocity of the Sioux enemy.

Figure 8.13 The iconic figure who led the battle at Little Bighorn River, Sitting Bull led Indians in what was their largest victory against American settlers. While the battle was a rout by the Sioux over Custer's troops, the ultimate outcome for his tribe and the men who had joined him was one of constant harassment, arrest, and death at the hands of federal troops.

AMERICAN INDIAN SUBMISSION

Despite their success at Little Bighorn, neither the Sioux nor any other Plains tribe followed this battle with any other armed encounter. Rather, they either returned to tribal life or fled out of fear of remaining troops, until the U.S. Army arrived in greater numbers and began to exterminate Indian encampments and force others to accept payment for forcible removal from their lands. Sitting Bull himself fled to Canada, although he later returned in 1881 and subsequently worked in Buffalo Bill's Wild West show. In Montana, the Blackfoot and Crow were forced to leave their tribal lands. In Colorado, the Utes gave up their lands after a brief period of resistance. In Idaho, most of the Nez Perce gave up their lands peacefully, although in an incredible episode, a band of some eight hundred Indians sought to evade U.S. troops and escape into Canada.

MY STORY

⚙ *I Will Fight No More: Chief Joseph's Capitulation*

Chief Joseph, known to his people as "Thunder Traveling to the Loftier Mountain Heights," was the chief of the Nez Perce tribe, and he had realized that they could not win against the whites. In order to avoid a war that would undoubtedly lead to the extermination of his people, he hoped to lead his tribe to Canada, where they could live freely. He led a full retreat of his people over fifteen hundred miles of mountains and harsh terrain, only to be caught within fifty miles of the Canadian border in late 1877. His speech has remained a poignant and vivid reminder of what the tribe had lost.

> Tell General Howard I know his heart. What he told me before, I have it in my heart. I am tired of fighting. Our Chiefs are killed; Looking Glass is dead, Ta Hool Hool Shute is dead. The old men are all dead. It is the young men who say yes or no. He who led on the young men is dead. It is cold, and we have no blankets; the little children are freezing to death. My people, some of them, have run away to the hills, and have no blankets, no food. No one knows where they are—perhaps freezing to death. I want to have time to look for my children, and see how many of them I can find. Maybe I shall find them among the dead. Hear me, my Chiefs! I am tired; my heart is sick and sad. From where the sun now stands I will fight no more forever.

—Chief Joseph, 1877

The final episode in the so-called Indian Wars occurred in 1890, at the **Battle of Wounded Knee** in South Dakota. On their reservation, the Sioux had begun to perform the "Ghost Dance," which told of an Indian Messiah who would deliver the tribe from its hardship, with such frequency that white settlers began to worry that another uprising would occur. The militia prepared to round up the Sioux. The tribe, after the death of Sitting Bull, who had been arrested, shot, and killed in 1890, prepared to surrender at Wounded Knee, South Dakota, on December 29, 1890. Although the accounts are unclear, an apparent accidental rifle discharge by a young male Indian preparing to lay down his weapon led the U.S. soldiers to begin firing indiscriminately upon the Indians. What little resistance the Indians mounted with a handful of concealed rifles at the outset of the fight diminished quickly, with the troops eventually massacring between 150 and 300 men, women, and children. The U.S. troops suffered twenty-five fatalities, some of which were the result of their own crossfire. Captain Edward Godfrey of the Seventh Cavalry later commented, "I know the men did not aim deliberately and they were greatly excited. I don't believe they saw their sights. They fired rapidly but it seemed to me only a few seconds till there was not a living thing before us; warriors, squaws, children, ponies, and dogs . . . went down before that unaimed fire." With this last show of brutality, the Indian Wars came to a close. U.S. government officials had already begun the process of seeking an alternative to the meaningless treaties and costly battles. A more effective means with which to address the public perception of the "Indian threat" was needed. **Americanization** provided the answer.

AMERICANIZATION

Through the years of the Indian Wars of the 1870s and early 1880s, opinion back east was mixed. There were many who felt, as General Philip Sheridan (appointed in 1867 to pacify the Plains Indians) allegedly said, that the only good Indian was a dead Indian. But increasingly, several American reformers who would later form the backbone of the Progressive Era had begun to criticize the violence, arguing that the Indians should be helped through "Americanization" to become assimilated into American society. Individual land ownership, Christian worship, and education for children became the cornerstones of this new, and final, assault on Indian life and culture.

Beginning in the 1880s, clergymen, government officials, and social workers all worked to assimilate Indians into American life. The government permitted reformers to remove Indian children from their homes and place them in boarding schools, such as the Carlisle Indian School or the Hampton Institute, where they were taught to abandon their tribal traditions and embrace the tools of American productivity, modesty, and sanctity through total immersion. Such schools not only acculturated Indian boys and girls, but also provided vocational training for males and domestic science classes for females. Adults were also targeted by religious reformers, specifically evangelical Protestants as well as a number of Catholics, who sought to convince Indians to abandon their language, clothing, and social customs for a more Euro-American lifestyle (**Figure 8.14**).

Figure 8.14 The federal government's policy towards the Indians shifted in the late 1880s from relocating them to assimilating them into the American ideal. Indians were given land in exchange for renouncing their tribe, traditional clothing, and way of life.

A vital part of the assimilation effort was land reform. During earlier negotiations, the government had respected that the Indian tribes used their land communally. Most Indian belief structures did not allow for the concept of individual land ownership; rather, land was available for all to use, and required responsibility from all to protect it. As a part of their plan to Americanize the tribes, reformers sought legislation to replace this concept with the popular Euro-American notion of real estate ownership and self-reliance. One such law was the Dawes Severalty Act of 1887, named after a reformer and senator from Massachusetts, which struck a deadly blow to the Indian way of life. In what was essentially an Indian version of the original Homestead Act, the Dawes Act permitted the federal government to divide the lands of any tribe and grant 160 acres of farmland or 320 acres of grazing land to each head of family, with lesser amounts to others. In a nod towards the paternal relationship with which whites viewed Indians—similar to the justification of the previous treatment of African American slaves—the Dawes Act permitted the federal government to hold an individual Indian's newly acquired land in trust for twenty-five years. Only then would he obtain full title and be granted the citizenship rights that land ownership entailed. It would not be until 1924 that formal citizenship was granted to all Native Americans. Under the Dawes Act, Indians were given the most arid, useless land. Further, inefficiencies and corruption in the government meant that much of the land due to be allotted to Indians was simply deemed "surplus" and claimed by settlers. Once all allotments were determined, the remaining tribal lands—as much as eighty million acres—were sold to white American settlers.

The final element of "Americanization" was the symbolic "last arrow" pageant, which often coincided with the formal redistribution of tribal lands under the Dawes Act. At these events, Indians were forced to assemble in their tribal garb, carrying a bow and arrow. They would then symbolically fire their "last arrow" into the air, enter a tent where they would strip away their Indian clothing, dress in a white farmer's coveralls, and emerge to take a plow and an American flag to show that they had converted to a new way of life. It was a seismic shift for the Indians, and one that left them bereft of their culture and history.

Click and Explore

Take a look at the **Carlisle Industrial Indian School** (http://openstaxcollege.org/l/carlisleschool) where Indian students were "civilized" from 1879 to 1918. It is worth looking through the photographs and records of the school to see how this well-intended program obliterated Indian culture.

8.5 The Impact of Expansion on Chinese Immigrants and Hispanic Citizens

By the end of this section, you will be able to:
- Describe the treatment of Chinese immigrants and Hispanic citizens during the westward expansion of the nineteenth century

As white Americans pushed west, they not only collided with Indian tribes but also with Hispanic Americans and Chinese immigrants. Hispanics in the Southwest had the opportunity to become American citizens at the end of the Mexican-American war, but their status was markedly second-class. Chinese immigrants arrived en masse during the California Gold Rush and numbered in the hundreds of thousands by the late 1800s, with the majority living in California, working menial jobs. These distinct cultural and ethnic groups strove to maintain their rights and way of life in the face of persistent racism and entitlement. But the large number of white settlers and government-sanctioned land acquisitions left them at a profound disadvantage. Ultimately, both groups withdrew into homogenous communities in which their language and culture could survive.

CHINESE IMMIGRANTS IN THE AMERICAN WEST

The initial arrival of Chinese immigrants to the United States began as a slow trickle in the 1820s, with barely 650 living in the U.S. by the end of 1849. However, as gold rush fever swept the country, Chinese immigrants, too, were attracted to the notion of quick fortunes. By 1852, over 25,000 Chinese immigrants had arrived, and by 1880, over 300,000 Chinese lived in the United States, most in California. While they had dreams of finding gold, many instead found employment building the first transcontinental railroad (**Figure 8.15**). Some even traveled as far east as the former cotton plantations of the Old South, which they helped to farm after the Civil War. Several thousand of these immigrants booked their passage to the United States using a "credit-ticket," in which their passage was paid in advance by American businessmen to whom the immigrants were then indebted for a period of work. Most arrivals were men: Few wives or children ever traveled to the United States. As late as 1890, less than 5 percent of the

Chinese population in the U.S. was female. Regardless of gender, few Chinese immigrants intended to stay permanently in the United States, although many were reluctantly forced to do so, as they lacked the financial resources to return home.

Figure 8.15 Building the railroads was dangerous and backbreaking work. On the western railroad line, Chinese migrants, along with other nonwhite workers, were often given the most difficult and dangerous jobs of all.

Prohibited by law since 1790 from obtaining U.S. citizenship through naturalization, Chinese immigrants faced harsh discrimination and violence from American settlers in the West. Despite hardships like the special tax that Chinese miners had to pay to take part in the Gold Rush, or their subsequent forced relocation into Chinese districts, these immigrants continued to arrive in the United States seeking a better life for the families they left behind. Only when the Chinese Exclusion Act of 1882 forbade further immigration from China for a ten-year period did the flow stop.

The Chinese community banded together in an effort to create social and cultural centers in cities such as San Francisco. In a haphazard fashion, they sought to provide services ranging from social aid to education, places of worship, health facilities, and more to their fellow Chinese immigrants. But only American Indians suffered greater discrimination and racial violence, legally sanctioned by the federal government, than did Chinese immigrants at this juncture in American history. As Chinese workers began competing with white Americans for jobs in California cities, the latter began a system of built-in discrimination. In the 1870s, white Americans formed "anti-coolie clubs" ("coolie" being a racial slur directed towards people of any Asian descent), through which they organized boycotts of Chinese-produced products and lobbied for anti-Chinese laws. Some protests turned violent, as in 1885 in Rock Springs, Wyoming, where tensions between white and Chinese immigrant miners erupted in a riot, resulting in over two dozen Chinese immigrants being murdered and many more injured.

Slowly, racism and discrimination became law. The new California constitution of 1879 denied naturalized Chinese citizens the right to vote or hold state employment. Additionally, in 1882, the U.S. Congress passed the Chinese Exclusion Act, which forbade further Chinese immigration into the United States for ten years. The ban was later extended on multiple occasions until its repeal in 1943. Eventually, some Chinese immigrants returned to China. Those who remained were stuck in the lowest-paying, most menial jobs. Several found assistance through the creation of benevolent associations designed to both support Chinese communities and defend them against political and legal discrimination; however, the history of Chinese immigrants to the United States remained largely one of deprivation and hardship well into the twentieth century.

Click and Explore

The **Central Pacific Railroad Photographic History Museum** (http://openstaxcollege.org/l/railroadchina) provides a context for the role of the Chinese who helped build the railroads. What does the site celebrate, and what, if anything, does it condemn?

DEFINING "AMERICAN"

⊙ *The Backs that Built the Railroad*

Below is a description of the construction of the railroad in 1867. Note the way it describes the scene, the laborers, and the effort.

> The cars now (1867) run nearly to the summit of the Sierras. . . . four thousand laborers were at work—one-tenth Irish, the rest Chinese. They were a great army laying siege to Nature in her strongest citadel. The rugged mountains looked like stupendous ant-hills. They swarmed with Celestials, shoveling, wheeling, carting, drilling and blasting rocks and earth, while their dull, moony eyes stared out from under immense basket-hats, like umbrellas. At several dining camps we saw hundreds sitting on the ground, eating soft boiled rice with chopsticks as fast as terrestrials could with soup-ladles. Irish laborers received thirty dollars per month (gold) and board; Chinese, thirty-one dollars, boarding themselves. After a little experience the latter were quite as efficient and far less troublesome.

> —Albert D. Richardson, *Beyond the Mississippi*

Several great American advancements of the nineteenth century were built with the hands of many other nations. It is interesting to ponder how much these immigrant communities felt they were building their own fortunes and futures, versus the fortunes of others. Is it likely that the Chinese laborers, many of whom died due to the harsh conditions, considered themselves part of "a great army"? Certainly, this account reveals the unwitting racism of the day, where workers were grouped together by their ethnicity, and each ethnic group was labeled monolithically as "good workers" or "troublesome," with no regard for individual differences among the hundreds of Chinese or Irish workers.

HISPANIC AMERICANS IN THE AMERICAN WEST

The Treaty of Guadalupe Hidalgo, which ended the Mexican-American War in 1848, promised U.S. citizenship to the nearly seventy-five thousand Hispanics now living in the American Southwest; approximately 90 percent accepted the offer and chose to stay in the United States despite their immediate relegation to second-class citizenship status. Relative to the rest of Mexico, these lands were sparsely populated and had been so ever since the country achieved its freedom from Spain in 1821. In fact, New Mexico—not Texas or California—was the center of settlement in the region in the years immediately preceding the war with the United States, containing nearly fifty thousand Mexicans. However, those who did settle the area were proud of their heritage and ability to develop *rancheros* of great size and success. Despite promises made in the treaty, these Californios—as they came to be known—quickly lost their land to white settlers who simply displaced the rightful landowners, by force if necessary. Repeated efforts at legal redress mostly fell upon deaf ears. In some instances, judges and lawyers would permit the legal cases to proceed through an expensive legal process only to the point where Hispanic landowners who insisted on holding their ground were rendered penniless for their efforts.

Much like Chinese immigrants, Hispanic citizens were relegated to the worst-paying jobs under the most terrible working conditions. They worked as *peóns* (manual laborers similar to slaves), *vaqueros* (cattle herders), and cartmen (transporting food and supplies) on the cattle ranches that white landowners possessed, or undertook the most hazardous mining tasks (**Figure 8.16**).

Figure 8.16 Mexican ranchers had worked the land in the American Southwest long before American "cowboys" arrived. In what ways might the Mexican *vaquero* pictured above have influenced the American cowboy?

In a few instances, frustrated Hispanic citizens fought back against the white settlers who dispossessed them of their belongings. In 1889–1890 in New Mexico, several hundred Mexican Americans formed *las Gorras Blancas* (the White Caps) to try and reclaim their land and intimidate white Americans, preventing further land seizures. White Caps conducted raids of white farms, burning homes, barns, and crops to express their growing anger and frustration. However, their actions never resulted in any fundamental changes. Several White Caps were captured, beaten, and imprisoned, whereas others eventually gave up, fearing harsh reprisals against their families. Some White Caps adopted a more political strategy, gaining election to local offices throughout New Mexico in the early 1890s, but growing concerns over the potential impact upon the territory's quest for statehood led several citizens to heighten their repression of the movement. Other laws passed in the United States intended to deprive Mexican Americans of their heritage as much as their lands. "Sunday Laws" prohibited "noisy amusements" such as bullfights, cockfights, and other cultural gatherings common to Hispanic communities at the time. "Greaser Laws" permitted the imprisonment of any unemployed Mexican American on charges of vagrancy. Although Hispanic Americans held tightly to their cultural heritage as their remaining form of self-identity, such laws did take a toll.

In California and throughout the Southwest, the massive influx of Anglo-American settlers simply overran the Hispanic populations that had been living and thriving there, sometimes for generations. Despite being U.S. citizens with full rights, Hispanics quickly found themselves outnumbered, outvoted, and, ultimately, outcast. Corrupt state and local governments favored whites in land disputes, and mining companies and cattle barons discriminated against them, as with the Chinese workers, in terms of pay and working conditions. In growing urban areas such as Los Angeles, *barrios*, or clusters of working-class homes, grew more isolated from the white American centers. Hispanic Americans, like the Native Americans and Chinese, suffered the fallout of the white settlers' relentless push west.

CHAPTER 9

Industrialization and the Rise of Big Business, 1870-1900

Figure 9.1 The Electrical Building, constructed in 1892 for the World's Columbian Exposition, included displays from General Electric and Westinghouse, and introduced the American public to alternating current and neon lights. The Chicago World's Fair, as the universal exposition was more commonly known, featured architecture, inventions, and design, serving as both a showcase for and an influence on the country's optimism about the Industrial Age.

Chapter Outline

9.1 Inventors of the Age
9.2 From Invention to Industrial Growth
9.3 Building Industrial America on the Backs of Labor
9.4 A New American Consumer Culture

Introduction

"The electric age was ushered into being in this last decade of the nineteenth century today when President Cleveland, by pressing a button, started the mighty machinery, rushing waters and revolving wheels in the World's Columbian exhibition." With this announcement about the official start of the Chicago World's Fair in 1893 (**Figure 9.1**), the *Salt Lake City Herald* captured the excitement and optimism of the machine age. "In the previous expositions," the editorial continued, "the possibilities of electricity had been limited to the mere starting of the engines in the machinery hall, but in this it made thousands of servants do its bidding . . . the magic of electricity did the duty of the hour."

The fair, which commemorated the four hundredth anniversary of Columbus's journey to America, was a potent symbol of the myriad inventions that changed American life and contributed to the significant economic growth of the era, as well as the new wave of industrialization that swept the country. While businessmen capitalized upon such technological innovations, the new industrial working class faced enormous challenges. Ironically, as the World's Fair welcomed its first visitors, the nation was spiraling downward into the worst depression of the century. Subsequent frustrations among working-class Americans laid the groundwork for the country's first significant labor movement.

9.1 Inventors of the Age

By the end of this section, you will be able to:
- Explain how the ideas and products of late nineteenth-century inventors contributed to the rise of big business
- Explain how the inventions of the late nineteenth century changed everyday American life

The late nineteenth century was an energetic era of inventions and entrepreneurial spirit. Building upon the mid-century Industrial Revolution in Great Britain, as well as answering the increasing call from Americans for efficiency and comfort, the country found itself in the grip of invention fever, with more people working on their big ideas than ever before. In retrospect, harnessing the power of steam and then electricity in the nineteenth century vastly increased the power of man and machine, thus making other advances possible as the century progressed.

Facing an increasingly complex everyday life, Americans sought the means by which to cope with it. Inventions often provided the answers, even as the inventors themselves remained largely unaware of the life-changing nature of their ideas. To understand the scope of this zeal for creation, consider the U.S. Patent Office, which, in 1790—its first decade of existence—recorded only 276 inventions. By 1860, the office had issued a total of 60,000 patents. But between 1860 and 1890, that number exploded to nearly 450,000, with another 235,000 in the last decade of the century. While many of these patents came to naught, some inventions became lynchpins in the rise of big business and the country's move towards an industrial-based economy, in which the desire for efficiency, comfort, and abundance could be more fully realized by most Americans.

AN EXPLOSION OF INVENTIVE ENERGY

From corrugated rollers that could crack hard, homestead-grown wheat into flour to refrigerated train cars and garment-sewing machines (**Figure 9.3**), new inventions fueled industrial growth around the

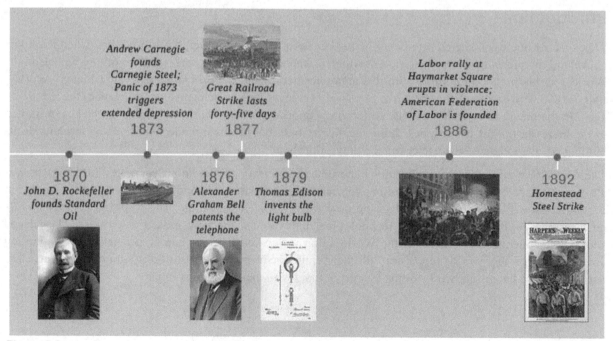

Figure 9.2

country. As late as 1880, fully one-half of all Americans still lived and worked on farms, whereas fewer than one in seven—mostly men, except for long-established textile factories in which female employees tended to dominate—were employed in factories. However, the development of commercial electricity by the close of the century, to complement the steam engines that already existed in many larger factories, permitted more industries to concentrate in cities, away from the previously essential water power. In turn, newly arrived immigrants sought employment in new urban factories. Immigration, urbanization, and industrialization coincided to transform the face of American society from primarily rural to significantly urban. From 1880 to 1920, the number of industrial workers in the nation quadrupled from 2.5 million to over 10 million, while over the same period urban populations doubled, to reach one-half of the country's total population.

Figure 9.3 Advertisements of the late nineteenth century promoted the higher quality and lower prices that people could expect from new inventions. Here, a knitting factory promotes the fact that its machines make seamless hose, while still acknowledging the traditional role of women in the garment industry, from grandmothers who used to sew by hand to young women who now used machines.

In offices, worker productivity benefited from the typewriter, invented in 1867, the cash register, invented in 1879, and the adding machine, invented in 1885. These tools made it easier than ever to keep up with the rapid pace of business growth. Inventions also slowly transformed home life. The vacuum cleaner arrived during this era, as well as the flush toilet. These indoor "water closets" improved public health through the reduction in contamination associated with outhouses and their proximity to water supplies and homes. Tin cans and, later, Clarence Birdseye's experiments with frozen food, eventually changed how women shopped for, and prepared, food for their families, despite initial health concerns over preserved foods. With the advent of more easily prepared food, women gained valuable time in their daily schedules, a step that partially laid the groundwork for the modern women's movement. Women who had the means to purchase such items could use their time to seek other employment outside of the home, as well as broaden their knowledge through education and reading. Such a transformation did not occur overnight, as these inventions also increased expectations for women to remain tied to the home and their domestic chores; slowly, the culture of domesticity changed.

Perhaps the most important industrial advancement of the era came in the production of steel. Manufacturers and builders preferred steel to iron, due to its increased strength and durability. After the Civil War, two new processes allowed for the creation of furnaces large enough and hot enough to melt the wrought iron needed to produce large quantities of steel at increasingly cheaper prices. The Bessemer process, named for English inventor Henry Bessemer, and the open-hearth process, changed the way the United States produced steel and, in doing so, led the country into a new industrialized age. As the new material became more available, builders eagerly sought it out, a demand that steel mill owners were happy to supply.

In 1860, the country produced thirteen thousand tons of steel. By 1879, American furnaces were producing over one million tons per year; by 1900, this figure had risen to ten million. Just ten years later, the United States was the top steel producer in the world, at over twenty-four million tons annually. As production increased to match the overwhelming demand, the price of steel dropped by over 80 percent. When quality steel became cheaper and more readily available, other industries relied upon it more heavily as a key to their growth and development, including construction and, later, the automotive industry. As a result, the steel industry rapidly became the cornerstone of the American economy, remaining the primary indicator of industrial growth and stability through the end of World War II.

ALEXANDER GRAHAM BELL AND THE TELEPHONE

Advancements in communications matched the pace of growth seen in industry and home life. Communication technologies were changing quickly, and they brought with them new ways for information to travel. In 1858, British and American crews laid the first transatlantic cable lines, enabling messages to pass between the United States and Europe in a matter of hours, rather than waiting the few weeks it could take for a letter to arrive by steamship. Although these initial cables worked for barely a month, they generated great interest in developing a more efficient telecommunications industry. Within twenty years, over 100,000 miles of cable crisscrossed the ocean floors, connecting all the continents. Domestically, Western Union, which controlled 80 percent of the country's telegraph lines, operated nearly 200,000 miles of telegraph routes from coast to coast. In short, people were connected like never before, able to relay messages in minutes and hours rather than days and weeks.

One of the greatest advancements was the telephone, which Alexander Graham Bell patented in 1876 (**Figure 9.4**). While he was not the first to invent the concept, Bell was the first one to capitalize on it; after securing the patent, he worked with financiers and businessmen to create the National Bell Telephone Company. Western Union, which had originally turned down Bell's machine, went on to commission Thomas Edison to invent an improved version of the telephone. It is actually Edison's version that is most like the modern telephone used today. However, Western Union, fearing a costly legal battle they were likely to lose due to Bell's patent, ultimately sold Edison's idea to the Bell Company. With the communications industry now largely in their control, along with an agreement from the federal government to permit such control, the Bell Company was transformed into the American Telephone and Telegraph Company, which still exists today as AT&T. By 1880, fifty thousand telephones were in use in the United States, including one at the White House. By 1900, that number had increased to 1.35 million, and hundreds of American cities had obtained local service for their citizens. Quickly and inexorably, technology was bringing the country into closer contact, changing forever the rural isolation that had defined America since its beginnings.

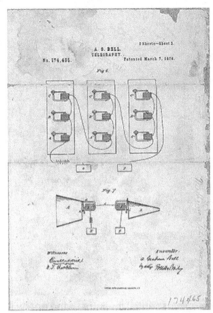

Figure 9.4 Alexander Graham Bell's patent of the telephone was one of almost 700,000 U.S. patents issued between 1850 and 1900. Although the patent itself was only six pages long, including two pages of illustrations, it proved to be one of the most contested and profitable of the nineteenth century. (credit: U.S. National Archives and Records Administration)

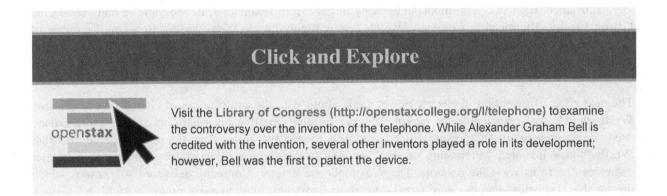

Click and Explore

Visit the **Library of Congress** (http://openstaxcollege.org/l/telephone) to examine the controversy over the invention of the telephone. While Alexander Graham Bell is credited with the invention, several other inventors played a role in its development; however, Bell was the first to patent the device.

THOMAS EDISON AND ELECTRIC LIGHTING

Although Thomas Alva Edison (**Figure 9.5**) is best known for his contributions to the electrical industry, his experimentation went far beyond the light bulb. Edison was quite possibly the greatest inventor of the turn of the century, saying famously that he "hoped to have a minor invention every ten days and a big thing every month or so." He registered 1,093 patents over his lifetime and ran a world-famous laboratory, Menlo Park, which housed a rotating group of up to twenty-five scientists from around the globe.

Edison became interested in the telegraph industry as a boy, when he worked aboard trains selling candy and newspapers. He soon began tinkering with telegraph technology and, by 1876, had devoted himself full time to lab work as an inventor. He then proceeded to invent a string of items that are still used today: the phonograph, the mimeograph machine, the motion picture projector, the dictaphone, and the storage battery, all using a factory-oriented assembly line process that made the rapid production of inventions possible.

Figure 9.5 Thomas Alva Edison was the quintessential inventor of the era, with a passion for new ideas and over one thousand patents to his name. Seen here with his incandescent light bulb, which he invented in 1879, Edison produced many inventions that subsequently transformed the country and the world.

In 1879, Edison invented the item that has led to his greatest fame: the incandescent light bulb. He allegedly explored over six thousand different materials for the filament, before stumbling upon tungsten as the ideal substance. By 1882, with financial backing largely from financier J. P. Morgan, he had created the Edison Electric Illuminating Company, which began supplying electrical current to a small number of customers in New York City. Morgan guided subsequent mergers of Edison's other enterprises, including a machine works firm and a lamp company, resulting in the creation of the Edison General Electric Company in 1889.

The next stage of invention in electric power came about with the contribution of George Westinghouse. Westinghouse was responsible for making electric lighting possible on a national scale. While Edison used "direct current" or DC power, which could only extend two miles from the power source, in 1886, Westinghouse invented "alternating current" or AC power, which allowed for delivery over greater distances due to its wavelike patterns. The Westinghouse Electric Company delivered AC power, which meant that factories, homes, and farms—in short, anything that needed power—could be served, regardless of their proximity to the power source. A public relations battle ensued between the Westinghouse and Edison camps, coinciding with the invention of the electric chair as a form of prisoner execution. Edison publicly proclaimed AC power to be best adapted for use in the chair, in the hope that such a smear campaign would result in homeowners becoming reluctant to use AC power in their houses. Although Edison originally fought the use of AC power in other devices, he reluctantly adapted to it as its popularity increased.

Click and Explore

Not all of Edison's ventures were successful. Read about Edison's Folly (http://openstaxcollege.org/l/edisonfail) to learn the story behind his greatest failure. Was there some benefit to his efforts? Or was it wasted time and money?

9.2 From Invention to Industrial Growth

By the end of this section, you will be able to:
- Explain how the inventions of the late nineteenth century contributed directly to industrial growth in America
- Identify the contributions of Andrew Carnegie, John Rockefeller, and J. P. Morgan to the new industrial order emerging in the late nineteenth century
- Describe the visions, philosophies, and business methods of the leaders of the new industrial order

As discussed previously, new processes in steel refining, along with inventions in the fields of communications and electricity, transformed the business landscape of the nineteenth century. The exploitation of these new technologies provided opportunities for tremendous growth, and business entrepreneurs with financial backing and the right mix of business acumen and ambition could make their fortunes. Some of these new millionaires were known in their day as **robber barons**, a negative term that connoted the belief that they exploited workers and bent laws to succeed. Regardless of how they were perceived, these businessmen and the companies they created revolutionized American industry.

RAILROADS AND ROBBER BARONS

Earlier in the nineteenth century, the first transcontinental railroad and subsequent spur lines paved the way for rapid and explosive railway growth, as well as stimulated growth in the iron, wood, coal, and other related industries. The railroad industry quickly became the nation's first "big business." A powerful, inexpensive, and consistent form of transportation, railroads accelerated the development of virtually every other industry in the country. By 1890, railroad lines covered nearly every corner of the United States, bringing raw materials to industrial factories and finished goods to consumer markets. The amount of track grew from 35,000 miles at the end of the Civil War to over 200,000 miles by the close of the century. Inventions such as car couplers, air brakes, and Pullman passenger cars allowed the volume of both freight and people to increase steadily. From 1877 to 1890, both the amount of goods and the number of passengers traveling the rails tripled.

Financing for all of this growth came through a combination of private capital and government loans and grants. Federal and state loans of cash and land grants totaled $150 million and 185 million acres of public land, respectively. Railroads also listed their stocks and bonds on the New York Stock Exchange to attract investors from both within the United States and Europe. Individual investors consolidated their power as railroads merged and companies grew in size and power. These individuals became some of the wealthiest Americans the country had ever known. Midwest farmers, angry at large railroad owners for their exploitative business practices, came to refer to them as "robber barons," as their business dealings were frequently shady and exploitative. Among their highly questionable tactics was the practice of differential shipping rates, in which larger business enterprises received discounted rates to transport their goods, as opposed to local producers and farmers whose higher rates essentially subsidized the discounts.

Jay Gould was perhaps the first prominent railroad magnate to be tarred with the "robber baron" brush. He bought older, smaller, rundown railroads, offered minimal improvements, and then capitalized on factory owners' desires to ship their goods on this increasingly popular and more cost-efficient form of transportation. His work with the Erie Railroad was notorious among other investors, as he drove the company to near ruin in a failed attempt to attract foreign investors during a takeover attempt. His model worked better in the American West, where the railroads were still widely scattered across the country, forcing farmers and businesses to pay whatever prices Gould demanded in order to use his trains. In addition to owning the Union Pacific Railroad that helped to construct the original transcontinental railroad line, Gould came to control over ten thousand miles of track across the United States, accounting for 15 percent of all railroad transportation. When he died in 1892, Gould had a personal worth of over $100 million, although he was a deeply unpopular figure.

In contrast to Gould's exploitative business model, which focused on financial profit more than on tangible industrial contributions, Commodore Cornelius Vanderbilt was a "robber baron" who truly cared about the success of his railroad enterprise and its positive impact on the American economy. Vanderbilt consolidated several smaller railroad lines, called trunk lines, to create the powerful New York Central Railroad Company, one of the largest corporations in the United States at the time (**Figure 9.6**). He later purchased stock in the major rail lines that would connect his company to Chicago, thus expanding his reach and power while simultaneously creating a railroad network to connect Chicago to New York City. This consolidation provided more efficient connections from Midwestern suppliers to eastern markets. It was through such consolidation that, by 1900, seven major railroad tycoons controlled over 70 percent of all operating lines. Vanderbilt's personal wealth at his death (over $100 million in 1877), placed him among the top three wealthiest individuals in American history.

Figure 9.6 "The Great Race for the Western Stakes," a Currier & Ives lithograph from 1870, depicts one of Cornelius Vanderbilt's rare failed attempts at further consolidating his railroad empire, when he lost his 1866–1868 battle with James Fisk, Jay Gould, and Daniel Drew for control of the Erie Railway Company.

GIANTS OF WEALTH: CARNEGIE, ROCKEFELLER, AND MORGAN

The post-Civil War inventors generated ideas that transformed the economy, but they were not big businessmen. The evolution from technical innovation to massive industry took place at the hands of the entrepreneurs whose business gambles paid off, making them some of the richest Americans of their day. Steel magnate Andrew Carnegie, oil tycoon John D. Rockefeller, and business financier J. P. Morgan were all businessmen who grew their respective businesses to a scale and scope that were unprecedented. Their companies changed how Americans lived and worked, and they themselves greatly influenced the growth of the country.

Andrew Carnegie and *The Gospel of Wealth*

Andrew Carnegie, steel magnate, has the prototypical rags-to-riches story. Although such stories resembled more myth than reality, they served to encourage many Americans to seek similar paths to fame and fortune. In Carnegie, the story was one of few derived from fact. Born in Scotland, Carnegie immigrated with his family to Pennsylvania in 1848. Following a brief stint as a "bobbin boy," changing spools of thread at a Pittsburgh clothing manufacturer at age thirteen, he subsequently became a telegram messenger boy. As a messenger, he spent much of his time around the Pennsylvania Railroad office and developed parallel interests in railroads, bridge building, and, eventually, the steel industry.

Ingratiating himself to his supervisor and future president of the Pennsylvania Railroad, Tom Scott, Carnegie worked his way into a position of management for the company and subsequently began to invest some of his earnings, with Scott's guidance. One particular investment, in the booming oil fields of northwest Pennsylvania in 1864, resulted in Carnegie earning over $1 million in cash dividends, thus providing him with the capital necessary to pursue his ambition to modernize the iron and steel industries, transforming the United States in the process. Having seen firsthand during the Civil War, when he served as Superintendent of Military Railways and telegraph coordinator for the Union forces, the importance of industry, particularly steel, to the future growth of the country, Carnegie was convinced of his strategy. His first company was the J. Edgar Thompson Steel Works, and, a decade later, he bought out the newly built Homestead Steel Works from the Pittsburgh Bessemer Steel Company. By the end of the century, his enterprise was running an annual profit in excess of $40 million (**Figure 9.7**).

Figure 9.7 Andrew Carnegie made his fortune in steel at such factories as the Carnegie Steel Works located in Youngstown, Ohio, where new technologies allowed the strong metal to be used in far more applications than ever before. Carnegie's empire grew to include iron ore mines, furnaces, mills, and steel works companies.

Although not a scientific expert in steel, Carnegie was an excellent promoter and salesman, able to locate financial backing for his enterprise. He was also shrewd in his calculations on consolidation and expansion, and was able to capitalize on smart business decisions. Always thrifty with the profits he earned, a trait owed to his upbringing, Carnegie saved his profits during prosperous times and used them to buy out other steel companies at low prices during the economic recessions of the 1870s and 1890s. He insisted on up-to-date machinery and equipment, and urged the men who worked at and managed his steel mills to constantly think of innovative ways to increase production and reduce cost.

Carnegie, more than any other businessman of the era, championed the idea that America's leading tycoons owed a debt to society. He believed that, given the circumstances of their successes, they should serve as benefactors to the less fortunate public. For Carnegie, poverty was not an abstract concept, as his family had been a part of the struggling masses. He desired to set an example of philanthropy for all other prominent industrialists of the era to follow. Carnegie's famous essay, *The Gospel of Wealth*, featured below, expounded on his beliefs. In it, he borrowed from Herbert Spencer's theory of **social Darwinism**, which held that society developed much like plant or animal life through a process of evolution in which the most fit and capable enjoyed the greatest material and social success.

MY STORY

✪ *Andrew Carnegie on Wealth*

Carnegie applauded American capitalism for creating a society where, through hard work, ingenuity, and a bit of luck, someone like himself could amass a fortune. In return for that opportunity, Carnegie wrote that the wealthy should find proper uses for their wealth by funding hospitals, libraries, colleges, the arts, and more. *The Gospel of Wealth* spelled out that responsibility.

> Poor and restricted are our opportunities in this life; narrow our horizon; our best work most imperfect; but rich men should be thankful for one inestimable boon. They have it in their power during their lives to busy themselves in organizing benefactions from which the masses of their fellows will derive lasting advantage, and thus dignify their own lives. . . .

> This, then, is held to be the duty of the man of Wealth: First, to set an example of modest, unostentatious living, shunning display or extravagance; to provide moderately for the legitimate wants of those dependent upon him; and after doing so to consider all surplus revenues which come to him simply as trust funds, which he is called upon to administer, and strictly bound as a matter of duty to administer in the manner which, in his judgment, is best calculated to produce the most beneficial results for the community—the man of wealth thus becoming the mere agent and trustee for his poorer brethren, bringing to their service his superior wisdom, experience and ability to administer, doing for them better than they would or could do for themselves. . . .

> In bestowing charity, the main consideration should be to help those who will help themselves; to provide part of the means by which those who desire to improve may do so; to give those who desire to use the aids by which they may rise; to assist, but rarely or never to do all. Neither the individual nor the race is improved by alms-giving. Those worthy of assistance, except in rare cases, seldom require assistance. The really valuable men of the race never do, except in cases of accident or sudden change. Every one has, of course, cases of individuals brought to his own knowledge where temporary assistance can do genuine good, and these he will not overlook. But the amount which can be wisely given by the individual for individuals is necessarily limited by his lack of knowledge of the circumstances connected with each. He is the only true reformer who is as careful and as anxious not to aid the unworthy as he is to aid the worthy, and, perhaps, even more so, for in alms-giving more injury is probably done by rewarding vice than by relieving virtue.

—Andrew Carnegie, *The Gospel of Wealth*

Social Darwinism added a layer of pseudoscience to the idea of the self-made man, a desirable thought for all who sought to follow Carnegie's example. The myth of the rags-to-riches businessman was a potent one. Author Horatio Alger made his own fortune writing stories about young enterprising boys who beat poverty and succeeded in business through a combination of "luck and pluck." His stories were immensely popular, even leading to a board game (**Figure 9.8**) where players could hope to win in the same way that his heroes did.

Figure 9.8 Based on a book by Horatio Alger, District Messenger Boy was a board game where players could achieve the ultimate goal of material success. Alger wrote hundreds of books on a common theme: A poor but hardworking boy can get ahead and make his fortune through a combination of "luck and pluck."

John D. Rockefeller and Business Integration Models

Like Carnegie, John D. Rockefeller was born in 1839 of modest means, with a frequently absent traveling salesman of a father who sold medicinal elixirs and other wares. Young Rockefeller helped his mother with various chores and earned extra money for the family through the sale of family farm products. When the family moved to a suburb of Cleveland in 1853, he had an opportunity to take accounting and bookkeeping courses while in high school and developed a career interest in business. While living in Cleveland in 1859, he learned of Colonel Edwin Drake who had struck "black gold," or oil, near Titusville, Pennsylvania, setting off a boom even greater than the California Gold Rush of the previous decade. Many sought to find a fortune through risky and chaotic "wildcatting," or drilling exploratory oil wells, hoping to strike it rich. But Rockefeller chose a more certain investment: refining crude oil into kerosene, which could be used for both heating and lamps. As a more efficient source of energy, as well as less dangerous to produce, kerosene quickly replaced whale oil in many businesses and homes. Rockefeller worked initially with family and friends in the refining business located in the Cleveland area, but by 1870, Rockefeller ventured out on his own, consolidating his resources and creating the Standard Oil Company of Ohio, initially valued at $1 million.

Rockefeller was ruthless in his pursuit of total control of the oil refining business. As other entrepreneurs flooded the area seeking a quick fortune, Rockefeller developed a plan to crush his competitors and create a true **monopoly** in the refining industry. Beginning in 1872, he forged agreements with several large railroad companies to obtain discounted freight rates for shipping his product. He also used the railroad companies to gather information on his competitors. As he could now deliver his kerosene at lower prices, he drove his competition out of business, often offering to buy them out for pennies on the dollar. He hounded those who refused to sell out to him, until they were driven out of business. Through his method of growth via mergers and acquisitions of similar companies—known as **horizontal**

integration —Standard Oil grew to include almost all refineries in the area. By 1879, the Standard Oil Company controlled nearly 95 percent of all oil refining businesses in the country, as well as 90 percent of all the refining businesses in the world. Editors of the *New York World* lamented of Standard Oil in 1880 that, "When the nineteenth century shall have passed into history, the impartial eyes of the reviewers will be amazed to find that the U.S. . . . tolerated the presence of the most gigantic, the most cruel, impudent, pitiless and grasping monopoly that ever fastened itself upon a country."

Seeking still more control, Rockefeller recognized the advantages of controlling the transportation of his product. He next began to grow his company through **vertical integration**, wherein a company handles all aspects of a product's lifecycle, from the creation of raw materials through the production process to the delivery of the final product. In Rockefeller's case, this model required investment and acquisition of companies involved in everything from barrel-making to pipelines, tanker cars to railroads. He came to own almost every type of business and used his vast power to drive competitors from the market through intense price wars. Although vilified by competitors who suffered from his takeovers and considered him to be no better than a robber baron, several observers lauded Rockefeller for his ingenuity in integrating the oil refining industry and, as a result, lowering kerosene prices by as much as 80 percent by the end of the century. Other industrialists quickly followed suit, including Gustavus Swift, who used vertical integration to dominate the U.S. meatpacking industry in the late nineteenth century.

In order to control the variety of interests he now maintained in industry, Rockefeller created a new legal entity, known as a **trust**. In this arrangement, a small group of trustees possess legal ownership of a business that they operate for the benefit of other investors. In 1882, all thirty-seven stockholders in the various Standard Oil enterprises gave their stock to nine trustees who were to control and direct all of the company's business ventures. State and federal challenges arose, due to the obvious appearance of a monopoly, which implied sole ownership of all enterprises composing an entire industry. When the Ohio Supreme Court ruled that the Standard Oil Company must dissolve, as its monopoly control over all refining operations in the U.S. was in violation of state and federal statutes, Rockefeller shifted to yet another legal entity, called a **holding company** model. The holding company model created a central corporate entity that controlled the operations of multiple companies by holding the majority of stock for each enterprise. While not technically a "trust" and therefore not vulnerable to anti-monopoly laws, this consolidation of power and wealth into one entity was on par with a monopoly; thus, progressive reformers of the late nineteenth century considered holding companies to epitomize the dangers inherent in capitalistic big business, as can be seen in the political cartoon below (**Figure 9.9**). Impervious to reformers' misgivings, other businessmen followed Rockefeller's example. By 1905, over three hundred business mergers had occurred in the United States, affecting more than 80 percent of all industries. By that time, despite passage of federal legislation such as the Sherman Anti-Trust Act in 1890, 1 percent of the country's businesses controlled over 40 percent of the nation's economy.

Figure 9.9 John D. Rockefeller, like Carnegie, grew from modest means to a vast fortune. Unlike Carnegie, however, his business practices were often predatory and aggressive. This cartoon from the era shows how his conglomerate, Standard Oil, was perceived by progressive reformers and other critics.

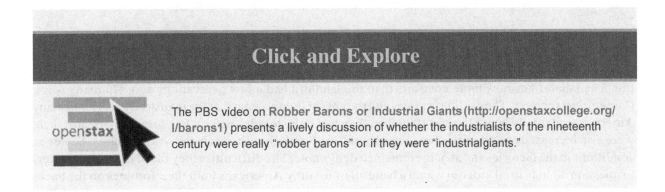

Click and Explore

The PBS video on **Robber Barons or Industrial Giants** (http://openstaxcollege.org/l/barons1) presents a lively discussion of whether the industrialists of the nineteenth century were really "robber barons" or if they were "industrial giants."

J. Pierpont Morgan

Unlike Carnegie and Rockefeller, J. P. Morgan was no rags-to-riches hero. He was born to wealth and became much wealthier as an investment banker, making wise financial decisions in support of the hard-working entrepreneurs building their fortunes. Morgan's father was a London banker, and Morgan the son moved to New York in 1857 to look after the family's business interests there. Once in America, he separated from the London bank and created the J. Pierpont Morgan and Company financial firm. The firm bought and sold stock in growing companies, investing the family's wealth in those that showed great promise, turning an enormous profit as a result. Investments from firms such as his were the key to the success stories of up-and-coming businessmen like Carnegie and Rockefeller. In return for his investment, Morgan and other investment bankers demanded seats on the companies' boards, which gave them even greater control over policies and decisions than just investment alone. There were many critics of Morgan and these other bankers, particularly among members of a U.S. congressional subcommittee who investigated the control that financiers maintained over key industries in the country. The subcommittee referred to Morgan's enterprise as a form of "money trust" that was even more powerful than the trusts operated by Rockefeller and others. Morgan argued that his firm, and others like it, brought stability and organization to a hypercompetitive capitalist economy, and likened his role to a kind of public service.

Ultimately, Morgan's most notable investment, and greatest consolidation, was in the steel industry, when he bought out Andrew Carnegie in 1901. Initially, Carnegie was reluctant to sell, but after repeated badgering by Morgan, Carnegie named his price: an outrageously inflated sum of $500 million. Morgan agreed without hesitation, and then consolidated Carnegie's holdings with several smaller steel firms to create the U.S. Steel Corporation. U.S. Steel was subsequently capitalized at $1.4 billion. It was the country's first billion-dollar firm. Lauded by admirers for the efficiency and modernization he brought to investment banking practices, as well as for his philanthropy and support of the arts, Morgan was also criticized by reformers who subsequently blamed his (and other bankers') efforts for contributing to the artificial bubble of prosperity that eventually burst in the Great Depression of the 1930s. What none could doubt was that Morgan's financial aptitude and savvy business dealings kept him in good stead. A subsequent U.S. congressional committee, in 1912, reported that his firm held 341 directorships in 112 corporations that controlled over $22 billion in assets. In comparison, that amount of wealth was greater than the assessed value of all the land in the United States west of the Mississippi River.

9.3 Building Industrial America on the Backs of Labor

By the end of this section, you will be able to:
- Explain the qualities of industrial working-class life in the late nineteenth century
- Analyze both workers' desire for labor unions and the reasons for unions' inability to achieve their goals

The growth of the American economy in the last half of the nineteenth century presented a paradox. The standard of living for many American workers increased. As Carnegie said in *The Gospel of Wealth*, "the poor enjoy what the rich could not before afford. What were the luxuries have become the necessaries of life. The laborer has now more comforts than the landlord had a few generations ago." In many ways, Carnegie was correct. The decline in prices and the cost of living meant that the industrial era offered many Americans relatively better lives in 1900 than they had only decades before. For some Americans, there were also increased opportunities for upward mobility. For the multitudes in the working class, however, conditions in the factories and at home remained deplorable. The difficulties they faced led many workers to question an industrial order in which a handful of wealthy Americans built their fortunes on the backs of workers.

WORKING-CLASS LIFE

Between the end of the Civil War and the turn of the century, the American workforce underwent a transformative shift. In 1865, nearly 60 percent of Americans still lived and worked on farms; by the early 1900s, that number had reversed itself, and only 40 percent still lived in rural areas, with the remainder living and working in urban and early suburban areas. A significant number of these urban and suburban dwellers earned their wages in factories. Advances in farm machinery allowed for greater production with less manual labor, thus leading many Americans to seek job opportunities in the burgeoning factories in the cities. Not surprisingly, there was a concurrent trend of a decrease in American workers being self-employed and an increase of those working for others and being dependent on a factory wage system for their living.

Yet factory wages were, for the most part, very low. In 1900, the average factory wage was approximately twenty cents per hour, for an annual salary of barely six hundred dollars. According to some historical estimates, that wage left approximately 20 percent of the population in industrialized cities at, or below, the poverty level. An average factory work week was sixty hours, ten hours per day, six days per week, although in steel mills, the workers put in twelve hours per day, seven days a week. Factory owners had little concern for workers' safety. According to one of the few available accurate measures, as late as 1913, nearly 25,000 Americans lost their lives on the job, while another 700,000 workers suffered from injuries that resulted in at least one missed month of work. Another element of hardship for workers was the increasingly dehumanizing nature of their work. Factory workers executed repetitive tasks throughout the long hours of their shifts, seldom interacting with coworkers or supervisors. This solitary and repetitive work style was a difficult adjustment for those used to more collaborative and skill-based work, whether on farms or in crafts shops. Managers embraced Fredrick Taylor's principles of **scientific management**, also called "stop-watch management," where he used stop-watch studies to divide manufacturing tasks into short, repetitive segments. A mechanical engineer by training, Taylor encouraged factory owners to seek efficiency and profitability over any benefits of personal interaction. Owners adopted this model, effectively making workers cogs in a well-oiled machine.

One result of the new breakdown of work processes was that factory owners were able to hire women and children to perform many of the tasks. From 1870 through 1900, the number of women working outside the home tripled. By the end of this period, five million American women were wage earners, with one-quarter of them working factory jobs. Most were young, under twenty-five, and either immigrants themselves or the daughters of immigrants. Their foray into the working world was not seen as a step towards empowerment or equality, but rather a hardship born of financial necessity. Women's factory work tended to be in clothing or textile factories, where their appearance was less offensive to men who felt that heavy industry was their purview. Other women in the workforce worked in clerical positions as bookkeepers and secretaries, and as salesclerks. Not surprisingly, women were paid less than men, under the pretense that they should be under the care of a man and did not require a living wage.

Factory owners used the same rationale for the exceedingly low wages they paid to children. Children were small enough to fit easily among the machines and could be hired for simple work for a fraction of an adult man's pay. The image below (**Figure 9.10**) shows children working the night shift in a glass factory. From 1870 through 1900, child labor in factories tripled. Growing concerns among progressive reformers over the safety of women and children in the workplace would eventually result in the development of political lobby groups. Several states passed legislative efforts to ensure a safe workplace, and the lobby groups pressured Congress to pass protective legislation. However, such legislation would not be forthcoming until well into the twentieth century. In the meantime, many working-class immigrants still desired the additional wages that child and women labor produced, regardless of the harsh working conditions.

Figure 9.10 A photographer took this image of children working in a New York glass factory at midnight. There, as in countless other factories around the country, children worked around the clock in difficult and dangerous conditions.

WORKER PROTESTS AND VIOLENCE

Workers were well aware of the vast discrepancy between their lives and the wealth of the factory owners. Lacking the assets and legal protection needed to organize, and deeply frustrated, some working communities erupted in spontaneous violence. The coal mines of eastern Pennsylvania and the railroad yards of western Pennsylvania, central to both respective industries and home to large, immigrant, working enclaves, saw the brunt of these outbursts. The combination of violence, along with several other factors, blunted any significant efforts to organize workers until well into the twentieth century.

Business owners viewed organization efforts with great mistrust, capitalizing upon widespread anti-union sentiment among the general public to crush unions through open shops, the use of strikebreakers, yellow-dog contracts (in which the employee agrees to not join a union as a pre-condition of employment), and other means. Workers also faced obstacles to organization associated with race and ethnicity, as questions arose on how to address the increasing number of low-paid African American workers, in addition to the language and cultural barriers introduced by the large wave of southeastern European immigration to the United States. But in large part, the greatest obstacle to effective unionization was the general public's continued belief in a strong work ethic and that an individual work ethic—not organizing into radical collectives—would reap its own rewards. As violence erupted, such events seemed only to confirm widespread popular sentiment that radical, un-American elements were behind all union efforts.

In the 1870s, Irish coal miners in eastern Pennsylvania formed a secret organization known as the **Molly Maguires**, named for the famous Irish patriot. Through a series of scare tactics that included kidnappings, beatings, and even murder, the Molly Maguires sought to bring attention to the miners' plight, as well as to cause enough damage and concern to the mine owners that the owners would pay attention to their concerns. Owners paid attention, but not in the way that the protesters had hoped. They hired detectives to pose as miners and mingle among the workers to obtain the names of the Molly Maguires. By 1875, they had acquired the names of twenty-four suspected Maguires, who were subsequently convicted of murder and violence against property. All were convicted and ten were hanged in 1876, at a public "Day of the Rope." This harsh reprisal quickly crushed the remaining Molly Maguires movement. The only substantial gain the workers had from this episode was the knowledge that, lacking labor organization, sporadic violent protest would be met by escalated violence.

Public opinion was not sympathetic towards labor's violent methods as displayed by the Molly Maguires. But the public was further shocked by some of the harsh practices employed by government agents to crush the labor movement, as seen the following year in the Great Railroad Strike of 1877. After incurring a significant pay cut earlier that year, railroad workers in West Virginia spontaneously went on strike and blocked the tracks (**Figure 9.11**). As word spread of the event, railroad workers across the country joined in sympathy, leaving their jobs and committing acts of vandalism to show their frustration with the ownership. Local citizens, who in many instances were relatives and friends, were largely sympathetic to the railroad workers' demands.

Figure 9.11 This engraving of the "Blockade of Engines at Martinsburg, West Virginia" appeared on the front cover of *Harper's Weekly* on August 11, 1877, while the Great Railroad Strike was still underway.

The most significant violent outbreak of the railroad strike occurred in Pittsburgh, beginning on July 19. The governor ordered militiamen from Philadelphia to the Pittsburgh roundhouse to protect railroad property. The militia opened fire to disperse the angry crowd and killed twenty individuals while wounding another twenty-nine. A riot erupted, resulting in twenty-four hours of looting, violence, fire, and mayhem, and did not die down until the rioters wore out in the hot summer weather. In a subsequent skirmish with strikers while trying to escape the roundhouse, militiamen killed another twenty individuals. Violence erupted in Maryland and Illinois as well, and President Hayes eventually sent federal troops into major cities to restore order. This move, along with the impending return of cooler weather that brought with it the need for food and fuel, resulted in striking workers nationwide returning to the railroad. The strike had lasted for forty-five days, and they had gained nothing but a reputation for violence and aggression that left the public less sympathetic than ever. Dissatisfied laborers began to realize that there would be no substantial improvement in their quality of life until they found a way to better organize themselves.

WORKER ORGANIZATION AND THE STRUGGLES OF UNIONS

Prior to the Civil War, there were limited efforts to create an organized labor movement on any large scale. With the majority of workers in the country working independently in rural settings, the idea of organized labor was not largely understood. But, as economic conditions changed, people became more aware of the inequities facing factory wage workers. By the early 1880s, even farmers began to fully recognize the strength of unity behind a common cause.

Models of Organizing: The Knights of Labor and American Federation of Labor

In 1866, seventy-seven delegates representing a variety of different occupations met in Baltimore to form the National Labor Union (NLU). The NLU had ambitious ideas about equal rights for African Americans and women, currency reform, and a legally mandated eight-hour workday. The organization was successful in convincing Congress to adopt the eight-hour workday for federal employees, but their reach did not progress much further. The Panic of 1873 and the economic recession that followed as a result of overspeculation on railroads and the subsequent closing of several banks—during which workers actively sought any employment regardless of the conditions or wages—as well as the death of the NLU's founder, led to a decline in their efforts.

A combination of factors contributed to the debilitating Panic of 1873, which triggered what the public referred to at the time as the "Great Depression" of the 1870s. Most notably, the railroad boom that had occurred from 1840 to 1870 was rapidly coming to a close. Overinvestment in the industry had extended many investors' capital resources in the form of railroad bonds. However, when several economic developments in Europe affected the value of silver in America, which in turn led to a de facto gold standard that shrunk the U.S. monetary supply, the amount of cash capital available for railroad investments rapidly declined. Several large business enterprises were left holding their wealth in all but worthless railroad bonds. When Jay Cooke & Company, a leader in the American banking industry, declared bankruptcy on the eve of their plans to finance the construction of a new transcontinental railroad, the panic truly began. A chain reaction of bank failures culminated with the New York Stock Exchange suspending all trading for ten days at the end of September 1873. Within a year, over one hundred railroad enterprises had failed; within two years, nearly twenty thousand businesses had failed. The loss of jobs and wages sent workers throughout the United States seeking solutions and clamoring for scapegoats.

Although the NLU proved to be the wrong effort at the wrong time, in the wake of the Panic of 1873 and the subsequent frustration exhibited in the failed Molly Maguires uprising and the national railroad strike, another, more significant, labor organization emerged. The Knights of Labor (KOL) was more able to attract a sympathetic following than the Molly Maguires and others by widening its base and appealing to more members. Philadelphia tailor Uriah Stephens grew the KOL from a small presence during the Panic of 1873 to an organization of national importance by 1878. That was the year the KOL held their first general assembly, where they adopted a broad reform platform, including a renewed call for an eight-hour workday, equal pay regardless of gender, the elimination of convict labor, and the creation of greater cooperative enterprises with worker ownership of businesses. Much of the KOL's strength came from its concept of "One Big Union"—the idea that it welcomed all wage workers, regardless of occupation, with the exception of doctors, lawyers, and bankers. It welcomed women, African Americans, Native Americans, and immigrants, of all trades and skill levels. This was a notable break from the earlier tradition of craft unions, which were highly specialized and limited to a particular group. In 1879, a new leader, Terence V. Powderly, joined the organization, and he gained even more followers due to his marketing and promotional efforts. Although largely opposed to strikes as effective tactics, through their sheer size, the Knights claimed victories in several railroad strikes in 1884–1885, including one against notorious "robber baron" Jay Gould, and their popularity consequently rose among workers. By 1886, the KOL had a membership in excess of 700,000.

In one night, however, the KOL's popularity—and indeed the momentum of the labor movement as a whole—plummeted due to an event known as the **Haymarket affair**, which occurred on May 4, 1886, in Chicago's Haymarket Square (**Figure 9.12**). There, an anarchist group had gathered in response to a death at an earlier nationwide demonstration for the eight-hour workday. At the earlier demonstration, clashes between police and strikers at the International Harvester Company of Chicago led to the death of a striking worker. The anarchist group decided to hold a protest the following night in Haymarket Square, and, although the protest was quiet, the police arrived armed for conflict. Someone in the crowd threw a bomb at the police, killing one officer and injuring another. The seven anarchists speaking at the protest were arrested and charged with murder. They were sentenced to death, though two were later pardoned and one committed suicide in prison before his execution.

Figure 9.12 The Haymarket affair, as it was known, began as a rally for the eight-hour workday. But when police broke it up, someone threw a bomb into the crowd, causing mayhem. The organizers of the rally, although not responsible, were sentenced to death. The affair and subsequent hangings struck a harsh blow against organized labor.

The press immediately blamed the KOL as well as Powderly for the Haymarket affair, despite the fact that neither the organization nor Powderly had anything to do with the demonstration. Combined with the American public's lukewarm reception to organized labor as a whole, the damage was done. The KOL saw its membership decline to barely 100,000 by the end of 1886. Nonetheless, during its brief success, the Knights illustrated the potential for success with their model of "industrial unionism," which welcomed workers from all trades.

AMERICANA

☸ *The Haymarket Rally*

On May 1, 1886, recognized internationally as a day for labor celebration, labor organizations around the country engaged in a national rally for the eight-hour workday. While the number of striking workers varied around the country, estimates are that between 300,000 and 500,000 workers protested in New York, Detroit, Chicago, and beyond. In Chicago, clashes between police and protesters led the police to fire into the crowd, resulting in fatalities. Afterward, angry at the deaths of the striking workers, organizers quickly organized a "mass meeting," per the poster below (**Figure 9.13**).

Figure 9.13 This poster invited workers to a meeting denouncing the violence at the labor rally earlier in the week. Note that the invitation is written in both English and German, evidence of the large role that the immigrant population played in the labor movement.

While the meeting was intended to be peaceful, a large police presence made itself known, prompting one of the event organizers to state in his speech, "There seems to prevail the opinion in some quarters that this meeting has been called for the purpose of inaugurating a riot, hence these warlike preparations on the part of so-called 'law and order.' However, let me tell you at the beginning that this meeting has not been called for any such purpose. The object of this meeting is to explain the general situation of the eight-hour movement and to throw light upon various incidents in connection with it." The mayor of Chicago later corroborated accounts of the meeting, noted that it was a peaceful rally, but as it was winding down, the police marched into the crowd, demanding they disperse. Someone in the crowd threw a bomb, killing one policeman immediately and wounding many others, some of whom died later. Despite the aggressive actions of the police, public opinion was strongly against the striking laborers. The *New York Times*, after the events played out, reported on it with the headline "Rioting and Bloodshed in the Streets of Chicago: Police Mowed Down with Dynamite." Other papers echoed the tone and often exaggerated the chaos, undermining organized labor's efforts and leading to the ultimate conviction and hanging of the rally organizers. Labor activists considered those hanged after the Haymarket affair to be martyrs for the cause and created an informal memorial at their gravesides in Park Forest, Illinois.

Click and Explore

This article about the "Rioting and Bloodshed in the Streets of Chicago" (http://openstaxcollege.org/l/haymarket) reveals how the *New York Times* reported on the Haymarket affair. Assess whether the article gives evidence of the information it lays out. Consider how it portrays the events, and how different, more sympathetic coverage might have changed the response of the general public towards immigrant workers and labor unions.

During the effort to establish industrial unionism in the form of the KOL, craft unions had continued to operate. In 1886, twenty different craft unions met to organize a national federation of autonomous craft unions. This group became the American Federation of Labor (AFL), led by Samuel Gompers from its inception until his death in 1924. More so than any of its predecessors, the AFL focused almost all of its efforts on economic gains for its members, seldom straying into political issues other than those that had a direct impact upon working conditions. The AFL also kept a strict policy of not interfering in each union's individual business. Rather, Gompers often settled disputes between unions, using the AFL to represent all unions of matters of federal legislation that could affect all workers, such as the eight-hour workday.

By 1900, the AFL had 500,000 members; by 1914, its numbers had risen to one million, and by 1920 they claimed four million working members. Still, as a federation of craft unions, it excluded many factory workers and thus, even at its height, represented only 15 percent of the nonfarm workers in the country. As a result, even as the country moved towards an increasingly industrial age, the majority of American workers still lacked support, protection from ownership, and access to upward mobility.

The Decline of Labor: The Homestead and Pullman Strikes

While workers struggled to find the right organizational structure to support a union movement in a society that was highly critical of such worker organization, there came two final violent events at the close of the nineteenth century. These events, the Homestead Steel Strike of 1892 and the Pullman Strike of 1894, all but crushed the labor movement for the next forty years, leaving public opinion of labor strikes lower than ever and workers unprotected.

At the Homestead factory of the Carnegie Steel Company, workers represented by the Amalgamated Association of Iron and Steel Workers enjoyed relatively good relations with management until Henry C. Frick became the factory manager in 1889. When the union contract was up for renewal in 1892, Carnegie—long a champion of living wages for his employees—had left for Scotland and trusted Frick—noted for his strong anti-union stance—to manage the negotiations. When no settlement was reached by June 29, Frick ordered a lockout of the workers and hired three hundred Pinkerton detectives to protect company property. On July 6, as the Pinkertons arrived on barges on the river, union workers along the shore engaged them in a gunfight that resulted in the deaths of three Pinkertons and six workers. One week later, the Pennsylvania militia arrived to escort strike-breakers into the factory to resume production. Although the lockout continued until November, it ended with the union defeated and individual workers asking for their jobs back. A subsequent failed assassination attempt by anarchist Alexander Berkman on Frick further strengthened public animosity towards the union.

Two years later, in 1894, the Pullman Strike was another disaster for unionized labor. The crisis began in the company town of Pullman, Illinois, where Pullman "sleeper" cars were manufactured for America's railroads. When the depression of 1893 unfolded in the wake of the failure of several northeastern railroad companies, mostly due to overconstruction and poor financing, company owner George Pullman fired three thousand of the factory's six thousand employees, cut the remaining workers' wages by an average of 25 percent, and then continued to charge the same high rents and prices in the company homes and store where workers were required to live and shop. Workers began the strike on May 11, when Eugene V. Debs, the president of the American Railway Union, ordered rail workers throughout the country to stop handling any trains that had Pullman cars on them. In practicality, almost all of the trains fell into this category, and, therefore, the strike created a nationwide train stoppage, right on the heels of the depression of 1893. Seeking justification for sending in federal troops, President Grover Cleveland turned to his attorney general, who came up with a solution: Attach a mail car to every train and then send in troops to ensure the delivery of the mail. The government also ordered the strike to end; when Debs refused, he was arrested and imprisoned for his interference with the delivery of U.S. mail. The image below (**Figure 9.14**) shows the standoff between federal troops and the workers. The troops protected the hiring of new workers, thus rendering the strike tactic largely ineffective. The strike ended abruptly on July 13, with no labor gains and much lost in the way of public opinion.

Figure 9.14 In this photo of the Pullman Strike of 1894, the Illinois National Guard and striking workers face off in front of a railroad building.

MY STORY

⊙ *George Estes on the Order of Railroad Telegraphers*

The following excerpt is a reflection from George Estes, an organizer and member of the Order of Railroad Telegraphers, a labor organization at the end of the nineteenth century. His perspective on the ways that labor and management related to each other illustrates the difficulties at the heart of their negotiations. He notes that, in this era, the two groups saw each other as enemies and that any gain by one was automatically a loss by the other.

> I have always noticed that things usually have to get pretty bad before they get any better. When inequities pile up so high that the burden is more than the underdog can bear, he gets his dander up and things begin to happen. It was that way with the telegraphers' problem. These exploited individuals were determined to get for themselves better working conditions—higher pay, shorter hours, less work which might not properly be classed as telegraphy, and the high and mighty Mr. Fillmore [railroad company president] was not going to stop them. It was a bitter fight. At the outset, Mr. Fillmore let it be known, by his actions and comments, that he held the telegraphers in the utmost contempt.

> With the papers crammed each day with news of labor strife—and with two great labor factions at each other's throats, I am reminded of a parallel in my own early and more active career. Shortly before the turn of the century, in 1898 and 1899 to be more specific, I occupied a position with regard to a certain class of skilled labor, comparable to that held by the Lewises and Greens of today. I refer, of course, to the telegraphers and station agents. These hard-working gentlemen—servants of the public—had no regular hours, performed a multiplicity of duties, and, considering the service they rendered, were sorely and inadequately paid. A telegrapher's day included a considerable number of chores that present-day telegraphers probably never did or will do in the course of a day's work. He used to clean and fill lanterns, block lights, etc. Used to do the janitor work around the small town depot, stoke the pot-bellied stove of the waiting-room, sweep the floors, picking up papers and waiting-room litter. . . .

> Today, capital and labor seem to understand each other better than they did a generation or so ago. Capital is out to make money. So is labor—and each is willing to grant the other a certain amount of tolerant leeway, just so he doesn't go too far. In the old days there was a breach as wide as the Pacific separating capital and labor. It wasn't money altogether in those days, it was a matter of principle. Capital and labor couldn't see eye to eye on a single point. Every gain that either made was at the expense of the other, and was fought tooth and nail. No difference seemed ever possible of amicable settlement. Strikes were riots. Murder and mayhem was common. Railroad labor troubles were frequent. The railroads, in the nineties, were the country's largest employers. They were so big, so powerful, so perfectly organized themselves—I mean so in accord among themselves as to what treatment they felt like offering the man who worked for them—that it was extremely difficult for labor to gain a single advantage in the struggle for better conditions.

—George Estes, interview with Andrew Sherbert, 1938

9.4 A New American Consumer Culture

By the end of this section, you will be able to:
- Describe the characteristics of the new consumer culture that emerged at the end of the nineteenth century

Despite the challenges workers faced in their new roles as wage earners, the rise of industry in the United States allowed people to access and consume goods as never before. The rise of big business had turned

America into a culture of consumers desperate for time-saving and leisure commodities, where people could expect to find everything they wanted in shops or by mail order. Gone were the days where the small general store was the only option for shoppers; at the end of the nineteenth century, people could take a train to the city and shop in large department stores like Macy's in New York, Gimbel's in Philadelphia, and Marshall Fields in Chicago. Chain stores, like A&P and Woolworth's, both of which opened in the 1870s, offered options to those who lived farther from major urban areas and clearly catered to classes other than the wealthy elite. Industrial advancements contributed to this proliferation, as new construction techniques permitted the building of stores with higher ceilings for larger displays, and the production of larger sheets of plate glass lent themselves to the development of larger store windows, glass countertops, and display cases where shoppers could observe a variety of goods at a glance. L. Frank Baum, of *Wizard of Oz* fame, later founded the National Association of Window Trimmers in 1898, and began publishing *The Store Window* journal to advise businesses on space usage and promotion.

Even families in rural America had new opportunities to purchase a greater variety of products than ever before, at ever decreasing prices. Those far from chain stores could benefit from the newly developed business of mail-order catalogs, placing orders by telephone. Aaron Montgomery Ward established the first significant mail-order business in 1872, with Sears, Roebuck & Company following in 1886. Sears distributed over 300,000 catalogs annually by 1897, and later broke the one million annual mark in 1907. Sears in particular understood that farmers and rural Americans sought alternatives to the higher prices and credit purchases they were forced to endure at small-town country stores. By clearly stating the prices in his catalog, Richard Sears steadily increased his company's image of their catalog serving as "the consumer's bible." In the process, Sears, Roebuck & Company supplied much of America's hinterland with products ranging from farm supplies to bicycles, toilet paper to automobiles, as seen below in a page from the catalog (**Figure 9.15**).

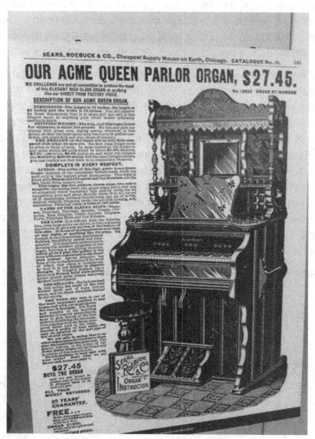

Figure 9.15 This page from the Sears, Roebuck & Co. catalog illustrates how luxuries that would only belong to wealthy city dwellers were now available by mail order to those all around the country.

The tremendous variety of goods available for sale required businesses to compete for customers in ways they had never before imagined. Suddenly, instead of a single option for clothing or shoes, customers were faced with dozens, whether ordered by mail, found at the local chain store, or lined up in massive rows at department stores. This new level of competition made advertising a vital component of all businesses. By 1900, American businesses were spending almost $100 million annually on advertising. Competitors offered "new and improved" models as frequently as possible in order to generate interest. From toothpaste and mouthwash to books on entertaining guests, new goods were constantly offered. Newspapers accommodated the demand for advertising by shifting their production to include full-page advertisements, as opposed to the traditional column width, agate-type advertisements that dominated mid-nineteenth century newspapers (similar to classified advertisements in today's publications). Likewise, professional advertising agencies began to emerge in the 1880s, with experts in consumer demand bidding for accounts with major firms.

It may seem strange that, at a time when wages were so low, people began buying readily; however, the slow emergence of a middle class by the end of the century, combined with the growing practice of buying on credit, presented more opportunities to take part in the new consumer culture. Stores allowed people to open accounts and purchase on credit, thus securing business and allowing consumers to buy without ready cash. Then, as today, the risks of buying on credit led many into debt. As advertising expert Roland Marchand described in his *Parable on the Democracy of Goods*, in an era when access to products became more important than access to the means of production, Americans quickly accepted the notion that they could live a better lifestyle by purchasing the right clothes, the best hair cream, and the shiniest shoes, regardless of their class. For better or worse, American consumerism had begun.

AMERICANA

☉ *Advertising in the Industrial Age: Credit, Luxury, and the Advent of "New and Improved"*

Before the industrial revolution, most household goods were either made at home or purchased locally, with limited choices. By the end of the nineteenth century, factors such as the population's move towards urban centers and the expansion of the railroad changed how Americans shopped for, and perceived, consumer goods. As mentioned above, advertising took off, as businesses competed for customers.

Many of the elements used widely in nineteenth-century advertisements are familiar. Companies sought to sell luxury, safety, and, as the ad for the typewriter below shows (**Figure 9.16**), the allure of the new-and-improved model. One advertising tactic that truly took off in this era was the option to purchase on credit. For the first time, mail order and mass production meant that the aspiring middle class could purchase items that could only be owned previously by the wealthy. While there was a societal stigma for buying everyday goods on credit, certain items, such as fine furniture or pianos, were considered an investment in the move toward entry into the middle class.

Figure 9.16 This typewriter advertisement, like others of the era, tried to lure customers by offering a new model.

Additionally, farmers and housewives purchased farm equipment and sewing machines on credit, considering these items investments rather than luxuries. For women, the purchase of a sewing machine meant that a shirt could be made in one hour, instead of fourteen. The Singer Sewing Machine Company was one of the most aggressive at pushing purchase on credit. They advertised widely, and their "Dollar Down, Dollar a Week" campaign made them one of the fastest-growing companies in the country.

For workers earning lower wages, these easy credit terms meant that the middle-class lifestyle was within their reach. Of course, it also meant they were in debt, and changes in wages, illness, or other unexpected expenses could wreak havoc on a household's tenuous finances. Still, the opportunity to own new and luxurious products was one that many Americans, aspiring to improve their place in society, could not resist.

CHAPTER 10

The Growing Pains of Urbanization, 1870-1900

Figure 10.1 For the millions of immigrants arriving by ship in New York City's harbor, the sight of the Statue of Liberty, as in *Unveiling the Statue of Liberty* (1886) by Edward Moran, stood as a physical representation of the new freedoms and economic opportunities they hoped to find.

Chapter Outline

Introduction

"We saw the big woman with spikes on her head." So begins Sadie Frowne's first memory of arriving in the United States. Many Americans experienced in their new home what the thirteen-year-old Polish girl had seen in the silhouette of the Statue of Liberty (**Figure 10.1**): a wondrous world of new opportunities fraught with dangers. Sadie and her mother, for instance, had left Poland after her father's death. Her mother died shortly thereafter, and Sadie had to find her own way in New York, working in factories and slowly assimilating to life in a vast multinational metropolis. Her story is similar to millions of others, as people came to the United States seeking a better future than the one they had at home.

The future they found, however, was often grim. While many believed in the land of opportunity, the reality of urban life in the United States was more chaotic and difficult than people expected. In addition to the challenges of language, class, race, and ethnicity, these new arrivals dealt with low wages, overcrowded buildings, poor sanitation, and widespread disease. The land of opportunity, it seemed, did not always deliver on its promises.

10.1 Urbanization and Its Challenges

By the end of this section, you will be able to:
- Explain the growth of American cities in the late nineteenth century
- Identify the key challenges that Americans faced due to urbanization, as well as some of the possible solutions to those challenges

Urbanization occurred rapidly in the second half of the nineteenth century in the United States for a number of reasons. The new technologies of the time led to a massive leap in industrialization, requiring large numbers of workers. New electric lights and powerful machinery allowed factories to run twenty-four hours a day, seven days a week. Workers were forced into grueling twelve-hour shifts, requiring them to live close to the factories.

While the work was dangerous and difficult, many Americans were willing to leave behind the declining prospects of preindustrial agriculture in the hope of better wages in industrial labor. Furthermore, problems ranging from famine to religious persecution led a new wave of immigrants to arrive from central, eastern, and southern Europe, many of whom settled and found work near the cities where they first arrived. Immigrants sought solace and comfort among others who shared the same language and customs, and the nation's cities became an invaluable economic and cultural resource.

Although cities such as Philadelphia, Boston, and New York sprang up from the initial days of colonial settlement, the explosion in urban population growth did not occur until the mid-nineteenth century (**Figure 10.3**). At this time, the attractions of city life, and in particular, employment opportunities, grew exponentially due to rapid changes in industrialization. Before the mid-1800s, factories, such as the early textile mills, had to be located near rivers and seaports, both for the transport of goods and the necessary water power. Production became dependent upon seasonal water flow, with cold, icy winters all but stopping river transportation entirely. The development of the steam engine transformed this need, allowing businesses to locate their factories near urban centers. These factories encouraged more and more people to move to urban areas where jobs were plentiful, but hourly wages were often low and the work was routine and grindingly monotonous.

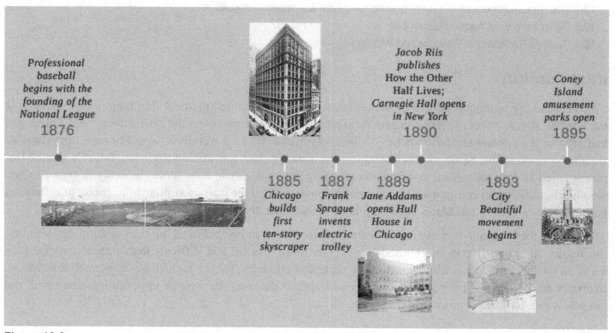

Figure 10.2

Rural and Urban Populations in the United States, 1860–1920		
Year	Rural	Urban
1860	25,226,803	6,216,518
1870	28,656,010	9,902,361
1880	36,059,474	14,129,735
1890	40,873,501	22,106,265
1900	45,997,336	30,214,832
1910	50,164,495	42,064,001
1920	51,768,255	54,253,282
Source: Bureau of the Census		

(a)

Populations of Major Cities in the United States, 1860–1900			
City	1860	1880	1900
New York	1,174,800	1,912,000	3,437,000
Philadelphia	565,500	847,000	1,294,000
Boston	177,800	363,000	561,000
Baltimore	212,400	332,000	509,000
Cincinnati	161,000	255,000	326,000
St. Louis	160,800	350,000	575,000
Chicago	109,300	503,000	1,698,000

(b)

Figure 10.3 As these panels illustrate, the population of the United States grew rapidly in the late 1800s (a). Much of this new growth took place in urban areas (defined by the census as twenty-five hundred people or more), and this urban population, particularly that of major cities (b), dealt with challenges and opportunities that were unknown in previous generations.

Eventually, cities developed their own unique characters based on the core industry that spurred their growth. In Pittsburgh, it was steel; in Chicago, it was meat packing; in New York, the garment and financial industries dominated; and Detroit, by the mid-twentieth century, was defined by the automobiles it built. But all cities at this time, regardless of their industry, suffered from the universal problems that rapid expansion brought with it, including concerns over housing and living conditions, transportation, and communication. These issues were almost always rooted in deep class inequalities, shaped by racial divisions, religious differences, and ethnic strife, and distorted by corrupt local politics.

Click and Explore

This 1884 Bureau of Labor Statistics report (http://openstaxcollege.org/l/clothingfact) from Boston looks in detail at the wages, living conditions, and moral code of the girls who worked in the clothing factories there.

THE KEYS TO SUCCESSFUL URBANIZATION

As the country grew, certain elements led some towns to morph into large urban centers, while others did not. The following four innovations proved critical in shaping urbanization at the turn of the century: electric lighting, communication improvements, intracity transportation, and the rise of skyscrapers. As people migrated for the new jobs, they often struggled with the absence of basic urban infrastructures, such as better transportation, adequate housing, means of communication, and efficient sources of light and energy. Even the basic necessities, such as fresh water and proper sanitation—often taken for granted in the countryside—presented a greater challenge in urban life.

Electric Lighting

Thomas Edison patented the incandescent light bulb in 1879. This development quickly became common in homes as well as factories, transforming how even lower- and middle-class Americans lived. Although slow to arrive in rural areas of the country, electric power became readily available in cities when the first commercial power plants began to open in 1882. When Nikola Tesla subsequently developed the AC (alternating current) system for the Westinghouse Electric & Manufacturing Company, power supplies for lights and other factory equipment could extend for miles from the power source. AC power transformed the use of electricity, allowing urban centers to physically cover greater areas. In the factories, electric lights permitted operations to run twenty-four hours a day, seven days a week. This increase in production required additional workers, and this demand brought more people to cities.

Gradually, cities began to illuminate the streets with electric lamps to allow the city to remain alight throughout the night. No longer did the pace of life and economic activity slow substantially at sunset, the way it had in smaller towns. The cities, following the factories that drew people there, stayed open all the time.

Communications Improvements

The telephone, patented in 1876, greatly transformed communication both regionally and nationally. The telephone rapidly supplanted the telegraph as the preferred form of communication; by 1900, over 1.5 million telephones were in use around the nation, whether as private lines in the homes of some middle- and upper-class Americans, or jointly used "party lines" in many rural areas. By allowing instant communication over larger distances at any given time, growing telephone networks made urban sprawl possible.

In the same way that electric lights spurred greater factory production and economic growth, the telephone increased business through the more rapid pace of demand. Now, orders could come constantly via telephone, rather than via mail-order. More orders generated greater production, which in turn required still more workers. This demand for additional labor played a key role in urban growth, as expanding companies sought workers to handle the increasing consumer demand for their products.

Intracity Transportation

As cities grew and sprawled outward, a major challenge was efficient travel within the city—from home to factories or shops, and then back again. Most transportation infrastructure was used to connect cities to each other, typically by rail or canal. Prior to the 1880s, the most common form of transportation within cities was the omnibus. This was a large, horse-drawn carriage, often placed on iron or steel tracks to provide a smoother ride. While omnibuses worked adequately in smaller, less congested cities, they were not equipped to handle the larger crowds that developed at the close of the century. The horses had to stop and rest, and horse manure became an ongoing problem.

In 1887, Frank Sprague invented the electric trolley, which worked along the same concept as the omnibus, with a large wagon on tracks, but was powered by electricity rather than horses. The electric trolley could run throughout the day and night, like the factories and the workers who fueled them. But it also modernized less important industrial centers, such as the southern city of Richmond, Virginia. As early as 1873, San Francisco engineers adopted pulley technology from the mining industry to introduce cable cars and turn the city's steep hills into elegant middle-class communities. However, as crowds continued to grow in the largest cities, such as Chicago and New York, trolleys were unable to move efficiently through the crowds of pedestrians (**Figure 10.4**). To avoid this challenge, city planners elevated the trolley lines above the streets, creating elevated trains, or L-trains, as early as 1868 in New York City, and quickly spreading to Boston in 1887 and Chicago in 1892. Finally, as skyscrapers began to dominate the air, transportation evolved one step further to move underground as subways. Boston's subway system began operating in 1897, and was quickly followed by New York and other cities.

(a)   (b)

Figure 10.4 Although trolleys were far more efficient than horse-drawn carriages, populous cities such as New York experienced frequent accidents, as depicted in this 1895 illustration from *Leslie's Weekly* (a). To avoid overcrowded streets, trolleys soon went underground, as at the Public Gardens Portal in Boston (b), where three different lines met to enter the Tremont Street Subway, the oldest subway tunnel in the United States, opening on September 1, 1897.

The Rise of Skyscrapers

The last limitation that large cities had to overcome was the ever-increasing need for space. Eastern cities, unlike their midwestern counterparts, could not continue to grow outward, as the land surrounding them was already settled. Geographic limitations such as rivers or the coast also hampered sprawl. And in all cities, citizens needed to be close enough to urban centers to conveniently access work, shops, and other core institutions of urban life. The increasing cost of real estate made upward growth attractive, and so did the prestige that towering buildings carried for the businesses that occupied them. Workers completed the first skyscraper in Chicago, the ten-story Home Insurance Building, in 1885 (**Figure 10.5**). Although engineers had the capability to go higher, thanks to new steel construction techniques, they required another vital invention in order to make taller buildings viable: the elevator. In 1889, the Otis Elevator Company, led by inventor James Otis, installed the first electric elevator. This began the skyscraper craze, allowing developers in eastern cities to build and market prestigious real estate in the hearts of crowded eastern metropoles.

Figure 10.5 While the technology existed to engineer tall buildings, it was not until the invention of the electric elevator in 1889 that skyscrapers began to take over the urban landscape. Shown here is the Home Insurance Building in Chicago, considered the first modern skyscraper.

DEFINING "AMERICAN"

☉ *Jacob Riis and the Window into "How the Other Half Lives"*

Jacob Riis was a Danish immigrant who moved to New York in the late nineteenth century and, after experiencing poverty and joblessness first-hand, ultimately built a career as a police reporter. In the course of his work, he spent much of his time in the slums and tenements of New York's working poor. Appalled by what he found there, Riis began documenting these scenes of squalor and sharing them through lectures and ultimately through the publication of his book, *How the Other Half Lives*, in 1890 (Figure 10.6).

Figure 10.6 In photographs such as *Bandit's Roost* (1888), taken on Mulberry Street in the infamous Five Points neighborhood of Manhattan's Lower East Side, Jacob Riis documented the plight of New York City slums in the late nineteenth century.

By most contemporary accounts, Riis was an effective storyteller, using drama and racial stereotypes to tell his stories of the ethnic slums he encountered. But while his racial thinking was very much a product of his time, he was also a reformer; he felt strongly that upper and middle-class Americans could and should care about the living conditions of the poor. In his book and lectures, he argued against the immoral landlords and useless laws that allowed dangerous living conditions and high rents. He also suggested remodeling existing tenements or building new ones. He was not alone in his concern for the plight of the poor; other reporters and activists had already brought the issue into the public eye, and Riis's photographs added a new element to the story.

To tell his stories, Riis used a series of deeply compelling photographs. Riis and his group of amateur photographers moved through the various slums of New York, laboriously setting up their tripods and explosive chemicals to create enough light to take the photographs. His photos and writings shocked the public, made Riis a well-known figure both in his day and beyond, and eventually led to new state legislation curbing abuses in tenements.

THE IMMEDIATE CHALLENGES OF URBAN LIFE

Congestion, pollution, crime, and disease were prevalent problems in all urban centers; city planners and inhabitants alike sought new solutions to the problems caused by rapid urban growth. Living conditions for most working-class urban dwellers were atrocious. They lived in crowded tenement houses and cramped apartments with terrible ventilation and substandard plumbing and sanitation. As a result, disease ran rampant, with typhoid and cholera common. Memphis, Tennessee, experienced waves of cholera (1873) followed by yellow fever (1878 and 1879) that resulted in the loss of over ten thousand lives. By the late 1880s, New York City, Baltimore, Chicago, and New Orleans had all introduced sewage pumping systems to provide efficient waste management. Many cities were also serious fire hazards. An average working-class family of six, with two adults and four children, had at best a two-bedroom tenement. By one 1900 estimate, in the New York City borough of Manhattan alone, there were nearly fifty thousand tenement houses. The photographs of these tenement houses are seen in Jacob Riis's book, *How the Other Half Lives*, discussed in the feature above. Citing a study by the New York State Assembly at this time, Riis found New York to be the most densely populated city in the world, with as many as eight hundred residents per square acre in the Lower East Side working-class slums, comprising the Eleventh and Thirteenth Wards.

Click and Explore

Visit New York City, Tenement Life (http://openstaxcollege.org/l/tenement) to get an impression of the everyday life of tenement dwellers on Manhattan's Lower East Side.

Churches and civic organizations provided some relief to the challenges of working-class city life. Churches were moved to intervene through their belief in the concept of the **social gospel**. This philosophy stated that all Christians, whether they were church leaders or social reformers, should be as concerned about the conditions of life in the secular world as the afterlife, and the Reverend Washington Gladden was a major advocate. Rather than preaching sermons on heaven and hell, Gladden talked about social changes of the time, urging other preachers to follow his lead. He advocated for improvements in daily life and encouraged Americans of all classes to work together for the betterment of society. His sermons included the message to "love thy neighbor" and held that all Americans had to work together to help the masses. As a result of his influence, churches began to include gymnasiums and libraries as well as offer evening classes on hygiene and health care. Other religious organizations like the Salvation Army and the Young Men's Christian Association (YMCA) expanded their reach in American cities at this time as well. Beginning in the 1870s, these organizations began providing community services and other benefits to the urban poor.

In the secular sphere, the **settlement house movement** of the 1890s provided additional relief. Pioneering women such as Jane Addams in Chicago and Lillian Wald in New York led this early progressive reform movement in the United States, building upon ideas originally fashioned by social reformers in England. With no particular religious bent, they worked to create settlement houses in urban centers where they could help the working class, and in particular, working-class women, find aid. Their help included child daycare, evening classes, libraries, gym facilities, and free health care. Addams opened her now-famous Hull House (**Figure 10.7**) in Chicago in 1889, and Wald's Henry Street Settlement opened in New York six years later. The movement spread quickly to other cities, where they not only provided relief to working-class women but also offered employment opportunities for women graduating college in the growing field of social work. Oftentimes, living in the settlement houses among the women they helped, these college graduates experienced the equivalent of living social classrooms in which to practice their skills, which also frequently caused friction with immigrant women who had their own ideas of reform and self-improvement.

Figure 10.7 Jane Addams opened Hull House in Chicago in 1889, offering services and support to the city's working poor.

The success of the settlement house movement later became the basis of a political agenda that included pressure for housing laws, child labor laws, and worker's compensation laws, among others. Florence Kelley, who originally worked with Addams in Chicago, later joined Wald's efforts in New York; together, they created the National Child Labor Committee and advocated for the subsequent creation of the Children's Bureau in the U.S. Department of Labor in 1912. Julia Lathrop—herself a former resident of Hull House—became the first woman to head a federal government agency, when President William Howard Taft appointed her to run the bureau. Settlement house workers also became influential leaders in the women's suffrage movement as well as the antiwar movement during World War I.

MY STORY

✧ *Jane Addams Reflects on the Settlement House Movement*

Jane Addams was a social activist whose work took many forms. She is perhaps best known as the founder of Hull House in Chicago, which later became a model for settlement houses throughout the country. Here, she reflects on the role that the settlement played.

> Life in the Settlement discovers above all what has been called 'the extraordinary pliability of human nature,' and it seems impossible to set any bounds to the moral capabilities which might unfold under ideal civic and educational conditions. But in order to obtain these conditions, the Settlement recognizes the need of cooperation, both with the radical and the conservative, and from the very nature of the case the Settlement cannot limit its friends to any one political party or economic school.
>
> The Settlement casts side none of those things which cultivated men have come to consider reasonable and goodly, but it insists that those belong as well to that great body of people who, because of toilsome and underpaid labor, are unable to procure them for themselves. Added to this is a profound conviction that the common stock of intellectual enjoyment should not be difficult of access because of the economic position of him who would approach it, that those 'best results of civilization' upon which depend the finer and freer aspects of living must be incorporated into our common life and have free mobility through all elements of society if we would have our democracy endure.
>
> The educational activities of a Settlement, as well its philanthropic, civic, and social undertakings, are but differing manifestations of the attempt to socialize democracy, as is the very existence of the Settlement itself.

In addition to her pioneering work in the settlement house movement, Addams also was active in the women's suffrage movement as well as an outspoken proponent for international peace efforts. She was instrumental in the relief effort after World War I, a commitment that led to her winning the Nobel Peace Prize in 1931.

10.2 The African American "Great Migration" and New European Immigration

By the end of this section, you will be able to:
- Identify the factors that prompted African American and European immigration to American cities in the late nineteenth century
- Explain the discrimination and anti-immigration legislation that immigrants faced in the late nineteenth century

New cities were populated with diverse waves of new arrivals, who came to the cities to seek work in the businesses and factories there. While a small percentage of these newcomers were white Americans seeking jobs, most were made up of two groups that had not previously been factors in the urbanization movement: African Americans fleeing the racism of the farms and former plantations in the South, and southern and eastern European immigrants. These new immigrants supplanted the previous waves of northern and western European immigrants, who had tended to move west to purchase land. Unlike their predecessors, the newer immigrants lacked the funds to strike out to the western lands and instead remained in the urban centers where they arrived, seeking any work that would keep them alive.

THE AFRICAN AMERICAN "GREAT MIGRATION"

Between the end of the Civil War and the beginning of the Great Depression, nearly two million African Americans fled the rural South to seek new opportunities elsewhere. While some moved west, the vast majority of this **Great Migration**, as the large exodus of African Americans leaving the South in the early twentieth century was called, traveled to the Northeast and Upper Midwest. The following cities were the primary destinations for these African Americans: New York, Chicago, Philadelphia, St. Louis, Detroit, Pittsburgh, Cleveland, and Indianapolis. These eight cities accounted for over two-thirds of the total population of the African American migration.

A combination of both "push" and "pull" factors played a role in this movement. Despite the end of the Civil War and the passage of the Thirteenth, Fourteenth, and Fifteenth Amendments to the U.S. Constitution (ensuring freedom, the right to vote regardless of race, and equal protection under the law, respectively), African Americans were still subjected to intense racial hatred. The rise of the Ku Klux Klan in the immediate aftermath of the Civil War led to increased death threats, violence, and a wave of lynchings. Even after the formal dismantling of the Klan in the late 1870s, racially motivated violence continued. According to researchers at the Tuskegee Institute, there were thirty-five hundred racially motivated lynchings and other murders committed in the South between 1865 and 1900. For African Americans fleeing this culture of violence, northern and midwestern cities offered an opportunity to escape the dangers of the South.

In addition to this "push" out of the South, African Americans were also "pulled" to the cities by factors that attracted them, including job opportunities, where they could earn a wage rather than be tied to a landlord, and the chance to vote (for men, at least), supposedly free from the threat of violence. Although many lacked the funds to move themselves north, factory owners and other businesses that sought cheap labor assisted the migration. Often, the men moved first then sent for their families once they were ensconced in their new city life. Racism and a lack of formal education relegated these African American workers to many of the lower-paying unskilled or semi-skilled occupations. More than 80 percent of African American men worked menial jobs in steel mills, mines, construction, and meat packing. In the railroad industry, they were often employed as porters or servants (**Figure 10.8**). In other businesses, they worked as janitors, waiters, or cooks. African American women, who faced discrimination due to both their race and gender, found a few job opportunities in the garment industry or laundries, but were more often employed as maids and domestic servants. Regardless of the status of their jobs, however, African Americans earned higher wages in the North than they did for the same occupations in the South, and typically found housing to be more available.

(a)   (b)

Figure 10.8 African American men who moved north as part of the Great Migration were often consigned to menial employment, such as working in construction or as porters on the railways (a), such as in the celebrated Pullman dining and sleeping cars (b).

However, such economic gains were offset by the higher cost of living in the North, especially in terms of rent, food costs, and other essentials. As a result, African Americans often found themselves living in overcrowded, unsanitary conditions, much like the tenement slums in which European immigrants lived in the cities. For newly arrived African Americans, even those who sought out the cities for the opportunities they provided, life in these urban centers was exceedingly difficult. They quickly learned that racial discrimination did not end at the Mason-Dixon Line, but continued to flourish in the North as well as the South. European immigrants, also seeking a better life in the cities of the United States, resented the arrival of the African Americans, whom they feared would compete for the same jobs or offer to work at lower wages. Landlords frequently discriminated against them; their rapid influx into the cities created severe housing shortages and even more overcrowded tenements. Homeowners in traditionally white neighborhoods later entered into covenants in which they agreed not to sell to African American buyers; they also often fled neighborhoods into which African Americans had gained successful entry. In addition, some bankers practiced mortgage discrimination, later known as "redlining," in order to deny home loans to qualified buyers. Such pervasive discrimination led to a concentration of African Americans in some of the worst slum areas of most major metropolitan cities, a problem that remained ongoing throughout most of the twentieth century.

So why move to the North, given that the economic challenges they faced were similar to those that African Americans encountered in the South? The answer lies in noneconomic gains. Greater educational opportunities and more expansive personal freedoms mattered greatly to the African Americans who made the trek northward during the Great Migration. State legislatures and local school districts allocated more funds for the education of both blacks and whites in the North, and also enforced compulsory school attendance laws more rigorously. Similarly, unlike the South where a simple gesture (or lack of a deferential one) could result in physical harm to the African American who committed it, life in larger, crowded northern urban centers permitted a degree of anonymity—and with it, personal freedom—that enabled African Americans to move, work, and speak without deferring to every white person with whom they crossed paths. Psychologically, these gains more than offset the continued economic challenges that black migrants faced.

THE CHANGING NATURE OF EUROPEAN IMMIGRATION

Immigrants also shifted the demographics of the rapidly growing cities. Although immigration had always been a force of change in the United States, it took on a new character in the late nineteenth century. Beginning in the 1880s, the arrival of immigrants from mostly southern and eastern European countries rapidly increased while the flow from northern and western Europe remained relatively constant (**Table 10.1**).

Table 10.1 Cumulative Total of the Foreign-Born Population in the United States, 1870–1910 (by major country of birth and European region)

Region Country	1870	1880	1890	1900	1910
Northern and Western Europe	4,845,679	5,499,889	7,288,917	7,204,649	7,306,325
Germany	1,690,533	1,966,742	2,784,894	2,663,418	2,311,237
Ireland	1,855,827	1,854,571	1,871,509	1,615,459	1,352,251
England	550,924	662,676	908,141	840,513	877,719
Sweden	97,332	194,337	478,041	582,014	665,207
Austria	30,508	38,663	123,271	275,907	626,341
Norway	114,246	181,729	322,665	336,388	403,877
Scotland	140,835	170,136	242,231	233,524	261,076
Southern and Eastern Europe	93,824	248,620	728,851	1,674,648	4,500,932
Italy	17,157	44,230	182,580	484,027	1,343,125
Russia	4,644	35,722	182,644	423,726	1,184,412
Poland	14,436	48,557	147,440	383,407	937,884
Hungary	3,737	11,526	62,435	145,714	495,609
Czechoslovakia	40,289	85,361	118,106	156,891	219,214

The previous waves of immigrants from northern and western Europe, particularly Germany, Great Britain, and the Nordic countries, were relatively well off, arriving in the country with some funds and often moving to the newly settled western territories. In contrast, the newer immigrants from southern and eastern European countries, including Italy, Greece, and several Slavic countries including Russia, came over due to "push" and "pull" factors similar to those that influenced the African Americans arriving from the South. Many were "pushed" from their countries by a series of ongoing famines, by the need to escape religious, political, or racial persecution, or by the desire to avoid compulsory military service. They were also "pulled" by the promise of consistent, wage-earning work.

Whatever the reason, these immigrants arrived without the education and finances of the earlier waves of immigrants, and settled more readily in the port towns where they arrived, rather than setting out to seek their fortunes in the West. By 1890, over 80 percent of the population of New York would be either foreign-born or children of foreign-born parentage. Other cities saw huge spikes in foreign populations as well, though not to the same degree, due in large part to Ellis Island in New York City being the primary port of entry for most European immigrants arriving in the United States.

The number of immigrants peaked between 1900 and 1910, when over nine million people arrived in the United States. To assist in the processing and management of this massive wave of immigrants, the Bureau of Immigration in New York City, which had become the official port of entry, opened Ellis Island in 1892. Today, nearly half of all Americans have ancestors who, at some point in time, entered the country through the portal at Ellis Island. Doctors or nurses inspected the immigrants upon arrival, looking for any signs of infectious diseases (**Figure 10.9**). Most immigrants were admitted to the country with only a cursory glance at any other paperwork. Roughly 2 percent of the arriving immigrants were denied entry due to a medical condition or criminal history. The rest would enter the country by way of the streets of New York, many unable to speak English and totally reliant on finding those who spoke their native tongue.

Figure 10.9 This photo shows newly arrived immigrants at Ellis Island in New York. Inspectors are examining them for contagious health problems, which could require them to be sent back. (credit: NIAID)

Seeking comfort in a strange land, as well as a common language, many immigrants sought out relatives, friends, former neighbors, townspeople, and countrymen who had already settled in American cities. This led to a rise in ethnic enclaves within the larger city. Little Italy, Chinatown, and many other communities developed in which immigrant groups could find everything to remind them of home, from local language newspapers to ethnic food stores. While these enclaves provided a sense of community to their members, they added to the problems of urban congestion, particularly in the poorest slums where immigrants could afford housing.

Click and Explore

This Library of Congress exhibit on the history of Jewish immigration (http://openstaxcollege.org/l/jewishimmig) to the United States illustrates the ongoing challenge immigrants felt between the ties to their old land and a love for America.

The demographic shift at the turn of the century was later confirmed by the Dillingham Commission, created by Congress in 1907 to report on the nature of immigration in America; the commission reinforced this ethnic identification of immigrants and their simultaneous discrimination. The report put it simply: These newer immigrants looked and acted differently. They had darker skin tone, spoke languages with which most Americans were unfamiliar, and practiced unfamiliar religions, specifically Judaism and Catholicism. Even the foods they sought out at butchers and grocery stores set immigrants apart. Because of these easily identifiable differences, new immigrants became easy targets for hatred and discrimination. If jobs were hard to find, or if housing was overcrowded, it became easy to blame the immigrants. Like African Americans, immigrants in cities were blamed for the problems of the day.

Growing numbers of Americans resented the waves of new immigrants, resulting in a backlash. The Reverend Josiah Strong fueled the hatred and discrimination in his bestselling book, *Our Country: Its Possible Future and Its Present Crisis*, published in 1885. In a revised edition that reflected the 1890 census records, he clearly identified undesirable immigrants—those from southern and eastern European countries—as a key threat to the moral fiber of the country, and urged all good Americans to face the challenge. Several thousand Americans answered his call by forming the American Protective Association, the chief political activist group to promote legislation curbing immigration into the United States. The group successfully lobbied Congress to adopt both an English language literacy test for immigrants, which eventually passed in 1917, and the Chinese Exclusion Act (discussed in a previous chapter). The group's political lobbying also laid the groundwork for the subsequent Emergency Quota Act of 1921 and the Immigration Act of 1924, as well as the National Origins Act.

Click and Explore

The **global timeline of immigration** (http://openstaxcollege.org/l/immig1) at the Library of Congress offers a summary of immigration policies and the groups affected by it, as well as a compelling overview of different ethnic groups' immigration stories. Browse through to see how different ethnic groups made their way in the United States.

10.3 Relief from the Chaos of Urban Life

By the end of this section, you will be able to:

- Identify how each class of Americans—working class, middle class, and upper class—responded to the challenges associated with urban life
- Explain the process of machine politics and how it brought relief to working-class Americans

Settlement houses and religious and civic organizations attempted to provide some support to working-class city dwellers through free health care, education, and leisure opportunities. Still, for urban citizens, life in the city was chaotic and challenging. But how that chaos manifested and how relief was sought differed greatly, depending on where people were in the social caste—the working class, the upper class, or the newly emerging professional middle class—in addition to the aforementioned issues of race and ethnicity. While many communities found life in the largest American cities disorganized and overwhelming, the ways they answered these challenges were as diverse as the people who lived there. Broad solutions emerged that were typically class specific: The rise of machine politics and popular culture provided relief to the working class, higher education opportunities and suburbanization benefitted the professional middle class, and reminders of their elite status gave comfort to the upper class. And everyone, no matter where they fell in the class system, benefited from the efforts to improve the physical landscapes of the fast-growing urban environment.

THE LIFE AND STRUGGLES OF THE URBAN WORKING CLASS

For the working-class residents of America's cities, one practical way of coping with the challenges of urban life was to take advantage of the system of machine politics, while another was to seek relief in the variety of popular culture and entertainment found in and around cities. Although neither of these forms of relief was restricted to the working class, they were the ones who relied most heavily on them.

Machine Politics

The primary form of relief for working-class urban Americans, and particularly immigrants, came in the form of **machine politics**. This phrase referred to the process by which every citizen of the city, no matter their ethnicity or race, was a ward resident with an alderman who spoke on their behalf at city hall. When everyday challenges arose, whether sanitation problems or the need for a sidewalk along a muddy road, citizens would approach their alderman to find a solution. The aldermen knew that, rather than work through the long bureaucratic process associated with city hall, they could work within the "machine" of local politics to find a speedy, mutually beneficial solution. In machine politics, favors were exchanged for votes, votes were given in exchange for fast solutions, and the price of the solutions included a kickback to the boss. In the short term, everyone got what they needed, but the process was neither transparent nor democratic, and it was an inefficient way of conducting the city's business.

One example of a machine political system was the Democratic political machine **Tammany Hall** in New York, run by machine boss William Tweed with assistance from George Washington Plunkitt (**Figure 10.10**). There, citizens knew their immediate problems would be addressed in return for their promise of political support in future elections. In this way, machines provided timely solutions for citizens and votes for the politicians. For example, if in Little Italy there was a desperate need for sidewalks in order to improve traffic to the stores on a particular street, the request would likely get bogged down in the bureaucratic red tape at city hall. Instead, store owners would approach the machine. A district captain would approach the "boss" and make him aware of the problem. The boss would contact city politicians and strongly urge them to appropriate the needed funds for the sidewalk in exchange for the promise that the boss would direct votes in their favor in the upcoming election. The boss then used the funds to pay one of his friends for the sidewalk construction, typically at an exorbitant cost, with a financial kickback to the boss, which was known as **graft**. The sidewalk was built more quickly than anyone hoped, in exchange for the citizens' promises to vote for machine-supported candidates in the next elections. Despite its corrupt nature, Tammany Hall essentially ran New York politics from the 1850s until the 1930s. Other large cities, including Boston, Philadelphia, Cleveland, St. Louis, and Kansas City, made use of political machines as well.

"THAT'S WHAT'S THE MATTER."

Boss Tweed. "As long as I count the Votes, what are you going to do about it? say?"

Figure 10.10 This political cartoon depicts the control of Boss Tweed, of Tammany Hall, over the election process in New York. Why were people willing to accept the corruption involved in machine politics?

Popular Culture and Entertainment

Working-class residents also found relief in the diverse and omnipresent offerings of popular culture and entertainment in and around cities. These offerings provided an immediate escape from the squalor and difficulties of everyday life. As improved means of internal transportation developed, working-class residents could escape the city and experience one of the popular new forms of entertainment—the amusement park. For example, Coney Island on the Brooklyn shoreline consisted of several different amusement parks, the first of which opened in 1895 (**Figure 10.11**). At these parks, New Yorkers enjoyed wild rides, animal attractions, and large stage productions designed to help them forget the struggles of their working-day lives. Freak "side" shows fed the public's curiosity about physical deviance. For a mere ten cents, spectators could watch a high-diving horse, take a ride to the moon to watch moon maidens eat green cheese, or witness the electrocution of an elephant, a spectacle that fascinated the public both with technological marvels and exotic wildlife. The treatment of animals in many acts at Coney Island and other public amusement parks drew the attention of middle-class reformers such as the American Society for the Prevention of Cruelty to Animals. Despite questions regarding the propriety of many of the acts, other cities quickly followed New York's lead with similar, if smaller, versions of Coney Island's attractions.

Figure 10.11 The Dreamland Amusement Park tower was just one of Coney Island's amusements.

Click and Explore

The American Experience Timeline of Coney Island (http://openstaxcollege.org/l/coney) shows a timeline, photo gallery, and other elements of Coney Island. Look to see what elements of American culture, from the hot dog to the roller coaster, debuted there.

Another common form of popular entertainment was vaudeville—large stage variety shows that included everything from singing, dancing, and comedy acts to live animals and magic. The vaudeville circuit gave rise to several prominent performers, including magician Harry Houdini, who began his career in these variety shows before his fame propelled him to solo acts. In addition to live theater shows, it was primarily working-class citizens who enjoyed the advent of the nickelodeon, a forerunner to the movie theater. The first nickelodeon opened in Pittsburgh in 1905, where nearly one hundred visitors packed into a storefront theater to see a traditional vaudeville show interspersed with one-minute film clips. Several theaters initially used the films as "chasers" to indicate the end of the show to the live audience so they would clear the auditorium. However, a vaudeville performers' strike generated even greater interest in the films, eventually resulting in the rise of modern movie theaters by 1910.

One other major form of entertainment for the working class was professional baseball (**Figure 10.12**). Club teams transformed into professional baseball teams with the Cincinnati Red Stockings, now the Cincinnati Reds, in 1869. Soon, professional teams sprang up in several major American cities. Baseball games provided an inexpensive form of entertainment, where for less than a dollar, a person could enjoy a double-header, two hot dogs, and a beer. But more importantly, the teams became a way for newly relocated Americans and immigrants of diverse backgrounds to develop a unified civic identity, all cheering for one team. By 1876, the National League had formed, and soon after, cathedral-style ballparks began to spring up in many cities. Fenway Park in Boston (1912), Forbes Field in Pittsburgh (1909), and the Polo Grounds in New York (1890) all became touch points where working-class Americans came together to support a common cause.

Figure 10.12 Boston's Fenway Park opened in 1912 and was a popular site for working-class Bostonians to spend their leisure time. The "Green Monster," the iconic, left field wall, makes it one of the most recognizable stadiums in baseball today.

Other popular sports included prize-fighting, which attracted a predominantly male, working- and middle-class audience who lived vicariously through the triumphs of the boxers during a time where opportunities for individual success were rapidly shrinking, and college football, which paralleled a modern corporation in its team hierarchy, divisions of duties, and emphasis on time management.

THE UPPER CLASS IN THE CITIES

The American financial elite did not need to crowd into cities to find work, like their working-class counterparts. But as urban centers were vital business cores, where multi-million-dollar financial deals were made daily, those who worked in that world wished to remain close to the action. The rich chose to be in the midst of the chaos of the cities, but they were also able to provide significant measures of comfort, convenience, and luxury for themselves.

Wealthy citizens seldom attended what they considered the crass entertainment of the working class. Instead of amusement parks and baseball games, urban elites sought out more refined pastimes that underscored their knowledge of art and culture, preferring classical music concerts, fine art collections, and social gatherings with their peers. In New York, Andrew Carnegie built Carnegie Hall in 1891, which quickly became the center of classical music performances in the country. Nearby, the Metropolitan Museum of Art opened its doors in 1872 and still remains one of the largest collections of fine art in the world. Other cities followed suit, and these cultural pursuits became a way for the upper class to remind themselves of their elevated place amid urban squalor.

As new opportunities for the middle class threatened the austerity of upper-class citizens, including the newer forms of transportation that allowed middle-class Americans to travel with greater ease, wealthier Americans sought unique ways to further set themselves apart in society. These included more expensive excursions, such as vacations in Newport, Rhode Island, winter relocation to sunny Florida, and frequent trips aboard steamships to Europe. For those who were not of the highly respected "old money," but only recently obtained their riches through business ventures, the relief they sought came in the form of one book—the annual *Social Register*. First published in 1886 by Louis Keller in New York City, the register became a directory of the wealthy socialites who populated the city. Keller updated it annually, and people would watch with varying degrees of anxiety or complacency to see their names appear in print. Also called the *Blue Book*, the register was instrumental in the planning of society dinners, balls, and other social events. For those of newer wealth, there was relief found simply in the notion that they and others witnessed their wealth through the publication of their names in the register.

A NEW MIDDLE CLASS

While the working class were confined to tenement houses in the cities by their need to be close to their work and the lack of funds to find anyplace better, and the wealthy class chose to remain in the cities to stay close to the action of big business transactions, the emerging middle class responded to urban challenges with their own solutions. This group included the managers, salesmen, engineers, doctors, accountants, and other salaried professionals who still worked for a living, but were significantly better educated and compensated than the working-class poor. For this new middle class, relief from the trials of the cities came through education and suburbanization.

In large part, the middle class responded to the challenges of the city by physically escaping it. As transportation improved and outlying communities connected to urban centers, the middle class embraced a new type of community—the suburbs. It became possible for those with adequate means to work in the city and escape each evening, by way of a train or trolley, to a house in the suburbs. As the number of people moving to the suburbs grew, there also grew a perception among the middle class that the farther one lived from the city and the more amenities one had, the more affluence one had achieved.

Although a few suburbs existed in the United States prior to the 1880s (such as Llewellyn Park, New Jersey), the introduction of the electric railway generated greater interest and growth during the last decade of the century. The ability to travel from home to work on a relatively quick and cheap mode of transportation encouraged more Americans of modest means to consider living away from the chaos of the city. Eventually, Henry Ford's popularization of the automobile, specifically in terms of a lower price, permitted more families to own cars and thus consider suburban life. Later in the twentieth century, both the advent of the interstate highway system, along with federal legislation designed to allow families to construct homes with low-interest loans, further sparked the suburban phenomenon.

New Roles for Middle-Class Women

Social norms of the day encouraged middle-class women to take great pride in creating a positive home environment for their working husbands and school-age children, which reinforced the business and educational principles that they practiced on the job or in school. It was at this time that the magazines *Ladies Home Journal* and *Good Housekeeping* began distribution, to tremendous popularity (**Figure 10.13**).

Figure 10.13 The middle-class family of the late nineteenth century largely embraced a separation of gendered spheres that had first emerged during the market revolution of the antebellum years. Whereas the husband earned money for the family outside the home, the wife oversaw domestic chores, raised the children, and tended to the family's spiritual, social, and cultural needs. The magazine *Good Housekeeping*, launched in 1885, capitalized on the middle-class woman's focus on maintaining a pride-worthy home.

While the vast majority of middle-class women took on the expected role of housewife and homemaker, some women were finding paths to college. A small number of men's colleges began to open their doors to women in the mid-1800s, and co-education became an option. Some of the most elite universities created affiliated women's colleges, such as Radcliffe College with Harvard, and Pembroke College with Brown University. But more importantly, the first women's colleges opened at this time. Mount Holyoke, Vassar, Smith, and Wellesley Colleges, still some of the best known women's schools, opened their doors between 1865 and 1880, and, although enrollment was low (initial class sizes ranged from sixty-one students at Vassar to seventy at Wellesley, seventy-one at Smith, and up to eighty-eight at Mount Holyoke), the opportunity for a higher education, and even a career, began to emerge for young women. These schools offered a unique, all-women environment in which professors and a community of education-seeking young women came together. While most college-educated young women still married, their education offered them new opportunities to work outside the home, most frequently as teachers, professors, or in the aforementioned settlement house environments created by Jane Addams and others.

Education and the Middle Class

Since the children of the professional class did not have to leave school and find work to support their families, they had opportunities for education and advancement that would solidify their position in the middle class. They also benefited from the presence of stay-at-home mothers, unlike working-class children, whose mothers typically worked the same long hours as their fathers. Public school enrollment exploded at this time, with the number of students attending public school tripling from seven million in 1870 to twenty-one million in 1920. Unlike the old-fashioned one-room schoolhouses, larger schools slowly began the practice of employing different teachers for each grade, and some even began hiring discipline-specific instructors. High schools also grew at this time, from one hundred high schools nationally in 1860 to over six thousand by 1900.

The federal government supported the growth of higher education with the Morrill Acts of 1862 and 1890. These laws set aside public land and federal funds to create land-grant colleges that were affordable to middle-class families, offering courses and degrees useful in the professions, but also in trade, commerce, industry, and agriculture (**Figure 10.14**). Land-grant colleges stood in contrast to the expensive, private Ivy League universities such as Harvard and Yale, which still catered to the elite. Iowa became the first state to accept the provisions of the original Morrill Act, creating what later became Iowa State University. Other states soon followed suit, and the availability of an affordable college education encouraged a boost in enrollment, from 50,000 students nationwide in 1870 to over 600,000 students by 1920.

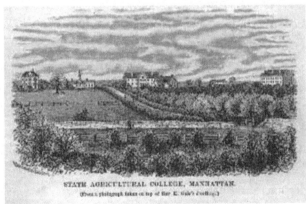

Figure 10.14 This rendering of Kansas State University in 1878 shows an early land-grant college, created by the Morrill Act. These newly created schools allowed many more students to attend college than the elite Ivy League system, and focused more on preparing them for professional careers in business, medicine, and law, as well as business, agriculture, and other trades.

College curricula also changed at this time. Students grew less likely to take traditional liberal arts classes in rhetoric, philosophy, and foreign language, and instead focused on preparing for the modern work world. Professional schools for the study of medicine, law, and business also developed. In short, education for the children of middle-class parents catered to class-specific interests and helped ensure that parents could establish their children comfortably in the middle class as well.

"CITY BEAUTIFUL"

While the working poor lived in the worst of it and the wealthy elite sought to avoid it, all city dwellers at the time had to deal with the harsh realities of urban sprawl. Skyscrapers rose and filled the air, streets were crowded with pedestrians of all sorts, and, as developers worked to meet the always-increasing demand for space, the few remaining green spaces in the city quickly disappeared. As the U.S. population became increasingly centered in urban areas while the century drew to a close, questions about the quality of city life—particularly with regard to issues of aesthetics, crime, and poverty—quickly consumed many reformers' minds. Those middle-class and wealthier urbanites who enjoyed the costlier amenities presented by city life—including theaters, restaurants, and shopping—were free to escape to the suburbs, leaving behind the poorer working classes living in squalor and unsanitary conditions. Through the **City Beautiful** movement, leaders such as Frederick Law Olmsted and Daniel Burnham sought to champion middle- and upper-class progressive reforms. They improved the quality of life for city dwellers, but also cultivated middle-class-dominated urban spaces in which Americans of different ethnicities, racial origins, and classes worked and lived.

Olmsted, one of the earliest and most influential designers of urban green space, and the original designer of Central Park in New York, worked with Burnham to introduce the idea of the City Beautiful movement at the Columbian Exposition in 1893. There, they helped to design and construct the "White City"—so named for the plaster of Paris construction of several buildings that were subsequently painted a bright white—an example of landscaping and architecture that shone as an example of perfect city planning. From wide-open green spaces to brightly painted white buildings, connected with modern transportation services and appropriate sanitation, the "White City" set the stage for American urban city planning for the next generation, beginning in 1901 with the modernization of Washington, DC. This model encouraged city planners to consider three principal tenets: First, create larger park areas inside cities; second, build wider boulevards to decrease traffic congestion and allow for lines of trees and other greenery between lanes; and third, add more suburbs in order to mitigate congested living in the city itself (**Figure 10.15**). As each city adapted these principles in various ways, the City Beautiful movement became a cornerstone of urban development well into the twentieth century.

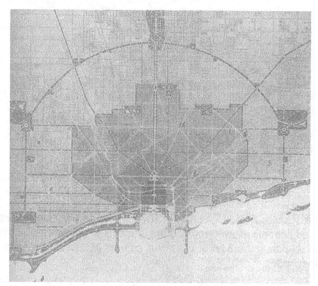

Figure 10.15 This blueprint shows Burnham's vision for Chicago, an example of the City Beautiful movement. His goal was to preserve much of the green space along the city's lakefront, and to ensure that all city dwellers had access to green space.

10.4 Change Reflected in Thought and Writing

By the end of this section, you will be able to:
- Explain how American writers, both fiction and nonfiction, helped Americans to better understand the changes they faced in the late nineteenth and early twentieth centuries
- Identify some of the influential women and African American writers of the era

In the late nineteenth century, Americans were living in a world characterized by rapid change. Western expansion, dramatic new technologies, and the rise of big business drastically influenced society in a matter of a few decades. For those living in the fast-growing urban areas, the pace of change was even faster and harder to ignore. One result of this time of transformation was the emergence of a series of notable authors, who, whether writing fiction or nonfiction, offered a lens through which to better understand the shifts in American society.

UNDERSTANDING SOCIAL PROGRESS

One key idea of the nineteenth century that moved from the realm of science to the murkier ground of social and economic success was Charles Darwin's theory of evolution. Darwin was a British naturalist who, in his 1859 work *On the Origin of Species*, made the case that species develop and evolve through natural selection, not through divine intervention. The idea quickly drew fire from the Anglican Church (although a liberal branch of Anglicans embraced the notion of natural selection being part of God's plan) and later from many others, both in England and abroad, who felt that the theory directly contradicted the role of God in the earth's creation. Although biologists, botanists, and most of the scientific establishment widely accepted the theory of evolution at the time of Darwin's publication, which they felt synthesized much of the previous work in the field, the theory remained controversial in the public realm for decades.

Political philosopher Herbert Spencer took Darwin's theory of evolution further, coining the actual phrase "survival of the fittest," and later helping to popularize the phrase social Darwinism to posit that society evolved much like a natural organism, wherein some individuals will succeed due to racially and ethnically inherent traits, and their ability to adapt. This model allowed that a collection of traits and skills, which could include intelligence, inherited wealth, and so on, mixed with the ability to adapt, would let all Americans rise or fall of their own accord, so long as the road to success was accessible to all. William Graham Sumner, a sociologist at Yale, became the most vocal proponent of social Darwinism. Not surprisingly, this ideology, which Darwin himself would have rejected as a gross misreading of his scientific discoveries, drew great praise from those who made their wealth at this time. They saw their success as proof of biological fitness, although critics of this theory were quick to point out that those who did not succeed often did not have the same opportunities or equal playing field that the ideology of social Darwinism purported. Eventually, the concept fell into disrepute in the 1930s and 1940s, as eugenicists began to utilize it in conjunction with their racial theories of genetic superiority.

Other thinkers of the day took Charles Darwin's theories in a more nuanced direction, focusing on different theories of **realism** that sought to understand the truth underlying the changes in the United States. These thinkers believed that ideas and social constructs must be proven to work before they could be accepted. Philosopher William James was one of the key proponents of the closely related concept of **pragmatism**, which held that Americans needed to experiment with different ideas and perspectives to find the truth about American society, rather than assuming that there was truth in old, previously accepted models. Only by tying ideas, thoughts, and statements to actual objects and occurrences could one begin to identify a coherent truth, according to James. His work strongly influenced the subsequent avant-garde and modernist movements in literature and art, especially in understanding the role of the observer, artist, or writer in shaping the society they attempted to observe. John Dewey built on the idea of pragmatism to create a theory of **instrumentalism**, which advocated the use of education in the search for truth. Dewey believed that education, specifically observation and change through the scientific method, was the best tool by which to reform and improve American society as it continued to grow ever more complex. To that end, Dewey strongly encouraged educational reforms designed to create an informed American citizenry that could then form the basis for other, much-needed progressive reforms in society.

In addition to the new medium of photography, popularized by Riis, novelists and other artists also embraced realism in their work. They sought to portray vignettes from real life in their stories, partly in response to the more sentimental works of their predecessors. Visual artists such as George Bellows, Edward Hopper, and Robert Henri, among others, formed the Ashcan School of Art, which was interested primarily in depicting the urban lifestyle that was quickly gripping the United States at the turn of the century. Their works typically focused on working-class city life, including the slums and tenement houses, as well as working-class forms of leisure and entertainment (**Figure 10.16**).

Figure 10.16 Like most examples of works by Ashcan artists, *The Cliff Dwellers*, by George Wesley Bellows, depicts the crowd of urban life realistically. (credit: Los Angeles County Museum of Art)

Novelists and journalists also popularized realism in literary works. Authors such as Stephen Crane, who wrote stark stories about life in the slums or during the Civil War, and Rebecca Harding Davis, who in 1861 published *Life in the Iron Mills*, embodied this popular style. Mark Twain also sought realism in his books, whether it was the reality of the pioneer spirit, seen in *The Adventures of Huckleberry Finn*, published in 1884, or the issue of corruption in *The Gilded Age*, co-authored with Charles Dudley Warner in 1873. The narratives and visual arts of these realists could nonetheless be highly stylized, crafted, and even fabricated, since their goal was the effective portrayal of social realities they thought required reform. Some authors, such as Jack London, who wrote *Call of the Wild*, embraced a school of thought called **naturalism**, which concluded that the laws of nature and the natural world were the only truly relevant laws governing humanity (**Figure 10.17**).

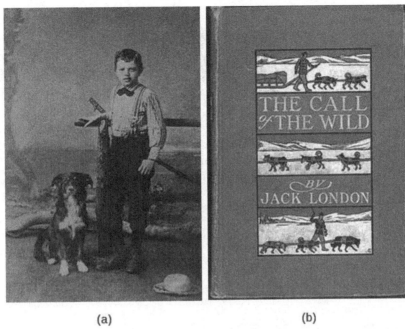

(a)   (b)

Figure 10.17 Jack London poses with his dog Rollo in 1885 (a). The cover of Jack London's *Call of the Wild* (b) shows the dogs in the brutal environment of the Klondike. The book tells the story of Buck, a dog living happily in California until he is sold to be a sled dog in Canada. There, he must survive harsh conditions and brutal behavior, but his innate animal nature takes over and he prevails. The story clarifies the struggle between humanity's nature versus the nurturing forces of society.

Kate Chopin, widely regarded as the foremost woman short story writer and novelist of her day, sought to portray a realistic view of women's lives in late nineteenth-century America, thus paving the way for more explicit feminist literature in generations to come. Although Chopin never described herself as a feminist per se, her reflective works on her experiences as a southern woman introduced a form of creative nonfiction that captured the struggles of women in the United States through their own individual experiences. She also was among the first authors to openly address the race issue of miscegenation. In her work *Desiree's Baby*, Chopin specifically explores the Creole community of her native Louisiana in depths that exposed the reality of racism in a manner seldom seen in literature of the time.

African American poet, playwright, and novelist of the realist period, Paul Laurence Dunbar dealt with issues of race at a time when most reform-minded Americans preferred to focus on other issues. Through his combination of writing in both standard English and black dialect, Dunbar delighted readers with his rich portrayals of the successes and struggles associated with African American life. Although he initially struggled to find the patronage and financial support required to develop a full-time literary career, Dunbar's subsequent professional relationship with literary critic and *Atlantic Monthly* editor William Dean Howells helped to firmly cement his literary credentials as the foremost African American writer of his generation. As with Chopin and Harding, Dunbar's writing highlighted parts of the American experience that were not well understood by the dominant demographic of the country. In their work, these authors provided readers with insights into a world that was not necessarily familiar to them and also gave hidden communities—be it iron mill workers, southern women, or African American men—a sense of voice.

Click and Explore

Mark Twain's lampoon of author Horatio Alger (http://openstaxcollege.org/l/twain1) demonstrates Twain's commitment to realism by mocking the myth set out by Alger, whose stories followed a common theme in which a poor but honest boy goes from rags to riches through a combination of "luck and pluck." See how Twain twists Alger's hugely popular storyline in this piece of satire.

DEFINING "AMERICAN"

◎ *Kate Chopin: An Awakening in an Unpopular Time*

Author Kate Chopin grew up in the American South and later moved to St. Louis, where she began writing stories to make a living after the death of her husband. She published her works throughout the late 1890s, with stories appearing in literary magazines and local papers. It was her second novel, *The Awakening*, which gained her notoriety and criticism in her lifetime, and ongoing literary fame after her death (Figure 10.18).

(a)   (b)

Figure 10.18 Critics railed against Kate Chopin, the author of the 1899 novel *The Awakening*, criticizing its stark portrayal of a woman struggling with societal confines and her own desires. In the twentieth century, scholars rediscovered Chopin's work and *The Awakening* is now considered part of the canon of American literature.

The Awakening, set in the New Orleans society that Chopin knew well, tells the story of a woman struggling with the constraints of marriage who ultimately seeks her own fulfillment over the needs of her family. The book deals far more openly than most novels of the day with questions of women's sexual desires. It also flouted nineteenth-century conventions by looking at the protagonist's struggles with the traditional role expected of women.

While a few contemporary reviewers saw merit in the book, most criticized it as immoral and unseemly. It was censored, called "pure poison," and critics railed against Chopin herself. While Chopin wrote squarely in the tradition of realism that was popular at this time, her work covered ground that was considered "too real" for comfort. After the negative reception of the novel, Chopin retreated from public life and discontinued writing. She died five years after its publication. After her death, Chopin's work was largely ignored, until scholars rediscovered it in the late twentieth century, and her books and stories came back into print. *The Awakening* in particular has been recognized as vital to the earliest edges of the modern feminist movement.

Click and Explore

Excerpts from interviews (http://openstaxcollege.org/l/katechopin) with David Chopin, Kate Chopin's grandson, and a scholar who studies her work provide interesting perspectives on the author and her views.

CRITICS OF MODERN AMERICA

While many Americans at this time, both everyday working people and theorists, felt the changes of the era would lead to improvements and opportunities, there were critics of the emerging social shifts as well. Although less popular than Twain and London, authors such as Edward Bellamy, Henry George, and Thorstein Veblen were also influential in spreading critiques of the industrial age. While their critiques were quite distinct from each other, all three believed that the industrial age was a step in the wrong direction for the country.

In the 1888 novel *Looking Backward, 2000-1887*, Edward Bellamy portrays a utopian America in the year 2000, with the country living in peace and harmony after abandoning the capitalist model and moving to a socialist state. In the book, Bellamy predicts the future advent of credit cards, cable entertainment, and "super-store" cooperatives that resemble a modern day Wal-Mart. *Looking Backward* proved to be a popular bestseller (third only to *Uncle Tom's Cabin* and *Ben Hur* among late nineteenth-century publications) and appealed to those who felt the industrial age of big business was sending the country in the wrong direction. Eugene Debs, who led the national Pullman Railroad Strike in 1894, later commented on how Bellamy's work influenced him to adopt socialism as the answer to the exploitative industrial capitalist model. In addition, Bellamy's work spurred the publication of no fewer than thirty-six additional books or articles by other writers, either supporting Bellamy's outlook or directly criticizing it. In 1897, Bellamy felt compelled to publish a sequel, entitled *Equality*, in which he further explained ideas he had previously introduced concerning educational reform and women's equality, as well as a world of vegetarians who speak a universal language.

Another author whose work illustrated the criticisms of the day was nonfiction writer Henry George, an economist best known for his 1879 work *Progress and Poverty*, which criticized the inequality found in an industrial economy. He suggested that, while people should own that which they create, all land and natural resources should belong to all equally, and should be taxed through a "single land tax" in order to disincentivize private land ownership. His thoughts influenced many economic progressive reformers, as well as led directly to the creation of the now-popular board game, Monopoly.

Another critique of late nineteenth-century American capitalism was Thorstein Veblen, who lamented in *The Theory of the Leisure Class* (1899) that capitalism created a middle class more preoccupied with its own comfort and consumption than with maximizing production. In coining the phrase "conspicuous consumption," Veblen identified the means by which one class of nonproducers exploited the working class that produced the goods for their consumption. Such practices, including the creation of business trusts, served only to create a greater divide between the haves and have-nots in American society, and resulted in economic inefficiencies that required correction or reform.

CHAPTER 11

Politics in the Gilded Age, 1870-1900

Figure 11.1 L. Frank Baum's story of a Kansas girl and the magical land of Oz has become a classic of both film and screen, but it may have originated in part as an allegory of late nineteenth-century politics and the rise of the Populist movement.

Chapter Outline

11.1 Political Corruption in Postbellum America

11.2 The Key Political Issues: Patronage, Tariffs, and Gold

11.3 Farmers Revolt in the Populist Era

11.4 Social and Labor Unrest in the 1890s

Introduction

L. Frank Baum was a journalist who rose to prominence at the end of the nineteenth century. Baum's most famous story, *The Wizard of Oz* (**Figure 11.1**), was published in 1900, but "Oz" first came into being years earlier, when he told a story to a group of schoolchildren visiting his newspaper office in South Dakota. He made up a tale of a wonderful land, and, searching for a name, he allegedly glanced down at his file cabinet, where the bottom drawer was labeled "O-Z." Thus was born the world of Oz, where a girl from struggling Kansas hoped to get help from a "wonderful wizard" who proved to be a fraud. Since then, many have speculated that the story reflected Baum's political sympathies for the Populist Party, which galvanized midwestern and southern farmers' demands for federal reform. Whether he intended the story to act as an allegory for the plight of farmers and workers in late nineteenth-century America, or whether he simply wanted to write an "American fairy tale" set in the heartland, Populists looked for answers much like Dorothy did. And the government in Washington proved to be meek rather than magical.

11.1 Political Corruption in Postbellum America

By the end of this section, you will be able to:
- Discuss the national political scene during the Gilded Age
- Analyze why many critics considered the Gilded Age a period of ineffective national leadership

The challenges Americans faced in the post-Civil War era extended far beyond the issue of Reconstruction and the challenge of an economy without slavery. Political and social repair of the nation was paramount, as was the correlative question of race relations in the wake of slavery. In addition, farmers faced the task of cultivating arid western soils and selling crops in an increasingly global commodities market, while workers in urban industries suffered long hours and hazardous conditions at stagnant   wages.

Farmers, who still composed the largest percentage of the U.S. population, faced mounting debts as agricultural prices spiraled downward. These lower prices were due in large part to the cultivation of more acreage using more productive farming tools and machinery, global market competition, as well as price manipulation by commodity traders, exorbitant railroad freight rates, and costly loans upon which farmers depended. For many, their hard work resulted merely in a continuing decline in prices and even greater debt. These farmers, and others who sought leaders to heal the wounds left from the Civil War, organized in different states, and eventually into a national third-party challenge, only to find that, with the end of Reconstruction, federal political power was stuck in a permanent partisan stalemate, and corruption was widespread at both the state and federal levels.

As the **Gilded Age** unfolded, presidents had very little power, due in large part to highly contested elections in which relative popular majorities were razor-thin. Two presidents won the Electoral College without a popular majority. Further undermining their efficacy was a Congress comprising mostly politicians operating on the principle of political patronage. Eventually, frustrated by the lack of leadership in Washington, some Americans began to develop their own solutions, including the establishment of new political parties and organizations to directly address the problems they faced. Out of the   frustration

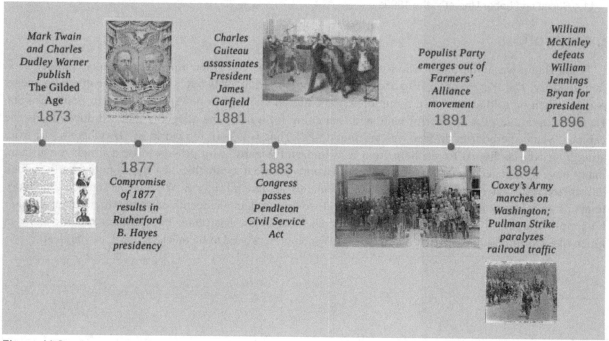

Figure 11.2

wrought by war and presidential political impotence, as well as an overwhelming pace of industrial change, farmers and workers formed a new grassroots reform movement that, at the end of the century, was eclipsed by an even larger, mostly middle-class, Progressive movement. These reform efforts did bring about change—but not without a fight.

THE GILDED AGE

Mark Twain coined the phrase "Gilded Age" in a book he co-authored with Charles Dudley Warner in 1873, *The Gilded Age: A Tale of Today*. The book satirized the corruption of post-Civil War society and politics. Indeed, popular excitement over national growth and industrialization only thinly glossed over the stark economic inequalities and various degrees of corruption of the era (**Figure 11.3**). Politicians of the time largely catered to business interests in exchange for political support and wealth. Many participated in graft and bribery, often justifying their actions with the excuse that corruption was too widespread for a successful politician to resist. The machine politics of the cities, specifically Tammany Hall in New York, illustrate the kind of corrupt, but effective, local and national politics that dominated the era.

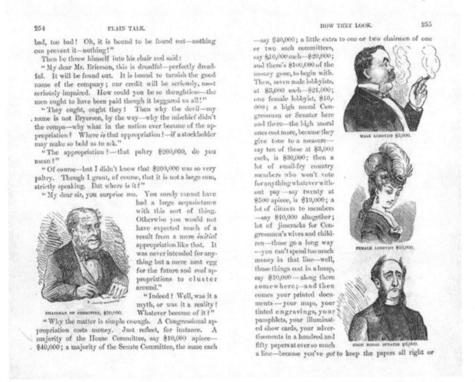

Figure 11.3 Pages from Mark Twain's *The Gilded Age*, published in 1873. The illustrations in this chapter reveal the cost of doing business in Washington in this new age of materialism and corruption, with the cost of obtaining a female lobbyist's support set at $10,000, while that of a male lobbyist or a "high moral" senator can be had for $3,000.

Nationally, between 1872 and 1896, the lack of clear popular mandates made presidents reluctant to venture beyond the interests of their traditional supporters. As a result, for nearly a quarter of a century, presidents had a weak hold on power, and legislators were reluctant to tie their political agendas to such weak leaders. On the contrary, weakened presidents were more susceptible to support various legislators' and lobbyists' agendas, as they owed tremendous favors to their political parties, as well as to key financial contributors, who helped them garner just enough votes to squeak into office through the Electoral College. As a result of this relationship, the rare pieces of legislation passed were largely responses to the desires of businessmen and industrialists whose support helped build politicians' careers.

What was the result of this political malaise? Not surprisingly, almost nothing was accomplished on the federal level. However, problems associated with the tremendous economic growth during this time continued to mount. More Americans were moving to urban centers, which were unable to accommodate the massive numbers of working poor. Tenement houses with inadequate sanitation led to widespread illness. In rural parts of the country, people fared no better. Farmers were unable to cope with the challenges of low prices for their crops and exorbitant costs for everyday goods. All around the country, Americans in need of solutions turned further away from the federal government for help, leading to the rise of fractured and corrupt political groups.

DEFINING "AMERICAN"

⚙ *Mark Twain and the Gilded Age*

Mark Twain (**Figure 11.4**) wrote *The Gilded Age: A Tale of Today* with his neighbor, Charles Dudley Warner, as a satire about the corrupt politics and lust for power that he felt characterized American society at the time. The book, the only novel Twain ever co-authored, tells of the characters' desire to sell their land to the federal government and become rich. It takes aim at both the government in Washington and those Americans, in the South and elsewhere, whose lust for money and status among the newly rich in the nation's capital leads them to corrupt and foolish choices.

Figure 11.4 Mark Twain was a noted humorist, recognized by most Americans as the greatest writer of his day. He co-wrote the novel *The Gilded Age: A Tale of Today* with Charles Dudley Warner in 1873.

In the following conversation from Chapter Fifty-One of the book, Colonel Sellers instructs young Washington Hawkins on the routine practices of Congress:

> "Now let's figure up a little on, the preliminaries. I think Congress always tries to do as near right as it can, according to its lights. A man can't ask any fairer than that. The first preliminary it always starts out on, is to clean itself, so to speak. It will arraign two or three dozen of its members, or maybe four or five dozen, for taking bribes to vote for this and that and the other bill last winter."
>
> "It goes up into the dozens, does it?"
>
> "Well, yes; in a free country likes ours, where any man can run for Congress and anybody can vote for him, you can't expect immortal purity all the time—it ain't in nature. Sixty or eighty or a hundred and fifty people are bound to get in who are not angels in disguise, as young Hicks the correspondent says; but still it is a very good average; very good indeed. . . . Well, after they have finished the bribery cases, they will take up cases of members who have bought their seats with money. That will take another four weeks."
>
> "Very good; go on. You have accounted for two-thirds of the session."
>
> "Next they will try each other for various smaller irregularities, like the sale of appointments to West Point cadetships, and that sort of thing— . . ."
>
> "How long does it take to disinfect itself of these minor impurities?"
>
> "Well, about two weeks, generally."
>
> "So Congress always lies helpless in quarantine ten weeks of a session. That's encouraging."

The book was a success, in part because it amused people even as it excoriated the politics of the day. For this humor, as well as its astute analysis, Twain and Warner's book still offers entertainment and insight today.

Click and Explore

Visit the **PBS Scrap Book** (http://openstaxcollege.org/l/gage) for information on Mark Twain's life and marriage at the time he wrote *The Gilded Age: A Tale of Today.*

THE ELECTION OF 1876 SETS THE TONE

In many ways, the presidential election of 1876 foreshadowed the politics of the era, in that it resulted in one of the most controversial results in all of presidential history. The country was in the middle of the economic downturn caused by the Panic of 1873, a downturn that would ultimately last until 1879, all but assuring that Republican incumbent Ulysses S. Grant would not be reelected. Instead, the Republican Party nominated a three-time governor from Ohio, Rutherford B. Hayes. Hayes was a popular candidate who advocated for both "hard money"—an economy based upon gold currency transactions—to protect against inflationary pressures and **civil service** reform, that is, recruitment based upon merit and qualifications, which was to replace the practice of handing out government jobs as "spoils." Most importantly, he had no significant political scandals in his past, unlike his predecessor Grant, who suffered through the Crédit Mobilier of America scandal. In this most notorious example of Gilded Age corruption, several congressmen accepted cash and stock bribes in return for appropriating inflated federal funds for the construction of the transcontinental railroad.

The Democrats likewise sought a candidate who could champion reform against growing political corruption. They found their man in Samuel J. Tilden, governor of New York and a self-made millionaire, who had made a successful political career fighting corruption in New York City, including spearheading the prosecution against Tammany Hall Boss William Tweed, who was later jailed. Both parties tapped into the popular mood of the day, each claiming to champion reform and promising an end to the corruption that had become rampant in Washington (**Figure 11.5**). Likewise, both parties promised an end to post-Civil War Reconstruction.

(a)   **(b)**

Figure 11.5 These campaign posters for Rutherford B. Hayes (a) and Samuel Tilden (b) underscore the tactics of each party, which remained largely unchanged, regardless of the candidates. The Republican placard highlights the party's role in preserving "liberty and union" in the wake of the Civil War, hoping to tap into the northern voters' pride in victory over secession. The Democratic poster addresses the economic turmoil and corruption of the day, specifically that of the Grant administration, promising "honesty, reform, and prosperity" for all.

The campaign was a typical one for the era: Democrats shone a spotlight on earlier Republican scandals, such as the Crédit Mobilier affair, and Republicans relied upon the **bloody shirt campaign**, reminding the nation of the terrible human toll of the war against southern confederates who now reappeared in national politics under the mantle of the Democratic Party. President Grant previously had great success with the "bloody shirt" strategy in the 1868 election, when Republican supporters attacked Democratic candidate Horatio Seymour for his sympathy with New York City draft rioters during the war. In 1876, true to the campaign style of the day, neither Tilden nor Hayes actively campaigned for office, instead relying upon supporters and other groups to promote their causes.

Fearing a significant African American and white Republican voter turnout in the South, particularly in the wake of the Civil Rights Act of 1875, which further empowered African Americans with protection in terms of public accommodations, Democrats relied upon white supremacist terror organizations to intimidate blacks and Republicans, including physically assaulting many while they attempted to vote. The Redshirts, based in Mississippi and the Carolinas, and the White League in Louisiana, relied upon intimidation tactics similar to the Ku Klux Klan but operated in a more open and organized fashion with the sole goal of restoring Democrats to political predominance in the South. In several instances, Redshirts would attack freedmen who attempted to vote, whipping them openly in the streets while simultaneously hosting barbecues to attract Democratic voters to the polls. Women throughout South Carolina began to sew red flannel shirts for the men to wear as a sign of their political views; women themselves began wearing red ribbons in their hair and bows about their waists.

The result of the presidential election, ultimately, was close. Tilden won the popular vote by nearly 300,000 votes; however, he had only 184 electoral votes, with 185 needed to proclaim formal victory. Three states, Florida, Louisiana, and South Carolina, were in dispute due to widespread charges of voter fraud and miscounting. Questions regarding the validity of one of the three electors in Oregon cast further doubt on the final vote; however, that state subsequently presented evidence to Congress confirming all three electoral votes for Hayes.

As a result of the disputed election, the House of Representatives established a special electoral commission to determine which candidate won the challenged electoral votes of these three states. In what later became known as the Compromise of 1877, Republican Party leaders offered southern Democrats an enticing deal. The offer was that if the commission found in favor of a Hayes victory, Hayes would order the withdrawal of the remaining U.S. troops from those three southern states, thus allowing the collapse of the radical Reconstruction governments of the immediate post-Civil War era. This move would permit southern Democrats to end federal intervention and control their own states' fates in the wake of the end of slavery (**Figure 11.6**).

Figure 11.6 Titled "A Truce not a Compromise," this cartoon suggests the lack of consensus after the election of 1876 could have ended in another civil war.

After weeks of deliberation, the electoral commission voted eight to seven along straight party lines, declaring Hayes the victor in each of the three disputed states. As a result, Hayes defeated Tilden in the electoral vote by a count of 185–184 and became the next president. By April of that year, radical Reconstruction ended as promised, with the removal of federal troops from the final two Reconstruction states, South Carolina and Louisiana. Within a year, Redeemers—largely Southern Democrats—had regained control of the political and social fabric of the South.

Although unpopular among the voting electorate, especially among African Americans who referred to it as "The Great Betrayal," the compromise exposed the willingness of the two major political parties to avoid a "stand-off" via a southern Democrat filibuster, which would have greatly prolonged the final decision regarding the election. Democrats were largely satisfied to end Reconstruction and maintain "home rule" in the South in exchange for control over the White House. Likewise, most realized that Hayes would likely be a one-term president at best and prove to be as ineffectual as his pre-Civil War predecessors.

Perhaps most surprising was the lack of even greater public outrage over such a transparent compromise, indicative of the little that Americans expected of their national government. In an era where voter turnout remained relatively high, the two major political parties remained largely indistinguishable in their agendas as well as their propensity for questionable tactics and backroom deals. Likewise, a growing belief in laissez-faire principles as opposed to reforms and government intervention (which many Americans believed contributed to the outbreak of the Civil War) led even more Americans to accept the nature of an inactive federal government (**Figure 11.7**).

Figure 11.10 Garfield's shooting and the subsequent capture of the assassin, Charles Guiteau, are depicted in this illustration for a newspaper of the day. The president clung to life for another two months after the assassination.

DEFINING "AMERICAN"

The Assassination of a President

I executed
the Divine command.
And Garfield did remove,
To save my party,
and my country
From the bitter fate of War.
—Charles Guiteau

Charles Guiteau was a lawyer and supporter of the Republican Party, although not particularly well known in either area. But he gave a few speeches, to modest crowds, in support of the Republican nominee James Garfield, and ultimately deluded himself that his speeches influenced the country enough to cause Garfield's victory. After the election, Guiteau immediately began pressuring the new president, requesting a post as ambassador. When his queries went unanswered, Guiteau, out of money and angry that his supposed help had been ignored, planned to kill the president.

He spent significant time planning his attack and considered weapons as diverse as dynamite and a stiletto before deciding on a gun, stating, "I wanted it done in an American manner." He followed the president around the Capitol and let several opportunities pass, unwilling to kill Garfield in front of his wife or son. Frustrated with himself, Guiteau recommitted to the plan and wrote a letter to the White House, explaining how this act would "unite the Republican Party and save the Republic."

Guiteau shot the president from behind and continued to shoot until police grabbed him and hauled him away. He went to jail, and, the following November after Garfield had died, he stood trial for murder. His poor mental health, which had been evident for some time, led to eccentric courtroom behavior that the newspapers eagerly reported and the public loved. He defended his case with a poem that used religious imagery and suggested that God had ordered him to commit the murder. He defended himself in court by saying, "The doctors killed Garfield, I just shot him." While this in fact was true, it did not save him. Guiteau was convicted and hanged in the summer of 1882.

Click and Explore

Take a look at America's Story (http://openstaxcollege.org/l/guiteau) from the Library of Congress, which highlights the fact that Guiteau in fact did not kill the president, but rather infection from his medical treatment did.

Surprising both his party and the Democrats when he assumed the office of president, Chester Arthur immediately distanced himself from the Stalwarts. Although previously a loyal party man, Arthur understood that he owed his current position to no particular faction or favor. He was in the unique position to usher in a wave a civil service reform unlike any other political candidate, and he chose to do just that. In 1883, he signed into law the Pendleton Civil Service Act, the first significant piece of antipatronage legislation. This law created the Civil Service Commission, which listed all government patronage jobs and then set aside 15 percent of the list as appointments to be determined through a competitive civil service examination process. Furthermore, to prevent future presidents from undoing this reform, the law declared that future presidents could enlarge the list but could never shrink it by moving a civil service job back into the patronage column.

TARIFFS IN THE GILDED AGE

In addition to civil service, President Arthur also carried the reformist spirit into the realm of tariffs, or taxes on international imports to the United States. Tariffs had long been a controversial topic in the United States, especially as the nineteenth century came to a close. Legislators appeared to be bending to the will of big businessmen who desired higher tariffs in order to force Americans to buy their domestically produced goods rather than higher-priced imports. Lower tariffs, on the other hand, would reduce prices and lower the average American's cost of living, and were therefore favored by many working-class families and farmers, to the extent that any of them fully understood such economic forces beyond the prices they paid at stores. Out of growing concern for the latter group, Arthur created the U.S. Tariff Commission in 1882 to investigate the propriety of increasingly high tariffs. Despite his concern, along with the commission's recommendation for a 25 percent rollback in most tariffs, the most Arthur could accomplish was the "Mongrel Tariff" of 1883, which lowered tariff rates by barely 5 percent.

Such bold attempts at reform further convinced Republican Party leaders, as the 1884 election approached, that Arthur was not their best option to continue in the White House. Arthur quickly found himself a man without a party. As the 1884 election neared, the Republican Party again searched their ranks for a candidate who could restore some semblance of the spoils system while maintaining a reformist image. Unable to find such a man, the predominant Half-Breeds again turned to their own leader, Senator Blaine. However, when news of his many personal corrupt bargains began to surface, a significant portion of the party chose to break from the traditional Stalwarts-versus-Half-Breeds debate and form their own faction, the **Mugwumps**, a name taken from the Algonquin phrase for "great chief."

Anxious to capitalize on the disarray within the Republican Party, as well as to return to the White House for the first time in nearly thirty years, the Democratic Party chose to court the Mugwump vote by nominating Grover Cleveland, the reform governor from New York who had built a reputation by attacking machine politics in New York City. Despite several personal charges against him for having fathered a child out of wedlock, Cleveland managed to hold on for a close victory with a margin of less than thirty thousand votes.

Cleveland's record on civil service reform added little to the initial blows struck by President Arthur. After electing the first Democratic president since 1856, the Democrats could actually make great use of the spoils system. Cleveland was, however, a notable reform president in terms of business regulation and tariffs. When the U.S. Supreme Court ruled in 1886 that individual states could not regulate interstate transportation, Cleveland urged Congress to pass the Interstate Commerce Act of 1887. Among several other powers, this law created the Interstate Commerce Commission (ICC) to oversee railroad prices and ensure that they remained reasonable to all customers. This was an important shift. In the past, railroads had granted special rebates to big businesses, such as John D. Rockefeller's Standard Oil, while charging small farmers with little economic muscle exorbitant rates. Although the act eventually provided for real regulation of the railroad industry, initial progress was slow due to the lack of enforcement power held by the ICC. Despite its early efforts to regulate railroad rates, the U.S. Supreme Court undermined the commission in *Interstate Commerce Commission v. Cincinnati, New Orleans, and Texas Pacific Railway Cos.* in 1897. Rate regulations were limits on profits that, in the opinion of a majority of the justices, violated the Fourteenth Amendment protection against depriving persons of their property without due process of the law.

As for tariff reform, Cleveland agreed with Arthur's position that tariffs remained far too high and were clearly designed to protect big domestic industries at the expense of average consumers who could benefit from international competition. While the general public applauded Cleveland's efforts at both civil service and tariff reform, influential businessmen and industrialists remained adamant that the next president must restore the protective tariffs at all costs.

To counter the Democrats' re-nomination of Cleveland, the Republican Party turned to Benjamin Harrison, grandson of former president William Henry Harrison. Although Cleveland narrowly won the overall popular vote, Harrison rode the influential coattails of several businessmen and party bosses to win the key electoral states of New York and New Jersey, where party officials stressed Harrison's support for a higher tariff, and thus secure the White House. Not surprisingly, after Harrison's victory, the United States witnessed a brief return to higher tariffs and a strengthening of the spoils system. In fact, the McKinley Tariff raised some rates as much as 50 percent, which was the highest tariff in American history to date.

Some of Harrison's policies were intended to offer relief to average Americans struggling with high costs and low wages, but remained largely ineffective. First, the Sherman Anti-Trust Act of 1890 sought to prohibit business monopolies as "conspiracies in restraint of trade," but it was seldom enforced during the first decade of its existence. Second, the Sherman Silver Purchase Act of the same year required the U.S. Treasury to mint over four million ounces of silver into coins each month to circulate more cash into the economy, raise prices for farm goods, and help farmers pay their way out of debt. But the measure could not undo the previous "hard money" policies that had deflated prices and pulled farmers into well-entrenched cycles of debt. Other measures proposed by Harrison intended to support African Americans, including a Force Bill to protect voters in the South, as well as an Education Bill designed to support public education and improve literacy rates among African Americans, also met with defeat.

MONETARY POLICIES AND THE ISSUE OF GOLD VS SILVER

Although political corruption, the spoils system, and the question of tariff rates were popular discussions of the day, none were more relevant to working-class Americans and farmers than the issue of the nation's monetary policy and the ongoing debate of gold versus silver (**Figure 11.11**). There had been frequent attempts to establish a bimetallic standard, which in turn would have created inflationary pressures and placed more money into circulation that could have subsequently benefitted farmers. But the government remained committed to the gold standard, including the official demonetizing of silver altogether in 1873. Such a stance greatly benefitted prominent businessmen engaged in foreign trade while forcing more farmers and working-class Americans into greater debt.

Figure 11.11 This cartoon illustrates the potential benefits of a bimetal system, but the benefits did not actually extend to big business, which preferred the gold standard and worked to keep it.

As farmers and working-class Americans sought the means by which to pay their bills and other living expenses, especially in the wake of increased tariffs as the century came to a close, many saw adherence to a strict gold standard as their most pressing problem. With limited gold reserves, the money supply remained constrained. At a minimum, a return to a bimetallic policy that would include the production of silver dollars would provide some relief. However, the aforementioned Sherman Silver Purchase Act was largely ineffective to combat the growing debts that many Americans faced. Under the law, the federal government purchased 4.5 million ounces of silver on a monthly basis in order to mint silver dollars. However, many investors exchanged the bank notes with which the government purchased the silver for gold, thus severely depleting the nation's gold reserve. Fearing the latter, President Grover Cleveland signed the act's repeal in 1893. This lack of meaningful monetary measures from the federal government would lead one group in particular who required such assistance—American farmers—to attempt to take control over the political process itself.

11.3 Farmers Revolt in the Populist Era

By the end of this section, you will be able to:
- Understand how the economic and political climate of the day promoted the formation of the farmers' protest movement in the latter half of the nineteenth century
- Explain how the farmers' revolt moved from protest to politics

The challenges that many American farmers faced in the last quarter of the nineteenth century were significant. They contended with economic hardships born out of rapidly declining farm prices, prohibitively high tariffs on items they needed to purchase, and foreign competition. One of the largest challenges they faced was overproduction, where the glut of their products in the marketplace drove the price lower and lower.

Overproduction of crops occurred in part due to the westward expansion of homestead farms and in part because industrialization led to new farm tools that dramatically increased crop yields. As farmers fell deeper into debt, whether it be to the local stores where they bought supplies or to the railroads that shipped their produce, their response was to increase crop production each year in the hope of earning more money with which to pay back their debt. The more they produced, the lower prices dropped. To a hard-working farmer, the notion that their own overproduction was the greatest contributing factor to their debt was a completely foreign concept (**Figure 11.12**).

Figure 11.12 This North Dakota sod hut, built by a homesteading farmer for his family, was photographed in 1898, two years after it was built. While the country was quickly industrializing, many farmers still lived in rough, rural conditions.

In addition to the cycle of overproduction, tariffs were a serious problem for farmers. Rising tariffs on industrial products made purchased items more expensive, yet tariffs were *not* being used to keep farm prices artificially high as well. Therefore, farmers were paying inflated prices but not receiving them. Finally, the issue of gold versus silver as the basis of U.S. currency was a very real problem to many farmers. Farmers needed more money in circulation, whether it was paper or silver, in order to create inflationary pressure. Inflationary pressure would allow farm prices to increase, thus allowing them to earn more money that they could then spend on the higher-priced goods in stores. However, in 1878, federal law set the amount of paper money in circulation, and, as mentioned above, Harrison's Sherman Silver Act, intended to increase the amount of silver coinage, was too modest to do any real good, especially in light of the unintended consequence of depleting the nation's gold reserve. In short, farmers had a big stack of bills and wanted a big stack of money—be it paper or silver—to pay them. Neither was forthcoming from a government that cared more about issues of patronage and how to stay in the White House for more than four years at a time.

FARMERS BEGIN TO ORGANIZE

The initial response by increasingly frustrated and angry farmers was to organize into groups that were similar to early labor unions. Taking note of how the industrial labor movement had unfolded in the last quarter of the century, farmers began to understand that a collective voice could create significant pressure among political leaders and produce substantive change. While farmers had their own challenges, including that of geography and diverse needs among different types of famers, they believed this model to be useful to their cause.

One of the first efforts to organize farmers came in 1867 with Oliver Hudson Kelly's creation of the Patrons of Husbandry, more popularly known as the **Grange**. In the wake of the Civil War, the Grangers quickly grew to over 1.5 million members in less than a decade (**Figure 11.13**). Kelly believed that farmers could best help themselves by creating farmers' cooperatives in which they could pool resources and obtain better shipping rates, as well as prices on seeds, fertilizer, machinery, and other necessary inputs. These cooperatives, he believed, would let them self-regulate production as well as collectively obtain better rates from railroad companies and other businesses.

Figure 11.13 This print from the early 1870s, with scenes of farm life, was a promotional poster for the Grangers, one of the earliest farmer reform groups.

At the state level, specifically in Wisconsin, Minnesota, Illinois, and Iowa, the Patrons of Husbandry did briefly succeed in urging the passage of Granger Laws, which regulated some railroad rates along with the prices charged by grain elevator operators. The movement also created a political party—the Greenback Party, so named for its support of print currency (or "greenbacks") not based upon a gold standard—which saw brief success with the election of fifteen congressmen. However, such successes were short-lived and had little impact on the lives of everyday farmers. In the Wabash case of 1886, brought by the Wabash, St. Louis, and Pacific Railroad Company, the U.S. Supreme Court ruled against the State of Illinois for passing Granger Laws controlling railroad rates; the court found such laws to be unconstitutional. Their argument held that states did not have the authority to control interstate commerce. As for the Greenback Party, when only seven delegates appeared at an 1888 national convention of the group, the party faded from existence.

Click and Explore

Explore Rural Life in the Late Nineteenth Century (http://openstaxcollege.org/l/rurallife) to study photographs, firsthand reports, and other information about how farmers lived and struggled at the end of the nineteenth century.

The **Farmers' Alliance**, a conglomeration of three regional alliances formed in the mid-1880s, took root in the wake of the Grange movement. In 1890, Dr. Charles Macune, who led the Southern Alliance, which was based in Texas and had over 100,000 members by 1886, urged the creation of a national alliance between his organization, the Northwest Alliance, and the Colored Alliance, the largest African American organization in the United States. Led by Tom Watson, the Colored Alliance, which was founded in Texas but quickly spread throughout the Old South, counted over one million members. Although they originally advocated for self-help, African Americans in the group soon understood the benefits of political organization and a unified voice to improve their plight, regardless of race. While racism kept the alliance splintered among the three component branches, they still managed to craft a national agenda that appealed to their large membership. All told, the Farmers' Alliance brought together over 2.5 million members, 1.5 million white and 1 million black (**Figure 11.14**).

Figure 11.14 The Farmers' Alliance flag displays the motto: "The most good for the most PEOPLE," clearly a sentiment they hoped that others would believe.

The alliance movement, and the subsequent political party that emerged from it, also featured prominent roles for women. Nearly 250,000 women joined the movement due to their shared interest in the farmers' worsening situation as well as the promise of being a full partner with political rights within the group, which they saw as an important step towards advocacy for women's suffrage on a national level. The ability to vote and stand for office within the organization encouraged many women who sought similar rights on the larger American political scene. Prominent alliance spokeswoman, Mary Elizabeth Lease of Kansas, often spoke of membership in the Farmers' Alliance as an opportunity to "raise less corn and more hell!"

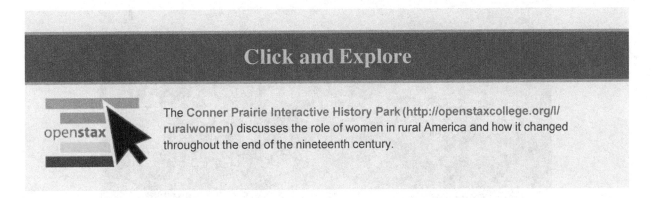

The alliance movement had several goals similar to those of the original Grange, including greater regulation of railroad prices and the creation of an inflationary national monetary policy. However, most creative among the solutions promoted by the Farmers' Alliance was the call for a subtreasury plan. Under this plan, the federal government would store farmers' crops in government warehouses for a brief period of time, during which the government would provide loans to farmers worth 80 percent of the current crop prices. Thus, farmers would have immediate cash on hand with which to settle debts and purchase goods, while their crops sat in warehouses and farm prices increased due to this control over supply at the market. When market prices rose sufficiently high enough, the farmer could withdraw his crops, sell at the higher price, repay the government loan, and still have profit remaining.

Economists of the day thought the plan had some merit; in fact, a greatly altered version would subsequently be adopted during the Great Depression of the 1930s, in the form of the Agricultural Adjustment Act. However, the federal government never seriously considered the plan, as congressmen questioned the propriety of the government serving as a rural creditor making loans to farmers with no assurance that production controls would result in higher commodity prices. The government's refusal to act on the proposal left many farmers wondering what it would take to find solutions to their growing indebtedness.

FROM ORGANIZATION TO POLITICAL PARTY

Angry at the federal government's continued unwillingness to substantively address the plight of the average farmer, Charles Macune and the Farmers' Alliance chose to create a political party whose representatives—if elected—could enact real change. Put simply, if the government would not address the problem, then it was time to change those elected to power.

In 1891, the alliance formed the **Populist Party**, or People's Party, as it was more widely known. Beginning with nonpresidential-year elections, the Populist Party had modest success, particularly in Kansas, Nebraska, and the Dakotas, where they succeeded in electing several state legislators, one governor, and a handful of congressmen. As the 1892 presidential election approached, the Populists chose to model themselves after the Democratic and Republican Parties in the hope that they could shock the country with a "third-party" victory.

At their national convention that summer in Omaha, Nebraska, they wrote the Omaha Platform to more fully explain to all Americans the goals of the new party (**Figure 11.15**). Written by Ignatius Donnelly, the platform statement vilified railroad owners, bankers, and big businessmen as all being part of a widespread conspiracy to control farmers. As for policy changes, the platform called for adoption of the subtreasury plan, government control over railroads, an end to the national bank system, the creation of a federal income tax, the direct election of U.S. senators, and several other measures, all of which aimed at a more proactive federal government that would support the economic and social welfare of all Americans. At the close of the convention, the party nominated James B. Weaver as its presidential candidate.

Figure 11.15 The People's Party gathered for its nominating convention in Nebraska, where they wrote the Omaha Platform to state their concerns and goals.

In a rematch of the 1888 election, the Democrats again nominated Grover Cleveland, while Republicans went with Benjamin Harrison. Despite the presence of a third-party challenger, Cleveland won another close popular vote to become the first U.S. president to be elected to nonconsecutive terms. Although he finished a distant third, Populist candidate Weaver polled a respectable one million votes. Rather than being disappointed, several Populists applauded their showing—especially for a third party with barely two years of national political experience under its belt. They anxiously awaited the 1896 election, believing that if the rest of the country, in particular industrial workers, experienced hardships similar to those that farmers already faced, a powerful alliance among the two groups could carry the Populists to victory.

11.4 Social and Labor Unrest in the 1890s

By the end of this section, you will be able to:
- Explain how the Depression of 1893 helped the Populist Party to grow in popularity in the 1890s
- Understand the forces that contributed to the Populist Party's decline following the 1896 presidential election

Insofar as farmers wanted the rest of the country to share their plight, they got their wish. Soon after Cleveland's election, the nation catapulted into the worst economic depression in its history to date. As the government continued to fail in its efforts to address the growing problems, more and more Americans sought relief outside of the traditional two-party system. To many industrial workers, the Populist Party began to seem like a viable solution.

FROM FARMERS' HARDSHIPS TO A NATIONAL DEPRESSION

The late 1880s and early 1890s saw the American economy slide precipitously. As mentioned above, farmers were already struggling with economic woes, and the rest of the country followed quickly. Following a brief rebound from the speculation-induced Panic of 1873, in which bank investments in railroad bonds spread the nation's financial resources too thin—a rebound due in large part to the protective tariffs of the 1880s—a greater economic catastrophe hit the nation, as the decade of the 1890s began to unfold.

The causes of the Depression of 1893 were manifold, but one major element was the speculation in railroads over the previous decades. The rapid proliferation of railroad lines created a false impression of growth for the economy as a whole. Banks and investors fed the growth of the railroads with fast-paced investment in industry and related businesses, not realizing that the growth they were following was built on a bubble. When the railroads began to fail due to expenses outpacing returns on their construction, the supporting businesses, from banks to steel mills, failed also.

Beginning with the closure of the Philadelphia & Reading Railroad Company in 1893, several railroads ceased their operations as a result of investors cashing in their bonds, thus creating a ripple effect throughout the economy. In a single year, from 1893 to 1894, unemployment estimates increased from 3 percent to nearly 19 percent of all working-class Americans. In some states, the unemployment rate soared even higher: over 35 percent in New York State and 43 percent in Michigan. At the height of this depression, over three million American workers were unemployed. By 1895, Americans living in cities grew accustomed to seeing the homeless on the streets or lining up at soup kitchens.

Immediately following the economic downturn, people sought relief through their elected federal government. Just as quickly, they learned what farmers had been taught in the preceding decades: A weak, inefficient government interested solely in patronage and the spoils system in order to maintain its power was in no position to help the American people face this challenge. The federal government had little in place to support those looking for work or to provide direct aid to those in need. Of course, to be fair, the government had seldom faced these questions before. Americans had to look elsewhere.

A notable example of the government's failure to act was the story of **Coxey's Army**. In the spring of 1894, businessman Jacob Coxey led a march of unemployed Ohioans from Cincinnati to Washington, DC, where leaders of the group urged Congress to pass public works legislation for the federal government to hire unemployed workers to build roads and other public projects. From the original one hundred protesters, the march grew five hundred strong as others joined along the route to the nation's capital. Upon their arrival, not only were their cries for federal relief ignored, but Coxey and several other marchers were arrested for trespassing on the grass outside the U.S. Capitol. Frustration over the event led many angry works to consider supporting the Populist Party in subsequent elections.

AMERICANA

✪ *L. Frank Baum: Did Coxey's Army inspire Dorothy and the Wizard of Oz?*

Scholars, historians, and economists have long argued inconclusively that L. Frank Baum intended the story of *The Wizard of Oz* as an allegory for the politics of the day. Whether that actually was Baum's intention is up for debate, but certainly the story could be read as support for the Populist Party's crusade on behalf of American farmers. In 1894, Baum witnessed Coxey's Army's march firsthand, and some feel it may have influenced the story (**Figure 11.16**).

THE COMMONWEAL ARMY LEAVING BRIGHTWOOD CAMP.

Figure 11.16 This image of Coxey's Army marching on Washington to ask for jobs may have helped inspire L. Frank Baum's story of Dorothy and her friends seeking help from the Wizard of Oz.

According to this theory, the Scarecrow represents the American farmer, the Tin Woodman is the industrial worker, and the Cowardly Lion is William Jennings Bryan, a prominent "Silverite" (strong supporters of the Populist Party who advocated for the free coinage of silver) who, in 1900 when the book was published, was largely criticized by the Republicans as being cowardly and indecisive. In the story, the characters march towards Oz, much as Coxey's Army marched to Washington. Like Dorothy and her companions, Coxey's Army gets in trouble, before being turned away with no help.

Following this reading, the seemingly powerful but ultimately impotent Wizard of Oz is a representation of the president, and Dorothy only finds happiness by wearing the silver slippers—they only became ruby slippers in the later movie version—along the Yellow Brick Road, a reference to the need for the country to move from the gold standard to a two-metal silver and gold plan. While no literary theorists or historians have proven this connection to be true, it is possible that Coxey's Army inspired Baum to create Dorothy's journey on the yellow brick road.

Several strikes also punctuated the growing depression, including a number of violent uprisings in the coal regions of Ohio and Pennsylvania. But the infamous Pullman Strike of 1894 was most notable for its nationwide impact, as it all but shut down the nation's railroad system in the middle of the depression. The strike began immediately on the heels of the Coxey's Army march when, in the summer of 1894, company owner George Pullman fired over two thousand employees at Pullman Co.—which made railroad cars, such as Pullman sleeper cars—and reduced the wages of the remaining three thousand workers. Since the factory operated in the company town of Pullman, Illinois, where workers rented homes from George Pullman and shopped at the company store owned by him as well, unemployment also meant eviction. Facing such harsh treatment, all of the Pullman workers went on strike to protest the decisions. Eugene V. Debs, head of the American Railway Union, led the strike.

In order to bring the plight of Pullman, Illinois, to Americans all around the country, Debs adopted the strike strategy of ordering all American Railroad Union members to refuse to handle any train that had Pullman cars on it. Since virtually every train in the United States operated with Pullman cars, the strike truly brought the transportation industry to its knees. Fearful of his ability to end the economic depression with such a vital piece of the economy at a standstill, President Cleveland turned to his attorney general for the answer. The attorney general proposed a solution: use federal troops to operate the trains under the pretense of protecting the delivery of the U.S. mail that was typically found on all trains. When Debs and the American Railway Union refused to obey the court injunction prohibiting interference with the mail, the troops began operating the trains, and the strike quickly ended. Debs himself was arrested, tried, convicted, and sentenced to six months in prison for disobeying the court injunction. The American Railway Union was destroyed, leaving workers even less empowered than before, and Debs was in prison, contemplating alternatives to a capitalist-based national economy. The Depression of 1893 left the country limping towards the next presidential election with few solutions in sight.

THE ELECTION OF 1896

As the final presidential election of the nineteenth century unfolded, all signs pointed to a possible Populist victory. Not only had the ongoing economic depression convinced many Americans—farmers and factory workers alike—of the inability of either major political party to address the situation, but also the Populist Party, since the last election, benefited from four more years of experience and numerous local victories. As they prepared for their convention in St. Louis that summer, the Populists watched with keen interest as the Republicans and Democrats hosted their own conventions.

The Republicans remained steadfast in their defense of a gold-based standard for the American economy, as well as high protective tariffs. They turned to William McKinley, former congressman and current governor of Ohio, as their candidate. At their convention, the Democrats turned to William Jennings Bryan—a congressman from Nebraska. Bryan defended the importance of a silver-based monetary system and urged the government to coin more silver. Furthermore, being from farm country, he was very familiar with the farmers' plight and saw some merit in the subtreasury system proposal. In short, Bryan could have been the ideal Populist candidate, but the Democrats got to him first. The Populist Party subsequently endorsed Bryan as well, with their party's nomination three weeks later (**Figure 11.17**).

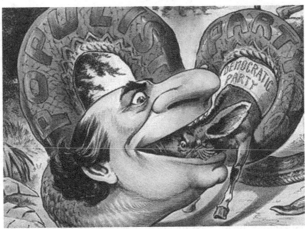

Figure 11.17 Republicans portrayed presidential candidate Bryan as a grasping politician whose Populist leanings could swallow the Democratic Party. Bryan was in fact not a Populist at all, but a Democrat whose views aligned with the Populists on some issues. He was formally nominated by the Democratic Party, the Populist Party, and the Silver Republican Party for the 1896 presidential election.

Click and Explore

Browse through the cartoons and commentary at 1896 (http://openstaxcollege.org/l/1896election) at Vassar College, a site that contains a wealth of information about the major players and themes of the presidential election of 1896.

As the Populist convention unfolded, the delegates had an important decision to make: either locate another candidate, even though Bryan would have been an excellent choice, or join the Democrats and support Bryan as the best candidate but risk losing their identity as a third political party as a result. The Populist Party chose the latter and endorsed Bryan's candidacy. However, they also nominated their own vice-presidential candidate, Georgia Senator Tom Watson, as opposed to the Democratic nominee, Arthur Sewall, presumably in an attempt to maintain some semblance of a separate identity.

The race was a heated one, with McKinley running a typical nineteenth-century style "front porch" campaign, during which he espoused the long-held Republican Party principles to visitors who would call on him at his Ohio home. Bryan, to the contrary, delivered speeches all throughout the country, bringing his message to the people that Republicans "shall not crucify mankind on a cross of gold."

DEFINING "AMERICAN"

✪ *William Jennings Bryan and the "Cross of Gold"*

William Jennings Bryan was a politician and speechmaker in the late nineteenth century, and he was particularly well known for his impassioned argument that the country move to a bimetal or silver standard. He received the Democratic presidential nomination in 1896, and, at the nominating convention, he gave his most famous speech. He sought to argue against Republicans who stated that the gold standard was the only way to ensure stability and prosperity for American businesses. In the speech he said:

> We say to you that you have made the definition of a business man too limited in its application. The man who is employed for wages is as much a business man as his employer; the attorney in a country town is as much a business man as the corporation counsel in a great metropolis; the merchant at the cross-roads store is as much a business man as the merchant of New York; the farmer who goes forth in the morning and toils all day, who begins in spring and toils all summer, and who by the application of brain and muscle to the natural resources of the country creates wealth, is as much a business man as the man who goes upon the Board of Trade and bets upon the price of grain; . . . We come to speak of this broader class of business men.

This defense of working Americans as critical to the prosperity of the country resonated with his listeners, as did his passionate ending when he stated, "Having behind us the producing masses of this nation and the world, supported by the commercial interests, the laboring interests, and the toilers everywhere, we will answer their demand for a gold standard by saying to them: 'You shall not press down upon the brow of labor this crown of thorns; you shall not crucify mankind upon a cross of gold.'"

The speech was an enormous success and played a role in convincing the Populist Party that he was the candidate for them.

The result was a close election that finally saw a U.S. president win a majority of the popular vote for the first time in twenty-four years. McKinley defeated Bryan by a popular vote of 7.1 million to 6.5 million. Bryan's showing was impressive by any standard, as his popular vote total exceeded that of any other presidential candidate in American history to that date—winner or loser. He polled nearly one million more votes than did the previous Democratic victor, Grover Cleveland; however, his campaign also served to split the Democratic vote, as some party members remained convinced of the propriety of the gold standard and supported McKinley in the election.

Amid a growing national depression where Americans truly recognized the importance of a strong leader with sound economic policies, McKinley garnered nearly two million more votes than his Republican predecessor Benjamin Harrison. Put simply, the American electorate was energized to elect a strong candidate who could adequately address the country's economic woes. Voter turnout was the largest in American history to that date; while both candidates benefitted, McKinley did more so than Bryan (**Figure 11.18**).

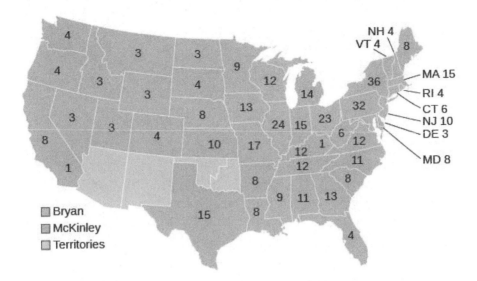

Figure 11.18 The electoral vote map of the 1896 election illustrates the stark divide in the country between the industry-rich coasts and the rural middle.

In the aftermath, it is easy to say that it was Bryan's defeat that all but ended the rise of the Populist Party. Populists had thrown their support to the Democrats who shared similar ideas for the economic rebound of the country and lost. In choosing principle over distinct party identity, the Populists aligned themselves to the growing two-party American political system and would have difficulty maintaining party autonomy afterwards. Future efforts to establish a separate party identity would be met with ridicule by critics who would say that Populists were merely "Democrats in sheep's clothing."

But other factors also contributed to the decline of Populism at the close of the century. First, the discovery of vast gold deposits in Alaska during the Klondike Gold Rush of 1896–1899 (also known as the "Yukon Gold Rush") shored up the nation's weakening economy and made it possible to thrive on a gold standard. Second, the impending Spanish-American War, which began in 1898, further fueled the economy and increased demand for American farm products. Still, the Populist spirit remained, although it lost some momentum at the close of the nineteenth century. As will be seen in a subsequent chapter, the reformist zeal took on new forms as the twentieth century unfolded.

CHAPTER 12

Age of Empire: American Foreign Policy, 1890-1914

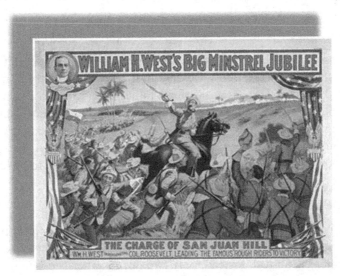

Figure 12.1 This poster advertises a minstrel show wherein an actor playing Theodore Roosevelt reenacts his leadership of the Rough Riders in the Spanish-American War and illustrates the American public's zeal for tales of American expansionist glory.

Chapter Outline

Introduction

As he approached the rostrum to speak before historians gathered in Chicago in 1893, Frederick Jackson Turner appeared nervous. He was presenting a conclusion that would alarm all who believed that westward expansion had fostered the nation's principles of democracy. His conclusion: The frontier—the encounter between European traditions and the native wilderness—had played a fundamental role in shaping American character, but the American frontier no longer existed. Turner's statement raised questions. How would Americans maintain their unique political culture and innovative spirit in the absence of the frontier? How would the nation expand its economy if it could no longer expand its territory?

Later historians would see Turner's Frontier Thesis as deeply flawed, a gross mischaracterization of the West. But the young historian's work greatly influenced politicians and thinkers of the day. Like a muckraker, Turner exposed the problem; others found a solution by seeking out new frontiers in the creation of an American empire. The above advertisement for a theater reenactment of the Spanish-American War (**Figure 12.1**) shows the American appetite for expansion. Many Americans felt that it was time for their nation to offer its own brand of international leadership and dominance as an alternative to the land-grabbing empires of Europe.

12.1 Turner, Mahan, and the Roots of Empire

By the end of this section, you will be able to:
- Explain the evolution of American interest in foreign affairs from the end of the Civil War through the early 1890s
- Identify the contributions of Frederick Jackson Turner and Alfred Thayer Mahan to the conscious creation of an American empire

During the time of Reconstruction, the U.S. government showed no significant initiative in foreign affairs. Western expansion and the goal of Manifest Destiny still held the country's attention, and American missionaries proselytized as far abroad as China, India, the Korean Peninsula, and Africa, but reconstruction efforts took up most of the nation's resources. As the century came to a close, however, a variety of factors, from the closing of the American frontier to the country's increased industrial production, led the United States to look beyond its borders. Countries in Europe were building their empires through global power and trade, and the United States did not want to be left behind.

AMERICA'S LIMITED BUT AGGRESSIVE PUSH OUTWARD

On the eve of the Civil War, the country lacked the means to establish a strong position in international diplomacy. As of 1865, the U.S. State Department had barely sixty employees and no ambassadors representing American interests abroad. Instead, only two dozen American foreign ministers were located in key countries, and those often gained their positions not through diplomatic skills or expertise in foreign affairs but through bribes. Further limiting American potential for foreign impact was the fact that a strong international presence required a strong military—specifically a navy—which the United States, after the Civil War, was in no position to maintain. Additionally, as late as 1890, with the U.S. Navy significantly reduced in size, a majority of vessels were classified as "Old Navy," meaning a mixture of iron hulled and wholly wooden ships. While the navy had introduced the first all-steel, triple-hulled steam engine vessels seven years earlier, they had only thirteen of them in operation by 1890.

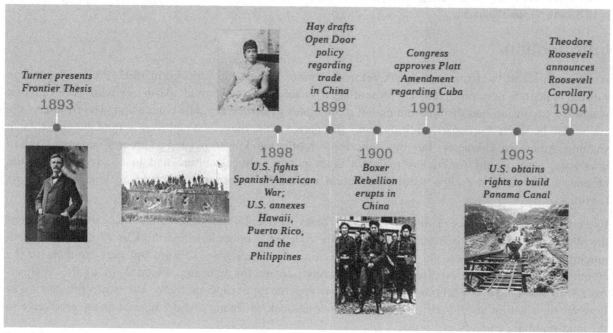

Figure 12.2

Despite such widespread isolationist impulses and the sheer inability to maintain a strong international position, the United States moved ahead sporadically with a modest foreign policy agenda in the three decades following the Civil War. Secretary of State William Seward, who held that position from 1861 through 1869, sought to extend American political and commercial influence in both Asia and Latin America. He pursued these goals through a variety of actions. A treaty with Nicaragua set the early course for the future construction of a canal across Central America. He also pushed through the annexation of the Midway Islands in the Pacific Ocean, which subsequently opened a more stable route to Asian markets. In frequent conversations with President Lincoln, among others, Seward openly spoke of his desire to obtain British Columbia, the Hawaiian Islands, portions of the Dominican Republic, Cuba, and other territories. He explained his motives to a Boston audience in 1867, when he professed his intention to give the United States "control of the world."

Most notably, in 1867, Seward obtained the Alaskan Territory from Russia for a purchase price of $7.2 million. Fearing future loss of the territory through military conflict, as well as desiring to create challenges for Great Britain (which they had fought in the Crimean War), Russia had happily accepted the American purchase offer. In the United States, several newspaper editors openly questioned the purchase and labeled it "**Seward's Folly**" (**Figure 12.3**). They highlighted the lack of Americans to populate the vast region and lamented the challenges in attempting to govern the native peoples in that territory. Only if gold were to be found, the editors decried, would the secretive purchase be justified. That is exactly what happened. Seward's purchase added an enormous territory to the country—nearly 600,000 square miles—and also gave the United States access to the rich mineral resources of the region, including the gold that trigged the Klondike Gold Rush at the close of the century. As was the case elsewhere in the American borderlands, Alaska's industrial development wreaked havoc on the region's indigenous and Russian cultures.

Figure 12.3 Although mocked in the press at the time as "Seward's Folly," Secretary of State William Seward's acquisition of Alaska from Russia was a strategic boon to the United States.

Seward's successor as Secretary of State, Hamilton Fish, held the position from 1869 through 1877. Fish spent much of his time settling international disputes involving American interests, including claims that British assistance to the Confederates prolonged the Civil War for about two years. In these so-called Alabama claims, a U.S. senator charged that the Confederacy won a number of crucial battles with the help of one British cruiser and demanded $2 billion in British reparations. Alternatively, the United States would settle for the rights to Canada. A joint commission representing both countries eventually settled on a British payment of $15 million to the United States. In the negotiations, Fish also suggested adding the Dominican Republic as a territorial possession with a path towards statehood, as well as discussing the construction of a transoceanic canal with Columbia. Although neither negotiation ended in the desired result, they both expressed Fish's intent to cautiously build an American empire without creating any unnecessary military entanglements in the wake of the Civil War.

BUSINESS, RELIGIOUS, AND SOCIAL INTERESTS SET THE STAGE FOR EMPIRE

While the United States slowly pushed outward and sought to absorb the borderlands (and the indigenous cultures that lived there), the country was also changing how it functioned. As a new industrial United States began to emerge in the 1870s, economic interests began to lead the country toward a more expansionist foreign policy. By forging new and stronger ties overseas, the United States would gain access to international markets for export, as well as better deals on the raw materials needed domestically. The concerns raised by the economic depression of the early 1890s further convinced business owners that they needed to tap into new markets, even at the risk of foreign entanglements.

As a result of these growing economic pressures, American exports to other nations skyrocketed in the years following the Civil War, from $234 million in 1865 to $605 million in 1875. By 1898, on the eve of the Spanish-American War, American exports had reached a height of $1.3 billion annually. Imports over the same period also increased substantially, from $238 million in 1865 to $616 million in 1898. Such an increased investment in overseas markets in turn strengthened Americans' interest in foreign affairs.

Businesses were not the only ones seeking to expand. Religious leaders and Progressive reformers joined businesses in their growing interest in American expansion, as both sought to increase the democratic and Christian influences of the United States abroad. Imperialism and Progressivism were compatible in the minds of many reformers who thought the Progressive impulses for democracy at home translated overseas as well. Editors of such magazines as *Century*, *Outlook*, and *Harper's* supported an imperialistic stance as the democratic responsibility of the United States. Several Protestant faiths formed missionary societies in the years after the Civil War, seeking to expand their reach, particularly in Asia. Influenced by such works as Reverend Josiah Strong's *Our Country: Its Possible Future and Its Present Crisis* (1885), missionaries sought to spread the gospel throughout the country and abroad. Led by the American Board of Commissioners for Foreign Missions, among several other organizations, missionaries conflated Christian ethics with American virtues, and began to spread both gospels with zeal. This was particularly true among women missionaries, who composed over 60 percent of the overall missionary force. By 1870, missionaries abroad spent as much time advocating for the American version of a modern civilization as they did teaching the Bible.

Social reformers of the early Progressive Era also performed work abroad that mirrored the missionaries. Many were influenced by recent scholarship on race-based intelligence and embraced the implications of social Darwinist theory that alleged inferior races were destined to poverty on account of their lower evolutionary status. While certainly not all reformers espoused a racist view of intelligence and civilization, many of these reformers believed that the Anglo-Saxon race was mentally superior to others and owed the presumed less evolved populations their stewardship and social uplift—a service the British writer Rudyard Kipling termed "the white man's burden."

By trying to help people in less industrialized countries achieve a higher standard of living and a better understanding of the principles of democracy, reformers hoped to contribute to a noble cause, but their approach suffered from the same paternalism that hampered Progressive reforms at home. Whether reformers and missionaries worked with native communities in the borderlands such as New Mexico; in the inner cities, like the Salvation Army; or overseas, their approaches had much in common. Their good intentions and willingness to work in difficult conditions shone through in the letters and articles they wrote from the field. Often in their writing, it was clear that they felt divinely empowered to change the lives of other, less fortunate, and presumably, less enlightened, people. Whether oversees or in the urban slums, they benefitted from the same passions but expressed the same paternalism.

MY STORY

⚙ *Lottie Moon, Missionary*

Lottie Moon was a Southern Baptist missionary who spent more than forty years living and working in China. She began in 1873 when she joined her sister in China as a missionary, teaching in a school for Chinese women. Her true passion, however, was to evangelize and minister, and she undertook a campaign to urge the Southern Baptist missionaries to allow women to work beyond the classroom. Her letter campaign back to the head of the Mission Board provided a vivid picture of life in China and exhorted the Southern Baptist women to give more generously of their money and their time. Her letters appeared frequently in religious publications, and it was her suggestion—that the week before Christmas be established as a time to donate to foreign missions—that led to the annual Christmas giving tradition. Lottie's rhetoric caught on, and still today, the annual Christmas offering is done in her name.

> We had the best possible voyage over the water—good weather, no headwinds, scarcely any rolling or pitching—in short, all that reasonable people could ask. . . . I spent a week here last fall and of course feel very natural to be here again. I do so love the East and eastern life! Japan fascinated my heart and fancy four years ago, but now I honestly believe I love China the best, and actually, which is stranger still, like the Chinese best.
> —Charlotte "Lottie" Moon, 1877

Lottie remained in China through famines, the Boxer Rebellion, and other hardships. She fought against foot binding, a cultural tradition where girls' feet were tightly bound to keep them from growing, and shared her personal food and money when those around her were suffering. But her primary goal was to evangelize her Christian beliefs to the people in China. She won the right to minister and personally converted hundreds of Chinese to Christianity. Lottie's combination of moral certainty and selfless service was emblematic of the missionary zeal of the early American empire.

TURNER, MAHAN, AND THE PLAN FOR EMPIRE

The initial work of businesses, missionaries, and reformers set the stage by the early 1890s for advocates of an expanded foreign policy and a vision of an American empire. Following decades of an official stance of isolationism combined with relatively weak presidents who lacked the popular mandate or congressional support to undertake substantial overseas commitments, a new cadre of American leaders—many of whom were too young to fully comprehend the damage inflicted by the Civil War—assumed leadership roles. Eager to be tested in international conflict, these new leaders hoped to prove America's might on a global stage. The Assistant Secretary of the Navy, Theodore Roosevelt, was one of these leaders who sought to expand American influence globally, and he advocated for the expansion of the U.S. Navy, which at the turn of the century was the only weapons system suitable for securing overseas expansion.

Turner (**Figure 12.4**) and naval strategist Alfred Thayer Mahan were instrumental in the country's move toward foreign expansion, and writer Brooks Adams further dramatized the consequences of the nation's loss of its frontier in his *The Law of Civilization and Decay* in 1895. As mentioned in the chapter opening, Turner announced his **Frontier Thesis**—that American democracy was largely formed by the American frontier—at the Chicago World's Colombian Exposition. He noted that "for nearly three centuries the dominant fact in American life has been expansion." He continued: "American energy will continually demand a wider field for its exercise."

Figure 12.4 Historian Fredrick Jackson Turner's Frontier Thesis stated explicitly that the existence of the western frontier forged the very basis of the American identity.

Although there was no more room for these forces to proceed domestically, they would continue to find an outlet on the international stage. Turner concluded that "the demands for a vigorous foreign policy, for an interoceanic canal, for a revival of our power upon our seas, and for the extension of American influence to outlying islands and adjoining countries are indications that the forces [of expansion] will continue." Such policies would permit Americans to find new markets. Also mindful of the mitigating influence of a frontier—in terms of easing pressure from increased immigration and population expansion in the eastern and midwestern United States—he encouraged new outlets for further population growth, whether as lands for further American settlement or to accommodate more immigrants. Turner's thesis was enormously influential at the time but has subsequently been widely criticized by historians. Specifically, the thesis underscores the pervasive racism and disregard for the indigenous communities, cultures, and individuals in the American borderlands and beyond.

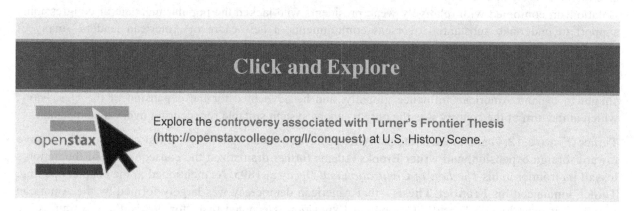

Click and Explore

Explore the controversy associated with Turner's Frontier Thesis (http://openstaxcollege.org/l/conquest) at U.S. History Scene.

While Turner provided the idea for an empire, Mahan provided the more practical guide. In his 1890 work, *The Influence of Seapower upon History*, he suggested three strategies that would assist the United States in both constructing and maintaining an empire. First, noting the sad state of the U.S. Navy, he called for the government to build a stronger, more powerful version. Second, he suggested establishing a network of naval bases to fuel this expanding fleet. Seward's previous acquisition of the Midway Islands served this purpose by providing an essential naval coaling station, which was vital, as the limited reach of steamships and their dependence on coal made naval coaling stations imperative for increasing the navy's geographic reach. Future acquisitions in the Pacific and Caribbean increased this naval supply network (**Figure 12.5**). Finally, Mahan urged the future construction of a canal across the isthmus of Central America, which would decrease by two-thirds the time and power required to move the new navy from the Pacific to the Atlantic oceans. Heeding Mahan's advice, the government moved quickly, passing the Naval Act of 1890, which set production levels for a new, modern fleet. By 1898, the government had succeeded in increasing the size of the U.S. Navy to an active fleet of 160 vessels, of which 114 were newly built of steel. In addition, the fleet now included six battleships, compared to zero in the previous decade. As a naval power, the country catapulted to the third strongest in world rankings by military experts, trailing only Spain and Great Britain.

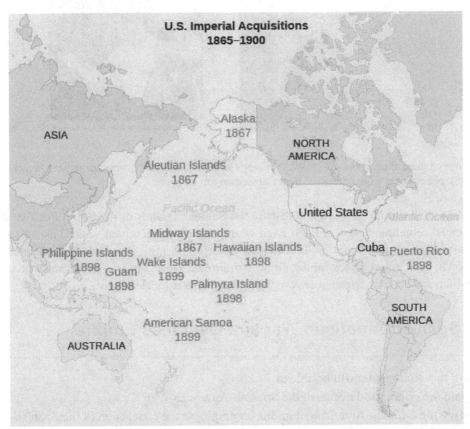

Figure 12.5 American imperial acquisitions as of the end of the Spanish-American War in 1898. Note how the spread of island acquisitions across the Pacific Ocean fulfills Alfred Mahan's call for more naval bases in order to support a larger and more effective U.S. Navy rather than mere territorial expansion.

The United States also began to expand its influence to other Pacific Islands, most notably Samoa and Hawaii. With regard to the latter, American businessmen were most interested in the lucrative sugar industry that lay at the heart of the Hawaiian Islands' economy. By 1890, through a series of reciprocal trade agreements, Hawaiians exported nearly all of their sugar production to the United States, tariff-free. When Queen Liliuokalani tapped into a strong anti-American resentment among native Hawaiians over the economic and political power of exploitative American sugar companies between 1891 and 1893, worried businessmen worked with the American minister to Hawaii, John Stevens, to stage a quick, armed revolt to counter her efforts and seize the islands as an American protectorate (**Figure 12.6**). Following five more years of political wrangling, the United States annexed Hawaii in 1898, during the Spanish-American War.

(a)   (b)

Figure 12.6 Queen Liliuokalani of Hawaii (a) was unhappy with the one-sided trade agreement Hawaii held with the United States (b), but protests were squashed by an American-armed revolt.

The United States had similar strategic interests in the Samoan Islands of the South Pacific, most notably, access to the naval refueling station at Pago Pago where American merchant vessels as well as naval ships could take on food, fuel, and supplies. In 1899, in an effort to mitigate other foreign interests and still protect their own, the United States joined Great Britain and Germany in a three-party protectorate over the islands, which assured American access to the strategic ports located there.

12.2 The Spanish-American War and Overseas Empire

By the end of this section, you will be able to:
- Explain the origins and events of the Spanish-American War
- Analyze the different American opinions on empire at the conclusion of the Spanish-American War
- Describe how the Spanish-American War intersected with other American expansions to solidify the nation's new position as an empire

The Spanish-American War was the first significant international military conflict for the United States since its war against Mexico in 1846; it came to represent a critical milestone in the country's development as an empire. Ostensibly about the rights of Cuban rebels to fight for freedom from Spain, the war had, for the United States at least, a far greater importance in the country's desire to expand its global reach.

The Spanish-American War was notable not only because the United States succeeded in seizing territory from another empire, but also because it caused the global community to recognize that the United States was a formidable military power. In what Secretary of State John Hay called "a splendid little war," the United States significantly altered the balance of world power, just as the twentieth century began to unfold (**Figure 12.7**).

LA FATLERA DEL ONCLE SAM (per M. MOLINÉ).

Guardarse l' isla perque no 's perdi.

Figure 12.7 Whereas Americans thought of the Spanish colonial regime in Cuba as a typical example of European imperialism, this 1896 Spanish cartoon depicts the United States as a land-grabbing empire. The caption, written in Catalan, states "Keep the island so it won't get lost."

THE CHALLENGE OF DECLARING WAR

Despite its name, the Spanish-American War had less to do with the foreign affairs between the United States and Spain than Spanish control over Cuba and its possessions in the Far East. Spain had dominated Central and South America since the late fifteenth century. But, by 1890, the only Spanish colonies that had not yet acquired their independence were Cuba and Puerto Rico. On several occasions prior to the war, Cuban independence fighters in the Cuba Libre movement had attempted unsuccessfully to end Spanish control of their lands. In 1895, a similar revolt for independence erupted in Cuba; again, Spanish forces under the command of General Valeriano Weyler repressed the insurrection. Particularly notorious was their policy of re-concentration in which Spanish troops forced rebels from the countryside into military-controlled camps in the cities, where many died from harsh conditions.

As with previous uprisings, Americans were largely sympathetic to the Cuban rebels' cause, especially as the Spanish response was notably brutal. Evoking the same rhetoric of independence with which they fought the British during the American Revolution, several people quickly rallied to the Cuban fight for freedom. Shippers and other businessmen, particularly in the sugar industry, supported American intervention to safeguard their own interests in the region. Likewise, the "Cuba Libre" movement founded by José Martí, who quickly established offices in New York and Florida, further stirred American interest in the liberation cause. The difference in this uprising, however, was that supporters saw in the renewed U.S. Navy a force that could be a strong ally for Cuba. Additionally, the late 1890s saw the height of **yellow journalism**, in which newspapers such as the *New York Journal*, led by William Randolph Hearst, and the *New York World*, published by Joseph Pulitzer, competed for readership with sensationalistic stories. These publishers, and many others who printed news stories for maximum drama and effect, knew that war would provide sensational copy.

However, even as sensationalist news stories fanned the public's desire to try out their new navy while supporting freedom, one key figure remained unmoved. President William McKinley, despite commanding a new, powerful navy, also recognized that the new fleet—and soldiers—were untested. Preparing for a reelection bid in 1900, McKinley did not see a potential war with Spain, acknowledged to be the most powerful naval force in the world, as a good bet. McKinley did publicly admonish Spain for its actions against the rebels, and urged Spain to find a peaceful solution in Cuba, but he remained resistant to public pressure for American military intervention.

McKinley's reticence to involve the United States changed in February 1898. He had ordered one of the newest navy battleships, the USS *Maine*, to drop anchor off the coast of Cuba in order to observe the situation, and to prepare to evacuate American citizens from Cuba if necessary. Just days after it arrived, on February 15, an explosion destroyed the *Maine*, killing over 250 American sailors (**Figure 12.8**). Immediately, yellow journalists jumped on the headline that the explosion was the result of a Spanish attack, and that all Americans should rally to war. The newspaper battle cry quickly emerged, "Remember the Maine!" Recent examinations of the evidence of that time have led many historians to conclude that the explosion was likely an accident due to the storage of gun powder close to the very hot boilers. But in 1898, without ready evidence, the newspapers called for a war that would sell papers, and the American public rallied behind the cry.

Figure 12.8 Although later reports would suggest the explosion was due to loose gunpowder onboard the ship, the press treated the explosion of the USS *Maine* as high drama. Note the lower headline citing that the ship was destroyed by a mine, despite the lack of evidence.

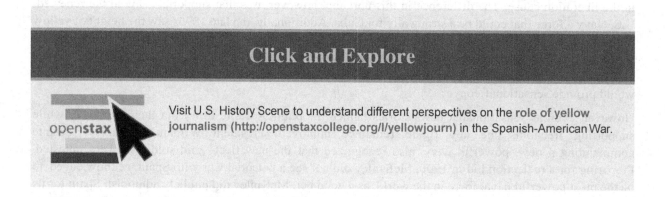

Click and Explore

Visit U.S. History Scene to understand different perspectives on the **role of yellow journalism** (http://openstaxcollege.org/l/yellowjourn) in the Spanish-American War.

McKinley made one final effort to avoid war, when late in March, he called on Spain to end its policy of concentrating the native population in military camps in Cuba, and to formally declare Cuba's independence. Spain refused, leaving McKinley little choice but to request a declaration of war from

Congress. Congress received McKinley's war message, and on April 19, 1898, they officially recognized Cuba's independence and authorized McKinley to use military force to remove Spain from the island. Equally important, Congress passed the Teller Amendment to the resolution, which stated that the United States would not annex Cuba following the war.

WAR: BRIEF AND DECISIVE

The Spanish-American War lasted approximately ten weeks, and the outcome was clear: The United States triumphed in its goal of helping liberate Cuba from Spanish control. Despite the positive result, the conflict did present significant challenges to the United States military. Although the new navy was powerful, the ships were, as McKinley feared, largely untested. Similarly untested were the American soldiers. The country had fewer than thirty thousand soldiers and sailors, many of whom were unprepared to do battle with a formidable opponent. But volunteers sought to make up the difference. Over one million American men—many lacking a uniform and coming equipped with their own guns—quickly answered McKinley's call for able-bodied men. Nearly ten thousand African American men also volunteered for service, despite the segregated conditions and additional hardships they faced, including violent uprisings at a few American bases before they departed for Cuba. The government, although grateful for the volunteer effort, was still unprepared to feed and supply such a force, and many suffered malnutrition and malaria for their sacrifice.

To the surprise of the Spanish forces who saw the conflict as a clear war over Cuba, American military strategists prepared for it as a war for empire. More so than simply the liberation of Cuba and the protection of American interests in the Caribbean, military strategists sought to further Mahan's vision of additional naval bases in the Pacific Ocean, reaching as far as mainland Asia. Such a strategy would also benefit American industrialists who sought to expand their markets into China. Just before leaving his post for volunteer service as a lieutenant colonel in the U.S. cavalry, Assistant Secretary of the Navy Theodore Roosevelt ordered navy ships to attack the Spanish fleet in the Philippines, another island chain under Spanish control. As a result, the first significant military confrontation took place not in Cuba but halfway around the world in the Philippines. Commodore George Dewey led the U.S. Navy in a decisive victory, sinking all of the Spanish ships while taking almost no American losses. Within a month, the U.S. Army landed a force to take the islands from Spain, which it succeeded in doing by mid-August 1899.

The victory in Cuba took a little longer. In June, seventeen thousand American troops landed in Cuba. Although they initially met with little Spanish resistance, by early July, fierce battles ensued near the Spanish stronghold in Santiago. Most famously, Theodore Roosevelt led his **Rough Riders**, an all-volunteer cavalry unit made up of adventure-seeking college graduates, and veterans and cowboys from the Southwest, in a charge up Kettle Hill, next to San Juan Hill, which resulted in American forces surrounding Santiago. The victories of the Rough Riders are the best known part of the battles, but in fact, several African American regiments, made up of veteran soldiers, were instrumental to their success. The Spanish fleet made a last-ditch effort to escape to the sea but ran into an American naval blockade that resulted in total destruction, with every Spanish vessel sunk. Lacking any naval support, Spain quickly lost control of Puerto Rico as well, offering virtually no resistance to advancing American forces. By the end of July, the fighting had ended and the war was over. Despite its short duration and limited number of casualties—fewer than 350 soldiers died in combat, about 1,600 were wounded, while almost 3,000 men died from disease—the war carried enormous significance for Americans who celebrated the victory as a reconciliation between North and South.

DEFINING "AMERICAN"

⊙ *"Smoked Yankees": Black Soldiers in the Spanish-American War*

The most popular image of the Spanish-American War is of Theodore Roosevelt and his Rough Riders, charging up San Juan Hill. But less well known is that the Rough Riders struggled mightily in several battles and would have sustained far more serious casualties, if not for the experienced black veterans—over twenty-five hundred of them—who joined them in battle (Figure 12.9). These soldiers, who had been fighting the Indian wars on the American frontier for many years, were instrumental in the U.S. victory in Cuba.

Figure 12.9 The decision to fight or not was debated in the black community, as some felt they owed little to a country that still granted them citizenship in name only, while others believed that proving their patriotism would enhance their opportunities. (credit: Library of Congress)

The choice to serve in the Spanish-American War was not a simple one. Within the black community, many spoke out both for and against involvement in the war. Many black Americans felt that because they were not offered the true rights of citizenship it was not their burden to volunteer for war. Others, in contrast, argued that participation in the war offered an opportunity for black Americans to prove themselves to the rest of the country. While their presence was welcomed by the military which desperately needed experienced soldiers, the black regiments suffered racism and harsh treatment while training in the southern states before shipping off to battle.

Once in Cuba, however, the "Smoked Yankees," as the Cubans called the black American soldiers, fought side-by-side with Roosevelt's Rough Riders, providing crucial tactical support to some of the most important battles of the war. After the Battle of San Juan, five black soldiers received the Medal of Honor and twenty-five others were awarded a certificate of merit. One reporter wrote that "if it had not been for the Negro cavalry, the Rough Riders would have been exterminated." He went on to state that, having grown up in the South, he had never been fond of black people before witnessing the battle. For some of the soldiers, their recognition made the sacrifice worthwhile. Others, however, struggled with American oppression of Cubans and Puerto Ricans, feeling kinship with the black residents of these countries now under American rule.

ESTABLISHING PEACE AND CREATING AN EMPIRE

As the war closed, Spanish and American diplomats made arrangements for a peace conference in Paris. They met in October 1898, with the Spanish government committed to regaining control of the Philippines, which they felt were unjustly taken in a war that was solely about Cuban independence. While the Teller Amendment ensured freedom for Cuba, President McKinley was reluctant to relinquish the strategically useful prize of the Philippines. He certainly did not want to give the islands back to Spain, nor did he want another European power to step in to seize them. Neither the Spanish nor the Americans considered giving the islands their independence, since, with the pervasive racism and cultural stereotyping of the day, they believed the Filipino people were not capable of governing themselves. William Howard Taft, the first American governor-general to oversee the administration of the new U.S. possession, accurately captured American sentiments with his frequent reference to Filipinos as "our little brown brothers."

As the peace negotiations unfolded, Spain agreed to recognize Cuba's independence, as well as recognize American control of Puerto Rico and Guam. McKinley insisted that the United States maintain control over the Philippines as an annexation, in return for a $20 million payment to Spain. Although Spain was reluctant, they were in no position militarily to deny the American demand. The two sides finalized the Treaty of Paris on December 10, 1898. With it came the international recognition that there was a new American empire that included the Philippines, Puerto Rico, and Guam. The American press quickly glorified the nation's new reach, as expressed in the cartoon below, depicting the glory of the American eagle reaching from the Philippines to the Caribbean (**Figure 12.10**).

Ten thousand miles from tip to tip.—Philadelphia Press.

Figure 12.10 This cartoon from the *Philadelphia Press*, showed the reach of the new American empire, from Puerto Rico to the Philippines.

Domestically, the country was neither unified in their support of the treaty nor in the idea of the United States building an empire at all. Many prominent Americans, including Jane Addams, former President Grover Cleveland, Andrew Carnegie, Mark Twain, and Samuel Gompers, felt strongly that the country should not be pursuing an empire, and, in 1898, they formed the **Anti-Imperialist League** to oppose this expansionism. The reasons for their opposition were varied: Some felt that empire building went against the principles of democracy and freedom upon which the country was founded, some worried about competition from foreign workers, and some held the xenophobic viewpoint that the assimilation of other races would hurt the country. Regardless of their reasons, the group, taken together, presented a formidable challenge. As foreign treaties require a two-thirds majority in the U.S. Senate to pass, the Anti-Imperialist League's pressure led them to a clear split, with the possibility of defeat of the treaty seeming imminent. Less than a week before the scheduled vote, however, news of a Filipino uprising against American forces reached the United States. Undecided senators were convinced of the need to maintain an American presence in the region and preempt the intervention of another European power, and the Senate formally ratified the treaty on February 6, 1899.

The newly formed American empire was not immediately secure, as Filipino rebels, led by Emilio Aguinaldo (**Figure 12.11**), fought back against American forces stationed there. The Filipinos' war for independence lasted three years, with over four thousand American and twenty thousand Filipino combatant deaths; the civilian death toll is estimated as high as 250,000. Finally, in 1901, President McKinley appointed William Howard Taft as the civil governor of the Philippines in an effort to disengage the American military from direct confrontations with the Filipino people. Under Taft's leadership, Americans built a new transportation infrastructure, hospitals, and schools, hoping to win over the local population. The rebels quickly lost influence, and Aguinaldo was captured by American forces and forced to swear allegiance to the United States. The Taft Commission, as it became known, continued to introduce reforms to modernize and improve daily life for the country despite pockets of resistance that continued to fight through the spring of 1902. Much of the commission's rule centered on legislative reforms to local government structure and national agencies, with the commission offering appointments to resistance leaders in exchange for their support. The Philippines continued under American rule until they became self-governing in 1946.

Figure 12.11 Philippine president Emilio Aguinaldo was captured after three years of fighting with U.S. troops. He is seen here boarding the USS *Vicksburg* after taking an oath of loyalty to the United States in 1901.

After the conclusion of the Spanish-American War and the successful passage of the peace treaty with Spain, the United States continued to acquire other territories. Seeking an expanded international presence, as well as control of maritime routes and naval stations, the United States grew to include Hawaii, which was granted territorial status in 1900, and Alaska, which, although purchased from Russia decades earlier, only became a recognized territory in 1912. In both cases, their status as territories granted U.S. citizenship to their residents. The Foraker Act of 1900 established Puerto Rico as an American territory with its own civil government. It was not until 1917 that Puerto Ricans were granted American citizenship. Guam and Samoa, which had been taken as part of the war, remained under the control of the U.S. Navy. Cuba, which after the war was technically a free country, adopted a constitution based on the U.S. Constitution. While the Teller Amendment had prohibited the United States from annexing the country, a subsequent amendment, the Platt Amendment, secured the right of the United States to interfere in Cuban affairs if threats to a stable government emerged. The Platt Amendment also guaranteed the United States its own naval and coaling station on the island's southern Guantanamo Bay and prohibited Cuba from making treaties with other countries that might eventually threaten their independence. While Cuba remained an independent nation on paper, in all practicality the United States governed Cuba's foreign policy and economic agreements.

Click and Explore

Explore the resources at U.S. History Scene to better understand the long and involved **history of Hawaii** (http://openstaxcollege.org/l/createHawaii) with respect to its intersection with the United States.

12.3 Economic Imperialism in East Asia

By the end of this section, you will be able to:
- Explain how economic power helped to expand America's empire in China
- Describe how the foreign partitioning of China in the last decade of the nineteenth century influenced American policy

While American forays into empire building began with military action, the country concurrently grew its scope and influence through other methods as well. In particular, the United States used its economic and industrial capacity to add to its empire, as can be seen in a study of the China market and the "Open Door notes" discussed below.

WHY CHINA?

Since the days of Christopher Columbus's westward journey to seek a new route to the East Indies (essentially India and China, but loosely defined as all of Southeast Asia), many westerners have dreamt of the elusive "China Market." With the defeat of the Spanish navy in the Atlantic and Pacific, and specifically with the addition of the Philippines as a base for American ports and coaling stations, the United States was ready to try and make the myth a reality. Although China originally accounted for only a small percentage of American foreign trade, captains of American industry dreamed of a vast market of Asian customers desperate for manufactured goods they could not yet produce in large quantities for themselves.

American businesses were not alone in seeing the opportunities. Other countries—including Japan, Russia, Great Britain, France, and Germany—also hoped to make inroads in China. Previous treaties between Great Britain and China in 1842 and 1844 during the Opium Wars, when the British Empire militarily coerced the Chinese empire to accept the import of Indian opium in exchange for its tea, had forced an "open door" policy on China, in which all foreign nations had free and equal access to Chinese ports. This was at a time when Great Britain maintained the strongest economic relationship with China; however, other western nations used the new arrangement to send Christian missionaries, who began to work across inland China. Following the Sino-Japanese War of 1894–1895 over China's claims to Korea, western countries hoped to exercise even greater influence in the region. By 1897, Germany had obtained exclusive mining rights in northern coastal China as reparations for the murder of two German missionaries. In 1898, Russia obtained permission to build a railroad across northeastern Manchuria. One by one, each country carved out their own **sphere of influence**, where they could control markets through tariffs and transportation, and thus ensure their share of the Chinese market.

Alarmed by the pace at which foreign powers further divided China into pseudo-territories, and worried that they had no significant piece for themselves, the United States government intervened. In contrast to

European nations, however, American businesses wanted the whole market, not just a share of it. They wanted to do business in China with no artificially constructed spheres or boundaries to limit the extent of their trade, but without the territorial entanglements or legislative responsibilities that anti-imperialists opposed. With the blessing and assistance of Secretary of State John Hay, several American businessmen created the American Asiatic Association in 1896 to pursue greater trade opportunities in China.

THE OPEN DOOR NOTES

In 1899, Secretary of State Hay made a bold move to acquire China's vast markets for American access by introducing **Open Door notes**, a series of circular notes that Hay himself drafted as an expression of U.S. interests in the region and sent to the other competing powers (**Figure 12.12**). These notes, if agreed to by the other five nations maintaining spheres of influences in China, would erase all spheres and essentially open all doors to free trade, with no special tariffs or transportation controls that would give unfair advantages to one country over another. Specifically, the notes required that all countries agree to maintain free access to all treaty ports in China, to pay railroad charges and harbor fees (with no special access), and that only China would be permitted to collect any taxes on trade within its borders. While on paper, the Open Door notes would offer equal access to all, the reality was that it greatly favored the United States. Free trade in China would give American businesses the ultimate advantage, as American companies were producing higher-quality goods than other countries, and were doing so more efficiently and less expensively. The "open doors" would flood the Chinese market with American goods, virtually squeezing other countries out of the market.

Figure 12.12 This political cartoon shows Uncle Sam standing on a map of China, while Europe's imperialist nations (from left to right: Germany, Spain, Great Britain, Russia, and France) try to cut out their "sphere of influence."

Although the foreign ministers of the other five nations sent half-hearted replies on behalf of their respective governments, with some outright denying the viability of the notes, Hay proclaimed them the new official policy on China, and American goods were unleashed throughout the nation. China was quite welcoming of the notes, as they also stressed the U.S. commitment to preserving the Chinese government and territorial integrity.

The notes were invoked barely a year later, when a group of Chinese insurgents, the Righteous and Harmonious Fists—also known as the Boxer Rebellion—fought to expel all western nations and their influences from China (**Figure 12.13**). The United States, along with Great Britain and Germany, sent over two thousand troops to withstand the rebellion. The troops signified American commitment to the territorial integrity of China, albeit one flooded with American products. Despite subsequent efforts, by Japan in particular, to undermine Chinese authority in 1915 and again during the Manchurian crisis of 1931, the United States remained resolute in defense of the open door principles through World War II. Only when China turned to communism in 1949 following an intense civil war did the principle become relatively meaningless. However, for nearly half a century, U.S. military involvement and a continued relationship with the Chinese government cemented their roles as preferred trading partners, illustrating how the country used economic power, as well as military might, to grow its empire.

Figure 12.13 The Boxer Rebellion in China sought to expel all western influences, including Christian missionaries and trade partners. The Chinese government appreciated the American, British, and German troops that helped suppress the rebellion.

Click and Explore

Browse the U.S. State Department's Milestones: 1899—1913 (http://openstaxcollege.org/l/haychina) to learn more about Secretary of State John Hay and the strategy and thinking behind the Open Door notes.

12.4 Roosevelt's "Big Stick" Foreign Policy

By the end of this section, you will be able to:
- Explain the meaning of "big stick" foreign policy
- Describe Theodore Roosevelt's use of the "big stick" to construct the Panama Canal
- Explain the role of the United States in ending the Russo-Japanese War

While President McKinley ushered in the era of the American empire through military strength and economic coercion, his successor, Theodore Roosevelt, established a new foreign policy approach, allegedly based on a favorite African proverb, "speak softly, and carry a big stick, and you will go far" (**Figure 12.14**). At the crux of his foreign policy was a thinly veiled threat. Roosevelt believed that in light of the country's recent military successes, it was unnecessary to *use* force to achieve foreign policy goals, so long as the military could *threaten* force. This rationale also rested on the young president's philosophy, which he termed the "strenuous life," and that prized challenges overseas as opportunities to instill American men with the resolve and vigor they allegedly had once acquired in the Trans-Mississippi West.

THE BIG STICK IN THE CARIBBEAN SEA

Figure 12.14 Roosevelt was often depicted in cartoons wielding his "big stick" and pushing the U.S. foreign agenda, often through the power of the U.S. Navy.

Roosevelt believed that while the coercive power wielded by the United States could be harmful in the wrong hands, the Western Hemisphere's best interests were also the best interests of the United States. He felt, in short, that the United States had the right and the obligation to be the policeman of the hemisphere. This belief, and his strategy of "speaking softly and carrying a big stick," shaped much of Roosevelt's foreign policy.

THE CONSTRUCTION OF THE PANAMA CANAL

As early as the mid-sixteenth century, interest in a canal across the Central American isthmus began to take root, primarily out of trade interests. The subsequent discovery of gold in California in 1848 further spurred interest in connecting the Atlantic and Pacific Oceans, and led to the construction of the Panama Railway, which began operations in 1855. Several attempts by France to construct a canal between 1881 and 1894 failed due to a combination of financial crises and health hazards, including malaria and yellow fever, which led to the deaths of thousands of French workers.

Upon becoming president in 1901, Roosevelt was determined to succeed where others had failed. Following the advice that Mahan set forth in his book *The Influence of Seapower upon History*, he sought to achieve the construction of a canal across Central America, primarily for military reasons associated with empire, but also for international trade considerations. The most strategic point for the construction was across the fifty-mile isthmus of Panama, which, at the turn of the century, was part of the nation of Colombia. Roosevelt negotiated with the government of Colombia, sometimes threatening to take the project away and build through Nicaragua, until Colombia agreed to a treaty that would grant the United States a lease on the land across Panama in exchange for a payment of $10 million and an additional $250,000 annual rental fee. The matter was far from settled, however. The Colombian people were outraged over the loss of their land to the United States, and saw the payment as far too low. Influenced by the public outcry, the Colombian Senate rejected the treaty and informed Roosevelt there would be no canal.

Undaunted, Roosevelt chose to now wield the "big stick." In comments to journalists, he made it clear that the United States would strongly support the Panamanian people should they choose to revolt against Colombia and form their own nation. In November 1903, he even sent American battleships to the coast of Colombia, ostensibly for practice maneuvers, as the Panamanian revolution unfolded. The warships effectively blocked Colombia from moving additional troops into the region to quell the growing Panamanian uprising. Within a week, Roosevelt immediately recognized the new country of Panama, welcoming them to the world community and offering them the same terms—$10 million plus the annual $250,000 rental fee—he had previously offered Colombia. Following the successful revolution, Panama became an American protectorate, and remained so until 1939.

Once the Panamanian victory was secured, with American support, construction on the canal began in May 1904. For the first year of operations, the United States worked primarily to build adequate housing, cafeterias, warehouses, machine shops, and other elements of infrastructure that previous French efforts had failed to consider. Most importantly, the introduction of fumigation systems and mosquito nets following Dr. Walter Reed's discovery of the role of mosquitoes in the spread of malaria and yellow fever reduced the death rate and restored the fledgling morale among workers and American-born supervisors. At the same time, a new wave of American engineers planned for the construction of the canal. Even though they decided to build a lock-system rather than a sea-level canal, workers still had to excavate over 170 million cubic yards of earth with the use of over one hundred new rail-mounted steam shovels (**Figure 12.15**). Excited by the work, Roosevelt became the first sitting U.S. president to leave the country while in office. He traveled to Panama where he visited the construction site, taking a turn at the steam shovel and removing dirt. The canal opened in 1914, permanently changing world trade and military defense patterns.

Figure 12.15 Recurring landslides made the excavation of the Culebra Cut one of the most technically challenging elements in the construction of the Panama Canal.

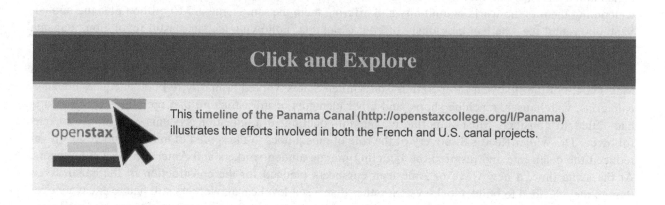

Click and Explore

This timeline of the Panama Canal (http://openstaxcollege.org/l/Panama) illustrates the efforts involved in both the French and U.S. canal projects.

THE ROOSEVELT COROLLARY

With the construction of the canal now underway, Roosevelt next wanted to send a clear message to the rest of the world—and in particular to his European counterparts—that the colonization of the Western Hemisphere had now ended, and their interference in the countries there would no longer be tolerated. At the same time, he sent a message to his counterparts in Central and South America, should the United States see problems erupt in the region, that it would intervene in order to maintain peace and stability throughout the hemisphere.

Roosevelt articulated this seeming double standard in a 1904 address before Congress, in a speech that became known as the **Roosevelt Corollary**. The Roosevelt Corollary was based on the original Monroe Doctrine of the early nineteenth century, which warned European nations of the consequences of their interference in the Caribbean. In this addition, Roosevelt states that the United States would use military force "as an international police power" to correct any "chronic wrongdoing" by any Latin American nation that might threaten stability in the region. Unlike the Monroe Doctrine, which proclaimed an American policy of noninterference with its neighbors' affairs, the Roosevelt Corollary loudly proclaimed the right and obligation of the United States to involve itself whenever necessary.

Roosevelt immediately began to put the new corollary to work. He used it to establish protectorates over Cuba and Panama, as well as to direct the United States to manage the Dominican Republic's custom service revenues. Despite growing resentment from neighboring countries over American intervention in their internal affairs, as well as European concerns from afar, knowledge of Roosevelt's previous actions in Colombia concerning acquisition of land upon which to build the Panama Canal left many fearful of American reprisals should they resist. Eventually, Presidents Herbert Hoover and Franklin Roosevelt softened American rhetoric regarding U.S. domination of the Western Hemisphere, with the latter proclaiming a new "Good Neighbor Policy" that renounced American intervention in other nations' affairs. However, subsequent presidents would continue to reference aspects of the Roosevelt Corollary to justify American involvement in Haiti, Nicaragua, and other nations throughout the twentieth century. The map below (**Figure 12.16**) shows the widespread effects of Roosevelt's policies throughout Latin America.

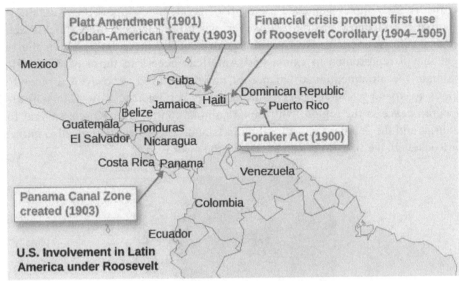

Figure 12.16 From underwriting a revolution in Panama with the goal of building a canal to putting troops in Cuba, Roosevelt vastly increased the U.S. impact in Latin America.

DEFINING "AMERICAN"

⚙ *The Roosevelt Corollary and Its Impact*

In 1904, Roosevelt put the United States in the role of the "police power" of the Western Hemisphere and set a course for the U.S. relationship with Central and Latin America that played out over the next several decades. He did so with the Roosevelt Corollary, in which he stated:

> It is not true that the United States feels any land hunger or entertains any projects as regards the other nations of the Western Hemisphere save as such are for their welfare. All that this country desires is to see the neighboring countries stable, orderly, and prosperous. Any country whose people conduct themselves well can count upon our hearty friendship. . . . Chronic wrongdoing, or an impotence which results in a general loosening of the ties of civilized society, may in America, as elsewhere, require intervention by some civilized nation, and in the Western Hemisphere the adherence of the United States to the Monroe Doctrine may force the United States, however, reluctantly, in flagrant cases of such wrongdoing or impotence, to the exercise of an international police power."

In the twenty years after he made this statement, the United States would use military force in Latin America over a dozen times. The Roosevelt Corollary was used as a rationale for American involvement in the Dominican Republic, Nicaragua, Haiti, and other Latin American countries, straining relations between Central America and its dominant neighbor to the north throughout the twentieth century.

AMERICAN INTERVENTION IN THE RUSSO-JAPANESE WAR

Although he supported the Open Door notes as an excellent economic policy in China, Roosevelt lamented the fact that the United States had no strong military presence in the region to enforce it. Clearly, without a military presence there, he could not as easily use his "big stick" threat credibly to achieve his foreign policy goals. As a result, when conflicts did arise on the other side of the Pacific, Roosevelt adopted a policy of maintaining a balance of power among the nations there. This was particularly evident when the Russo-Japanese War erupted in 1904.

In 1904, angered by the massing of Russian troops along the Manchurian border, and the threat it represented to the region, Japan launched a surprise naval attack upon the Russian fleet. Initially, Roosevelt supported the Japanese position. However, when the Japanese fleet quickly achieved victory after victory, Roosevelt grew concerned over the growth of Japanese influence in the region and the continued threat that it represented to China and American access to those markets (**Figure 12.17**). Wishing to maintain the aforementioned balance of power, in 1905, Roosevelt arranged for diplomats from both nations to attend a secret peace conference in Portsmouth, New Hampshire. The resultant negotiations secured peace in the region, with Japan gaining control over Korea, several former Russian bases in Manchuria, and the southern half of Sakhalin Island. These negotiations also garnered the Nobel Peace Prize for Roosevelt, the first American to receive the award.

Figure 12.17 Japan's defense against Russia was supported by President Roosevelt, but when Japan's ongoing victories put the United States' own Asian interests at risk, he stepped in.

When Japan later exercised its authority over its gains by forcing American business interests out of Manchuria in 1906–1907, Roosevelt felt he needed to invoke his "big stick" foreign policy, even though the distance was great. He did so by sending the U.S. Great White Fleet on maneuvers in the western Pacific Ocean as a show of force from December 1907 through February 1909. Publicly described as a goodwill tour, the message to the Japanese government regarding American interests was equally clear. Subsequent negotiations reinforced the Open Door policy throughout China and the rest of Asia. Roosevelt had, by both the judicious use of the "big stick" and his strategy of maintaining a balance of power, kept U.S. interests in Asia well protected.

Click and Explore

Browse the **Smithsonian National Portrait Gallery** (http://openstaxcollege.org/l/RooseveltIcon) to follow Theodore Roosevelt from Rough Rider to president and beyond.

12.5 Taft's "Dollar Diplomacy"

By the end of this section, you will be able to:

- Explain how William Howard Taft used American economic power to protect the nation's interests in its new empire

When William Howard Taft became president in 1909, he chose to adapt Roosevelt's foreign policy philosophy to one that reflected American economic power at the time. In what became known as "**dollar diplomacy**," Taft announced his decision to "substitute dollars for bullets" in an effort to use foreign policy to secure markets and opportunities for American businessmen (**Figure 12.18**). Not unlike Roosevelt's threat of force, Taft used the threat of American economic clout to coerce countries into agreements to benefit the United States.

Figure 12.18 Although William Howard Taft was Theodore Roosevelt's hand-picked successor to the presidency, he was less inclined to use Roosevelt's "big stick," choosing instead to use the economic might of the United States to influence foreign affairs.

Of key interest to Taft was the debt that several Central American nations still owed to various countries in Europe. Fearing that the debt holders might use the monies owed as leverage to use military intervention in the Western Hemisphere, Taft moved quickly to pay off these debts with U.S. dollars. Of course, this move made the Central American countries indebted to the United States, a situation that not all nations wanted. When a Central American nation resisted this arrangement, however, Taft responded with military force to achieve the objective. This occurred in Nicaragua when the country refused to accept American loans to pay off its debt to Great Britain. Taft sent a warship with marines to the region to pressure the government to agree. Similarly, when Mexico considered the idea of allowing a Japanese corporation to gain significant land and economic advantages in its country, Taft urged Congress to pass the Lodge Corollary, an addendum to the Roosevelt Corollary, stating that no foreign corporation—other than American ones—could obtain strategic lands in the Western Hemisphere.

In Asia, Taft's policies also followed those of Theodore Roosevelt. He attempted to bolster China's ability to withstand Japanese interference and thereby maintain a balance of power in the region. Initially, he experienced tremendous success in working with the Chinese government to further develop the railroad industry in that country through arranging international financing. However, efforts to expand the Open Door policy deeper into Manchuria met with resistance from Russia and Japan, exposing the limits of the American government's influence and knowledge about the intricacies of diplomacy. As a result, he reorganized the U.S. State Department to create geographical divisions (such as the Far East Division, the Latin American Division, etc.) in order to develop greater foreign policy expertise in each area.

Taft's policies, although not as based on military aggression as his predecessors, did create difficulties for the United States, both at the time and in the future. Central America's indebtedness would create economic concerns for decades to come, as well as foster nationalist movements in countries resentful of American's interference. In Asia, Taft's efforts to mediate between China and Japan served only to heighten tensions between Japan and the United States. Furthermore, it did not succeed in creating a balance of power, as Japan's reaction was to further consolidate its power and reach throughout the region.

As Taft's presidency came to a close in early 1913, the United States was firmly entrenched on its path towards empire. The world perceived the United States as the predominant power of the Western Hemisphere—a perception that few nations would challenge until the Soviet Union during the Cold War era. Likewise, the United States had clearly marked its interests in Asia, although it was still searching for an adequate approach to guard and foster them. The development of an American empire had introduced with it several new approaches to American foreign policy, from military intervention to economic coercion to the mere threat of force.

The playing field would change one year later in 1914 when the United States witnessed the unfolding of World War I, or "the Great War." A new president would attempt to adopt a new approach to diplomacy—one that was well-intentioned but at times impractical. Despite Woodrow Wilson's best efforts to the contrary, the United States would be drawn into the conflict and subsequently attempt to reshape the world order as a result.

Click and Explore

Read this brief biography of President Taft (http://openstaxcollege.org/l/Taft) to understand his foreign policy in the context of his presidency.

APPENDIX A
Presidents of the United States of America

Table A1 Presidents of the United States of America

Order	Election Year	President
1	1788–1789	George Washington
2	1792	George Washington
3	1796	John Adams
4	1800	Thomas Jefferson
5	1804	Thomas Jefferson
6	1808	James Madison
7	1812	James Madison
8	1816	James Monroe
9	1820	James Monroe
10	1824	John Quincy Adams
11	1828	Andrew Jackson
12	1832	Andrew Jackson
13	1836	Martin Van Buren
14	1840	William Henry Harrison
15	1844	James K. Polk
16	1848	Zachary Taylor
17	1852	Franklin Pierce
18	1856	James Buchanan
19	1860	Abraham Lincoln
20	1864	Abraham Lincoln
21	1868	Ulysses S. Grant
22	1872	Ulysses S. Grant
23	1876	Rutherford B. Hayes
24	1880	James A. Garfield

Table A1 Presidents of the United States of America

Order	Election Year	President
25	1884	Grover Cleveland
26	1888	Benjamin Harrison
27	1892	Grover Cleveland
28	1896	William McKinley
29	1900	William McKinley
30	1904	Theodore Roosevelt
31	1908	William Howard Taft
32	1912	Woodrow Wilson
33	1916	Woodrow Wilson
34	1920	Warren G. Harding
35	1924	Calvin Coolidge
36	1928	Herbert Hoover
37	1932	Franklin D. Roosevelt
38	1936	Franklin D. Roosevelt
39	1940	Franklin D. Roosevelt
40	1944	Franklin D. Roosevelt
41	1948	Harry S. Truman
42	1952	Dwight D. Eisenhower
43	1956	Dwight D. Eisenhower
44	1960	John F. Kennedy
45	1964	Lyndon B. Johnson
46	1968	Richard Nixon
47	1972	Richard Nixon
48	1976	Jimmy Carter
49	1980	Ronald Reagan
50	1984	Ronald Reagan
51	1988	George H. W. Bush

Table A1 Presidents of the United States of America

Order	Election Year	President
52	1992	Bill Clinton
53	1996	Bill Clinton
54	2000	George W. Bush
55	2004	George W. Bush
56	2008	Barack Obama
57	2012	Barack Obama

APPENDIX B

U.S. Political Map

Figure B1   (credit: U.S. Department of the Interior, U.S. Geological Survey, The National Atlas of the United States of America/nationalatlas.gov)

APPENDIX C

U.S. Topographical Map

APPENDIX D

United States Population Chart

Table D1 United States Population Chart[1]

Census Year	Population	Census Year	Population
1610	350	1820	9,638,453
1620	2,302	1830	12,866,020
1630	4,646	1840	17,069,453
1640	26,634	1850	23,191,876
1650	50,368	1860	31,443,321
1660	75,058	1870	38,558,371
1670	111,935	1880	50,189,209
1680	151,507	1890	62,979,766
1690	210,372	1900	76,212,168
1700	250,888	1910	92,228,496
1710	331,711	1920	106,021,537
1720	466,185	1930	123,202,624
1730	629,445	1940	132,164,569
1740	905,563	1950	151,325,798
1750	1,170,760	1960	179,323,175
1760	1,593,625	1970	203,211,926
1770	2,148,076	1980	226,656,805
1780	2,780,369	1990	248,709,873
1790	3,929,214	2000	281,421,906
1800	5,308,483	2010	308,745,538
1810	7,239,881		

1. Population figures for the decades before the first U.S. census in 1790 are estimates.

CPSIA information can be obtained
at www.ICGtesting.com
Printed in the USA
FSOW03n0206300316
18481FS